Taking
SIDES

Clashing Views on Controversial Educational Issues

Eighth Edition

Taking SIDES

Clashing Views on Controversial Educational Issues

Eighth Edition

Edited, Selected, and with Introductions by

James Wm. Noll
University of Maryland

The Dushkin Publishing Group, Inc.

For Stephanie and Sonja

Photo Acknowledgments

Part 1   Digital Stock, Incorporated
Part 2   The Apple® Macintosh® Classic® personal computer

Cover Art Acknowledgment

Charles Vitelli

Manufactured in the United States of America

Eighth Edition

10 9 8 7 6 5 4 3 2 1

Library of Congress Cataloging-in-Publication Data

Main entry under title:
  Taking sides: clashing views on controversial educational issues/edited, selected, and with introductions by James Wm. Noll.—8th ed.
    Includes bibliographical references and index.
    1. Education—United States—Aims and objectives. 2. Education—United States. I. Noll, James Wm., *comp.*
      LA217.2.T35   370′.973—dc20
      1-56134-330-7   94-47628

 Printed on Recycled Paper

The Dushkin Publishing Group, Inc.

PREFACE

Controversy is the basis of change and, hopefully, improvement. Its lack signifies the presence of complacency, the authoritarian limitation of viewpoint expression, or the absence of realistic alternatives to the existing circumstances. An articulate presentation of a point of view on a controversial matter breathes new life into abiding human and social concerns. Controversy prompts reexamination and perhaps renewal.

Education is controversial. Arguments over the most appropriate aims, the most propitious means, and the most effective control have raged over the centuries. Particularly in the United States, where the systematic effort to provide education has been more democratically dispersed and more varied than elsewhere, educational issues have been contentiously debated. Philosophers, psychologists, sociologists, professional educators, lobbyists, government officials, school boards, local pressure groups, taxpayers, parents, and students have all voiced their views.

This book aims to present opposing or sharply varying viewpoints on issues, both fundamental and of current concern, in the field of education. Those that address fundamental issues, such as the purposes of education, the control of schooling, the moral development of the young, and the equalization of opportunity, are taken from the works of prominent and seminal thinkers whose ideas are much discussed.

With the background provided by the examination of arguments on fundamental issues, the student is better prepared to analyze specific issues currently undergoing heated debate. These include "choice" plans for schools, the influence of religious fundamentalists, the problem of gender bias, Afrocentric education, discipline, tracking, educating disabled students, bilingual education, sexuality education, community service, and outcome-based education.

I have made every effort to select views from a wide range of thinkers —philosophers, psychologists, sociologists, professional educators, political leaders, historians, researchers, and gadflies.

Each issue is accompanied by an *introduction*, which sets the stage for debate, and each issue concludes with a *postscript* that considers other views on the issue and suggests additional readings. By combining the material in this volume with the informational background provided by a good introductory textbook, the student should be prepared to address the problems confronting the schools today.

My hope is that students will find challenges in the material presented here—provocations that will inspire them to better understand the roots of educational controversy, to attain a greater awareness of possible alternatives

i

in dealing with the various issues, and to stretch their personal powers of creative thinking in the search for more promising resolutions of the problems.

Changes to this edition   This eighth edition represents a considerable revision. There are 10 completely new issues: *Can "Character Education" Reverse Moral Decline?* (Issue 4); *Should Multiculturalism Permeate the Curriculum?* (Issue 6); *Has Court-Mandated School Desegregation Failed?* (Issue 7); *Should National Goals and Standards Guide School Reform?* (Issue 9); *Are Religious Fundamentalists Damaging Public Education?* (Issue 11); *Are Major Policy Changes Needed to Fight Gender Bias in the Schools?* (Issue 12); *Is Full Inclusion of Disabled Students Desirable?* (Issue 13); *Should Schools Offer Condoms to Students?* (Issue 19); *Can Outcome-Based Education Transform America's Schools?* (Issue 20); and *Is Mandatory Community Service Desirable and Legal?* (Issue 21). In all, there are 20 new selections.

A word to the instructor   An *Instructor's Manual With Test Questions* (multiple-choice and essay) is available through the publisher for the instructor using *Taking Sides* in the classroom. A general guidebook, called *Using Taking Sides in the Classroom*, which discusses methods and techniques for integrating the pro-con approach into any classroom setting, is also available.

Acknowledgments   I am thankful for the kind and efficient assistance given to me by Mimi Egan, publisher for the Taking Sides series, and the staff at The Dushkin Publishing Group. I was also greatly assisted in my work by the suggestions from the many users of *Taking Sides* who responded to a questionnaire sent by the publisher. Their comments have enhanced the quality of this edition of the book and are reflected in the new issues as well as the issues that have been retained. Special thanks go to those who responded with specific suggestions for the eighth edition:

Billy E. Askins
Texas Tech University

James K. Baum
West Georgia College

Anthea L. Bojar
Cardinal Stritch College

Deron Boyles
Georgia State University

Rick A. Breault
University of Indianapolis

Robert W. Bruinsma
The Kings College

Dexter E. Bryan, Jr.
California State University,
    Dominguez Hills

Patrick Collins
Hobart and William Smith
  Colleges

Paul Crutchfield
Flagler College

Debbie Dewitt
Coastal Carolina University

John W. Donaldson
Liberty University

Sheila Drake
Kansas Wesleyan University

Clifford H. Edwards
Brigham Young University

David W. Eggebrecht
Concordia University

Bernard J. Fleury
Westfield State College

Gail Sabella Fraser
University of Bridgeport

Bill Gile
Bethel College

Sharon Hartnett
Whitworth College

Wm. Ray Heitzmann
Villanova University

Ted Hipple
University of Tennessee

David Julian Hodges
Hunter College

Catherine S. Jarjisian
Oberlin College

Harry J. Klein
La Salle University

Lorraine S. Lange
Roanoke College

Letty Lincoln
Wilmington College

Bennett J. Lombardo
Rhode Island College

B. Edward McClellan
Indiana University

John McKay
University of Nebraska

Sarah A. Merrill
Purdue University

James C. Moses
Lewis University

M. Everett Myer
University of Tennessee

Thomas Nagel
San Diego State University

Alyce Oosterhuis
The Kings College

Charlene S. Plowcha
Mansfield University

Richard Rizzo
Sonoma State University

Michael Romanowski
Alabama State University

Patricia Ryan
Otterbein College

Pamela B. Schachter
Marymount College

Donald S. Seckinger
University of Wyoming

Clement A. Seldin
University of
    Massachusetts–Amherst

Eugene F. Sensel, Jr.
Elmira College

William T. Shannon
Grove City College

Rodena E. Smith
Longwood College

Frank Sottile
University of Scranton

G. Temp Sparkman
University of Kansas

Ellen C. Stewart
Adelphi University

Kevin Walsh
University of Alabama

Henry R. Weinstock
University of Missouri

James Wm. Noll
University of Maryland

CONTENTS IN BRIEF

CONTENTS

Philosopher John Dewey suggests that educators should reconsider traditional approaches to schooling and give fuller attention to the social environment of the students. Noted educator Robert M. Hutchins argues for a liberal arts education geared to the development of intellectual powers.

Writer and editor Clifton Fadiman argues that standardized subject matter sets the stage for successful and meaningful interaction in the world. Educator John Holt feels that an imposed curriculum usurps a basic human right to select one's own path of development.

B. F. Skinner, influential proponent of behaviorism and professor of psychology, argues that learning and motivation are linked to the influence of external forces. Professor of psychology and psychiatry Carl R. Rogers offers the "humanistic" alternative to behaviorism and insists that there are subjective forces in human motivation.

Developmental psychologist Thomas Lickona, a leading exponent of the new character education, charts a course of action to deal with the moral decline of American youth. Education professor Alan L. Lockwood asserts that values instilled through character education do not determine actual individual behavior.

Professor emeritus of education R. Freeman Butts warns that current efforts to redefine the relationship between religion and schooling are eroding the Constitution's intent. Professor of political science Robert L. Cord offers a more accommodating interpretation of this intent and argues that none of the school practices currently being allowed violate the First Amendment's establishment clause.

Education professor James A. Banks, a leading advocate of multicultural education, identifies what he feels are some of the current misconceptions about multicultural education and promotes its further implementation in the schools. Linda Chavez, director of the Center for the New American Community, accuses multiculturalists of following a political agenda designed to culturally divide America.

Social critic and educator Jonathan Kozol argues that the desegregation of U.S. schools called for in the 1954 Supreme Court decision of *Brown v. Board of Education* has been practically invalidated by subsequent rulings and actions. History professor Roger Wilkins argues that, overall, *Brown* has "destroyed American apartheid" and enriched the whole society.

Sociology professor Ruth Sidel supports Jonathan Kozol's arguments for the equalization of funding, as outlined in his controversial book, *Savage Inequalities.* Journalist Peter Schrag argues that Kozol's analysis is sometimes simplistic and often impractical.

Senator Edward M. Kennedy (D-Massachusetts) argues that the "Goals 2000" education reform legislation will render America's schools more effective. Legal studies professor Stephen Arons maintains that the national curriculum standards aspect of the legislation will threaten cultural diversity.

Political science researchers John E. Chubb and Terry M. Moe make the case for choice as a means of true reform. Frances C. Fowler of Miami University in Oxford, Ohio, finds an antidemocratic tone in the premises underlying the proposals of Chubb and Moe.

Zita Arocha, a freelance writer who specializes in education and social issues, argues that various ultraconservative groups have hidden agendas that include redefining school curricula. Christian Coalition leader Ralph E. Reed, Jr., and Robert L. Simonds, president of Citizens for Excellence in Education, maintain that the educational goals of the religious right represent mainstream ideology and the concerns of many parents.

The American Association of University Women (AAUW), an organization of college and university graduates that works for the advancement of women, argues that a wide variety of policy changes are necessary to balance the educational inequities that exist between boys and girls in the American school system. Rita Kramer, a writer who specializes in education issues, argues that the recommendations for change made by the AAUW are self-serving and anti-intellectual.

Attorney Jean B. Arnold and school superintendent Harold W. Dodge assert that the federal Individuals with Disabilities Education Act can benefit all students. Teachers' union president Albert Shanker maintains that the full inclusion ideology is not the best way to educate students with disabilities.

Black studies professor Molefi Kete Asante maintains that providing black
students with an Afrocentric frame of reference will enhance their self-esteem
and learning. Noted historian Arthur M. Schlesinger, Jr., documents his concerns about the recent spread of Afrocentric programs and the multiculturalization of the curriculum.

History of education professor Diane Ravitch argues that bilingual education
programs have not proven successful. Donaldo Macedo, an associate professor of linguistics, expresses concern about the pedagogical and political
implications of abandoning such programs.

Social scientist Jeannie Oakes argues that tracking contributes to mediocre
schooling for many who are placed in middle or lower tracks. Charles Nevi,
director of Curriculum and Instruction for the Puyallup School District in
Washington, feels that tracking accommodates individual differences while
making quality education available to all.

Lee Canter, developer of the Assertive Discipline program, argues that a positive approach to behavior management produces favorable results. John F. Covaleskie of Syracuse University claims that the behavioral approach fails to shape character.

Professor of education Kevin Ryan argues that sex education programs should be based in a firmer moral grounding. Peter Scales, a leading advocate of sexuality education, feels that current objections to sex education programs are unwarranted.

Margaret Pruitt Clark, director of the Center for Population Options, argues that the growing threat of acquiring sexually transmitted diseases through unprotected sexual activity make condom availability in the schools absolutely necessary. Education dean Edwin J. Delattre asserts that a policy of distributing condoms through the schools sends to students misguided messages about responsibility and morality.

William G. Spady, director of the High Success Network, advocates the outcome-based education (OBE) approach to teaching. Journalist John O'Neil maintains that there is little evidence that OBE will lead to major changes in the schools.

Education professor Vito Perrone asserts that community service learning can revitalize the schools and build a service ethic in students. The Institute for Justice, a nonprofit public interest law center in Washington, D.C., argues that government-mandated service negates the spirit of voluntarism.

INTRODUCTION

Ways of Thinking About Educational Issues

James Wm. Noll

Concern about the quality of education has been expressed by philosophers, politicians, and parents for centuries. There has been a perpetual and unresolved debate regarding the definition of education, the relationship between school and society, the distribution of decision-making power in educational matters, and the means for improving all aspects of the educational enterprise.

In recent decades the growing influence of thinking drawn from the humanities and the behavioral and social sciences has brought about the development of interpretive, normative, and critical perspectives, which have sharpened the focus on educational concerns. These perspectives have allowed scholars and researchers to closely examine the contextual variables, value orientations, and philosophical and political assumptions that shape both the status quo and reform efforts.

The study of education involves the application of many perspectives to the analysis of "what is and how it got that way" and "what can be and how we can get there." Central to such study are the prevailing philosophical assumptions, theories, and visions that find their way into real-life educational situations. The application situation, with its attendant political pressures, sociocultural differences, community expectations, parental influence, and professional problems, provides a testing ground for contending theories and ideals.

This "testing ground" image applies only insofar as the status quo is malleable enough to allow the examination and trial of alternative views. Historically, institutionalized education has been characteristically rigid. As a "testing ground" of ideas, it has often lacked an orientation encouraging innovation and futuristic thinking. Its political grounding has usually been conservative.

As social psychologist Allen Wheelis points out in *Quest for Identity*, social institutions by definition tend toward solidification and protectionism. His depiction of the dialectical development of civilizations centers on the tension between the security and authoritarianism of "institutional processes" and the dynamism and change-orientation of "instrumental processes."

The field of education seems to graphically illustrate this observation. Educational practices are primarily tradition-bound. The twentieth-century reform movement, spurred by the ideas of John Dewey, A. S. Neill, and a host of critics who campaigned for change in the 1960s, challenged the structural rigidity of schooling. The current situation is one of contending forces: those who wish to continue the struggle for true reform, those who demand a return to a more traditional or "basic" model, and those who are shaping a new form of procedural conformity around the tenets of behaviorism and competency-based approaches.

We are left with the abiding questions: What is an "educated" person? What should be the primary purpose of organized education? Who should control the decisions influencing the educational process? Should the schools follow society or lead it toward change? Should schooling be compulsory?

Long-standing forces have molded a wide variety of responses to these fundamental questions. The religious impetus, nationalistic fervor, philosophical ideas, the march of science and technology, varied interpretations of "societal needs," and the desire to use the schools as a means for social reform have been historically influential. In recent times other factors have emerged to contribute to the complexity of the search for answers—social class differences, demographic shifts, increasing bureaucratization, the growth of the textbook industry, the changing financial base for schooling, teacher unionization, and strengthening of parental and community pressure groups.

The struggle to find the most appropriate answers to these questions now involves, as in the past, an interplay of societal aims, educational purposes, and individual intentions. Moral development, the quest for wisdom, citizenship training, socioeconomic improvement, mental discipline, the rational control of life, job preparation, liberation of the individual, freedom of inquiry —these and many others continue to be topics of discourse on education.

A detailed historical perspective on these questions and topics may be gained by reading the interpretations of noted scholars in the field. R. Freeman Butts has written a brief but effective summary portrayal in "Search for Freedom—The Story of American Education," *NEA Journal* (March 1960). A partial listing of other sources includes R. Freeman Butts and Lawrence Cremin, *A History of Education in American Culture*; S. E. Frost, Jr., *Historical and Philosophical Foundations of Western Education*; Harry Good and Edwin Teller, *A History of Education*; Adolphe Meyer, *An Educational History of the American People*; Robert L. Church and Michael W. Sedlak, *Education in the United States: An Interpretive History*; Merle Curti, *The Social Ideas of American Educators*; Henry J. Perkinson, *The Imperfect Panacea: American Faith in Education, 1865–1965*; Clarence Karier, *Man, Society, and Education*; V. T. Thayer, *Formative Ideas in American Education*; H. Warren Button and Eugene F. Provenzo, Jr., *History of Education and Culture in America*; David Tyack and Elisabeth Hansot, *Managers of Virtue: Public School Leadership in America, 1820–1980*; Joel Spring, *The American School, 1642–1990*; S. Alexander Rippa, *Education in a Free Society: An American History*; John D. Pulliam, *History of Education in America*; Edward Stevens and George H. Wood, *Justice, Ideology, and Education*; and Walter Feinberg and Jonas F. Soltis, *School and Society*.

These and other historical accounts of the development of schooling demonstrate the continuing need to address educational questions in terms of cultural and social dynamics. A careful analysis of contemporary education demands attention not only to the historical interpretation of developmental influences but also to the philosophical forces that define formal education and the social and cultural factors that form the basis of informal education.

EXAMINING VIEWPOINTS

In his book *A New Public Education*, Seymour Itzkoff examines the interplay between informal and formal education, concluding that economic and technological expansion have pulled people away from the informal culture by placing a premium on success in formal education. This has brought about a reactive search for new informal educational contexts within the informal cultural community, which recognizes the impact of individual personality in shaping educational experiences.

This search for a reconstructed philosophical base for education has produced a barrage of critical commentary. Those who seek radical change in education characterize the present schools as mindless, manipulative, factory-like, bureaucratic institutions that offer little sense of community, pay scant attention to personal meaning, fail to achieve curricular integration, and maintain a psychological atmosphere of competitiveness, tension, fear, and alienation. Others deplore the ideological movement away from the formal organization of education, fearing an abandonment of standards, a dilution of the curriculum, an erosion of intellectual and behavioral discipline, and a decline in adult and institutional authority.

Students of education (whether prospective teachers, practicing professionals, or interested laypeople) must examine closely the assumptions and values underlying alternative positions in order to clarify their own viewpoints. This tri-level task may best be organized around the basic themes of purpose, power, and reform. These themes offer access to the theoretical grounding of actions in the field of education, to the political grounding of such actions, and to the future orientation of action decisions.

A general model for the examination of positions on educational issues includes the following dimensions: identification of the viewpoint, recognition of the stated or implied assumptions underlying the viewpoint, analysis of the validity of the supporting argument, and evaluation of the conclusions and action-suggestions of the originator of the position. The stated or implied assumptions may be derived from a philosophical or religious orientation, from scientific theory, from social or personal values, or from accumulated experience. Acceptance by the reader of an author's assumptions opens the way for a receptive attitude regarding the specific viewpoint expressed and its implications for action. The argument offered in justification of the viewpoint may be based on logic, common experience, controlled experiments, information and data, legal precedents, emotional appeals, and/or a host of other persuasive devices.

Holding the basic model in mind, readers of the positions presented in this volume (or anywhere else, for that matter) can examine the constituent elements of arguments—basic assumptions, viewpoint statements, supporting evidence, conclusions, and suggestions for action. The careful reader will accept or reject the individual elements of the total position. One might see reasonableness in a viewpoint and its justification but be unable to accept the assumptions on which it is based. Or one might accept the flow of argument from assumptions to viewpoint to evidence but find illogic or impracticality in the stated conclusions and suggestions for action. In any event, the reader's personal view is tested and honed through the process of analyzing the views of others.

PHILOSOPHICAL CONSIDERATIONS

Historically, organized education has been initiated and instituted to serve many purposes—spiritual salvation, political socialization, moral uplift, societal stability, social mobility, mental discipline, vocational efficiency, and social reform, among others. The various purposes have usually reflected the dominant philosophical conception of human nature and the prevailing assumptions about the relationship between the individual and society. At any given time, competing conceptions may vie for dominance—social conceptions, economic conceptions, conceptions that emphasize spirituality, or conceptions that stress the uniqueness and dignity of the individual, for example.

These considerations of human nature and individual-society relationships are grounded in philosophical assumptions, and these assumptions find their way to such practical domains as schooling. In Western civilization there has been an identifiable (but far from consistent and clear-cut) historical trend in the basic assumptions about reality, knowledge, values, and the human condition. This trend, made manifest in the philosophical positions of idealism, realism, pragmatism, and existentialism, has involved a shift in emphasis from the spiritual world to nature to human behavior to the social individual to the free individual, and from eternal ideas to fixed natural laws to social interaction to the inner person.

The idealist tradition, which dominated much of philosophical and educational thought until the eighteenth and nineteenth centuries, separates the changing, imperfect material world and the permanent, perfect spiritual or mental world. As Plato saw it, for example, human beings and all other physical entities are particular manifestations of an ideal reality which, in material existence, humans can never fully know. The purpose of education is to bring us closer to the absolute ideals, pure forms, and universal standards that exist spiritually by awakening and strengthening our rational powers. For

Plato, a curriculum based on mathematics, logic, and music would serve this purpose, especially in the training of leaders whose rationality must exert control over emotionality and baser instincts.

Against this tradition, which shaped the liberal arts curriculum in schools for centuries, the realism of Aristotle, with its finding of the "forms" of things *within* the material world, brought an emphasis on scientific investigation and on environmental factors in the development of human potential. This fundamental view has influenced two philosophical movements in education: "naturalism," based on following or gently assisting nature (as in the approaches of John Amos Comenius, Jean-Jacques Rousseau, and Johann Heinrich Pestalozzi), and "scientific realism," based on uncovering the natural laws of human behavior and shaping the educational environment to maximize their effectiveness (as in the approaches of John Locke, Johann Friedrich Herbart, and Edward Thorndike).

In the twentieth century, two philosophical forces (pragmatism and existentialism) have challenged these traditions. Each has moved primary attention away from fixed spiritual or natural influences and toward the individual as shaper of knowledge and values. The pragmatic position, articulated in America by Charles Sanders Peirce, William James, and John Dewey, turns from metaphysical abstractions toward concrete results of action. In a world of change and relativity, human beings must forge their own truths and values as they interact with their environments and each other. The European-based philosophy of existentialism, emerging from such thinkers as Gabriel Marcel, Martin Buber, Martin Heidegger, and Jean-Paul Sartre, has more recently influenced education here. Existentialism places the burdens of freedom, choice, and responsibility squarely on the individual, viewing the current encroachment of external forces and the tendency of people to "escape from freedom" as a serious diminishment of our human possibilities.

These many theoretical slants contend for recognition and acceptance as we continue the search for broad purposes in education and as we attempt to create curricula, methodologies, and learning environments that fulfill our stated purposes. This is carried out, of course, in the real world of the public schools in which social, political, and economic forces often predominate.

POWER AND CONTROL

Plato, in the fourth century B.C., found existing education manipulative and confining and, in the *Republic*, described a meritocratic approach designed to nurture intellectual powers so as to form and sustain a rational society. Reform-oriented as Plato's suggestions were, he nevertheless insisted on certain restrictions and controls so that his particular version of the "ideal" could be met.

The ways and means of education have been fertile grounds for power struggles throughout history. Many educational efforts have been initiated by religious bodies, often creating a conflict situation when secular authorities have moved into the field. Schools have usually been seen as repositories of culture and social values and, as such, have been overseen by the more conservative forces in society. To others, bent on social reform, the schools have been treated as a spawning ground for change. Given these basic political forces, conflict is inevitable.

When one speaks of the control of education, the range of influence is indeed wide. Political influences, governmental actions, court decisions, professional militancy, parental power, and student assertion all contribute to the phenomenon of control. And the domain of control is equally broad—school finances, curriculum, instructional means and objectives, teacher certification, accountability, student discipline, censorship of school materials, determination of access and opportunity, and determination of inclusion and exclusion.

The general topic of power and control leads to a multitude of questions: Who should make policy decisions? Must the schools be puppets of the government? Can the schools function in the vanguard of social change? Can cultural indoctrination be avoided? Can the schools lead the way to full social integration? Can the effects of social class be eradicated? Can and should the schools teach values? Dealing with such questions is complicated by the increasing power of the federal government in educational matters. Congressional legislation has broadened substantially from the early land grants and aid to agricultural and vocational programs to more recent laws covering aid to federally impacted areas, school construction aid, student loans and fellowships, support for several academic areas of the curriculum, work-study programs, compensatory education, employment opportunities for youth, adult education, aid to libraries, teacher preparation, educational research, career education, education of the handicapped, and equal opportunity for females. This proliferation of areas of influence has caused the federal administrative bureaucracy to blossom from its meager beginnings in 1867 into a cabinet-level Department of Education in 1979.

State legislatures and state departments of education have also grown in power, handling greater percentages of school appropriations and controlling basic curricular decisions, attendance laws, accreditation, research, etc. Local school boards, once the sole authorities in policy making, now share the role with higher governmental echelons as the financial support sources shift away from the local scene. Simultaneously, strengthened teacher organizations and increasingly vocal pressure groups at the local, state, and national levels have forced a widening of the base for policy decisions.

SOME CONCLUDING REMARKS

The schools often seem to be either facing backward or to be completely absorbed in the tribulations of the present, lacking a vision of possible futures that might guide current decisions. The present is inescapable, obviously, and certainly the historical and philosophical underpinnings of the present situation must be understood, but true improvement often requires a break with conventionality—a surge toward a desired future.

The radical reform critique of government-sponsored compulsory schooling has depicted organized education as a form of cultural or political imprisonment that traps young people in an artificial and mainly irrelevant environment and rewards conformity and docility while inhibiting curiosity and creativity. Constructive reform ideas that have come from this critique include the creation of "open" classrooms, the de-emphasis of external motivators, the diversification of educational experience, and the building of a true sense of "community" within the instructional environment.

Starting with Francis Wayland Parker's schools in Quincy, Massachusetts, and John Dewey's laboratory school at the University of Chicago around the turn of the century, the campaign to make schools into more productive and humane places has been relentless. The duplication of A. S. Neill's Summerhill model in the free school movement in the 1960s, the open classroom/open space trends of recent years, the several curricular variations on applications of "humanistic" ideals, and the emergence of schools without walls, storefront schools, and street academies in a number of urban areas testify to the desire to reform the present system or to build alternatives to it.

The progressive education movement, the development of "life adjustment" goals and curricula, and the "whole person" theories of educational psychology moved the schools toward an expanded concept of schooling that embraced new subject matters and new approaches to discipline during the first half of this century. Since the 1950s, however, pressure for a return to a narrower concept of schooling as intellectual training has sparked new waves of debate. Out of this situation have come attempts by educators and academicians to design new curricular approaches in the basic subject matter areas, efforts by private foundations to stimulate organizational innovations and to improve the training of teachers, and federal government support of the community school model and the career educational curriculum. Yet, criticism of the schools abounds. The schools, according to many who use their services, remain too factorylike, too age-segregated, and too custodial. Alternative paths are still sought—paths that would allow action-learning, work-study, and a diversity of ways to achieve success.

H. G. Wells has told us that human history becomes more and more a race between education and catastrophe. What is needed in order to win this race is the generation of new ideas regarding cultural change, human relationships, ethical norms, the uses of technology, and the quality of life. These new ideas, of course, may be old ideas newly applied. One could do worse, in thinking through the problem of improving the quality of education, than to turn to the third-century philosopher Plotinus, who called for an education directed to "the outer, the inner, and the whole." For Plotinus, "the outer" represented the public person, or the socioeconomic dimension of the total human being;

"the inner" reflected the subjective dimension, the uniquely experiencing individual, or the "I"; and "the whole" signified the universe of meaning and relatedness, or the realm of human, natural, and spiritual connectedness. It would seem that education must address all of these dimensions if it is to truly help people in the lifelong struggle to shape a meaningful existence. If educational experiences can be improved in these directions, the end result might be people who are not just filling space, filling time, or filling a social role, but who are capable of saying something worthwhile in their lives.

PART 1

Fundamental Issues

The issues discussed in this section are fundamental to any inquiry into education. The answers to the questions raised explore diverse views of human nature, educational aims, moral development, religion, equality of opportunity, and political influence as they relate to shaping educational policy.

- Should Schooling Be Based on Social Experiences?

- Should Schools Determine What Is Learned?

- Should Behaviorism Shape Educational Practices?

- Can "Character Education" Reverse Moral Decline?

- Is Church-State Separation Being Threatened?

- Should Multiculturalism Permeate the Curriculum?

- Has Court-Mandated School Desegregation Failed?

- Will Reforming School Funding Remove "Savage Inequalities"?

- Should National Goals and Standards Guide School Reform?

ISSUE 1

Should Schooling Be Based on Social Experiences?

YES: John Dewey, from *Experience and Education* (Macmillan, 1938)

NO: Robert M. Hutchins, from *The Conflict in Education* (Harper & Row, 1953)

ISSUE SUMMARY

YES: Philosopher John Dewey suggests a reconsideration of traditional approaches to schooling, giving fuller attention to the social development of the learner and the quality of his or her total experience.

NO: Noted educator and one-time chancellor of the University of Chicago Robert M. Hutchins argues for a liberal arts education geared to the development of intellectual powers.

Throughout history, organized education has served many purposes—the transmission of tradition, knowledge, and skills; the acculturation and socialization of the young; the building and preserving of political-economic systems; the provision of opportunity for social mobility; the enhancement of the quality of life; and the cultivation of individual potential, among others. At any given time, schools pursue a number of such goals, but the elucidation of a primary or overriding goal, which gives focus to all others, has been a source of continuous contention.

Schooling in America has been extended in the last 100 years to vast numbers of young people, and during this time the argument over aims has gained momentum. At the turn of the century, John Dewey was raising serious questions about the efficacy of the prevailing approach to schooling. He believed that schooling was often arid, pedantic, and detached from the real lives of children and youths. In establishing his laboratory school at the University of Chicago, Dewey hoped to demonstrate that experiences provided by schools could be meaningful extensions of the normal social activities of learners, having as their primary aim the full experiential growth of the individual.

In order to accomplish this, Dewey sought to bring the learner into an active and intimate relationship with the subject matter. The problem-solving or inquiry approach that he and his colleagues at Columbia University in New York City devised became the cornerstone of the "new education"—the progressive education movement.

In 1938, Dewey himself (as expressed in his article that follows) sounded a note of caution to progressive educators who may have abandoned too completely the traditional disciplines in their attempt to link schooling with the needs and interests of the learners. Having spawned an educational revolution, Dewey, in his later years, emerges as more of a compromiser.

In that same year, William C. Bagley, in "An Essentialists' Platform for the Advancement of American Education," harshly criticized what he felt were anti-intellectual excesses promulgated by progressivism. In the 1950s and 1960s this theme was elaborated on by other academics, among them Robert M. Hutchins, Hyman Rickover, Arthur Bestor, and Max Rafferty, who demanded a return to intellectual discipline, higher standards, and moral guidance.

Hutchins's critique of Dewey's pragmatic philosophy was perhaps the best reasoned. He felt that the emphasis on immediate needs and desires of students and the focus on change and relativism detracted from the development of the intellectual skills needed for the realization of human potential.

A renewal of scholarly interest in the philosophical and educational ideas of both Dewey and Hutchins has resulted in a number of books, among which are *John Dewey's Pragmatic Technology* (1990) by Larry A. Hickman; *The Influence of Plato and Aristotle on John Dewey's Philosophy* (1990) by J. J. Chambliss; *Hutchins' University: A Memoir of the University of Chicago* (1991) by William H. O'Neill; *Robert M. Hutchins: Portrait of an Educator* (1991) by Mary Ann Dzuback; *John Dewey and American Democracy* (1991) by Robert B. Westbrook; *The End of Epistemology: Dewey and His Allies on the Spectator Theory of Knowledge* (1992) by Christopher B. Kulp; and *The Promise of Pragmatism* (1994) by John Patrick Diggins. Their continuing influence is charted by Rene Vincente Arcilla in "Metaphysics in Education after Hutchins and Dewey," *Teachers College Record* (Winter 1991).

In the following selections, John Dewey charts the necessary shift from the abstractness and isolation of traditional schooling to the concreteness and vitality of the newer concept. Robert M. Hutchins dissects the assumptions underlying Dewey's position and puts forth his own theory based on the premise that human nature is constant and functions the same in every society.

YES

John Dewey

EXPERIENCE AND EDUCATION

Mankind likes to think in terms of extreme opposites. It is given to for-mulating its beliefs in terms of *Either-Ors*, between which it recognizes no intermediate possibilities. When forced to recognize that the extremes cannot be acted upon, it is still inclined to hold that they are all right in theory but that when it comes to practical matters circumstances compel us to compromise. Educational philosophy is no exception. The history of educational theory is marked by opposition between the idea that education is development from within and that it is formation from without; that it is based upon natural en-dowments and that education is a process of overcoming natural inclination and substituting in its place habits acquired under external pressure.

At present, the opposition, so far as practical affairs of the school are con-cerned, tends to take the form of contrast between traditional and progressive education. If the underlying ideas of the former are formulated broadly, with-out the qualifications required for accurate statement, they are found to be about as follows: The subject-matter of education consists of bodies of in-formation and of skills that have been worked out in the past; therefore, the chief business of the school is to transmit them to the new generation. In the past, there have also been developed standards and rules of conduct; moral training consists of forming habits of action in conformity with these rules and standards. Finally, the general pattern of school organization (by which I mean the relations of pupils to one another and to the teachers) constitutes the school as a kind of institution sharply marked off from other social insti-tutions. Call up in imagination the ordinary schoolroom, its time schedules, schemes of classification, of examination and promotion, of rules of order, and I think you will grasp what is meant by "pattern of organization." If then you contrast this scene with what goes on in the family, for example, you will appreciate what is meant by the school being a kind of institution sharply marked off from any other form of social organization.

The three characteristics just mentioned fix the aims and methods of in-struction and discipline. The main purpose or objective is to prepare the young for future responsibilities and for success in life, by means of acquisi-tion of the organized bodies of information and prepared forms of skill which comprehend the material of instruction. Since the subject-matter as well as standards of proper conduct are handed down from the past, the attitude of pupils must, upon the whole, be one of docility, receptivity, and obedience. Books, especially textbooks, are the chief representatives of the lore and wisdom of the past, while teachers are the organs through which pupils are brought into effective connection with the material. Teachers are the agents through which knowledge and skills are communicated and rules of conduct enforced.

I have not made this brief summary for the purpose of criticizing the underlying philosophy. The rise of what is called new education and progressive schools is of itself a product of discontent with traditional education. In effect it is a criticism of the latter. When the implied criticism is made explicit it reads somewhat as follows: The traditional scheme is, in essence, one of imposition from above and from outside. It imposes adult standards, subject-matter, and methods upon those who are only growing slowly toward maturity. The gap is so great that the required subject-matter, the methods of learning and of behaving are foreign to the existing capacities of the young. They are beyond the reach of the experience the young learners already possess. Consequently, they must be imposed; even though good teachers will use devices of art to cover up the imposition so as to relieve it of obviously brutal features.

But the gulf between the mature or adult products and the experience and abilities of the young is so wide that the very situation forbids much active participation by pupils in the development of what is taught. Theirs is to do—and learn, as it was the part of the six hundred to do and die. Learning here means acquisition of what already is incorporated in books and in the heads of the elders. Moreover, that which is taught is thought of as essentially static. It is taught as a finished product, with little regard either to the ways in which it was originally built up or to changes that will surely occur in the future. It is to a large extent the cultural product of societies that assumed the future would be much like the past, and yet it is used as educational food in a society where change is the rule, not the exception.

If one attempts to formulate the philosophy of education implicit in the practices of the new education, we may, I think, discover certain common principles amid the variety of progressive schools now existing. To imposition from above is opposed expression and cultivation of individuality; to external discipline is opposed free activity; to learning from texts and teachers, learning through experience; to acquisition of isolated skills and techniques by drill, is opposed acquisition of them as mean of attaining ends which make direct vital appeal; to preparation for a more or less remote future is opposed making the most of the opportunities of present life; to static aims and materials is opposed acquaintance with a changing world.

Now, all principles by themselves are abstract. They become concrete only in the consequences which result from their application. Just because the principles set forth are so fundamental and far-reaching, everything depends upon the interpretation given them as they are put into practice in the school and the home. It is at this point that the reference made earlier to *Either-Or* philosophies becomes peculiarly pertinent. The general philosophy of the new education may be sound, and yet the difference in abstract principles will not decide the way in which the moral and intellectual preference involved shall be worked out in practice. There is always the danger in a new movement that in rejecting the aims and methods of that which it would supplant, it may develop its principles negatively rather than positively and constructively. Then it takes its clew in practice from that which is rejected instead of from the constructive development its own philosophy.

I take it that the fundamental unity of the newer philosophy is found in the idea that there is an intimate and necessary relation between the processes of actual experience and education. If this be true, then a positive and constructive development of its own basic idea depends upon having a correct idea of experience. Take, for example, the question of organized subject-matter.... The problem for progressive education is: What is the place and meaning of subject-matter and of organization *within* experience? How does subject-matter function? Is there anything inherent in experience which tends towards progressive organization of its contents? What results follow when the materials of experience are not progressively organized? A philosophy which proceeds on the basis of rejection, of sheer opposition, will neglect these questions. It will tend to suppose that because the old education was based on ready-made organization, therefore it suffices to reject the principle of organization *in toto*, instead of striving to discover what it means and how it is to be attained on the basis of experience. We might go through all the points of difference between the new and the old education and reach similar conclusions. When external control is rejected, the problem becomes that of finding the factors of control that are inherent within experience. When external authority is rejected, it does not

follow that all authority should be rejected, but rather that there is need to search for a more effective source of authority. Because the older education imposed the knowledge, methods, and the rules of conduct of the mature person upon the young, it does not follow, except upon the basis of the extreme *Either-Or* philosophy, that the knowledge and skill of the mature person has no directive value for the experience of the immature. On the contrary, basing education upon personal experience may mean more multiplied and more intimate contacts between the mature and the immature than ever existed in the traditional school, and consequently more, rather than less, guidance by others. The problem, then, is: how these contacts can be established without violating the principle of learning through personal experience. The solution of this problem requires a well thought-out philosophy of the social factors that operate in the constitution of individual experience.

What is indicated in the foregoing remarks is that the general principles of the new education do not of themselves solve any of the problems of the actual or practical conduct and management of progressive schools. Rather, they set new problems which have to be worked out on the basis of a new philosophy of experience. The problems are not even recognized, to say nothing of being solved, when it is assumed that it suffices to reject the ideas and practices of the old education and then go to the opposite extreme. Yet I am sure that you will appreciate what is meant when I say that many of the newer schools tend to make little or nothing of organized subject-matter of study; to proceed as if any form of direction and guidance by adults were an invasion of individual freedom, and as if the idea that education should be concerned with the present and future meant that acquaintance with the past has little or no role to play in education. Without pressing these defects to the point of exaggeration, they at least illustrate what is meant by a theory and practice of education which proceeds negatively or by reaction against what has been current in education rather than by a positive and constructive development of purposes, methods, and subject-matter on the foundation of a theory of experience and its educational potentialities.

It is not too much to say that an educational philosophy which professes to be based on the idea of freedom may become as dogmatic as ever was the traditional education which is reacted against. For any theory and set of practices is dogmatic which is not based upon critical examination of its own underlying principles. Let us say that the new education emphasizes the freedom of the learner. Very well. A problem is now set. What does freedom mean and what are the conditions under which it is capable of realization? Let us say that the kind of external imposition which was so common in the traditional school limited rather than promoted the intellectual and moral development of the young. Again, very well. Recognition of this serious defect sets a problem. Just what is the role of the teacher and of books in promoting the educational development of the immature? Admit that traditional education employed as the subject-matter for study facts and ideas so bound up with the past as to give little help in dealing with the issues of the present and future. Very well. Now we have the problem of discovering the connection which actually exists *within*

experience between the achievements of the past and the issues of the present. We have the problem of ascertaining how acquaintance with the past may be translated into a potent instrumentality for dealing effectively with the future. We may reject knowledge of the past as the *end* of education and thereby only emphasize its importance as a *means*. When we do that we have a problem that is new in the story of education: How shall the young become acquainted with the past in such a way that the acquaintance is a potent agent in appreciation of the living present? ...

In short, the point I am making is that rejection of the philosophy and practice of traditional education sets a new type of difficult educational problem for those who believe in the new type of education. We shall operate blindly and in confusion until we recognize this fact; until we thoroughly appreciate that departure from the old solves no problems. What is said in the following pages is, accordingly, intended to indicate some of the main problems with which the newer education is confronted and to suggest the main lines along which their solution is to be sought. I assume that amid all uncertainties there is one permanent frame of reference: namely, the organic connection between education and personal experience; or, that the new philosophy of education is committed to some kind of empirical and experimental philosophy. But experience and experiment are not self-explanatory ideas. Rather, their meaning is part of the problem to be explored. To know the meaning of empiricism we need to understand what experience is.

The belief that all genuine education comes about through experience does not mean that all experiences are genuinely or equally educative. Experience and education cannot be directly equated to each other. For some experiences are miseducative. Any experience is miseducative that has the effect of arresting or distorting the growth of further experience. An experience may be such as to engender callousness; it may produce lack of sensitivity and of responsiveness. Then the possibilities of having richer experience in the future are restricted. Again, a given experience may increase a person's automatic skill in a particular direction and yet tend to land him in a groove or rut, the effect again to narrow the field of further experience. An experience may be immediately enjoyable and yet promote the formation of a slack and careless attitude; this attitude then operates to modify the quality of subsequent experiences so as to prevent a person from getting out of them what they have to give. Again, experiences may be so disconnected from one another that, while each is agreeable or even exciting in itself, they are not linked cumulatively to one another. Energy is then dissipated and a person becomes scatter-brained. Each experience may be lively, vivid, and "interesting," and yet their disconnectedness may artificially generate dispersive, disintegrated, centrifugal habits. The consequence of formation of such habits is inability to control future experiences. They are then taken, either by way of enjoyment or of discontent and revolt, just as they come. Under such circumstances, it is idle to talk of self-control.

Traditional education offers a plethora of examples of experiences of the kinds just mentioned. It is a great mistake to suppose, even tacitly, that the traditional schoolroom was not a place in which pupils had experiences. Yet this is tacitly assumed when progressive education as a plan of learning by experience is placed in sharp opposition to the old. The proper line of attack is that the experiences which were had, by pupils and teachers alike, were largely of a wrong kind. How many students, for example, were rendered callous to ideas, and how many lost the impetus to learn because of the way in which learning was experienced by them? How many acquired special skills by means of automatic drill so that their power of judgment and capacity to act intelligently in new situations was limited? How many came to associate the learning process with ennui and boredom? How many found what they did learn so foreign to the situations of life outside the school as to give them no power of control over the latter? How many came to associate books with dull drudgery, so that they were "conditioned" to all but flashy reading matter?

If I ask these questions, it is not for the sake of wholesale condemnation of the old education. It is for quite another purpose. It is to emphasize the fact, first, that young people in traditional schools do have experiences; and, secondly, that the trouble is not the absence of experiences, but their defective and wrong character—wrong and defective from the standpoint of connection with further experience. The positive side of this point is even more important in connection with progressive education. It is not enough to insist upon the necessity of experience, nor even of activity in experience. Everything depends upon the *quality* of the experience which is had. The quality of an experience has two aspects. There is an immediate aspect of agreeableness or disagreeableness, and there is its influence upon later experiences. The first is obvious and easy to judge. The *effect* of an experience is not borne on its face. It sets a problem to the educator. It is his business to arrange for the kind of experiences which, while they do not repel the student, but rather engage his activities are, nevertheless, more than immediately enjoyable since they promote having desirable future experiences. Just as no man lives or dies to himself, so no experience lives or dies to itself. Wholly independent of desire or intent, every experience lives on in further experiences. Hence the central problem of an education based upon experience is to select the kind of present experiences that live fruitfully and creatively in subsequent experiences. ... Here I wish simply to emphasize the importance of this principle [of the continuity of experience] for the philosophy of educative experience. A philosophy of education, like my theory, has to be stated in words, in symbols. But so far as it is more than verbal it is a plan for conducting education. Like any plan, it must be framed with reference to what is to be done and how it is to be done. The more definitely and sincerely it is held that education is a development within, by, and for experience, the more important it is that there shall be clear conceptions of what experience is. Unless experience is so conceived that the result is a plan for deciding upon subject-matter, upon methods of instruction and discipline, and upon material equipment and social organization of the school, it is wholly in the air. It is reduced to a form of words which may be emotionally stirring but for which any other set of words might equally well be substituted unless they indicate operations to be initiated and executed. Just because traditional education was a matter of routine in which the plans and programs were handed down from the past, it does not

follow that progressive education is a matter of planless improvisation.

The traditional school could get along without any consistently developed philosophy of education. About all it required in that line was a set of abstract words like culture, discipline, our great cultural heritage, etc., actual guidance being derived not from them but from custom and established routines. Just because progressive schools cannot rely upon established traditions and institutional habits, they must either proceed more or less haphazardly or be directed by ideas which, when they are made articulate and coherent, form a philosophy of education. Revolt against the kind of organization characteristic of the traditional school constitutes a demand for a kind of organization based upon ideas. I think that only slight acquaintance with the history of education is needed to prove that educational reformers and innovators alone have felt the need for a philosophy of education. Those who adhered to the established system needed merely a few fine-sounding words to justify existing practices. The real work was done by habits which were so fixed as to be institutional. The lesson for progressive education is that it requires in an urgent degree, a degree more pressing than was incumbent upon former innovators, a philosophy of education based upon a philosophy of experience.

I remarked incidentally that the philosophy in question is, to paraphrase the saying of Lincoln about democracy, one of education of, by, and for experience. No one of these words, *of, by,* or *for,* names anything which is self-evident. Each of them is a challenge to discover and put into operation a principle of order and organization which follows from understanding what education experience signifies.

It is, accordingly, a much more difficult task to work out the kinds of materials, of methods, and of social relationships that are appropriate to the new education than is the case with traditional education. I think many of the difficulties experienced in the conduct of progressive schools and many of the criticisms leveled against them arise from this source. The difficulties are aggravated and the criticisms are increased when it is supposed that the new education is somehow easier than the old. This belief is, I imagine, more or less current. Perhaps it illustrates again the *Either-Or* philosophy, springing from the idea that about all which is required is *not* to do what is done in traditional schools.

I admit gladly that the new education is *simpler* in principle than the old. It is in harmony with principles of growth, while there is very much which is artificial in the old selection and arrangement of subjects and methods, and artificiality always leads to unnecessary complexity. But the easy and the simple are not identical. To discover what is really simple and to act upon the discovery is an exceedingly difficult task. After the artificial and complex is once institutionally established and ingrained in custom and routine, it is easier to walk in the paths that have been beaten than it is, after taking a new point of view, to work out what is practically involved in the new point of view. The old Ptolemaic astronomical system was more complicated with its cycles and epicycles than the Copernican system. But until organization of actual astronomical phenomena on the ground of the latter principle had been effected the easiest course was to follow the line of least resistance provided by the old intellectual habit. So we come back to the idea that a coherent *theory* of experience, affording positive direction to selection and organization of appropriate educational methods and materials, is required by the attempt to give new direction to the work of the schools. The process is a slow and arduous one. It is a matter of growth, and there are many obstacles which tend to obstruct growth and to deflect it into wrong lines.

... [W]e must escape from the tendency to think of organization in terms of the *kind* of organization, whether of content (or subject matter), or of methods and social relations, that mark traditional education. I think that a good deal of the current opposition to the idea of organization is due to the fact that it is so hard to get away from the picture of the studies of the old school. The moment "organization" is mentioned imagination goes almost automatically to the kind of organization that is familiar, and in revolting against that we are led to shrink from the very idea of any organization. On the other hand, educational reactionaries, who are now gathering force, use the absence of adequate intellectual and moral organization in the newer type of school as proof not only of the need of organization, but to identify any and every kind of organization with that instituted before the rise of experimental science. Failure to develop a conception of organization upon the empirical and experimental basis gives reactionaries a too easy victory. But the fact that the empirical sciences now offer the best type of intellectual organization which can be found in any field shows that there is no reason why we, who call ourselves empiricists, should be "pushovers" in the matter of order and organization.

NO

Robert M. Hutchins

THE BASIS OF EDUCATION

The obvious failures of the doctrines of adaptation, immediate needs, social reform, and of the doctrine that we need no doctrine at all may suggest to us that we require a better definition of education. Let us concede that every society must have some system that attempts to adapt the young to their social and political environment. If the society is bad, in the sense, for example, in which the Nazi state was bad, the system will aim at the same bad ends. To the extent that it makes men bad in order that they may be tractable subjects of a bad state, the system may help to achieve the social ideals of the society. It may be what the society wants; it may even be what the society needs, if it is to perpetuate its form and accomplish its aims. In pragmatic terms, in terms of success in the society, it may be a "good" system.

But it seems to me clearer to say that, though it may be a system of training, or instruction, or adaptation, or meeting immediate needs, it is not a system of education. It seems clearer to say that the purpose of education is to improve men. Any system that tries to make them bad is not education, but something else. If, for example, democracy is the best form of society, a system that adapts the young to it will be an educational system. If despotism is a bad form of society, a system that adapts the young to it will not be an educational system, and the better it succeeds in adapting them the less educational it will be.

Every man has a function as a man. The function of a citizen or a subject may vary from society to society, and the system of training, or adaptation, or instruction, or meeting immediate needs may vary with it. But the function of a man as man is the same in every age and in every society, since it results from his nature as a man. The aim of an educational system is the same in every age and in every society where such a system can exist: it is to improve man as man.

If we are going to talk about improving men and societies, we have to believe that there is some difference between good and bad. This difference must not be, as the positivists think it is, merely conventional. We cannot tell this difference by any examination of the effectiveness of a given program as the pragmatists propose; the time required to estimate these effects is usually too long and the complexity of society is always too great for us to say that the consequences of a given program are altogether clear. We cannot discover the difference between good and bad by going to the laboratory, for men and societies are not laboratory animals. If we believe that there is no truth, there is no knowledge, and there are no values except those which are validated by laboratory experiment, we cannot talk about the improvement of men and societies, for we can have no standard of judging anything that takes place among men or in societies.

Society is to be improved, not by forcing a program of social reform down its throat, through the schools, or otherwise, but by the improvement of the individuals who compose it. As Plato said, "Governments reflect human nature. States are not made out of stone or wood, but out of the characters of their citizens: these turn the scale and draw everything after them." The individual is the heart of society....

Man is by nature free, and he is by nature social. To use his freedom rightly he needs discipline. To live in society he needs the moral virtues. Good moral and intellectual habits are required for the fullest development of the nature of man. To develop fully as a social, political animal man needs participation in his own government. A benevolent despotism will not do. You cannot expect the slave to show the virtues of the free man unless you first set him free. Only democracy, in which all men rule and are ruled in turn for the good life of the whole community, can be an absolutely good form of government....

Education deals with the development of the intellectual powers of men. Their moral and spiritual powers are the sphere of the family and the church. All three agencies must work in harmony; for, though a man has three aspects, he is still one man. But the schools cannot take over the role of the family and the church without promoting the atrophy of those institutions and failing in the task that is proper to the schools.

We cannot talk about the intellectual powers of men, though we can talk about training them, or amusing them, or adapting them, and meeting their immediate needs, unless our philosophy in general tells us that there is knowledge and that there is a difference between true and false. We must believe, too, that there are other means of obtaining knowledge than scientific experimentation. If knowledge can be sought only in the laboratory, many fields in which we thought we had knowledge will offer us nothing but opinion or superstition, and we shall be forced to conclude that we cannot know anything about the most important aspects of man and society. If we are to set about developing the intellectual powers of man through having them acquire knowledge of the most important subjects, we have to begin with the proposition that experimentation and empirical data will be of only limited use to us, contrary to the convictions of many American social scientists, and that philosophy, history, literature, and art give us knowledge, and significant knowledge, on the most significant issues.

If the object of education is the improvement of men, then any system of education that is without values is a contradiction in terms. A system that seeks bad values is bad. A system that denies the existence of values denies the possibility of education. Relativism, scientism, skepticism, and anti-intellectualism, the four horsemen of the philosophical apocalypse, have produced that chaos in education which will end in the disintegration of the West.

The prime object of education is to know what is good for man. It is to know the goods in their order. There is a hierarchy of values. The task of education is to help us understand it, establish it, and live by it. This Aristotle had in mind when he said: "It is not the possessions but the desires of men that must be equalized, and this is impossible unless they have a sufficient education according to the nature of things."

Such an education is far removed from the triviality of that produced by the doctrines of adaptation, of immediate needs, of social reform, or of the doctrine of no doctrine at all. Such an education will not adapt the young to a bad environment, but it will encourage them to make it good. It will not overlook immediate needs, but it will place these needs in their proper relationship to more distant, less tangible, and more important goods. It will be the only effective means of reforming society.

This is the education appropriate to free men. It is liberal education. If all men are to be free, all men must have this education. It makes no difference how they are to earn their living or what their special interests or aptitudes may be. They can learn to make a living, and they can develop their special interests and aptitudes, after they have laid the foundation of free and responsible manhood through liberal education. It will not do to say that they are incapable of such education. This claim is made by those who are too indolent or unconvinced to make the effort to give such education to the masses.

Nor will it do to say that there is not enough time to give everybody a liberal education before he becomes a specialist. In America, at least, the waste and frivolity of the educational system are so great that it would be possible through getting rid of them to give every citizen a liberal education and make him a qualified specialist, too, in less time than is now consumed in turning out uneducated specialists.

A liberal education aims to develop the powers of understanding and judgment. It is impossible that too many people can be educated in this sense, because there cannot be too many people with understanding and judgment. We hear a great deal today about the dangers that will come upon us through the frustration of educated people who have got educated in the expectation that education will get them a better job, and who then fail to get it. But surely this depends on the representations that are made to the young about what education is. If we allow them to believe that education will get them better jobs and encourage them to get educated with this end in view, they are entitled to a sense of frustration if, when they have got the education, they do not get the jobs. But, if we say that they should be educated in order to be men, and that everybody, whether he is ditch-digger or a bank president, should have this education because he is a man, then the ditch-digger may still feel frustrated, but not because of his education.

Nor is it possible for a person to have too much liberal education, because it is impossible to have too much understanding and judgment. But it is possible to undertake too much in the name of liberal education in youth. The object of liberal education in youth is not to teach the young all they will ever need to know. It is to give them the habits, ideas, and techniques that they need to continue to educate themselves. Thus the object of formal institutional liberal education in youth is to prepare the young to educate themselves throughout their lives.

I would remind you of the impossibility of learning to understand and judge many of the most important things in youth. The judgment and understanding of practical affairs can amount to little in the absence of experience with practical affairs. Subjects that cannot be understood without experience should not be taught to those who are without experience. Or, if these subjects are taught to those who are without experience, it should be clear that these subjects can be taught only by way of introduction and that their value to the student depends on his continuing to study them as he acquires experience. The tragedy in America is that economics, ethics, politics, history, and literature are studied in youth, and seldom studied again. Therefore the graduates of American universities seldom understand them.

This pedagogical principle, that subjects requiring experience can be learned only by the experienced, leads to the conclusion that the most important branch of education is the education of adults. We sometimes seem to think of education as something like the mumps, measles, whooping cough, or chicken pox. If a person has had education in childhood, he need not, in fact he cannot, have it again. But the pedagogical principle that the most important things can be learned only in mature life is supported by a sound philosophy in general. Men are rational animals. They achieve their terrestrial felicity by the use of reason. And this means that they have to use it for their entire lives. To say that they should learn only in childhood would mean that they were human only in childhood.

And it would mean that they were unfit to be citizens of a republic. A republic, a true *res publica*, can maintain justice, peace, freedom, and order only by the exercise of intelligence. When we speak of the consent of the governed, we mean, since men are not angels who seek the truth intuitively and do not have to learn it, that every act of assent on the part of the governed is a product of learning. A republic is really a common educational life in process. So Montesquieu said that, whereas the principle of a monarchy was honor, and the principle of a tyranny was fear, the principle of a republic was education.

Hence the ideal republic is the republic of learning. It is the utopia by which all actual political republics are measured. The goal toward which we started with the Athenians twenty-five centuries ago is an unlimited republic of learning and a worldwide political republic mutually supporting each other.

All men are capable of learning. Learning does not stop as long as a man lives, unless his learning power atrophies because he does not use it. Political freedom cannot endure unless it is accompanied by provision for the unlimited acquisition of knowledge. Truth is not long retained in human affairs without continual learning and relearning. Peace is unlikely unless there are continuous, unlimited opportunities for learning and unless men continuously avail themselves of them. The world of law and justice for which we yearn, the worldwide political republic, cannot be realized without the worldwide republic of learning. The civilization we seek will be achieved when all men are citizens of the world republic of law and justice and of the republic of learning all their lives long.

POSTSCRIPT

Should Schooling Be Based on Social Experiences?

Intellectual training versus social-emotional-mental growth—the argument between Dewey and Hutchins reflects a historical debate that flows from the ideas of Plato and Aristotle and which continues today. Psychologists, sociologists, curriculum and instruction specialists, and popular critics have joined philosophers in commenting on this central concern.

Followers of Dewey contend that training the mental powers cannot be isolated from other factors of development and, indeed, can be enhanced by attention to the concrete social situations in which learning occurs. Critics of Dewey worry that the expansion of effort into the social and emotional realm only detracts from the intellectual mission that is schooling's unique province.

Was the progressive education movement ruinous, or did it lay the foundation for the education of the future? A reasonably even-handed appraisal can be found in Lawrence Cremin's *The Transformation of the School* (1961). The free school movement of the 1960s, at least partly derived from progressivism, is analyzed in Allen Graubard's *Free the Children* (1973) and Jonathan Kozol's *Free Schools* (1972).

Other sources that represent a wide spectrum of views regarding primary goals for education include Paul Nash's *Models of Man* (1968); Edward J. Power's *Evolution of Educational Doctrine* (1969); Arthur Pearl's *The Atrocity of Education* (1972); Stephen K. Bailey's *The Purposes of Education* (1976); *Doctrines of the Great Educators* (1979) by Robert R. Rusk and James Scotland; Mortimer J. Adler's *The Paideia Proposal* (1982); John I. Goodlad's *A Place Called School* (1984); and Theodore R. Sizer's *Horace's Compromise* (1984) and *Horace's School* (1992).

Among the best of recent explorations of philosophical alternatives are Gerald L. Gutek's *Philosophical and Ideological Perspectives on Education* (1988); Edward J. Power's *Philosophy of Education: Studies in Philosophies, Schooling, and Educational Policies* (1990); and *Philosophical Foundations of Education* (1990) by Howard Ozmon and Samuel Craver.

Questions that must be addressed include: Can the "either/or" polarities of this basic argument be overcome? Is the articulation of overarching general aims essential to the charting of a productive and worthwhile educational experience? And how can the classroom teacher relate to general philosophical aims?

ISSUE 2

Should Schools Determine What Is Learned?

YES: Clifton Fadiman, from "The Case for Basic Education," in James D. Koerner, ed., *The Case for Basic Education* (Council for Basic Education, 1959)

NO: John Holt, from *Escape from Childhood* (E. P. Dutton, 1974)

ISSUE SUMMARY

YES: Writer and editor Clifton Fadiman argues that standardized subject matter rescues the learner from triviality and capriciousness and sets the stage for successful and meaningful interaction in the world.

NO: Educator John Holt feels that an imposed curriculum damages the individual and usurps a basic human right to select one's own path of development.

Controversy over the content of education has been particularly keen since the 1950s. The pendulum has swung from learner-centered progressive education to an emphasis on structured intellectual discipline to calls for radical reform in the direction of "openness" to the recent rally to go "back to basics."

The conservative viewpoint, articulated by such writers as Robert M. Hutchins, Clifton Fadiman, Jacques Barzun, Arthur Bestor, and James Koerner, arises from concerns about the drift toward informalism and the decline in academic achievement in recent decades. Taking philosophical cues from Plato's contention that certain subject matters have universal qualities that prompt mental and characterological development, the "basics" advocates argue against incidental learning, student choice, and diminution of structure and standards. Jacques Barzun summarizes the viewpoint succinctly: "Nonsense is at the heart of those proposals that would replace definable subject matters with vague activities copied from 'life' or with courses organized around 'problems' or 'attitudes.'"

The reform viewpoint, represented by John Holt, Paul Goodman, Ivan Illich, Charles Silberman, Edgar Friedenberg, and others, portrays the typical traditional school as a mindless, indifferent, social institution dedicated to producing fear, docility, and conformity. In such an atmosphere, the viewpoint holds, learners either become alienated from the established curriculum or learn to play the school "game" and thus achieve a hollow success. Taking cues from the ideas of John Dewey and A. S. Neill, the "radical reformers" have given rise to a flurry of alternatives to regular schooling during recent decades. Among these are free schools, which follow the Summerhill model; urban storefront schools, which attempt to develop a true sense of "community"; "schools without walls," which follow the Philadelphia Parkway Program model; "commonwealth" schools, in which students, parents, and teachers share responsibility; and various "humanistic education" projects within regular school systems, which emphasize students' self-concept development and choice-making ability.

The utilitarian tradition that has descended from Benjamin Franklin, Horace Mann, and Herbert Spencer, Dewey's theory of active experiencing, and Neill's insistence on free and natural development support the reform position. The ideology rejects the factory model of schooling with its rigidly set curriculum, its neglect of individual differences, its social engineering function, and its pervasive formalism. "Basics" advocates, on the other hand, express deep concern over the erosion of authority and the watering down of demands upon students that result from the reform ideology.

In the following pairing, Clifton Fadiman argues the case for basic education, emphasizing prescribed studies, drawing on his own experience of schooling, and demonstrating the meaningfulness of "old-fashioned" education. In opposition, John Holt goes beyond his earlier concerns about the oppressiveness of the school curriculum to propose complete freedom for the learner to determine all aspects of his or her educational development.

YES

Clifton Fadiman

THE CASE FOR BASIC EDUCATION

The present educational controversy, like all crucial controversies, has its roots in philosophy. One's attitude toward the proposals advanced in this book depends on one's conception of man. It depends on one's view of his nature, his powers, and his reason for existing.

If, consciously or unconsciously, one takes the position that his nature is essentially animal; that his powers lie largely in the area of social and biological adaptation; and that his reason for existence is either unknowable or (should he advance one) a form of self-delusion—then the case for basic education, and consequently for education itself, falls to the ground. By the same token the case for physical, social, and vocational training becomes irrefutable.

On the other hand, if one takes the position that man's nature is both animal *and* rational; that his powers lie not only in the area of adaptation but also in that of creation; and that his reason for existence is somehow bound up with the fullest possible evolution of his mental and spiritual capacities—then the case for basic education, and consequently for education itself, is established; and further discussion becomes a matter, however interesting and important, of detail.

A crisis period is not necessarily marked by disaster or violence or even revolutionary change. It is marked by the absence of any general, tacit adherence to an agreed-upon system of values. It is in such a crisis period that we live. Of the two positions briefly outlined above, a minority adheres to the first. Another minority adheres to the second. But most of us waver between the two or have never reflected on either. Our present educational system quite properly mirrors this uncertainty of the majority. It mirrors our own mental chaos. There is nothing else it *can* do, for ours is a democratic society, and all our institutions are representative.

Now neither of the positions is logically demonstrable, though some have tried to bend them to logic, as well as to propaganda. They are faiths. The scholars whose essays comprise this book deal explicitly with questions of curriculum. Implicitly, however, they are proclaiming the faith by which they live. Furthermore, they are proclaiming that this is the faith by which Western civilization lives.

Because all faiths are attackable, everything they say can be attacked. Indeed everything they say may be wrong. But the attack can only be sustained by the proclamation of an opposing faith. And if they are wrong, they are wrong only in the sense that no faith can be "proved" right.

Thus the *Metaphysics* of Aristotle opens with the well-known statement: "All men by nature desire to know." This is not a statement of fact in the sense that "All men are born with lungs" is a statement of fact. It is not statistically checkable. It is not a self-evident truth. Cursory observation of many men seems to give it the lie. Depending on whether we prefer the language of logic or the language of emotion we may call it either an assumption or a declaration of faith. If the assumption is denied, or the declaration countered by an opposing declaration, this book, as well as education itself, becomes an irrelevancy. But in that case the cultural fruits of civilization also become an irrelevancy, because they would appear to flow, not from some blind process of unending adaptation, but from Aristotle's proposition. Any doubt cast on that proposition also casts doubt on the permanent value of culture.

It may be that the proposition *is* untenable. Perhaps all men do not by nature desire to know. We can then fall back on a second line of defense. We can say that at least men have acted *as if* they did so desire. Aristotle's dictum may be an illusion. But it looks like a creative illusion.

He has another dictum. He tells us that man is a social animal. Put the two statements together. Were man not a social animal but an anarchic animal, his desire to know would have both its origin and its terminus located in himself. But, as he is a social and not an anarchic animal, he socializes and finally systematizes his desire to know. This socialization and systematization are what we mean by education. The main, though not the only, instrument of education is an odd invention, only three thousand years old, called the school. The primary job of the school is the efficient transmission and continual reappraisal of what we call tradition. Tradition is the mechanism by which all past men teach all future men.

Now arises the question: If all men by nature desire to know, and if that desire is best gratified by education and the transmission of tradition, what should be the character of that education and the content of that tradition? At once a vast, teeming chaos faces us: apparently men desire to know and transmit all kinds of matters, from how to tie a four-in-hand to the attributes of the Godhead.

Obviously this chaos cannot be taught. Hence in the past men have imposed upon it form, order, and hierarchy. They have selected certain areas of knowledge as the ones that, to the exclusion of others, both *can* and *should* be taught.

The structure of this hierarchy is not a matter of accident. Nor is it a matter of preference. The teacher may not teach only what happens to interest him. Nor may the student choose to be taught only what happens to interest him. The criteria of choice are many and far from immutable. But there is an essential one. Basic education concerns itself with those matters which, once learned, enable the student to learn all the other matters whether trivial or complex, that cannot properly be the subjects of elementary and secondary schooling. In other words, both logic and experience suggest that certain subjects have generative power and others do not have generative power. When we have learned to tie a four-in-hand, the subject is exhausted. It is self-terminating. Our knowledge is of no value for the acquisition of further knowledge. But once we have learned to read we can decipher instructions for the tieing of a four-in-hand. Once we have learned to listen and observe, we can learn from someone else how to tie a four-in-hand.

It has, up to our time, been the general experience of men that certain subjects and not others possess this generative power. Among these subjects are those that deal with language, whether or not one's own; forms, figures and numbers; the laws of nature; the past; and the shape and behavior of our common home, the earth. Apparently these master or generative subjects endow one with the ability to learn the minor or self-terminating subjects. They also endow one, of course, with the ability to learn the higher, more complex developments of the master subjects themselves.

To the question, "Just what are these master subjects?" the contributors to this book supply a specific answer. It happens to be a traditional answer. That is, these are, more or less, with modifications in each epoch, the subjects that Western civilization has up to recent times considered basic. That they are traditional is not an argument in their favor. The contributors believe that they are sanctioned not only by use and wont but by their intrinsic value.

The word *intrinsic* is troublesome. Is it possible that, as the environment changes, the number and names of the basic subjects must also change? At a certain time, our own for example, is it possible that driver-education is more basic than history? Many of us think so, or act as if we thought so. Again I would suggest that if we do think so, or act as if we thought so, it is not because we wish to lower the accident rate (though that is what we say) but because we unconsciously conceive of man primarily as an adaptive animal and not as a rational soul. For if he is primarily the first, then at the present moment in our human career driver-education *is* basic; but if he is primarily the second it is, though desirable, not basic.

I think the authors of this book would concede that with the environmental changes the relative importance of the basic subjects will also change. It is obvious that a post-Newtonian world must accord more attention to the mathematical and physical sciences than did the pre-Newtonian world. But *some* science has at all times been taught. Similarly in a hundred years the American high school student may be universally offered Russian rather than French or German. But this does not affect the principle that *some* systematic instruction in *some* leading foreign language will remain a basic necessity.

In other words, however their forms may be modified, a core of basic or generative subjects exists. This core is not lightly to be abandoned, for once it is abandoned we have lost the primary tools which enable us to make any kind of machine we wish. Other subjects may seem transiently attractive or of obvious utility. It is pleasant to square-dance, for instance and it is useful to know how to cook. Yet we cannot afford to be seduced by such "subjects." Hard though it may be, we must jettison them in favor of the basic subject matters. And there is no time for an eclectic mixture: only a few years are available in which [to] educe, to educate the rational soul. We cannot afford bypaths. We cannot afford pleasure. All education, Aristotle tells us, is accompanied by pain. Basic education is inescapably so accompanied, as well as by that magnificent pleasure that comes of stretching, rather than tickling, the mind.

I have briefly outlined the standard case for basic education insofar as it rests on an unchanging philosophic faith or view of human nature. But there is a more urgent, though less fundamental, argument still to be advanced. In sum it is this: while basic education is *always* a necessity, it is peculiarly so in our own time....

I am a very lucky man, for I believe that my generation was just about the last one to receive an undiluted basic education. As this is written, I am fifty-four years old. Thus I received my secondary school education from 1916 to 1920. Though I was not well educated by European standards, I was very well educated by present-day American ones....

My high school was part of the New York City system. It had no amenities. Its playground was asphalt and about the size of two large drawing rooms. It looked like a barracks. It made no provision for dramatics or square dancing. It didn't even have a psychiatrist —perhaps because we didn't need one. The students were all from what is known as the "underprivileged"—or what we used to call poor—class. Today this class is depended on to provide the largest quota of juvenile delinquents. During my four years in high school there was one scandalous case in which a student stole a pair of rubbers.

Academically my school was neither very good nor very bad. The same was true of me. As the area of elective subjects was strictly limited. I received approximately the same education my fellows did. (Unfortunately Latin was not compulsory: I had to learn it—badly —by myself later on.) Here is what— in addition to the standard minors of drawing, music, art and gym—I was taught some forty years ago:

Four years of English, including rigorous drill in composition, formal grammar and public speaking.

Four years of German.

Three years of French.

Three or four years (I am not sure which) of history, including classical, European and American, plus a no-nonsense factual course in civics....

One year of physics.

One year of biology.

Three years of mathematics, through trigonometry.

That, or its near equivalent, was the standard high school curriculum in New York forty years ago. That was all I learned, all any of us learned, all all of us learned. All these subjects can be, and often are, better taught today —when they are taught at all on this scale. However, I was taught French and German well enough so that in later years I made part of my living as a translator. I was taught rhetoric and composition well enough to make it possible for me to become a practicing journalist. I was taught public speaking well enough to enable me to replace my lower-class accent with at least a passable one; and I learned also the rudiments of enunciation, placing, pitch, and proper breathing so that in after years I found it not too difficult to get odd jobs as a public lecturer and radio-and-television handyman.

I adduce these practical arguments only to explode them. They may seem important to the life-adjuster. They are not important to me. One can make a living without French. One can even make a living without a knowledge of spelling. And it is perfectly possible to rise to high estate without any control whatsoever over the English language.

What *is* important about this old-fashioned basic education (itself merely a continuation and sophistication of the basic education then taught in the primary schools) is not that it prepared me for life or showed me how to get along with my fellow men. Its importance to me and, I believe, to most of my fellow students, irrespective of their later careers, is twofold:

(1) It furnished me with a foundation on which later on, within the limits of my abilities, I could erect any intellectual structure I fancied. It gave me the wherewithal for the self-education that should be every man's concern to the hour of his death.
(2) It precluded my ever becoming Lost.

In drawing the distinction between generative and self-terminating subjects we have already discussed (1).

I want now to explain (2) because the explanation should help to make clear why in our time basic education is needed not only in principle but as a kind of emergency measure....

Considered as a well-rounded American I am an extremely inferior product. I am a poor mechanic. I play no games beyond a little poorish tennis and I haven't played that for five years. I swim, type, dance and drive raggedly, though, with respect to the last, I hope non-dangerously. I have had to learn about sex and marriage without benefit of classroom instruction. I would like to be well-rounded and I admire those who are. But it is too late. I take no pleasure in my inferiorities but I accept the fact that I must live with them.

I feel inferior. Well and good. It seems to hurt nobody. But, though I feel inferior, I do not feel Lost. I have not felt lost since being graduated from high school. I do not expect ever to feel lost. This is not because I am wise, for I am not. It is not because I am learned, for I am not. It is not because I have mastered the art of getting along with my peers, for I do not know the first thing about it. I am often terrified by the world I live in, often horrified, usually unequal to its challenges. But I am not lost in it.

I know how I came to be an American citizen in 1959; what large general movements of history produced me; what my capacities and limitations are; what truly interests me; and how valuable or valueless these interests are. My tastes are fallible but not so fallible that I am easily seduced by the vulgar and transitory—though often enough I am unequal to a proper appreciation of the noble and the permanent. In a word, like tens of millions of others in this regard, I feel at home in the world. I am at times scared but I can truthfully say that I am not bewildered.

I do not owe this to any superiority of nature. I owe it, I sincerely believe, to the conventional basic education I received beginning about a half century ago. It taught me how to read, write, speak, calculate, and listen. It taught me the elements of reasoning and it put me on to the necessary business of drawing abstract conclusions from particular instances. It taught me how to locate myself in time and space and to survey the present in the light of an imperfect but ever-functioning knowledge of the past. It provided me with great models by which to judge my own lesser performances. And it gave me the ability to investigate for myself anything that interested me, provided my mind was equal to it. . . .

The average high school graduate today is just as intelligent as my fellow students were. He is just as educable. But he is Lost, in greater or lesser degree.

By that I mean he feels little relation to the whole world in time and space, and only the most formal relation to his own country. He may "succeed," he may become a good, law-abiding citizen, he may produce other good, law-abiding citizens, and on the whole he may live a pleasant—that is, not painful—life. Yet during most of that life, and particularly after his fortieth year or so, he will feel vaguely disconnected, rootless, purposeless. Like the very plague he will shun any searching questions as to his own worth, his own identity. He will die after having lived a fractional life.

Is this what he really wants? Perhaps it is. It all comes round again to what was said at the opening of these remarks. Again it depends on one's particular vision of man. If we see our youngster as an animal whose main function is biological and social adaptation on virtually a day-to-day basis, then his fractional life is not fractional at all. It is total. But in that case our school curriculum should reflect our viewpoint. It should include the rudiments of reading so that our high school graduate may decipher highway markers, lavatory signs, and perhaps the headlines of some undemanding newspaper. It should include a large number of electives, changing every year, that may be of use to him in job hunting. And primarily it should include as much play and sport as possible, for these are the proper activities of animals, and our boy is an animal.

Yet the doubt persists. *Is* this really what he wants? And once again the answer depends on our faith. For example, the "Rockefeller Report" on Education (published in 1958 and called *The Pursuit of Excellence*) did not issue, except indirectly, from surveys, analyses, polls or statistical abstracts. It issued from faith. The following sentences do not comprise a scientific conclusion. They are an expression of faith, like the Lord's Prayer:

"What most people, young or old, want is not merely security or comfort or luxury—although they are glad enough to have these. They want meaning in their lives. If their era and their culture and their leaders do not or cannot offer them great meanings, great objectives, great convictions, then they will settle for shallow and trivial meanings."

There is no compulsion to believe this. If we do not believe it, and unqualifiedly, there is no case for basic education. Which means that, except for the superior intellect, there is no case for traditional education at all. In that event we should at once start to overhaul our school system in the light of a conception of man that sees him as a continually adjusting, pleasure-seeking, pain-avoiding animal.

But if we do believe it, and unqualifiedly, then the proposals contained [here] might at least be considered as guidelines, subject to discussion and modification.

The root of our trouble does not lie in an unbalanced curriculum, or in an inadequate emphasis on any one subject, or in poor teaching methods, or in insufficient facilities, or in underpaid instructors. It lies in the circumstance that somehow the average high school graduate does not know who he is, where he is, or how he got there. It lies in the fact that naturally enough he "will settle for shallow and trivial meanings."

NO

John Holt

ESCAPE FROM CHILDHOOD

Young people should have the right to control and direct their own learning, that is, to decide what they want to learn, and when, where, how, how much, how fast, and with what help they want to learn it. To be still more specific, I want them to have the right to decide if, when, how much, and by whom they want to be *taught* and the right to decide whether they want to learn in a school and if so which one and for how much of the time.

No human right, except the right to life itself, is more fundamental than this. A person's freedom of learning is part of his freedom of thought, even more basic than his freedom of speech. If we take from someone his right to decide what he will be curious about, we destroy his freedom of thought. We say, in effect, you must think not about what interests and concerns *you*, but about what interests and concerns *us*.

We might call this the right of curiosity, the right to ask whatever questions are most important to us. As adults, we assume that we have the right to decide what does or does not interest us, what we will look into and what we will leave alone. We take this right for granted, cannot imagine that it might be taken away from us. Indeed, as far as I know, it has never been written into any body of law. Even the writers of our Constitution did not mention it. They thought it was enough to guarantee citizens the freedom of speech and the freedom to spread their ideas as widely as they wished and could. It did not occur to them that even the most tyrannical government would try to control people's minds, what they thought and knew. That idea was to come later, under the benevolent guise of compulsory universal education.

This right to each of us to control our own learning is now in danger. When we put into our laws the highly authoritarian notion that someone should and could decide what all young people were to learn and, beyond that, could do whatever might seem necessary (which now includes dosing them with drugs) to compel them to learn it, we took a long step down a very steep and dangerous path. The requirement that a child go to school, for about six hours a day, 180 days a year, for about ten years, whether or not he learns anything there, whether or not he already knows it or could learn it faster or better somewhere else, is such gross violation of civil liberties that few adults would stand for it. But the child who resists is treated as a criminal. With this requirement we created an industry, an army of people whose whole work was to tell young people what they had to learn and to try to make them learn it. Some of these people, wanting to exercise even more power over others, to be even more "helpful," or simply because the industry is not growing fast enough to hold all the people who want to get into it, are now beginning to say, "If it is good for children for us to decide what they shall learn and to make them learn it, why wouldn't it be good for everyone? If compulsory education is a good thing, how can there be too much of it? Why should we allow anyone, of any age, to decide that he has had enough of it? Why should we allow older people, any more than young, not to know what we know when their ignorance may have bad consequences for all of us? Why should we not *make* them know what they *ought* to know?"

They are beginning to talk, as one man did on a nationwide TV show, about "womb-to-tomb" schooling. If hours of homework every night are good for the young, why wouldn't they be good for us all—they would keep us away from the TV set and other frivolous pursuits. Some group of experts, somewhere, would be glad to decide what we all ought to know and then every so often check up on us to make sure we knew it—with, of course, appropriate penalties if we did not.

I am very serious in saying that I think this is coming unless we prepare against it and take steps to prevent it. The right I ask for the young is a right that I want to preserve for the rest of us, the right *to decide what goes into our minds*. This is much more than the right to decide whether or when or how much to go to school or what school you want to go to.

That right is important, but it is only part of a much larger and more fundamental right, which I might call the right to Learn, as opposed to being Educated, *i.e.*, made to learn what someone else thinks would be good for you. It is not just compulsory schooling but compulsory Education that I oppose and want to do away with.

That children might have the control of their own learning, including the right to decide if, when, how much, and where they wanted to go to school, frightens and angers many people. They ask me, "Are you saying that if the parents wanted the child to go to school, and the child didn't want to go, that he wouldn't have to go? Are you saying that if the parents wanted the child to go to one school, and the child wanted to go to another, that the child would have the right to decide?" Yes, that is what I say. Some people ask, "If school wasn't compulsory, wouldn't many parents take their children out of school to exploit their labors in one way or another?" Such questions are often both snobbish and hypocritical. The questioner assumes and implies (though rarely says) that these bad parents are people poorer and less schooled than he. Also, though he appears to be defending the right of children to go to school, what he really is defending is the right of the state to compel them to go whether they want to or not. What he wants, in short, is that children should be in school, not that they should have any choice about going.

But saying that children should have the right to choose to go or not to go to school does not mean that the ideas and wishes of the parents would have no weight. Unless he is estranged from his parents and rebelling against them, a child cares very much about what they think and want. Most of the time, he doesn't want to anger or worry or disappoint them. Right now, in families where the parents feel that they have some choice about their children's schooling, there is much bargaining about schools. Such parents, when their children are little, often ask them whether they want to go to nursery school or kindergarten. Or they may take them to school for a while to try it out. Or, if they have a choice of schools, they may take them to several to see which they think they will like the best. Later, they care whether the child likes his school. If he does not, they try to do something about it, get him out of it, find a school he will like.

I know some parents who for years had a running bargain with their children. "If on a given day you just can't stand the thought of school, you don't feel well, you are afraid of something that may happen, you have something of your own that you very much want to do—well, you can stay home." Needless to say, the schools, with their supporting experts, fight it with all their might—Don't Give into Your Child, Make Him Go to School, He's Got to Learn. Some parents, when their own plans make it possible for them to take an interesting trip, take their children with them. They don't ask the schools' permission, they just go. If the child doesn't want to make the trip and would rather stay in school, they work out a way for him to do that. Some parents, when their child is frightened, unhappy, and suffering in school, as many children are, just take him out. Hal Bennett, in his excellent book *No More Public School*, talks about ways to do this.

A friend of mine told me that when her boy was in third grade, he had a bad teacher, bullying, contemptuous, sarcastic, cruel. Many of the class switched to another section, but this eight-year-old, being tough, defiant, and stubborn, hung on. One day—his parents did not learn this until about two years later—having had enough of the teacher's meanness, he just got up from his desk and without saying a word, walked out of the room and went home. But for all his toughness and resiliency of spirit, the experience was hard on him. He grew more timid and quarrelsome, less outgoing and confident. He lost his ordinary good humor. Even his handwriting began to go to pieces—it was much worse in the spring of the school year than in the previous fall. One spring day he sat at breakfast, eating his cereal. After a while he stopped eating and sat silently thinking about the day ahead. His eyes filled up with tears, and two big ones slowly rolled down his cheeks. His mother, who ordinarily stays out of the school life of her children, saw this and knew what it was about. "Listen," she said to him, "we don't have to go on with this. If you've had enough of that teacher, if she's making school so bad for you that you don't want to go any more, I'll be perfectly happy just to pull you right out. We can manage it. Just say the word." He was horrified and indignant. "No!" he said, "I couldn't do that." "Okay," she said, "whatever you want is fine. Just let me know." And so they left it. He had decided that he was going to tough it out, and he did. But I am sure knowing that he had the support of his mother and the chance to give it up if it got too much for him gave him the strength he needed to go on.

To say that children should have the right to control and direct their own learning, to go to school or not as they choose, does not mean that the law would forbid the parents to express an opinion or wish or strong desire on the matter. It only means that if their natural authority is not strong enough the parents can't call in the cops to make the child do what they are not able to persuade him to do. And the law may say that there is no limit to the amount of pressure or coercion the parents can apply to the child to deny him a choice that he has a legal right to make.

When I urge that children should control their learning, there is one argument that people bring up so often that I feel I must anticipate and meet it here. It says that schools are a place where children can for a while be protected against the bad influences of the world outside, particularly from its greed, dishonesty, and commercialism. It says that in school children may have a glimpse of a higher way of life, of people acting from other and better motives than greed and fear. People say, "We know that society is bad enough as it is and that children go out into the larger world as soon as they wanted, they would be tempted and corrupted just that much sooner."

They seem to believe that schools are better, more honorable places than the world outside—what a friend of mine at Harvard once called "museums of virtue." Or that people in school, both children and adults, act from higher and better motives than people outside. In this they are mistaken. There are, of course, some good schools. But on the whole, far from being the opposite of, or an antidote to, the world outside, with all its envy, fear, greed, and obsessive competitiveness, the schools are very much like it. If anything, they are worse, a terrible, abstract, simplified caricature of it. In the world outside the school, some work, at least, is done honestly and well, for its own sake, not just to get ahead of others; people are not everywhere and always being set in competition against each other; people are not (or not yet) in every minute of their lives subject to the arbitrary, irrevocable orders and judgement of others. But in most schools, a student is every minute doing what others tell him, subject to their judgement, in situations in which he can only win at the expense of other students.

This is a harsh judgement. Let me say again, as I have before, that schools are worse than most of the people in them and that many of these people do many harmful things they would rather not do, and a great many other harmful things that they do not even see as harmful. The whole of school is much worse than the sum of its parts. There are very few people in the U.S. today (or perhaps anywhere, any time) in *any* occupation, who could be trusted with the kind of power that schools give most teachers over their students. Schools seem to me among the most anti-democratic, most authoritarian, most destructive, and most dangerous institutions of modern society. No other institution does more harm or more lasting harm to more people or destroys so much of their curiosity, independence, trust, dignity, and sense of identity and worth. Even quite kindly schools are inhibited and corrupted by the knowledge of children and teachers alike that they are *performing* for the judgement and approval of others—the children for the teachers; the teachers for the parents, supervisors, school board, or the state. No one is ever free from feeling that he is being judged all the time, or soon may be. Even after the best class experiences teachers must ask themselves, "Were we right to do that?

Can we prove we were right? Will it get us in trouble?"

What corrupts the school, and makes it so much worse than most of the people in it, or than they would like it to be, is its power—just as their powerlessness corrupts the students. The school is corrupted by the endless anxious demand of the parents to know how their child is doing—meaning is he ahead of the other kids—and their demand that he be kept ahead. Schools do not protect children from the badness of the world outside. They are at least as bad as the world outside, and the harm they do to the children in their power creates much of the badness of the world outside. The sickness of the modern world is in many ways a school-induced sickness. It is in school that most people learn to expect and accept that some expert can always place them in some sort of rank or hierarchy. It is in school that we meet, become used to, and learn to believe in the totally controlled society. We do not learn much science, but we learn to worship "scientists" and to believe that anything we might conceivably need or want can only come, and someday will come, from them. The school is the closest we have yet been able to come to Huxley's *Brave New World*, with its alphas and betas, deltas and epsilons—and now it even has its soma. Everyone, including children, should have the right to say "No!" to it.

POSTSCRIPT

Should Schools Determine What Is Learned?

The free/open school movement values small, personalized educational settings in which students engage in activities that have personal meaning. One of the movement's ideological assumptions, emanating from the philosophy of Jean-Jacques Rousseau, is that, given a reasonably unrestrictive atmosphere, the learner will pursue avenues of creative and intellectual self-development. This confidence in self-motivation is the cornerstone of Holt's advocacy of freedom for the learner, a position he elaborates upon in his books *Instead of Education* (1988) and *Teach Your Own* (1982). The argument has gained some potency with recent developments in home-based computer-assisted instruction.

A culmination of the Fadiman appraisal of the value of tightly organized schooling and the need for curricular clarity and certainty can be seen in the 1982 publication by the Institute for Philosophical Research of *The Paideia Proposal: An Educational Manifesto*. Written by Mortimer J. Adler, on behalf of a group of distinguished scholars and practitioners, the book charts the essential ingredients of an approach to schooling that aims at instilling in all students the general aspects of culture that will enable them to lead civilized lives. The proposal advocates a uniform course of study built around the acquisition of organized knowledge, the development of learning skills, and the understanding of ideas and values. The Institute for Philosophical Research's 1988 yearbook, *Content of the Curriculum*, edited by Ronald S. Brandt, seems to present a compromise portrait of a revitalized traditional curriculum.

The essentialist position articulated by Fadiman is echoed in a number of recent calls for a more standardized and challenging curriculum by such thinkers as E. D. Hirsch, Jr., Allen Bloom, William Bennett, Diane Ravitch, and Lynne Cheney. Holt's plea for freedom from an imposed curriculum has a new champion in John Taylor Gatto, New York City and New York State Teacher of the Year. Gatto has produced two provocative books, *Dumbing Us Down: The Hidden Curriculum of Compulsory Schooling* (1992) and *Confederacy of Dunces: The Tyranny of Compulsory Schooling* (1992), an excerpt from which appears in the Spring 1994 issue of *The Educational Forum*. Two other thought-stirring works that build upon Holt's basic views are Lewis J. Perelman's *School's Out: The New Technology and the End of Education* (1992) and George Leonard's "Notes: The End of School," *The Atlantic Monthly* (May 1992).

ISSUE 3

Should Behaviorism Shape Educational Practices?

YES: B. F. Skinner, from *Beyond Freedom and Dignity* (Alfred A. Knopf, 1971)

NO: Carl R. Rogers, from *Freedom to Learn* (Merrill, 1983)

ISSUE SUMMARY

YES: B. F. Skinner, influential proponent of behaviorism and professor of psychology critiques the concept of "inner freedom" and links learning and motivation to the influence of external forces.

NO: Professor of psychology and psychiatry Carl R. Rogers offers the "humanistic" alternative to behaviorism, insisting on the reality of subjective forces in human motivation.

Intimately enmeshed with considerations of aims and purposes and determination of curricular elements are the psychological base that affects the total setting in which learning takes place and the basic means of motivating learners. Historically, the atmosphere of schooling has often been characterized by harsh discipline, regimentation, and restriction. The prison metaphor often used by critics in describing school conditions rings true all too often.

Although calls to make schools pleasant have been sounded frequently, they have seldomly been heeded. Roman rhetorician Marcus Fabius Quintilian (ca. A.D. 35–ca. 100) advocated a constructive and enjoyable learning atmosphere. John Amos Comenius in the seventeenth century suggested a gardening metaphor in which learners were given kindly nurturance. Johann Heinrich Pestalozzi established a model school in the nineteenth century that replaced authoritarianism with love and respect.

Yet school as an institution retains the stigma of authoritarian control—attendance is compelled, social and psychological punishment is meted out, and the decision-making freedom of students is limited and often curtailed. These practices lead to rather obvious conclusions: either the prevailing belief is that young people are naturally evil and wild and therefore must be tamed in a restricting environment, or that schooling as such is so unpalatable that people must be forced and cajoled to reap its benefits—or both.

Certainly philosopher John Dewey (1895–1952) was concerned about this circumstance, citing at one time the superintendent of his native Burlington, Vermont, school district as admitting that the schools were a source of "grief and mortification" and were "unworthy of patronage." Dewey rejected both

32

the need for "taming" and the defeatist attitude that the school environment must remain unappealing. He hoped to create a motivational atmosphere that would engage learners in real problem-solving activities, thereby sustaining curiosity, creativity, and attachment. The rewards were to flow from the sense of accomplishment and freedom, which was to be achieved through the disciplined actions necessary to solve the problem at hand.

More recent treatment of the allied issues of freedom, control, and motivation has come from the two major camps in the field of educational psychology: the behaviorists (rooted in the early twentieth-century theories of Pavlov, Thorndike, and Watson) and the humanists (emanating from the Gestalt and field theory psychologies developed in Europe and America earlier in this century).

B. F. Skinner has been the dominant force in translating behaviorism into recommendations for school practices. He and his disciples, often referred to as neobehaviorists, have contributed to widely used innovations such as behavioral objectives in instruction and testing, competency-based education, mastery learning, assertive discipline, and outcome-based education. The humanistic viewpoint has been championed by Carl R. Rogers, Abraham Maslow, Fritz Perls, Rollo May, and Erich Fromm, most of whom ground their psychological theories in the philosophical assumptions of existentialism and phenomenology.

Skinner believes that "inner" states are merely convenient myths, that motives and behaviors are shaped by environmental factors. These shaping forces, however, need not be negative, nor must they operate in an uncontrolled manner. Our present understanding of human behavior allows us the freedom to shape the environmental forces, which in turn shape us. With this power, Skinner contends, we can replace aversive controls in schooling with positive reinforcements that heighten the students' motivation level and make learning more efficient. Skinner deals with the problem of freedom and control in the selection that follows.

Carl R. Rogers, representing humanistic psychology, critiques Skinner's behaviorist approach and sets forth his argument supporting the reality of freedom as an inner human state that is the wellspring of responsibility, will, and commitment.

YES
B. F. Skinner

FREEDOM THROUGH CONTROL

Almost all living things act to free themselves from harmful contacts. A kind of freedom is achieved by the relatively simple forms of behavior called reflexes. A person sneezes and frees his respiratory passages from irritating substances. He vomits and frees his stomach from indigestible or poisonous food. He pulls back his hand and frees it from a sharp or hot object. More elaborate forms of behavior have similar effects. When confined, people struggle ("in rage") and break free. When in danger they flee from or attack its source. Behavior of this kind presumably evolved because of its survival value; it is as much a part of what we call the human genetic endowment as breathing, sweating, or digesting food. And through conditioning similar behavior may be acquired with respect to novel objects which could have played no role in evolution. These are no doubt minor instances of the struggle to be free, but they are significant. We do not attribute them to any love of freedom; they are simply forms of behavior which have proved useful in reducing various threats to the individual and hence to the species in the course of evolution.

A much more important role is played by behavior which weakens harmful stimuli in another way. It is not acquired in the form of conditioned reflexes, but as the product of a different process called operant conditioning. When a bit of behavior is followed by a certain kind of consequence, it is more likely to occur again, and a consequence having this effect is called a reinforcer. Food, for example, is a reinforcer to a hungry organism; anything the organism does that is followed by the receipt of food is more likely to be done again whenever the organism is hungry. Some stimuli are called negative reinforcers; any response which reduces the intensity of such a stimulus—or ends it—is more likely to be emitted when the stimulus recurs. Thus, if a person escapes from a hot sun when he moves under cover, he is more likely to move under cover when the sun is again hot. The reduction in temperature reinforces the behavior it is "contingent upon"—that is, the behavior it follows. Operant conditioning also occurs when a person simply avoids a hot sun—when, roughly speaking, he escapes from the *threat* of a hot sun.

Negative reinforcers are called aversive in the sense that they are the things organisms "turn away from." The term suggests a spatial separation—moving or running away from something—but the essential relation is temporal. In a standard apparatus used to study the process in the laboratory, an arbitrary response simply weakens an aversive stimulus or brings it to an end. A great deal of physical technology is the result of this kind of struggle for freedom. Over the centuries, in erratic ways, men have constructed a world in which they are relatively free of many kinds of threatening or harmful stimuli—extremes of temperature, sources of infection, hard labor, danger, and even those minor aversive stimuli called discomfort.

Escape and avoidance play a much more important role in the struggle for freedom when the aversive conditions are generated by other people. Other people can be aversive without, so to speak, trying; they can be rude, dangerous, contagious, or annoying, and one escapes from them or avoids them accordingly. They may also be "intentionally" aversive—that is, they may treat other people aversively because of what follows. Thus, a slave driver induces a slave to work by whipping him when he stops; by resuming work the slave escapes from the whipping (and incidentally reinforces the slave driver's behavior in using the whip). A parent nags a child until the child performs a task; by performing the task the child escapes nagging (and reinforces the parent's behavior). The blackmailer threatens exposure unless the victim pays; by paying, the victim escapes from the threat (and reinforces the practice). A teacher threatens corporal punishment or failure until his students pay attention; by paying attention the students escape from the threat of punishment (and reinforce the teacher for threatening it). In one form or another intentional aversive control is the pattern of

most social coordination—in ethics, religion, government, economics, education, psychotherapy, and family life.

A person escapes from or avoids aversive treatment by behaving in ways which reinforce those who treated him aversively until he did so, but he may escape in other ways. For example, he may simply move out of range. A person may escape from slavery, emigrate or defect from a government, desert from an army, become an apostate from a religion, play truant, leave home, or drop out of a culture as a hobo, hermit, or hippie. Such behavior is as much a product of the aversive conditions as the behavior the conditions were designed to evoke. The latter can be guaranteed only by sharpening the contingencies or by using stronger aversive stimuli.

Another anomalous mode of escape is to attack those who arrange aversive conditions and weaken or destroy their power. We may attack those who crowd us or annoy us, as we attack the weeds in our garden, but again the struggle for freedom is mainly directed toward intentional controllers—toward those who treat others aversively in order to induce them to behave in particular ways. Thus, a child may stand up to his parents, a citizen may overthrow a government, a communicant may reform a religion, a student may attack a teacher or vandalize a school, and a dropout may work to destroy a culture.

It is possible that man's genetic endowment supports this kind of struggle for freedom: when treated aversively people tend to act aggressively or to be reinforced by signs of having worked aggressive damage. Both tendencies should have had evolutionary advantages, and they can easily be demonstrated. If two organisms which have been coexisting peacefully receive painful shocks, they immediately exhibit characteristic patterns of aggression toward each other. The aggressive behavior is not necessarily directed toward the actual source of stimulation; it may be "displaced" toward any convenient person or object. Vandalism and riots are often forms of undirected or misdirected aggression. An organism which has received a painful shock will also, if possible, act to gain access to another organism toward which it can act aggressively. The extent to which human aggression exemplifies innate tendencies is not clear, and many of the ways in which people attack and thus weaken or destroy the power of intentional controllers are quite obviously learned.

What we may call the "literature of freedom" has been designed to induce people to escape from or attack those who act to control them aversively. The content of the literature is the philosophy of freedom, but philosophies are among those inner causes which need to be scrutinized. We say that a person behaves in a given way because he possesses a philosophy, but we infer the philosophy from the behavior and therefore cannot use it in any satisfactory way as an explanation, at least until it is in turn explained. The literature of freedom, on the other hand, has a simple objective status. It consists of books, pamphlets, manifestoes, speeches, and other verbal products, designed to induce people to act to free themselves from various kinds of intentional control. It does not impart a philosophy of freedom; it induces people to act.

The literature often emphasizes the aversive conditions under which people live, perhaps by contrasting them with conditions in a freer world. It thus makes the conditions more aversive, "increasing the misery" of those it is trying to rescue. It also identifies those from whom one is to escape or those whose power is to be weakened through attack. Characteristic villains of the literature are tyrants, priests, generals, capitalists, martinet teachers, and domineering parents.

The literature also prescribes modes of action. It has not been much concerned with escape, possibly because advice has not been needed; instead, it has emphasized how controlling power may be weakened or destroyed. Tyrants are to be overthrown, ostracized, or assassinated. The legitimacy of a government is to be questioned. The ability of a religious agency to mediate supernatural sanctions is to be challenged. Strikes and boycotts are to be organized to weaken the economic power which supports aversive practices. The argument is strengthened by exhorting people to act, describing likely results, reviewing successful instances on the model of the advertising testimonial, and so on.

The would-be controllers do not, of course, remain inactive. Governments make escape impossible by banning travel or severely punishing or incarcerating defectors. They keep weapons and other sources of power out of the hands of revolutionaries. They destroy the written literature of freedom and imprison or kill those who carry it orally. If the struggle for freedom is to succeed, it must then be intensified.

The importance of the literature of freedom can scarcely be questioned. Without help or guidance people submit to aversive conditions in the most surprising way. This is true even when the aversive conditions are part of the natural environment. Darwin observed, for example, that the Fuegians seemed to make no effort to protect themselves from the cold; they wore only scant clothing and made little use of it against the weather. And one of the most striking things about the struggle for freedom from intentional control is how often it has been lacking. Many people have submitted to the most obvious religious, governmental, and economic controls for centuries, striking for freedom only sporadically, if at all. The literature of freedom has made an essential contribution to the elimination of many aversive practices in government, religion, education, family life, and the production of goods.

The contributions of the literature of freedom, however, are not usually described in these terms. Some traditional theories could conceivably be said to define freedom as the absence of aversive control, but the emphasis has been on how the condition *feels*. Other traditional theories could conceivably be said to define freedom as a person's condition when he is behaving under nonaversive control, but the emphasis has been upon a state of mind associated with doing what one wants. According to John Stuart Mill, "Liberty consists in doing what one desires." The literature of freedom has been important in changing practice (it has changed practices whenever it has had any effect whatsoever), but it has nevertheless defined its task as the changing of states of mind and feelings. Freedom is a "possession." A person escapes from or destroys the power of a controller in order to feel free, and once he feels free and can do what he desires, no further action is recommended and none is prescribed by the literature of freedom, except perhaps eternal vigilance lest control be resumed.

The feeling of freedom becomes an unreliable guide to action as soon as would-be controllers turn to nonaversive measures, as they are likely to do to avoid the problems raised when the controllee escapes or attacks. Nonaversive measures are not as conspicuous as aversive and are likely to be acquired more slowly, but they have obvious advantages which promote their use. Productive labor, for example, was once the result of punishment: the slave worked to avoid the consequences of not working. Wages exemplify a different principle; a person is paid when he behaves in a given way so that he will continue to behave in that way. Although it has long been recognized that rewards have useful effects, wage systems have evolved slowly. In the nineteenth century it was believed that an industrial society required a hungry labor force; wages would be effective only if the hungry worker could exchange them for food. By making labor less aversive—for instance, by shortening hours and improving conditions—it has been possible to get men to work for lesser rewards. Until recently teaching was almost entirely aversive: the student studies to escape the consequences of not studying, but nonaversive techniques are gradually being discovered and used. The skillful parent learns to reward a child for good behavior rather than punish him for bad. Religious agencies move from the threat of hellfire to an emphasis on God's love, and governments turn from aversive sanctions to various kinds of inducements. . . . What the layman calls a reward is a "positive reinforcer," the effects of which have been exhaustively studied in the experimental analysis of operant behavior. The effects are not as easily recognized as those of aversive contingencies because they tend to be deferred, and applications have therefore been delayed, but techniques as powerful as the older aversive techniques are now available. . . .

The literature of freedom has never come to grips with techniques of control which do not generate escape or counterattack because it has dealt with the problem in terms of states of mind and feelings. In his book *Sovereignty*, Bertrand de Jouvenel quotes two important figures in that literature. According to Leibnitz, "Liberty consists in the power to do what one wants to do," and according to Voltaire, "When I can do what I want to do, there is my liberty for me." But both writers add a concluding phrase: Leibnitz, "... or in the power to want what can be got," and Voltaire, more candidly, "... but I can't help wanting what I do want." Jouvenel relegates these comments to a footnote, saying that the power to want is a matter of "interior liberty" (the freedom of the inner man!) which falls outside the "gambit of freedom."

A person wants something if he acts to get it when the occasion arises. A person who says "I want something to eat" will presumably eat when something becomes available. If he says "I want to get warm," he will presumably move into a warm place when he can. These acts have been reinforced in the past by whatever was wanted. What a person *feels* when he feels himself wanting something depends upon the circumstances. Food is reinforcing only in a state of deprivation, and a person who wants something to eat may feel parts of that state—for example, hunger pangs. A person who wants to get warm presumably feels cold. Conditions associated with a high probability of responding may also be felt, together with aspects of the present occasion which are similar to those of past occasions upon which behavior has been reinforced. Wanting is not, however, a feeling, nor is a feeling the reason a person acts to get what he wants. Certain contingencies have raised the probability of behavior and at the same time have created conditions which may be felt. Freedom is a matter of contingencies of reinforcement, not of the feelings the contingencies generate. The distinction is particularly important when the contingencies do not generate escape or counterattack....

The literature of freedom has encouraged escape from or attack upon all controllers. It has done so by making any indication of control aversive. Those who manipulate human behavior are said to be evil men, necessarily bent on exploitation. Control is clearly the opposite of freedom, and if freedom is good, control must be bad. What is overlooked is control which does not have aversive consequences at any time. Many social practices essential to the welfare of the species involve the control of one person by another, and no one can suppress them who has any concern for human achievements.... [I]n order to maintain the position that all control is wrong, it has been necessary to disguise or conceal the nature of useful practices, to prefer weak practices just because they can be disguised or concealed, and—a most extraordinary result indeed!—to perpetuate punitive measures.

The problem is to be free men, not from control, but from certain kinds of control, and it can be solved only if our analysis takes all consequences into account. How people feel about control, before or after the literature of freedom has worked on their feelings, does not lead to useful distinctions.

Were it not for the unwarranted generalization that all control is wrong, we should deal with the social environment as simply as we deal with the nonsocial.

Although technology has freed men from certain aversive features of the environment, it has not freed them from the environment. We accept the fact that we depend upon the world around us, and we simply change the nature of the dependency. In the same way, to make the social environment as free as possible of aversive stimuli, we do not need to destroy that environment or escape from it; we need to redesign it.

Man's struggle for freedom is not due to a will to be free, but to certain behavioral processes characteristic of the human organism, the chief effect of which is the avoidance of or escape from so-called "aversive" features of the environment. Physical and biological technologies have been mainly concerned with natural aversive stimuli; the struggle for freedom is concerned with stimuli intentionally arranged by other people. The literature of freedom has identified the other people and has proposed ways of escaping from them or weakening or destroying their power. It has been successful in reducing the aversive stimuli used in intentional control, but it has made the mistake of defining freedom in terms of states of mind or feelings, and it has therefore not been able to deal effectively with techniques of control which do not breed escape or revolt but nevertheless have aversive consequences. It has been forced to brand all control as wrong and to misrepresent many of the advantages to be gained from a social environment. It is unprepared for the next step, which is not to free men from control but to analyze and change the kinds of control to which they are exposed.

NO

Carl R. Rogers

FREEDOM AND COMMITMENT

One of the deepest issues in modern life, in modern man, is the question as to whether the concept of personal freedom has any meaning whatsoever in our present-day scientific world. The growing ability of the behavioral scientist to predict and to control behavior has brought the issue sharply to the fore. If we accept the logical positivism and strictly behavioristic emphases which are predominant in the American psychological scene, there is not even room for discussion....

But if we step outside the narrowness of the behavioral sciences, this question is not only *an* issue, it is one of the primary issues which define modern man. Friedman in his book (1963, p. 251) makes his topic "the problematic of modern man—the alienation, the divided nature, the unresolved tension between personal freedom and psychological compulsion which follows on 'the death of God'." The issues of personal freedom and personal commitment have become very sharp indeed in a world in which man feels unsupported by a supernatural religion, and experiences keenly the division between his awareness and those elements of his dynamic functioning of which he is unaware. If he is to wrest any meaning from a universe which for all he knows may be indifferent, he must arrive at some stance which he can hold in regard to these timeless uncertainties.

So, writing as both a behavioral scientist and as one profoundly concerned with the human, the personal, the phenomenological and the intangible, I should like to contribute what I can to this continuing dialogue regarding the meaning of and the possibility of freedom.

MAN IS UNFREE

... In the minds of most behavioral scientists, man is not free, nor can he as a free man commit himself to some purpose, since he is controlled by factors outside of himself. Therefore, neither freedom nor commitment is even a possible concept to modern behavioral science as it is usually understood.

To show that I am not exaggerating, let me quote a statement from Dr. B. F. Skinner of Harvard, who is one of the most consistent advocates of a strictly behavioristic psychology. He says,

> The hypothesis that man is not free is essential to the application of scientific method to the study of human behavior. The free inner man who is held responsible for his behavior is only a prescientific substitute for the kinds of causes which are discovered in the course of scientific analysis. All these alternative causes lie *outside* the individual (1953, p. 477).

This view is shared by many psychologists and others who feel, as does Dr. Skinner, that all the effective causes of behavior lie outside of the individual and that it is only through the external stimulus that behavior takes place. The scientific description of behavior avoids anything that partakes in any way of freedom. For example, Dr. Skinner (1964, pp. 90–91) describes an experiment in which a pigeon was conditioned to turn in a clockwise direction. The behavior of the pigeon was "shaped up" by rewarding any movement that approximated a clockwise turn until, increasingly, the bird was turning round and round in a steady movement. This is what is known as operant conditioning. Students who had watched the demonstration were asked to write an account of what they had seen. Their responses included the following ideas: that the pigeon was conditioned to *expect* reinforcement for the right kind of behavior; that the pigeon *hoped* that something would bring the food back again; that the pigeon *observed* that a certain behavior seemed to produce a particular result; that the pigeon *felt* that food would be given it because of its action; that the bird came to *associate* his action with the clock of the food dispenser. Skinner ridicules these statements because they all go beyond the observed behavior in using such words as *expect, hope, observe, felt,* and *associate.* The whole explanation from his point of view is that the bird was reinforced when it emitted a given kind of behavior; the pigeon walked around until the food container again appeared; a certain behavior produced a given result; food was given to the pigeon when it acted in a given way; the click of the food dispenser was related in time to the bird's action. These statements describe the pigeon's behavior from a scientific point of view.

Skinner goes on to point out that the students were undoubtedly reporting what they would have expected, felt and hoped under similar circumstances. But he then makes the case that there is no more reality to such ideas in the human being than there is in the pigeon, that it is only because such words have been reinforced by the verbal community in which the individual has developed, that such terms are used. He discusses the fact that the verbal community which conditioned them to use such terms saw no more of their behavior than they had seen of the pigeon's. In other words the internal events, if they indeed exist, have no scientific significance.

As to the methods used for changing the behavior of the pigeon, many people besides Dr. Skinner feel that through such positive reinforcement human behavior as well as animal behavior can be "shaped up" and controlled. In his book *Walden Two,* Skinner says,

> Now that we know how positive reinforcement works and how negative doesn't, we can be more deliberate and hence more successful in our cultural de-

sign. We can achieve a sort of control under which the controlled, though they are following a code much more scrupulously than was ever the case under the old system, nevertheless *feel free*. They are doing what they want to do, not what they are forced to do. That's the source of the tremendous power of positive reinforcement—there is no restraint and no revolt. By a careful cultural design we control not the final behavior but the *inclination* to behave—the motives, the desires, the wishes. The curious thing is that in that case *the question of freedom never arises* (1948, p. 218).

... I think it is clear from all of this that man is a machine—a complex machine, to be sure, but one which is increasingly subject to scientific control. Whether behavior will be managed through operant conditioning as in *Walden Two* or whether we will be "shaped up" by the unplanned forms of conditioning implied in social pressure, or whether we will be controlled by electrodes in the brain, it seems quite clear that science is making out of man an object and that the purpose of such science is not only understanding and prediction but control. Thus it would seem to be quite clear that there could be no concept so foreign to the facts as that man is free. Man is a machine, man is unfree, man cannot commit himself in any meaningful sense; he is simply controlled by planned or unplanned forces outside of himself.

MAN IS FREE

I am impressed by the scientific advances illustrated in the examples I have given. I regard them as a great tribute to the ingenuity, insight, and persistence of the individuals making the investigations. They have added enormously to our knowl-

edge. Yet for me they leave something very important unsaid. Let me try to illustrate this, first from my experience in therapy.

I think of a young man classed as schizophrenic with whom I had been working for a long time in a state hospital. He was a very inarticulate man, and during one hour he made a few remarks about individuals who had recently left the hospital; then he remained silent for almost forty minutes. When he got up to go, he mumbled almost under his breath, "If some of *them* can do it, maybe I can too." That was all—not a dramatic statement, not uttered with force and vigor, yet a statement of choice by this young man to work toward his own improvement and eventual release from the hospital. It is not too surprising that about eight months after that statement he was out of the hospital. I believe this experience of responsible choice is one of the deepest aspects of psychotherapy and one of the elements which most solidly underlies personality change.

I think of another young person, this time a young woman graduate student, who was deeply disturbed and on the borderline of a psychotic break. Yet after a number of interviews in which she talked very critically about all of the people who had failed to give her what she needed, she finally concluded: "Well, with that sort of a foundation, it's really up to *me*. I mean it seems to be really apparent to me that I can't depend on someone else to *give* me an education." And then she added very softly: "I'll really have to get it myself." She goes on to explore this experience of important and responsible choice. She finds it a frightening experience, and yet one which gives her a feeling of strength. A force seems to surge up within her which is big and strong, and yet she also feels very much alone and sort of cut off from support. She adds: "I am going to begin to do more things that I know I should do." And she did.

I could add many other examples. One young fellow talking about the way in which his whole life had been distorted and spoiled by his parents finally comes to the conclusion that, "Maybe now that I *see* that, it's up to *me*." ...

For those of you [who] have seen the film *David and Lisa*—and I hope that you have had that rich experience —I can illustrate exactly what I have been discussing. David, the adolescent schizophrenic, goes into a panic if he is touched by anyone. He feels that "touching kills," and he is deathly afraid of it, and afraid of the closeness in human relationships which touching implies. Yet toward the close of the film he makes a bold and positive choice of the kind I have been describing. He has been trying to be of help to Lisa, the girl who is out of touch with reality. He tries to help at first in an intellectually contemptuous way, then increasingly in a warmer and more personal way. Finally, in a highly dramatic movement, he says to her, "Lisa, take my hand." He *chooses*, with obvious conflict and fear, to leave behind the safety of his untouchableness, and to venture into the world of real human relationships where he is literally and figuratively in *touch* with another. You are an unusual person if the film does not grow a bit misty at this point.

Perhaps a behaviorist could try to account for the reaching out of his hand by saying that it was the result of intermittent reinforcement of partial movements. I find such an explanation both inaccurate and inadequate. It is the

meaning of the *decision* which is essential to understanding the act.

What I am trying to suggest in all of this is that I would be at a loss to explain the positive change which can occur in psychotherapy if I had to omit the importance of the sense of free and responsible choice on the part of my clients. I believe that this experience of freedom to choose is one of the deepest elements underlying change.

THE MEANING OF FREEDOM

Considering the scientific advances which I have mentioned, how can we even speak of freedom? In what sense is a client free? In what sense are any of us free? What possible definition of freedom can there be in the modern world? Let me attempt such a definition.

In the first place, the freedom that I am talking about is essentially an inner thing, something which exists in the living person quite aside from any of the outward choices of alternatives which we so often think of as constituting freedom. I am speaking of the kind of freedom which Viktor Frankl vividly describes in his experience of the concentration camp, when everything—possessions, status, identity—was taken from the prisoners. But even months and years in such an environment showed only "that everything can be taken from a man but one thing: the last of the human freedoms—to choose one's own attitude in any given set of circumstances, to choose one's own way" (1959, p. 65). It is this inner, subjective, existential freedom which I have observed. It is the realization that "I can live myself, here and now, by my own choice." It is the quality of courage which enables a person to step into the uncertainty of the unknown as he chooses himself. It is the discovery of meaning from within oneself, meaning which comes from listening, sensitively and openly to the complexities of what one is experiencing. It is the burden of being responsible for the self one chooses to be. It is the recognition of a person that he is an emerging process, not a static end product. The individual who is thus deeply and courageously thinking his own thoughts, becoming his own uniqueness, responsibly choosing himself, may be fortunate in having hundreds of objective outer alternatives from which to choose, or he may be unfortunate in having none. But his freedom exists regardless. So we are first of all speaking of something which exists within the individual, something phenomenological rather than external, but nonetheless to be prized.

The second point in defining this experience of freedom is that it exists not as a contradiction of the picture of the psychological universe as a sequence of cause and effect, but as a complement to such a universe. Freedom rightly understood is a fulfillment by the person of the ordered sequence of his life. The free man moves out voluntarily, freely, responsibly, to play his significant part in a world whose determined events move through him and through his spontaneous choice and will.

I see this freedom of which I am speaking, then, as existing in a different *dimension* than the determined sequence of cause and effect. I regard it as a freedom which exists in the subjective person, a freedom which he courageously uses to live his potentialities. The fact that this type of freedom seems completely irreconcilable with the behaviorist's picture of man is something which I will discuss a bit later....

THE EMERGENCE OF COMMITMENT

I have spoken thus far primarily about freedom. What about commitment? Certainly the disease of our age is lack of purpose, lack of meaning, lack of commitment on the part of individuals. Is there anything which I can say in regard to this?

It is clear to me that in therapy, as indicated in the examples that I have given, commitment to purpose and to meaning in life is one of the significant elements of change. It is only when the person decides, "I am someone, I am someone worth being: I am committed to being myself," that change becomes possible.

At a very interesting symposium at Rice University recently, Dr. Sigmund Koch sketched the revolution which is taking place in science, literature and the arts, in which a sense of commitment is again becoming evident after a long period in which that emphasis has been absent.

Part of what he meant by that may be illustrated by talking about Dr. Michael Polanyi, the philosopher of science, formerly a physicist, who has been presenting his notions about what science basically is. In his book, *Personal Knowledge*, Polanyi makes it clear that even scientific knowledge is personal knowledge, committed knowledge. We cannot rest comfortably on the belief that scientific knowledge is impersonal and "out there," that it has nothing to do with the individual who has discovered it. Instead, every aspect of science is pervaded by disciplined personal commitment, and Polanyi makes the case very persuasively that the whole attempt to divorce science from the person is a completely unrealistic one.

I think I am stating his belief correctly when I say that in his judgment logical positivism and all the current structure of science cannot save us from the fact that all knowing is uncertain, involves risk, and is grasped and comprehended only through the deep, personal commitment of a disciplined search.

Perhaps a brief quotation will give something of the flavor of his thinking. Speaking of great scientists, he says:

> So we see that both Kepler and Einstein approached nature with intellectual passions and with beliefs inherent in these passions, which led them to their triumphs and misguided them to their errors. These passions and beliefs were theirs, personally, even universally. I believe that they were competent to follow these impulses, even though they risked being misled by them. And again, what I accept of their work today, I accept personally, guided by passions and beliefs similar to theirs, holding in my turn that my impulses are valid, universally, even though I must admit the possibility that they may be mistaken (1959, p. 145).

Thus we see that a modern philosopher of science believes that deep personal commitment is the only possible basis on which science can firmly stand. This is a far cry indeed from the logical positivism of twenty or thirty years ago, which placed knowledge far out in impersonal space.

Let me say a bit more about what I mean by commitment in the psychological sense. I think it is easy to give this word a much too shallow meaning, indicating that the individual has, simply by conscious choice, committed himself to one course of action or another. I think the meaning goes far deeper than that. Commitment is a total organismic direction involving not only the conscious mind but the whole direction of the organism as well.

In my judgment, commitment is something that one *discovers* within oneself. It is a trust of one's total reaction rather than of one's mind only. It has much to do with creativity. Einstein's explanation of how he moved toward his formulation of relativity without any clear knowledge of his goal is an excellent example of what I mean by the sense of commitment based on a total organismic reaction. He says:

> "During all those years there was a feeling of direction, of going straight toward something concrete. It is, of course, very hard to express that feeling in words but it was decidedly the case and clearly to be distinguished from later considerations about the rational form of the solution" (quoted in Wertheimer, 1945, p. 183–184).

Thus commitment is more than a decision. It is the functioning of an individual who is searching for the directions which are emerging within himself. Kierkegaard has said, "The truth exists only in the process of becoming, in the process of appropriation" (1941, p. 72). It is this individual creation of a tentative personal truth through action which is the essence of commitment.

Man is most successful in such a commitment when he is functioning as an integrated, whole, unified individual. The more that he is functioning in this total manner the more confidence he has in the directions which he unconsciously chooses. He feels a trust in his experiencing, of which, even if he is fortunate, he has only partial glimpses in his awareness.

Thought of in the sense in which I am describing it, it is clear that commitment is an achievement. It is the kind of purposeful and meaningful direction which is only gradually achieved by the individual who has come increasingly to live closely in relationship with his own experiencing—a relationship in which his unconscious tendencies are as much respected as are his conscious choices. This is the kind of commitment toward which I believe individuals can move. It is an important aspect of living in a fully functioning way.

THE IRRECONCILABLE CONTRADICTION

I trust it will be very clear that I have given two sharply divergent and irreconcilably contradictory points of view. On the one hand, modern psychological science and many other forces in modern life as well, hold the view that man is unfree, that he is controlled, that words such as purpose, choice, commitment have no significant meaning, that man is nothing but an object which we can more fully understand and more fully control. Enormous strides have been and are being made in implementing this perspective. It would seem heretical indeed to question this view.

Yet, as Polanyi has pointed out in another of his writings (1957), the dogmas of science can be in error. He says:

In the days when an idea could be silenced by showing that it was contrary to religion, theology was the greatest single source of fallacies. Today, when any human thought can be discredited by branding it as unscientific, the power previously exercised by theology has passed over to science; hence science has become in its turn the greatest single source of error.

So I am emboldened to say that over against this view of man as unfree, as an object, is the evidence from therapy, from subjective living, and from objective research as well, that personal freedom and responsibility have a crucial significance, that one cannot live a complete life without such personal freedom and responsibility, and that self-understanding and responsible choice make a sharp and measurable difference in the behavior of the individual. In this context, commitment does have meaning. Commitment is the emerging and changing total direction of the individual, based on a close and acceptant relationship between the person and all of the trends in his life, conscious and unconscious. Unless, as individuals and as a society, we can make constructive use of this capacity for freedom and commitment, mankind, it seems to me, is set on a collision course with fate. . . .

A part of modern living is to face the paradox that, viewed from one perspective, man is a complex machine. We are every day moving toward a more precise understanding and a more precise control of this objective mechanism which we call man. On the other hand, in another significant dimension of his existence, man is subjectively free; his personal choice and responsibility account for the shape of his life; he is in fact the architect of himself. A truly crucial part of his existence is the discovery of his own meaningful commitment to life with all of his being.

POSTSCRIPT

Should Behaviorism Shape Educational Practices?

The freedom-determinism or freedom-control argument has raged in philosophical, political, and psychological circles down through the ages. Is freedom of choice and action a central, perhaps *the* central, characteristic of being human? Or is freedom only an illusion, a refusal to acknowledge the external shaping of all human actions?

Moving the debate into the field of education, John Dewey depicts a developmental freedom that is acquired through improving one's ability to cope with problems. A. S. Neill (*Summerhill: A Radical Approach to Child Rearing*), who advanced the ideas of early twentieth-century progressive educators and the establishment of free schools, sees a more natural inborn freedom in human beings, which must be protected and allowed to flourish. B. F. Skinner refuses to recognize this "inner autonomous man" but sees freedom resulting from the scientific reshaping of the environment that influences us.

Just as Skinner has struggled to remove the stigma from the word *control,* arguing that it is the true gateway to freedom, John Holt, in *Freedom and Beyond* (1972), points out that freedom and free activities are not "unstructured"— indeed, that the structure of an open classroom is vastly more complicated than the structure of a traditional classroom.

If both of these views have validity, then we are in a position, as Dewey counselled, to go beyond either-or polemics on these matters and build a more constructive educational atmosphere. Jerome S. Bruner has consistently suggested ways in which free inquiry and subject matter structure can be effectively blended. Arthur W. Combs, in journal articles and in a report titled *Humanistic Education: Objectives and Assessment* (1978), has helped to bridge the ideological gap between humanists and behaviorists by demonstrating that subjective outcomes can be assessed by direct or modified behavioral techniques.

Other perspectives on the learning atmosphere in schools may be found in William Glasser's *Control Theory in the Classroom* (1986) and *The Quality School* (1990) and in Howard Gardner's *The Unschooled Mind: How Children Think and How Schools Should Teach* (1991).

B. F. Skinner's death in 1990 prompted a number of evaluations, among them "Skinner's Stimulus: The Legacy of Behaviorism's Grand Designer," Jeff Meade, *Teacher* (November/December 1990); "The Life and Contributions of Burrhus Frederic Skinner," Robert P. Hawkins, *Education and Treatment of Children* (August 1990); and Fred S. Keller, "Burrhus Frederic Skinner (1904–1990) (A Thank You)," *Journal of Applied Behavior Analysis* (Winter 1990).

ISSUE 4

Can "Character Education" Reverse Moral Decline?

YES: Thomas Lickona, from "The Return of Character Education," *Educational Leadership* (November 1993)

NO: Alan L. Lockwood, from "A Letter to Character Educators," *Educational Leadership* (November 1993)

ISSUE SUMMARY

YES: Developmental psychologist Thomas Lickona, a leading exponent of the new character education, details the rationale behind the movement and charts a course of action to deal with the moral decline of American youth.

NO: Education professor Alan L. Lockwood asserts that there is no relationship between values instilled through character education and actual individual behavior.

Do schools have a moral purpose? Can virtue be taught? Should the shaping of character be as important as the training of the intellect? Should value-charged issues be discussed in the classroom?

Much of the history of education chronicles the ways in which philosophers, theorists, educators, politicians, and the general public have responded to these and similar questions. In almost all countries (and certainly in early America), the didactic teaching of moral values, often those of a particular religious interpretation, was central to the process of schooling. Although the direct connection between religion and public education in the United States has faded, the image of the teacher as a value model persists, and the ethical dimension of everyday activities and human relations insinuates itself into the school atmosphere. Normative discourse inundates the educational environment; school is often a world of "rights" and "wrongs" and "oughts" and "don'ts."

Problems emerge when the attempt is made to delineate the school's proper role in setting value guidelines: Can school efforts supplement the efforts of home and church? Can the schools avoid representing a "middle-class morality" that disregards the cultural base of minority group values? Should the schools do battle against the value-manipulating forces of the mass media and the popular culture?

During the 1960s and 1970s a number of psychology-based approaches supplanted the traditional didacticism. Psychologist Lawrence Kohlberg fashioned strategies that link ethical growth to levels of cognitive maturity, moving the student through a range of stages that demand increasingly sophisticated types of moral reasoning. Another approach popularized during this period was "values clarification," developed and refined by Louis Raths, Merrill Harmin, Sidney Simon, and Howard Kirschenbaum. This moral education program attempted to assist learners in understanding their own attitudes, preferences, and values, as well as those of others, and placed central emphasis on feelings, emotions, sensitivity, and shared perceptions.

The current concern that many people have about the moral condition of American society and its young people in particular is prompting a reevaluation of the school's role in teaching values. "The schools are failing to provide the moral education they once did; they have abandoned moral teaching," says William Kilpatrick, author of *Why Johnny Can't Tell Right from Wrong* (1992). "If we want our children to possess the traits of character we most admire, we need to teach them what those traits are and why they deserve both admiration and allegiance," says William J. Bennett in the introduction to his best-selling book *The Book of Virtues* (1993). Both of these thinkers reject the moral relativism associated with values clarification and with similar approaches, and they call for a character-development strategy based upon time-tested materials that contribute to "moral literacy."

In the selections that follow, Thomas Lickona makes the case for a new character education movement and charts the course this effort must take in order to have a pronounced effect on the moral life of students. Alan L. Lockwood cautions that the assumptions and claims of Lickona and others in support of character education are questionable.

YES

Thomas Lickona

THE RETURN OF CHARACTER EDUCATION

To educate a person in mind and not in morals is to educate a menace to society.

—Theodore Roosevelt

Increasing numbers of people across the ideological spectrum believe that our society is in deep moral trouble. The disheartening signs are everywhere: the breakdown of the family; the deterioration of civility in everyday life; rampant greed at a time when one in five children is poor; an omnipresent sexual culture that fills our television and movie screens with sleaze, beckoning the young toward sexual activity at ever earlier ages; the enormous betrayal of children through sexual abuse; and the 1992 report of the National Research Council that says the United States is now *the* most violent of all industrialized nations.

As we become more aware of this societal crisis, the feeling grows that schools cannot be ethical bystanders. As a result, character education is making a comeback in American schools.

EARLY CHARACTER EDUCATION

Character education is as old as education itself. Down through history, education has had two great goals: to help people become smart and to help them become good.

Acting on that belief, schools in the earliest days of our republic tackled character education head on—through discipline, the teacher's example, and the daily school curriculum. The Bible was the public school's sourcebook for both moral and religious instruction. When struggles eventually arose over whose Bible to use and which doctrines to teach, William McGuffey stepped onto the stage in 1836 to offer his McGuffey Readers, ultimately to sell more than 100 million copies.

McGuffey retained many favorite Biblical stories but added poems, exhortations, and heroic tales. While children practiced their reading or arithmetic,

From Thomas Lickona, "The Return of Character Education," *Educational Leadership,* vol. 51, no. 3 (November 1993), pp. 6–11. Copyright © 1993 by The Association for Supervision and Curriculum Development. Reprinted by permission. All rights reserved.

they also learned lessons about honesty, love of neighbor, kindness to animals, hard work, thriftiness, patriotism, and courage.

WHY CHARACTER EDUCATION DECLINED

In the 20th century, the consensus supporting character education began to crumble under the blows of several powerful forces.

Darwinism introduced a new metaphor—evolution—that led people to see all things, including morality, as being in flux.

The philosophy of logical positivism, arriving at American universities from Europe, asserted a radical distinction between *facts* (which could be scientifically proven) and *values* (which positivism held were mere expressions of feeling, not objective truth). As a result of positivism, morality was relativized and privatized—made to seem a matter of personal "value judgment," not a subject for public debate and transmission through the schools.

In the 1960s, a worldwide rise in personalism celebrated the worth, autonomy, and subjectivity of the person, emphasizing individual rights and freedom over responsibility. Personalism rightly protested societal oppression and injustice, but it also delegitimized moral authority, eroded belief in objective moral norms, turned people inward toward self-fulfillment, weakened social commitments (for example, to marriage and parenting), and fueled the socially destabilizing sexual revolution.

Finally, the rapidly intensifying pluralism of American society (Whose values should we teach?) and the increasing secularization of the public arena (Won't moral education violate the separation of church and state?), became two more barriers to achieving the moral consensus indispensable for character education in the public schools. Public schools retreated from their once central role as moral and character educators.

The 1970s saw a return of values education, but in new forms: values clarification and Kohlberg's moral dilemma discussions. In different ways, both expressed the individualist spirit of the age. Values clarification said, don't impose values; help students choose their values freely. Kohlberg said, develop students' powers of moral reasoning so they can judge which values are better than others.

Each approach made contributions, but each had problems. Values clarification, though rich in methodology, failed to distinguish between personal preferences (truly a matter of free choice) and moral values (a matter of obligation). Kohlberg focused on moral reasoning, which is necessary but not sufficient for good character, and underestimated the school's role as a moral socializer.

THE NEW CHARACTER EDUCATION

In the 1990s we are seeing the beginnings of a new character education movement, one which restores "good character" to its historical place as the central desirable outcome of the school's moral enterprise. No one knows yet how broad or deep this movement is; we have no studies to tell us what percentage of schools are making what kind of effort. But something significant is afoot.

In July 1992, the Josephson Institute of Ethics called together more than 30 educational leaders representing state school boards, teachers' unions, universities, ethics centers, youth organizations, and religious groups. This diverse assemblage drafted the Aspen Declaration on Character Education, setting forth eight principles of character education.[1]

The Character Education Partnership was launched in March 1993, as a national coalition committed to putting character development at the top of the nation's educational agenda. Members include representatives from business, labor, government, youth, parents, faith communities, and the media.

The last two years have seen the publication of a spate of books—such as *Moral, Character, and Civic Education in the Elementary School, Why Johnny Can't Tell Right From Wrong,* and *Reclaiming Our Schools: A Handbook on Teaching Character, Academics, and Discipline*—that make the case for character education and describe promising programs around the country. A new periodical, the *Journal of Character Education,* is devoted entirely to covering the field.[2]

WHY CHARACTER EDUCATION NOW?

Why this groundswell of interest in character education? There are at least three causes:

1. The decline of the family. The family, traditionally a child's primary moral teacher, is for vast numbers of children today failing to perform that role, thus creating a moral vacuum. In her recent book *When the Bough Breaks: The Cost of Neglecting Our Children,* economist Sylvia Hewlett documents that American children, rich and poor, suffer a level of neglect unique among developed nations (1991). Overall, child well-being has de-

clined despite a decrease in the number of children per family, an increase in the educational level of parents, and historically high levels of public spending in education.

In "Dan Quayle Was Right," (April 1993) Barbara Dafoe Whitehead synthesizes the social science research on the decline of the two biological-parent family in America:

> If current trends continue, less than half of children born today will live continuously with their own mother and father throughout childhood.... An increasing number of children will experience family break-up two or even three times during childhood.

Children of marriages that end in divorce and children of single mothers are more likely to be poor, have emotional and behavioral problems, fail to achieve academically, get pregnant, abuse drugs and alcohol, get in trouble with the law, and be sexually and physically abused. Children in stepfamilies are generally worse off (more likely to be sexually abused, for example) than children in single-parent homes.

No one has felt the impact of family disruption more than schools. Whitehead writes:

> Across the nation, principals report a dramatic rise in the aggressive, acting-out behavior characteristic of children, especially boys, who are living in single-parent families. Moreover, teachers find that many children are so upset and preoccupied by the explosive drama of their own family lives that they are unable to concentrate on such mundane matters as multiplication tables.

Family disintegration, then, drives the character education movement in two ways: schools have to teach the values kids aren't learning at home; and schools, in order to conduct teaching and learning, must become caring moral communities that help children from unhappy homes focus on their work, control their anger, feel cared about, and become responsible students.

2. *Troubling trends in youth character.* A second impetus for renewed character education is the sense that young people in general, not just those from fractured families, have been adversely affected by poor parenting (in intact as well as broken families); the wrong kind of adult role models; the sex, violence, and materialism portrayed in the mass media; and the pressures of the peer group. Evidence that this hostile moral environment is taking a toll on youth character can be found in 10 troubling trends: rising youth violence; increasing dishonesty (lying, cheating, and stealing); growing disrespect for authority; peer cruelty; a resurgence of bigotry on school campuses, from preschool through higher education; a decline in the work ethic; sexual precocity; a growing self-centeredness and declining civil responsibility; an increase in self-destructive behavior; and ethical illiteracy.

The statistics supporting these trends are overwhelming.[3] For example, the U.S. homicide rate for 15- to 24-year-old males is 7 times higher than Canada's and 40 times higher than Japan's. The U.S. has one of the highest teenage pregnancy rates, the highest teen abortion rate, and the highest level of drug use among young people in the developed world. Youth suicide has tripled in the past 25 years, and a survey of more than 2,000 Rhode Island students, grades six through nine, found that two out of three boys and one of two girls thought it

"acceptable for a man to force sex on a woman" if they had been dating for six months or more (Kikuchi 1988).

3. *A recovery of shared, objectively important ethical values.* Moral decline in society has gotten bad enough to jolt us out of the privatism and relativism dominant in recent decades. We are recovering the wisdom that we do share a basic morality, essential for our survival; that adults must promote this morality by teaching the young, directly and indirectly, such values as respect, responsibility, trustworthiness, fairness, caring, and civil virtue; and that these values are not merely subjective preferences but that they have objective worth and a claim on our collective conscience.

Such values affirm our human dignity, promote the good of the individual and the common good, and protect our human rights. They meet the classic ethical tests of reversibility (Would you want to be treated this way?) and universalizability (Would you want all persons to act this way in a similar situation?). They define our responsibilities in a democracy, and they are recognized by all civilized people and taught by all enlightened creeds. *Not* to teach children these core ethical values is grave moral failure.

WHAT CHARACTER EDUCATION MUST DO

In the face of a deteriorating social fabric, what must character education do to develop good character in the young?

First, it must have an adequate theory of what good character is, one which gives schools a clear idea of their goals. Character must be broadly conceived to encompass the cognitive, affective, and behavioral aspects of morality. Good character consists of knowing the good, desiring the good, and doing the good. Schools must help children *understand* the core values, *adopt* or commit to them, and then *act upon* them in their own lives.

The cognitive side of character includes at least six specific moral qualities: awareness of the moral dimensions of the situation at hand, knowing moral values and what they require of us in concrete cases, perspective-taking, moral reasoning, thoughtful decision making, and moral self-knowledge. All these powers of rational moral thought are required for full moral maturity and citizenship in a democratic society.

People can be very smart about matters of right and wrong, however, and still choose the wrong. Moral education that is merely intellectual misses the crucial emotional side of character, which serves as the bridge between judgment and action. The emotional side includes at least the following qualities: conscience (the felt obligation to do what one judges to be right), self-respect, empathy, loving the good, self-control, and humility (a willingness to both recognize and correct our moral failings).

At times, we know what we should do, feel strongly that we should do it, yet still fail to translate moral judgment and feeling into effective moral behavior. Moral action, the third part of character, draws upon three additional moral qualities: competence (skills such as listening, communicating, and cooperating), will (which mobilizes our judgment and energy), and moral habit (a reliable inner disposition to respond to situations in a morally good way).

DEVELOPING CHARACTER

Once we have a comprehensive concept of character, we need a comprehensive approach to developing it. This approach tells schools to look at themselves through a moral lens and consider how virtually everything that goes on there affects the values and character of students. Then, plan how to use all phases of classroom and school life as deliberate tools of character development.

If schools wish to maximize their moral clout, make a lasting difference in students' character, and engage and develop all three parts of character (knowing, feeling, and behavior), they need a comprehensive, holistic approach. Having a comprehensive approach includes asking, Do present school practices support, neglect, or contradict the school's professed values and character education aims?

In classroom practice, a comprehensive approach to character education calls upon the individual teacher to:

- *Act as caregiver, model, and mentor,* treating students with love and respect, setting a good example, supporting positive social behavior, and correcting hurtful actions through one-on-one guidance and whole-class discussion;
- *Create a moral community,* helping students know one another as persons, respect and care about one another, and feel valued membership in, and responsibility to, the group;
- *Practice moral discipline,* using the creation and enforcement of rules as opportunities to foster moral reasoning, voluntary compliance with rules, and a respect for others;
- *Create a democratic classroom environment,* involving students in decision

making and the responsibility for making the classroom a good place to be and learn;

- *Teach values through the curriculum*, using the ethically rich content of academic subjects (such as literature, history, and science), as well as outstanding programs (such as *Facing History and Ourselves*[4] and *The Heartwood Ethics Curriculum for Children*[5]), as vehicles for teaching values and examining moral questions;

- *Use cooperative learning* to develop students' appreciation of others, perspective taking, and ability to work with others toward common goals;

- *Develop the "conscience of craft"* by fostering students' appreciation of learning, capacity for hard work, commitment to excellence, and sense of work as affecting the lives of others;

- *Encourage moral reflection* through reading, research, essay writing, journal keeping, discussion, and debate;

- *Teach conflict resolution*, so that students acquire the essential moral skills of solving conflicts fairly and without force.

Besides making full use of the moral life of classrooms, a comprehensive approach calls upon the school *as a whole* to:

- *Foster caring beyond the classroom*, using positive role models to inspire altruistic behavior and providing opportunities at every grade level to perform school and community service;

- *Create a positive moral culture in the school*, developing a schoolwide ethos (through the leadership of the principal, discipline, a schoolwide sense of community, meaningful student government, a moral community among adults, and making time for moral concerns) that supports and amplifies the values taught in classrooms;

- *Recruit parents and the community as partners in character education*, letting parents know that the school considers them their child's first and most important moral teacher, giving parents specific ways they can reinforce the values the school is trying to teach, and seeking the help of the community, churches, businesses, local government, and the media in promoting the core ethical values.

THE CHALLENGES AHEAD

Whether character education will take hold in American schools remains to be seen. Among the factors that will determine the movement's long-range success are:

- *Support for schools.* Can schools recruit the help they need from the other key formative institutions that shape the values of the young—including families, faith communities, and the media? Will public policy act to strengthen and support families, and will parents make the stability of their families and the needs of their children their highest priority?

- *The role of religion.* Both liberal and conservative groups are asking, How can students be sensitively engaged in considering the role of religion in the origins and moral development of our nation? How can students be encouraged to use their intellectual and moral resources, including their faith traditions, when confronting social issues (For example, what is my obligation to the poor?) and making personal moral decisions (For example, should I have sex before marriage?)?

- *Moral leadership.* Many schools lack a positive, cohesive moral culture. Especially at the building level, it is absolutely essential to have moral leadership that sets, models, and consistently enforces high standards of respect and responsibility. Without a positive schoolwide ethos, teachers will feel demoralized in their individual efforts to teach good values.

- *Teacher education.* Character education is far more complex than teaching ~~MAIN UF JUUI~~ growth as well as skills development. Yet teachers typically receive almost no preservice or inservice training in the moral aspects of their craft. Many teachers do not feel comfortable or competent in the values domain. How will teacher education colleges and school staff development programs meet this need?

"Character is destiny," wrote the ancient Greek philosopher Heraclitus. As we confront the causes of our deepest societal problems, whether in our intimate relationships or public institutions, questions of character loom large. As we close out a turbulent century and ready our schools for the next, educating for character is a moral imperative if we care about the future of our society and our children.

NOTES

1. For a copy of the Aspen Declaration and the issue of *Ethics* magazine reporting on the conference, write the Josephson Institute of Ethics, 310 Washington Blvd., Suite 104, Marina del Rey, CA 90292.

2. For information write Mark Kann, Editor, *The Journal of Character Education,* Jefferson Center for Character Education, 202 S. Lake Ave., Suite 240, Pasadena, CA 91101.

3. For documentation of these youth trends, see T. Lickona, (1991), *Educating for Character: How Our Schools Can Teach Respect and Responsibility* (New York: Bantam Books).

4. *Facing History and Ourselves* is an 8-week Holocaust curriculum for 8th graders. Write Facing History and Ourselves National Foundation, 25 ~~Kennard Rd., Brookline, MA 02146~~

5. *The Heartwood Ethics Curriculum for Children* uses multicultural children's literature to teach universal values. Write The Heartwood Institute, 12300 Perry Highway, Wexford, PA 15090.

REFERENCES

Benninga, J. S., ed. (1991). *Moral, Character, and Civic Education in the Elementary School.* New York: Teachers College Press.

Hewlett, S. (1991). *When the Bough Breaks: The Cost of Neglecting Our Children.* New York: Basic Books.

Kikuchi, J. (Fall 1988). "Rhode Island Develops Successful Intervention Program for Adolescents." *National Coalition Against Sexual Assault Newsletter.*

National Research Council. (1992). *Understanding and Preventing Violence.* Washington, D.C.: National Research Council.

Whitehead, B. D. (April 1993) "Dan Quayle Was Right." *The Atlantic* 271: 47–84.

Wynne, E. A., and K. Ryan. (1992). *Reclaiming Our Schools: A Handbook on Teaching Character, Academics, and Discipline.* New York: Merrill.

NO

Alan L. Lockwood

A LETTER TO CHARACTER EDUCATORS

Dear Character Educators, I'm writing to ask you to respond to some concerns I have about character education. Through our correspondence, I hope to learn more precisely what you mean and what you want people to do. Things are rather murky right now.

When a colleague recently asked me to explain character education, my reply was that character educators advocate schooling that promotes particular values presumed to lead to respectful and responsible behavior. I based my response on a number of things you have said:

1. "By our definition, 'character' involves engaging in morally relevant conduct or words or refraining from certain conduct or words" (Wynne and Walberg 1985/86, p. 15).
2. "Character consists of *operative values*, values in action" (Lickona 1991, p. 51).
3. "Moral *action* is the bottom line" (Ryan 1989, p. 9).

MY UNDERSTANDING OF YOUR RATIONALE

As I perceive it, the reason you want schooling to focus on producing good behavior is that there is so much bad behavior around. Wynne cites stunning increases in the rates of homicide, suicide, and illegitimate births among young people (1985/86, p. 6). The sharpest rise began in the early 1960s. "Of all the moral problems that have fueled this concern," says Lickona, "none has been more disturbing than rising youth violence" (1991, p. 4).

I certainly agree that bad behavior is pandemic. Even the small midwestern city in which I live has seen growing instances of what used to be called big-city problems. The causes of bad behavior are, no doubt, many. While I am sure you acknowledge the multifarious etiology of good and bad behavior, you emphasize values as the key cause. Inadequate understanding of, commitment to, and appreciation of moral values is, for you, the wellspring of bad behavior.

Your emphasis on the role of values is clear. Wynne calls for "the deliberate transmission of moral values to students" (1985/86, p. 4). His assumption is

From Alan L. Lockwood, "A Letter to Character Educators," *Educational Leadership,* vol. 51, no. 3 (November 1993), pp. 72–75. Copyright © 1993 by The Association for Supervision and Curriculum Development. Reprinted by permission. All rights reserved.

that our failure to do this is largely responsible for the increases in destructive behavior that he reports. Speaking of irresponsible sexual behavior among young people, Lickona says flatly, "Sexual behavior is determined by values, not mere knowledge" (1993, p. 1). Kilpatrick also sees a close connection between a lack of moral values and ruinous behavior: "In addition to the fact that Johnny still can't read, we are now faced with the more serious problem that he can't tell right from wrong" (1992, p. 14).

In *Can We Teach Children to Be Good?*, philosopher Roger Straughan summarizes the "moralistic argument":

> Modern society is becoming more lawless, violent, undisciplined, and permissive, and this trend is most apparent among the younger generation. Statistics show that vandalism, violent crime, drug-taking, and sexual activity have risen and are rising among teenagers. Less sensational but equally significant, it is claimed, is a general decline in such things as respect for authority, politeness, and good manners, resulting in children today being ruder, using more bad language, and caring less about their appearance and dress than ever before.... Teachers are not doing enough to impart the right values to children and to ensure that their behavior is socially acceptable (1982, pp. 1–2).

Your mission seems to be threefold: You want young people to understand proper moral values, to heartily endorse these values, and to take action based on them (Lickona 1991, p. 51). Of these three, the last is most important. In your opinion, school people must mount a systematic effort to get young people to do the right thing.

VALUES AND BEHAVIOR: NO *DIRECT* LINK

One of my concerns is that the untutored reader of your views, enthralled at the prospect of reducing violence, crime, and other irresponsible behavior, may conclude there is a direct relationship between values and behavior. This would be a most unfortunate conclusion. If the public enthusiastically endorses programs based on this fallacious assumption, the resulting disappointment may doom all efforts at moral education. The character education movement of the '90s may relive the fate of a similar movement in the 1920s. It failed.

I know of no research that shows a direct connection between values and behavior. Conversely, lots of research shows there is none. For example, although they were strong advocates of character education, Hartshorne and colleagues (1929) found no systematic relationship between values and behavior. After extensive and inventive empirical studies, they concluded, "The scores on our moral knowledge test, purporting to measure general level of comprehension of ideal conduct, proved to have little in common with either deceptive or altruistic behavior" (p. 64). Kohlberg reached similar conclusions: "Half a dozen studies show no positive correlation between high school or college students' verbal expression of the value of honesty or the badness of cheating, and actual honesty in experimental situations" (1969, p. 392).

Other studies have shown apparent situational variance in behavior. Milgram's (1965) controversial studies of obedience to authority had subjects administer increasingly severe doses of electric shock as part of a supposed learning experiment. Although no real shock was administered, the subjects did not know this. As the experiment progressed, the white-coated scientist in charge of the experiment ordered the subjects to increase the level of shock to a potentially lethal dose. Only 34 percent of the subjects disobeyed the orders even though the "victim," in an adjoining room, would scream, beg for mercy, and eventually fall silent. The proportion of subjects who disobeyed their orders increased as the proximity of the "victim" was shortened. In one condition, the subject had to hold the hand of the "victim" onto a metal bar that delivered the shock. In that situation, 70 per cent eventually disobeyed the scientist. "In certain circumstances," Milgram concluded, "it is not so much the kind of person a man [sic] is, as the kind of situation in which he is placed that determines his actions" (p. 72).

Substantial situational variance in helping behavior has been found in other studies. For example, people are more likely to help others when alone than when in groups, and, oddly, people are more likely to help others in subways than in airline terminals (Macaulay and Berkowitz 1970).

These and other studies should not lead us to conclude there is no relationship between moral values and behavior. We *should* observe that the relationship is not a direct, one-on-one correspondence. Studies by Thoma and Rest indicate a low but relatively consistent relationship between some forms of moral judgment and behavior. On average, these forms of moral judgment account for .09 percent of the variance in behavior (1986, pp. 134–135). At minimum, some mix of psychological, situational, and sociological variables are involved in determining behavior. Moral values alone have low predictive power.

Massey describes your work as "built on a growing consensus in favor of teaching a set of traditional or 'core' ethical values in a more direct way" (1993, p. 1). She then indicates there is a belief that such teaching will reduce irresponsible behavior. I hope you will clarify your views before the erroneous assumption that teaching moral values will produce significant reductions in irresponsible behavior spreads.

WHEN VALUE CONFLICTS ARISE

Social scientists have had difficulty determining the antecedents of value-related behavior. Although this may be a result of inadequate theory and research methodology, *conceptually*, general moral values provide limited guidance for making moral decisions. This is because equally good values can come into conflict, and acting on a single moral value can be problematic (Lockwood 1985/86, 1991).

Value conflicts can arise in situations ranging from the mundane to the momentous, from the prosaic to the profound. For example, suppose my favorite aunt serves me a dish that I hate and asks me if I like it. Unfortunately, if I tell her I like it, I will be dishonest, and if I tell her I dislike it, I will be discourteous. How do I decide which value—honesty or courtesy—to honor?

At a more momentous level, consider John Dean. Presumably President Nixon wanted him to maintain the cover-up of the Watergate scandal. Assuming that Dean believed in honesty and obedience to authority, what should he do? These examples illustrate that the mere holding of values does not, in itself, provide an adequate guide for behavior when values come into conflict.

Even holding a single value does not necessarily guide action. Suppose a father asks his daughter to tend his fruit stand while he takes her sick mother to the hospital. Also suppose a number of police officers approach the stand and ask the girl to give them some apples. Her family can barely make ends meet, and yet she has been taught to obey legitimate authority. Again, holding a value is not enough to help us determine our behavior.

For me, the previous discussion leads to a clear conclusion: Any program that intends to promote good behavior by teaching values rests on a shaky foundation. Social scientific research indicates that moral values play a small role in predicting behavior. Philosophy shows the conceptual difficulty of making decisions based simply on the holding of particular moral values.

I do not pretend to have a definitive characterization of the key factors that influence moral behavior. I do know, however, that more than the issue of values is involved. Thoma and Rest, for example, have identified a factor they call the "utilizer" variable, which accounts for certain concepts of justice that we employ in our decision making (1986, p. 171). When this variable was combined with a measure of moral value judgment, the predictability of moral behavior doubled compared with the predictive power of moral value judgment alone. However, only a small portion of the variance in moral behavior was accounted for (p. 174; see also Rest 1986).

HOW TO APPROACH VALUES EDUCATION

I have additional concerns about character education. For example, you often dismiss the values clarification and moral development approaches as ineffective (Wynne 1985/86, p. 8; Wynne and Ryan 1993, p. 44). These approaches, while different in significant ways, engage young people in serious deliberation about moral and other value issues. You, on the other hand, advocate that teachers should indoctrinate young people into accepting particular values— through modeling, reading inspirational literature, and so on.

What I find curious is that, at times, you also appear to want children to reason things through on their own. For example:

> We stress the duty of the older generation to indoctrinate the young with what they are convinced are the essential moral realities and ethical truths the young will need to live well.... It is essential for the school continually to engage the child in reflection about moral principle.

In the same article, you say that students should think through various solutions to problems and "select the best (most ethical) solution, based on the solutions they came up with" (Wynne and Ryan 1993, p. 24).

Similarly, Lickona endorses both indoctrinative programs such as proabstinence sex education (1991, pp. 354–359) and non-indoctrinative programs such as Lockwood and Harris' (1985) *Reasoning with Democratic Values* (pp. 170–172). I find this most confusing. Are you saying that sometimes we must tell students what to think and do and other times help them make their own decisions? If so, when is each situation appropriate?

MORAL EDUCATION AT THE SECONDARY LEVEL

The success or failure of educational reforms ultimately depends on teachers' ability and willingness to enact them. Teachers, especially at the secondary level, are often reluctant to engage in any systematic efforts toward values education. This may partly explain why most successful interventions are at the elementary level (Lockwood, in press). This is especially troublesome because most serious acts of irresponsible behavior are committed by adolescents and adults. Even if we could overcome teachers' reluctance to engage in some form of values education, a potentially more serious problem remains. Evidence suggests that young people generally do not perceive the same social problems as do adults, and even if they do, they are unlikely to turn to teachers for advice.

In 1989 the Girl Scouts commissioned a study of the values and beliefs of American youth. More than 5,000 young people from grades 4–12 were surveyed and interviewed (Girl Scouts of the USA 1991). Two findings are particularly relevant. First, children ranked the "crisis" youth problems quite low as a major concern: teenage pregnancy (5 percent), suicide (3 percent), physical abuse to children (3 percent), violence in schools (2 percent), and alcohol abuse (1 percent) (1991, p. 6). Second, while one-third of the children said that teachers and coaches "really care for them," only 7 percent "would go to them for advice" (p. 5). To be effective, it appears that we must not only persuade teachers to be moral educators but also persuade young people to pay attention to them.

IN CLOSING

My points are not intended to hinder your efforts. I do, however, believe your work will be enhanced if you speak to the issues I've discussed here; namely, elaborate your psychology of moral behavior, address the problem of conflicting values, more fully explicate your views on indoctrinative versus non-indoctrinative approaches, and deal with issues of values education that concern secondary school teachers and adolescents.

I hope you find my comments worthwhile as you pursue your complex task. I look forward to hearing from you.

REFERENCES

Girl Scouts of the USA. (1991). *Girl Scouts Survey on the Beliefs and Moral Values of America's Children: Executive Summary.* New York: Girl Scouts of the USA.

Hartshorne, H., M. May, and J. B. Maller. (1929). *Studies in Service and Self-Control.* New York: Macmillan.

Kilpatrick, W. K. (1992). *Why Johnny Can't Tell Right from Wrong.* New York: Simon and Schuster.

Kohlberg, L. (1969). "Stage and Sequence: The Cognitive-Developmental Approach to Socialization." In *Handbook of Socialization Theory and Research,* edited by D. A. Goslin. Chicago: Rand McNally.

Lickona, T. (1991). *Educating for Character.* New York: Bantam Books.

Lickona, T. (1993). "Educating for Self-Control: A Moral Imperative for Character Education." *Character* 1, 3: 1–5.

Lockwood, A. L. (December 1985/January 1986). "Keeping Them in the Courtyard: A Response to Wynne." *Educational Leadership* 43, 4: 9–10.

Lockwood, A. L. (1991). "Character Education: The Ten Percent Solution." *Social Education* 55, 4: 246–248.

Lockwood, A. L. (In press). "Being Overly 'Aimful.'" *Theory and Research in Social Education.*

Lockwood, A. L., and D. E. Harris. (1985). *Reasoning with Democratic Values.* New York: Teachers College Press.

Macaulay, J., and L. Berkowitz, eds. (1970). *Altruism and Helping Behavior.* New York: Academic Press.

Massey, M. (1993). "Interest in Character Education Seen Growing." *ASCD Update* 35, 4: 1, 4–5.

Milgram, S. (1965). "Some Conditions of Obedience and Disobedience to Authority." *Human Relations:* 57–76.

Rest, J., with M. Bebeau and J. Volker. (1986). "An Overview of the Psychology of Morality." In *Moral Development,* edited by J. R. Rest. New York: Praeger.

Ryan, K. (1989). "In Defense of Character Education." In *Moral Development and Character Education* edited by L. P. Nucci. Berkeley: McCutchan.

Straughan, R. (1982). *Can We Teach Children to be Good?* London: George Allen and Unwin.

Thoma, S., and J. Rest, with R. Barnett. (1986). "Moral Judgment, Behavior, Decision Making, and Attitudes." In *Moral Development,* edited by J. R. Rest. New York: Praeger.

Wynne, E. A. (December 1985/January 1986). "The Great Tradition in Education: Transmitting Moral Values." *Educational Leadership* 43, 4: 4–9.

Wynne, E. A., and K. Ryan. (Spring 1993). "Curriculum as Moral Educator." *American Educator:* 20–48.

Wynne, E. A., and H. W. Walberg. (December 1985/January 1986). "The Complementary Goals of Character Development and Academic Excellence." *Educational Leadership* 43, 4: 15–18.

POSTSCRIPT

Can "Character Education" Reverse Moral Decline?

Former secretary of education William J. Bennett has stated that we must not permit disputes over political and theological matters to suffocate the obligation we have to instruct our young in the importance of good character (see "Moral Literacy and the Formation of Character," *NASSP Bulletin*, December 1988). Yet, in the public domain, questions of whose values should be presented and whether or not religion-based values can be proffered take on a political cast that is hard to dismiss. Two recent books address specific aspects of the dilemma: *The Moral Life of Schools* by Philip W. Jackson, Robert E. Boostrom, and David T. Hansen (1993), and *Reclaiming Our Schools* by Edward A. Wynne and Kevin Ryan (1993).

For a full perspective on the issue of values and moral education, review John Dewey, *Moral Principles in Education* (1911); Abraham Maslow, *New Knowledge in Human Values* (1959); Milton Rokeach, *The Nature of Human Values* (1973); and Robert Coles, *The Moral Life of Children* (1986).

Alternative approaches to moral education can be explored in the following: "Correct Habits and Moral Character: John Dewey and Traditional Education," by Patrick K. Dooley, *Journal of Thought* (Fall 1991); *Literature-Based Moral Education* by Linda Leonard Lamme, Suzanne Lowell Krogh, and Kathy A. Yachmetz (1992); Howard Kirschenbaum, "A Comprehensive Model of Values Education and Moral Education," *Phi Delta Kappan* (June 1992); *The Moral Self: Building a Better Paradigm* by Gil Noam and Thomas Wren, eds. (1993); "The Three Rs of Moral Education," by M. Jean Bouas, and "Education and Family Values," by John Martin Rich, *The Educational Forum* (Winter 1993); and "Restoring Our Moral Voice," by Amitai Etzioni, *The Public Interest* (Summer 1994).

A number of journals have produced issues around the theme of character education that can be valuable sources of information. Among them are *The Clearing House* (May–June 1991), featuring articles by Maxine Greene, Nel Noddings, John Martin Rich, Kevin Ryan, and Henry A. Giroux; *The Journal of Education* (Spring 1993), particularly an article by Edwin J. Dellattre and William E. Russell titled "Schooling, Moral Principles, and the Formation of Character"; and *Educational Leadership* (November 1993), which contains over 20 articles on the subject of character education. For an elaboration of Lickona's theories and opinions, see his 1991 book *Education for Character: How Our Schools Can Teach Respect and Responsibility*.

ISSUE 5

Is Church-State Separation Being Threatened?

YES: R. Freeman Butts, from "A History and Civics Lesson for All of Us," *Educational Leadership* (May 1987)

NO: Robert L. Cord, from "Church-State Separation and the Public Schools: A Re-evaluation," *Educational Leadership* (May 1987)

ISSUE SUMMARY

YES: Professor emeritus of education R. Freeman Butts warns that current efforts to redefine the relationship between religion and schooling are eroding the Constitution's intent.

NO: Professor of political science Robert L. Cord offers a more accommodating interpretation of this intent, one that allows for the school practices that Butts condemns as unconstitutional.

The religious grounding of early schooling in America certainly cannot be denied. Nor can the history of religious influences on the conduct of our governmental functions and our school practices. In the nineteenth century, however, protests against the prevailing Protestant influence in the public schools were lodged by Catholics, Jews, nonbelievers, and other groups, giving rise to a number of issues that revolve around interpretations of the "establishment of religion" and the "free exercise of religion" clauses of the Constitution.

Twentieth-century U.S. Supreme Court cases, such as *Cochran* (1930), *Everson* (1947), *McCollum* (1948), *Zorach* (1952), *Engel* (1962), and *Murray* (1963), attempted to clarify the relationship between religion and schooling. Most of these decisions bolstered the separation of church and state position. Only recently has a countermovement, led in some quarters by the Moral Majority organization of Reverend Jerry Falwell, sought to sway public and legal opinion toward an emphasis on the "free exercise" clause and toward viewing the influence of secular humanism in the schools as "an establishment of religion."

At both the legislative and judicial levels, attempts were made in the 1980s to secure an official place in public education for voluntary prayer, moments of silent meditation, and creationism in the science curriculum. Censorship of textbooks and other school materials, access to facilities by religious groups, and the right of parents to withdraw their children from instruction deemed to be morally offensive and damaging have also been promoted. Humanists (who may be either religious or nonreligious) find a good deal of distortion in these recent attacks on the "secularization" of schooling, and they argue that the materials used in the schools are consistent with the historical goals of character development while also being in tune with the realities of the present times.

John Buchanan of People for the American Way argues that public schools are places where young people of differing backgrounds and beliefs can come together and learn tolerance. He and others worry that parental veto power will undermine decision making and impair school effectiveness. Bill Keith of the Creation Science Legal Defense Fund contends that a parent's liberty with regard to a child's education is a fundamental right, an enduring American tradition.

Resolution of the philosophical questions regarding the content and conduct of public education has become increasingly politicized. Who should control the school curriculum and its materials—school boards, professional educators, community groups, the federal or state governments, parents, or students? Should censorship boards operate at the local, state, or national level—or none of the above? Where does the line get drawn between benevolent intervention and thought control? Can schools be value-neutral?

In the articles presented here, R. Freeman Butts makes the case that legal and historical scholarship points to the broader, separatist, and secular meaning of the First Amendment, which controls the answers to many of these questions. Robert L. Cord bases his argument for a more accommodating interpretation on his findings in primary historical sources and on the actions of the framers of the Constitution.

YES

R. Freeman Butts

A HISTORY AND CIVICS LESSON FOR ALL OF US

As chairman of the Commission on the Bicentennial of the U.S. Constitution, former Chief Justice Warren E. Burger urges that the occasion provide "a history and civics lesson for all of us." I heartily agree, but the lesson will depend on which version of history you read and believe.

From May 1982, when President Reagan advocated adoption of a constitutional amendment to permit organized prayer in public schools, Congress has been bitterly divided during the repeated efforts to pass legislation aimed either at amending the Constitution or stripping the Supreme Court and other federal courts of jurisdiction to decide cases about prayers in the public schools. Similar controversies have arisen over efforts of the Reagan administration to promote vouchers and tuition tax credits to give financial aid to parents choosing to send their children to private religious schools.

SCHOOL/RELIGION CONTROVERSIES

I would like to remind educators that the present controversies have a long history, and the way we understand that history makes a difference in our policy judgments. A watershed debate occurred, for example, in 1947 when the Supreme Court spelled out the meaning of the part of the First Amendment which reads, "Congress shall make no law respecting an establishment of religion." The occasion was a challenge to a New Jersey law giving tax money to Catholic parents to send their children by bus to parochial schools. The Court split 5-4 in that case, *Everson* v. *Board of Education*, on whether this practice was, in effect, "an establishment of religion" and thus unconstitutional, but there was no disagreement on the principle. Justice Hugo Black wrote for the majority.

> The "establishment of religion" clause of the First Amendment means at least this: Neither a state nor the Federal Government can pass laws which aid one religion, aid all religions, or prefer one religion over another.... No tax in any amount, large or small, can be levied to support any religious activities or institutions, whatever they may be called, or whatever form they may adopt to teach or

From R. Freeman Butts, "A History and Civics Lesson for All of Us," *Educational Leadership*, vol. 44, no. 8 (May 1987), pp. 21–25. Copyright © 1987 by The Association for Supervision and Curriculum Development. Reprinted by permission. All rights reserved.

practice religion.... In the words of Jefferson, the clause against establishment of religion by law was intended to erect "a wall of separation between Church and State."[1]

The *Everson* majority accepted this broad principle, but decided, nevertheless, that bus fares were merely welfare aid to parents and children and not aid to the religious schools themselves. The 1948 *McCollum* case prohibited released time for religious instruction in the public schools of Champaign, Illinois, because it violated the *Everson* principle.

These two cases set off a thunderous denunciation of the Supreme Court and calls for impeachment of the justices. They also sent historians of education scurrying to original sources to see how valid this broad and liberal interpretation was.

ESTABLISHMENT PRINCIPLE

The two books at that time that gave most attention to the establishment principle as it related to education were James M. O'Neill's *Religion and Education Under the Constitution*[2] and my own, *The American Tradition in Religion and Education*.[3] O'Neill found the Court's interpretation appalling; I found it basically true to Madison and the majority of the framers of the First Amendment. My book was cited in 1971 in the concurring opinions of Justices Brennan, Douglas, and Black in *Lemon* v. *Kurtzman*.[4] Chief Justice Burger summarized for a unanimous court the accumulated precedents since *Everson* and listed three tests of constitutional state action in education: a secular purpose; neither advancement nor inhi-

bition of religion; and no excessive government entanglement with religion.

With that decision, I concluded that my views of the framers' intentions had been pretty well accepted: namely, that "an establishment of religion" in the 1780s was "a multiple establishment" whereby public aid could go to several churches, and that this is what the majority of framers, particularly Madison, intended to prohibit in the First Amendment.

Indeed, single religious establishments had existed in nine of the early colonies, but by 1789 when the First Congress drafted the First Amendment, religious diversity had become such a powerful political force that seven states, which included the vast majority of Americans, had either disestablished their churches or had never established any. Only six state constitutions still permitted "an establishment of religion," and all six provided tax funds for several churches, not just one.[5] Naturally, some representatives and senators from those states did not want their multiple establishment threatened by a Bill of Rights in the new federal government. But Madison did.

Madison had prevented just such a multiple establishment in Virginia in 1785 and 1786 and managed instead the passage of Jefferson's powerful Statute for Religious Freedom. In his speech of 8 June 1789, when he introduced his Bill of Rights proposals in the House, he made a double-barreled approach to religious freedom. He proposed (1) to prohibit Congress from establishing religion on a national basis, and (2) to prohibit the states from infringing "equal rights of conscience."

After considerable discussion and some changes of language, the House of Representatives approved both of Madison's proposals and sent them to the Senate. The Senate, however, did not approve the prohibition on the states. Furthermore, a minority in the Senate made three attempts to narrow the wording of the First Amendment to prohibit Congress from establishing a single church or giving preference to one religious sect or denomination. The majority, however, rejected all such attempts to narrow Madison's proposal, and the Senate finally accepted the wording of Madison's conference committee. This was then finally adopted by both houses. Madison's broad and liberal interpretation of the establishment clause as applied to Congress had won.[6]

Neither Madison nor the majority of framers intended for government to disdain religion. They intended that republican government guarantee equal rights of conscience to all persons, but it took some 150 years before Madison's views were applied specifically to the states through the Fourteenth Amendment. That is what the Supreme Court did in *Everson*.

FRAMERS' INTENTIONS REDEFINED

But today, "a jurisprudence of original intention" has revived the debates of the 1940s and 1950s, expounding much the same views as those of O'Neill namely that "the framers" intended only to prohibit Congress from establishing a single national church, but would permit aid to all religions on a nonpreferential basis and would even permit the states to establish a single church if they wished. These arguments are now being resurrected or reincarnated (to use the secular meaning of those terms) with even more sophisticated scholarship by such authors as Walter Berns of Georgetown University, Michael Malbin of the Amer-

ican Enterprise Institute, and Robert L. Cord of Northeastern University.[7]

Their works have been cited in legal briefs in several state actions and in at least one federal district court decision, while an increasingly vigorous campaign has been launched by conservative members of Congress and the Reagan administration to appeal to the history of "original intention."

These efforts reached a crescendo of confrontation in summer and fall of 1985, following two Supreme Court decisions. In *Wallace* v. *Jaffree* on 4 June 1985, the Court reversed Federal Judge W. Brevard Hand's decision that Alabama's laws providing for prayer in the public schools were, indeed, permissible and did not violate the First Amendment's prohibition against "an establishment of religion." Relying in part on Cord's version of history, Judge Hand argued that the Supreme Court had long erred in its reading of the original intention of the framers of the First Amendment. He said that they intended solely to prevent the federal government from establishing a single national church such as the Church of England; therefore, the Congress could aid all churches if it did not give preference to any one; that a state was free to establish a state religion if it chose to do so and, thus, could require or permit prayers in its public schools.

The Supreme Court reversed this decision (6-3), and Justice John Paul Stevens, writing for the Court, rebuked Judge Hand by referring to his "newly discovered historical evidence" as a "remarkable conclusion" wholly at odds with the firmly established constitutional provision that "the several States have no greater power to restrain the individual freedoms protected by the First Amendment than does the Congress of the

United States." Justice Stevens emphasized that the Court had confirmed and endorsed time and time again the principle of incorporation, by which the Fourteenth Amendment imposes the same limitations on the states that it imposes on Congress regarding protection of civil liberties guaranteed by the First Amendment and the original Bill of Rights.[8]

However, the confrontations between these views of history were not over. In his long dissenting opinion in *Jaffree*, Associate Justice William H. Rehnquist, now Chief Justice, reasserted an "accommodationist" view of church and state relations. Relying on O'Neill's and Cord's version of history, he argued that the "wall of separation between church and state" is a metaphor based on bad history and that the *Everson* principle "should be frankly and explicitly abandoned." Justice Byron R. White's dissent also supported such "a basic reconsideration of our precedents."

Soon after, on 1 July 1985, the Supreme Court ruled in *Aguilar* v. *Fenton* (5-4) that the practices of New York City and Grand Rapids, Michigan, in sending public school teachers to private religious schools to teach remedial and enhancement programs for disadvantaged children, were also unconstitutional. Justice William J. Brennan, delivering the Court's opinion, cited the *Everson* principle that the state should remain neutral and not become entangled with churches in administering schools. Dissents were written by the Chief Justice and Justices Sandra Day O'Connor, White, and Rehnquist.[9]

These Supreme Court decisions were greeted with some surprise and considerable elation by liberals and with dismay by conservatives. Attorney General Edwin Meese III quickly and forcefully responded on 10 July 1985 in a speech before the American Bar Association. He explicitly criticized the Court's decisions on religion and education as a misreading of history and commended Justice Rehnquist's call for overruling *Everson*. Secretary of Education William Bennett echoed the complaint that the Supreme Court was misreading history. And, then, in October 1985 Justices Brennan and Stevens both gave speeches sharply criticizing the Attorney General's campaign for a "jurisprudence of original intention."

In addition, the White House, the Attorney General, the Justice Department, the Secretary of Education, the former Republican majority of the Senate Judiciary Committee, the new Chief Justice, and the conservative justices of the Supreme Court, by public statements are now ranged against the liberal and centrist members of the Supreme Court and such notable constitutional scholars as Laurence Tribe of Harvard, Herman Schwartz of American University, A. E. Dick Howard of the University of Virginia, and Leonard W. Levy of the Claremont Graduate School. They all appeal to history, but whose version of history do you read—and believe?

All in all, I think it fair to say that the predominant stream of constitutional, legal, and historical scholarship points to the broader, separatist, and secular meaning of the First Amendment against the narrower, cooperationist, or accommodationist meaning. A nonspecialist cannot encompass the vast literature on this subject, but a valuable and readily available source of evidence is the recently published book by Leonard Levy, professor of humanities and chairman of the Claremont University Graduate Faculty of History. He is editor of the *Encyclopedia of the American Constitution* and the author of a dozen books devoted mostly to the Bill of Rights.

In his book on the First Amendment's establishment clause Levy concludes, and I fully agree, that the meaning of "an establishment of religion" is as follows:

After the American Revolution seven of the fourteen states that comprised the Union in 1791 authorized establishments of religion by law. Not one state maintained a single or preferential establishment of religion. An establishment of religion meant to those who framed and ratified the First Amendment what it meant in those seven states, and in all seven it meant public support of religion on a nonpreferential basis. It was specifically this support on a nonpreferential basis that the establishment clause of the First Amendment sought to forbid.[10]

Acceptance of a narrow, accommodationist view of the history of the establishment clause must not be allowed to be turned into public policies that serve to increase public support for religious schools in any form: vouchers, tax credits, or aid for extremes of "parental choice." They must not be allowed to increase the role of religion in public schools by organized prayer, teaching of Creationism, censorship of textbooks on the basis of their "secular humanism," or "opting out" of required studies in citizenship on the grounds that they offend any sincerely held religious belief, as ruled by Federal District Judge Thomas Hull in Greeneville, Tennessee, in October 1986.[11]

These practices not only violate good public policy, but they also vitiate the thrust toward separation of church and state which, with minor exceptions, marked the entire careers of Madison and Jefferson. William Lee Miller, professor of religious studies at the University of Virginia, wrote the following succinct summary of their views:

Did "religious freedom" for Jefferson and Madison extend to atheists? Yes. To agnostics, unbelievers, and pagans? Yes. To heretics and blasphemers and the sacrilegious? Yes. To the Jew and the Gentile, the Christian and Mohametan, the Hindoo, and infidel of every denomination? Yes. To people who want freedom *from* religion? Yes. To people who want freedom *against* religion? Yes....

Did this liberty of belief for Jefferson and Madison entail separation of church and state? Yes. A ban on tax aid to religion? Yes. On state help to religion? Yes. Even religion-in-general? Yes. Even if it were extended without any favoritism among religious groups? Yes. The completely voluntary way in religion? Yes.

Did all the founders agree with Jefferson and Madison? Certainly not. Otherwise there wouldn't have been a fight.[12]

The fight not only continues, but seems to be intensifying on many fronts. So, it behooves educators to study these issues in depth, to consider the best historical scholarship available, and to judge present issues of religion and education accordingly.

NOTES

1. *Everson* v. *Board of Education*, 330 U.S. 1 (1947). Black was joined by Chief Justice Vinson and Justices Douglas, Murphy, and Reed.

2. James M. O'Neill, *Religion and Education Under the Constitution* (New York: Harper, 1949). O'Neill was chairman of the department of speech at Queens College, New York. See also Wilfrid Parsons, S.J., *The First Freedom: Considerations on Church and State in the United States* (New York: Declan X. McMullen, 1948).

3. R. Freeman Butts, *The American Tradition in Religion and Education* (Boston: Beacon Press, 1950). I was professor of education at Teachers College, Columbia University, teaching courses in the history of education. See O'Neill's review of my

book in *America,* 9 September 1950, pp. 579–583. See also Leo Pfeffer, *Church, State, and Freedom* (Boston: Beacon Press, 1953) for views similar to mine.

4. *Lemon* v. *Kurtzman,* 403 U.S. 602 (1971). The law struck down in Pennsylvania would have paid part of the salaries of private school teachers of nonreligious subjects.

5. Those six states were Massachusetts, Connecticut, New Hampshire, Maryland, South Carolina, and Georgia.

6. R. Freeman Butts, *Religion, Education, and the First Amendment: The Appeal to History* (Washington, D.C.: People for the American Way, 1985), 35. R. Freeman Butts, "James Madison, the Bill of Rights, and Education," *Teachers College Record* 60, 3 (December 1958): 123–128.

7. Walter Berns, *The First Amendment and the Future of American Democracy* (New York:Basic Books, 1976). Michael J. Malbin, *Religion and Politics: The Intentions of the Authors of the First Amendment* (Washington, D.C.: American Enterprise Institute, 1978). Robert L. Cord, *Separation of Church and State: Historical Fact and Current Fiction* (New York: Lambeth Press, 1982) with a Foreword by William F. Buckley, Jr.

8. *Wallace* v. *Jaffree,* 105 S.Ct. 2479 (1985).

9. *Aguilar* v. *Felton,* 105 S.Ct. 3232 (1985).

10. Leonard W. Levy, *The Establishment Clause: Religion and the First Amendment* (New York: Macmillan, 1986), p. xvi.

11. *Mozert* v. *Hawkins,* U.S. District Court for Eastern District of Tennessee, 24 October 1986.

12. *The Washington Post National Weekly Edition,* 13 October 1986, pp. 23–24.

NO

Robert L. Cord

CHURCH-STATE SEPARATION AND THE PUBLIC SCHOOLS: A RE-EVALUATION

For four decades—since the *Everson* v. *Board of Education*[1] decision in 1947—a volatile national debate has raged about the meaning and scope of the First Amendment's establishment clause that mandates separation of church and state. Many of the U.S. Supreme Court's decisions about this matter involve education; therefore, their importance is great to school administrators and teachers who establish and execute policy.

Because of the vagueness of Supreme Court decision making in this important area of constitutional law, public school educators have been accused of violating the First Amendment by allowing or disallowing, for example, the posting of the Ten Commandments, a meeting on school property of a student religious club, or a moment of silent meditation and/or prayer. Today even the very textbooks that students read have become a subject of litigation by parents against a school system, a controversy most likely to end before the Supreme Court.

As this national debate rages, most scholars generally agree that the Founding Fathers' intentions regarding church-state separation are still extremely relevant and important. While the framers of the Constitution and the First Amendment could not foresee many twentieth century problems—especially those growing from advanced technology—many church-state concerns that they addressed in 1787 and 1789 are similar to those we face today.

CONSTITUTION'S WORDS NOT TRIVIAL

Further, if a nation, such as the United States, proclaims that its written Constitution protects individual liberties and truly provides legal restrictions on the actions of government, the words of that organic law—and the principles derived from them—cannot be treated as irrelevant trivia by those who temporarily govern. That is the surest single way to undo constitutional government, for constitutional government requires that the general power of government be defined and limited by law *in fact* as well as in theory.[2]

From Robert L. Cord, "Church-State Separation and the Public Schools: A Re-evaluation," *Educational Leadership*, vol. 44, no. 8 (May 1987), pp 26–32. Copyright © 1987 by The Association for Supervision and Curriculum Development. Reprinted by permission. All rights reserved.

Published in 1979 to the praise of many respected constitutional scholars, the encyclopedic *Congressional Quarterly's Guide to the U.S. Supreme Court* provided the following meaning of the establishment clause.

The two men most responsible for its inclusion in the Bill of Rights construed the clause *absolutely.* Thomas Jefferson and James Madison thought that the prohibition of establishment meant that a presidential proclamation of Thanksgiving Day was just as improper as a tax exemption for churches.[3]

Despite this authoritative statement, the historical facts are that, as President, James Madison issued at least four Thanksgiving Day proclamations—9 July 1812, 23 July 1813, 16 November 1814, and 4 March 1815.[4] If Madison interpreted the establishment clause absolutely, he violated both his oath of office and the very instruments of government that he helped write and labored to have ratified.[5]

Similarly, if President Thomas Jefferson construed the establishment clause absolutely, he also violated his oath of office, his principles, and the Constitution when, in 1802, he signed into federal law tax exemption for the churches in Alexandria County, Virginia.[6]

Since Jefferson and Madison held the concept of separation of church and state most dear, in my judgment, neither man —as president or in any other public office under the federal Constitution— was an absolutist and neither violated his understanding of the First Amendment's establishment clause. For me, it therefore logically follows that President Madison did not think issuing Thanksgiving Day Proclamations violated the constitutional doctrine of church-state separation, and

that President Jefferson held the same view about tax exemption for churches.

Whoever wrote the paragraph quoted from the prestigious *Guide to the U.S. Supreme Court,* I assume, did not intend to deceive, but evidently did not check primary historical sources, was ignorant of Madison's and Jefferson's actions when each was president, and mistakenly relied on inadequate secondary historical writings considered authoritative, as no doubt the paragraph from the *Guide* is, too. This indicates that much misunderstanding and/or misinformation exists about the meaning of the constitutional concept of separation of church and state.

In that context, I examine ideas critical of my writing published in a monograph—*Religion, Education, and the First Amendment: The Appeal to History*—by the eminent scholar, R. Freeman Butts. There he characterized my book, *Separation of Church and State: Historical Fact and Current Fiction,* as a manifestation of some "conservative counterreformation," the purpose of which is "to attack once again the [U.S. Supreme] Court's adherence to the principle of separation between church and state" by characterizing that principle as a "myth" or a "fiction" or merely "rhetoric."[7] The very first paragraph of my book refutes this erroneous characterization.

Separation of Church and State is probably the most distinctive concept that the American constitutional system has contributed to the body of political ideas. In 1791, when the First Amendment's prohibition that "Congress shall make no law respecting an establishment of religion" was added to the United States Constitution, no other country had provided so carefully to prevent the combination of the power of religion with the power of the national government.[8]

While primary historical sources exist that substantiate the Founding Fathers' commitment to church-state separation, other primary sources convince me that much of what the United States Supreme Court and noted scholars have written about it is historically untenable and, in many instances, sheer fiction at odds with the words and actions of the statesmen who placed that very principle in our Constitution.

ABSOLUTE SEPARATION V. "NO PREFERENCE" DOCTRINE

In the 40-year-old *Everson* case the Supreme Court justices, while splitting 5-4 over the immediate issue, were unanimous in proclaiming that the purpose of the establishment clause—and the intention of its framers in the First Congress—was to create a "high and impregnable" wall of separation between church and state.[9]

Unlike the *Everson* Court, Professor Butts, and all "absolute separationist" scholars, I think the full weight of historical evidence—especially the documented public words and deeds of the First Amendment's framers, including James Madison and our early presidents and Congresses—indicates that they embraced a far narrower concept of church-state separation. In my judgment, they interpreted the First Amendment as prohibiting Congress from (1) creating a national religion or establishment, and (2) placing any one religion, religious sect, or religious tradition in a legally preferred position.[10]

Simply put, the framers of the establishment clause sought to preclude discriminatory government religious partisanship, not nondiscriminatory government accommodation or, in some instances, government collaboration with religion. When this "no religious preference" interpretation of the establishment clause is substituted for the Supreme Court's "high and impregnable wall" interpretation, it is easier to understand many historical documents at odds with the absolutists' position. They substantiate that all our early Congresses, including the one that proposed to the states what subsequently became the First Amendment, and all our early presidents, including Jefferson and Madison, in one way or another used sectarian means to achieve constitutional secular ends.

EVERSON CASE

In the *Everson* case, writing the Court's opinion, Justice Black sought to bolster his "high and impregnable wall" dictum with appeals to some carefully chosen actions of Madison, Jefferson, the Virginia Legislature of 1786, and the framers of the First Amendment. Omitted from all of the *Everson* opinions are any historical facts that run counter to that theory. In his writings, I think Professor Butts employs a similar technique of "history by omission." By this I mean that he fails to address indisputable historical facts that are irreconcilable with his absolute separationist views. A few examples will substantiate this extremely important point.

Mentioning Madison's successful Virginia battle against the "Bill Establishing a Provision for Teachers of the Christian Religion" and "Jefferson's historic statute for religious freedom in 1786,"[11] Professor Butts does not explain away Jefferson's Virginia "Bill for Punishing Disturbers of Religious Worship and Sabbath Breakers," which was introduced by Madison in the Virginia Assembly in 1785 and became law in 1786.[12] Further, while he emphasizes Madison's role in introducing and guiding the Bill of Rights through the First Congress,[13] Professor Butts does not explain why the "absolutist" Madison served as one of six members of a Congressional Committee which, without recorded dissent, recommended the establishment of a Congressional Chaplain System. Adopting the Committee's recommendation, the First Congress voted a $500 annual salary from public funds for a Senate chaplain and a like amount for a House chaplain, both of whom were to offer public prayers in Congress.[14]

Nor does Professor Butts explain why, as an absolute separationist, James Madison would, as president, issue discretionary proclamations of Thanksgiving, calling for a day "to be set apart for the devout purposes of rendering the Sovereign of the Universe and the Benefactor of Man [identified earlier in the proclamation by Madison as "Almighty God"] the public homage due to His holy attributes. . . ."[15]

Unexplained also is why Professor Butts' absolute separationist version of Thomas Jefferson would, as president, conclude a treaty with Kaskaskia Indians which, in part, called for the United States to build them a Roman Catholic Church and pay their priest, and subsequently would urge Congress to appropriate public funds to carry out the terms of the treaty.[16] An understanding of what the framers of our Constitution thought about church-state separation would also be furthered if we had explanations of why Presidents Washington, John Adams, and Jefferson apparently did not think they were breaching the "high and impregnable" wall when they signed into law Congressional bills that, in

effect, purchased with enormous grants of federal land, in controlling trusts, the services of the "Society of the United Brethren for propagating the Gospel among the Heathen" to minister to the needs of Christian and other Indians in the Ohio Territory.[17] Like the majority of the Supreme Court, Professor Butts does not comment on these historical documents and events.

When all the historical evidence is considered, I think it relatively clear that the establishment clause was designed to prevent Congress from either establishing a national religion or from putting any one religion, religious sect, or religious tradition into a legally preferred position. In *Everson*, the Supreme Court interpreted the Fourteenth Amendment as prohibiting state legislatures, or their instrumentalities such as school boards, from doing likewise. As a result, the interpretation of the establishment clause by Supreme Court decisions governs the permissible range of both state and federal legislative authority.

Professor Butts thinks my definition of an "establishment of religion" too narrow, and the prohibition which I think the framers intended "plausible but false."[18] Plausible because in the sixteenth and seventeenth centuries, establishments in Europe and in the early American colonies usually meant the establishment of a single church. False because Professor Butts contends that, by the end of the eighteenth century, in America the term "establishment of religion" had taken on a different meaning.

His argument is that "the idea of a single church as constituting 'an establishment of religion' was no longer embedded in the legal framework of any American state when the First Amendment was being debated in Congress in the summer of 1789." Adding that in all of the states that still retained establishments, "multiple establishments were the rule," Professor Butts concludes that "the founders and the framers could not have been ignorant of this fact; they knew very well that this is what the majority in the First Congress intended to prohibit at the federal level."[19]

BUTTS' ARGUMENT UNTENABLE

This argument is simply untenable when considered with the primary historical record. Professor Butts virtually ignored the documents most crucial to an understanding of what the religion clauses were designed to prohibit at the federal level—the suggested constitutional amendments from the various State Ratifying Conventions. Those documents show that they feared, among other things, that important individual rights might be infringed by the powerful new national legislature authorized by the adoption of the federal Constitution.

Their amendments indicate that the states feared interference with the individual's right of conscience and an exclusive religious establishment, *not a multiple national establishment*, as Professor Butts wants us to believe. Typical was the Maryland Ratifying Convention's proposed amendment stating "that there will be no national religion established by law; but that all persons be equally entitled to protection in their religious liberty."[20]

The Virginia Ratifying Convention proposed a "Declaration of Bill of Rights" as amendments to the Constitution that was echoed by North Carolina, Rhode Island, and New York Conventions.

Virginia's Article Twenty, adopted 27 June 1788, stated:

> That religion, or the duty which we owe to our Creator, and the manner of discharging it, can be directed only by reason and conviction, not by force or violence; and therefore all men have an equal, natural, and unalienable right to the free exercise of religion, according to the dictates of conscience, and that no particular religious sect or society ought to be favored or established, by law, in preference to others.[21]

STATES WANTED NONPREFERENCE

In short, when it came to religious establishments, the State Ratifying Conventions proposed "nonpreference" amendments.

With these proposals in mind, it is easier to understand the wording of Madison's original religion amendment: "The Civil rights of none shall be abridged on account of religious belief or worship, nor shall any national religion be established, nor shall the full and equal rights of Conscience be in any manner, or on any pretext, infringed."[22] Madison wanted the Constitution to forbid the federal government from interfering with the rights of conscience or establish an exclusive national religion—not religions —and the record said so.

The "nonpreference" interpretation is further bolstered by Madison's original wording of his own establishment clause and his later interpretation on the floor of the House of Representatives of the intended prohibitions of the amendment. On 15 August 1789, using virtually the same words employed by the petitioning State Ratifying Conventions,

> Mr. Madison said, he apprehended the meaning of the words to be, that

Congress should not establish a religion, and enforce the legal observation of it by law, nor compel men to worship God in any manner contrary to their conscience. Whether the words are necessary or not, he did not mean to say, but . . . he thought it as well expressed as the nature of the language would admit.[23]

Further, the House record indicates that Madison said that "he believed that the people feared one sect might obtain a preeminence, or two combine together, and establish a religion to which they would compel others to conform."[24] Certainly Madison's statements from the record of the First Congress and the other primary documents mentioned here run contrary to the "multiple establishment" thesis.

IMPLICATIONS FOR THE PUBLIC SCHOOLS

Professionals in education may wonder appropriately what the impact would be on public education should the U.S. Supreme Court now choose to reverse some of its major rulings and adopt the narrower interpretation of church-state separation which I believe was intended and embraced by the First Amendment's framers.

First, the establishment clause would continue to prohibit Congress and individual states from creating, in Madison's words, "a national religion."

Second, in keeping with the framers' intent, the establishment clause's "no preference" doctrine, applied directly to the federal government and to the states by the Fourteenth Amendment, would constitutionally preclude all governmental entities from placing any one religion, religious sect, or religious tradition into a preferred legal status. As a consequence,

in public schools, the recitation of the Lord's Prayer or readings taken solely from the New Testament would continue to be unconstitutional because they place the Christian religion in a preferred position.

Similarly, the posting of the Ten Commandments only or reading only from the Old Testament would place the Judeo-Christian tradition in an unconstitutionally favored religious status. However, unendorsed readings or postings from many writings considered sacred by various religions, such as the Book of Mormon, the interpretative writings of Mary Baker Eddy, the Bible, the Koran, the Analects of Confucius, would be constitutional. A decision to teach only "creationism" or Genesis would be unconstitutional, while a course in cosmology, exploring a full range of beliefs about the origin of life or the nature of the universe —religious, areligious, or nonreligious— would not violate the First Amendment any more than would a course on comparative religions without teacher endorsement.

In all circumstances where the state is pursuing a valid educational goal, and is religiously nonpartisan in doing so, the professional leadership of the educational unit would decide, as in any other policy, whether such an activity was educationally appropriate or desirable. This would be the case whether the educational unit was a school, a school district, or an entire state educational system. Consequently, adherence to the "no preference" doctrine would return many policy decisions to the appropriate educational authorities, elected or appointed, and reduce the all too frequent present pattern of government by judiciary.

Third, although the First Amendment's free exercise of religion clause would not be contracted by the "no preference" principle, that interpretation would, in some instances, expand the individual's free exercise of religion and other First Amendment rights. This would happen where "equal access" is currently denied public school students.

EQUAL ACCESS ACT

The Equal Access Act of 1984 (Public Law 98-377) prohibits public high schools receiving federal aid from preventing voluntary student groups, including religious ones, from meeting in school facilities before and after class hours or during a club period, if other extracurricular groups have access.[25] The constitutionality of refusing "equal access" to voluntary student religious organizations was litigated in the lower courts[26] before reaching the U.S. Supreme Court in *Bender* v. *Williamsport* in March 1986.[27]

In deciding equal access cases, the lower federal courts applied the Supreme Court's "three part *Lemon*" test to determine whether the establishment clause had been violated. Under this test, first described in *Lemon* v. *Kurtzman*, the Supreme Court held that in order to pass constitutional muster under the establishment clause, the challenged governmental policy or activity must (1) have a secular purpose, (2) be one that has a principal or primary effect which neither advances nor inhibits religion, and (3) not foster an excessive government entanglement with religion.[28]

The "no preference" doctrine, on the other hand, would provide a relatively clearer and easier-to-apply test. Alleged violations would be measured by two simple questions: (1) Is the governmental action within the constitutional power of the acting public body? and (2) Does the governmental action elevate any one religion, religious sect, or religious tradition into a preferred legal status? Either a "no" to the first question or a "yes" to the second would make the policy unconstitutional.

Unlike the *Lemon* interpretation, the "no preference" interpretation poses less danger to a student's individual First and Fourteenth Amendment liberty. The Third U.S. Circuit Court's decision in *Bender* v. *Williamsport* illustrates this point. There the court held that it was constitutional for a school board to refuse to permit a student-initiated nondenominational prayer club to meet during the regularly scheduled activity period in a public school room.[29] As I see it, that decision subordinated three First Amendment freedoms—free exercise of religion, freedom of speech, and voluntary assembly—to one misinterpreted First Amendment guarantee. Under the "no preference" doctrine, equal access would be guaranteed to *all* religious or, for that matter, irreligious student groups under the same conditions that apply to any other voluntary student group.

Application of the "no preference" interpretation also avoids enormous dangers to an "open society" possible under the *Lemon* test. Can we not see that a court which can hold today that a classroom could not be used by a voluntary religious student group because that use may have as its primary effect the advancement of religion, can tomorrow, by the same logic, bar meeting rooms to students who want to discuss atheism or a book negative about religion, such as Bertrand Russell's *Why I Am Not a Christian*, because the primary effect there might be said to inhibit religion? By the use of *Lemon's* "primary effect" test, books about religion or those said to be irreligious can be removed from public school libraries. Is C. S. Lewis' *The Screwtape Letters* safe? And what about *Inherit the Wind*, or Darwin's *Origin of the Species?* Are we so frightened of ourselves that we are willing to disallow, in our institutions of learning, scrutinization of ultimate issues and values because of fear about where an open marketplace of ideas may eventually take the nation?

Finally, while some actions such as an uncoerced moment of silence for meditation and/or prayer in a public schoolroom[30] or the teaching of educationally deprived students from low-income families for several hours each week in a parochial school by public school teachers, recently held unconstitutional,[31] would be constitutional under the "no preference" interpretation, that does not mean they would automatically become educational policy. In all public educational entities, large or small, what would become policy would be up to the legally empowered decision makers in each of those entities.

NOTES

1. 330 U.S. 1 (1947).

2. Charles H. McIlwain, *Constitutionalism: Ancient and Modern*, rev. ed. (Ithaca, N.Y.: Great Seal Books, 1958), 19-22.

3. *Congressional Quarterly's Guide to the United States Supreme Court* (Washington, D.C.: Congressional Quarterly, Inc., 1979), 461. Emphasis added. The First Amendment has two religion clauses, the "establishment" clause and the "free exercise" clause. U.S. Constitution Amendment I: "Congress shall make no law respecting an establishment of religion, or prohibiting the free exercise thereof...."

4. These proclamations, in their entirety, are published in James D. Richardson, *A Contemplation of the Messages and Papers of the Presidents, 1789-1897*, vol. I (Washington, D.C.: Bureau of National Literature and Art, 1901), 34-35; and Robert L. Cord, *Separation of Church and State: Historical Fact and Current Fiction* (Grand Rapids, Michigan: Baker Book House, 1988), 257-260.

5. After he had left the presidency, and toward the end of his life, Madison wrote a document commonly known as the "Detached Memoranda," which was first published as recently as 1946 in *William and Mary Quarterly* 3 (1946): 534. In it Madison *does* say that Thanksgiving Day proclamations are unconstitutional, as are chaplains in Congress. In light of his actions in public office, these were obviously not his views as a congressman and president. For a fuller discussion of Madison's "Detached Memoranda," see Cord, *Separation*, 29-36.

6. *2 Statutes at Large* 194, Seventh Congress, Sess. 1, Chap. 52. Jefferson *did* believe Thanksgiving Proclamation violated the First Amendment and, unlike Washington, John Adams, and James Madison, declined to issue them.

7. R. Freeman Butts, *Religion, Education, and the First Amendment: The Appeal to History* (Washington, D.C.: People for the American Way, 1986), 9. Butts, an educational historian, is William F. Russell Professor Emeritus, Teachers College, Columbia University; Senior Fellow of the Kettering Foundation; and Visiting Scholar at the Hoover Institution, Stanford University.

8. Cord, *Separation*, XIII.

9. For an extensive critique of the *Everson* case and its interpretation of the establishment clause, see Cord, *Separation*, 103-133.

10. For in-depth study of the "no preference" principle, see Robert L. Cord, "Church-State Separation: Restoring the 'No Preference' Doctrine of the First Amendment," *Harvard Journal of Law & Public Policy* 9 (1986): 129.

11. Butts, *Religion*, 18.

12. Cord, *Separation*, 215-218.

13. Butts, *Religion*, 18-21.

14. Cord, *Separation*, 22-26.

15. Quoted from President Madison's "Proclamation" of "the 9th day of July A.D. 1812." This proclamation is republished in its entirety in Cord, *Separation*, 257.

16. For the entire text of the treaty, see Ibid., 261-263.

17. The full texts of these laws are republished in Cord, 263-270.

18. Butts, *Religion*, 16.

19. Ibid., 18.

20. Jonathan Elliott, *Debates on the Federal Constitution*, vol. II (Philadelphia: J.B. Lippincott Co., 1901), 553.

21. Ibid., vol. III, 659.

22. *Annals of the Congress of the United States, The Debates and Proceedings in the Congress of the United States*, vol. I, Compiled from Authentic Materials, by Joseph Gales, Senior (Washington, D.C.: Gales and Seaton, 1834), 434.

23. Ibid., 730.

24. Ibid., 731.

25. *Congressional Quarterly Weekly Report*, vols. 42, p. 1545, 1854; 43, p. 1807.

26. *Brandon* v. *Board of Education*, 635 F. 2nd 971 (2d Cir. 1980); *cert. denied*, 454 U.S. 1123 (1981); *Lubbock Civil Liberties Union* v. *Lubbock Independent School District*, 669 F. 2d 1038 (5th Cir. 1982), *cert. denied*, 459 U.S. 1155 (1983).

27. *Bender* v. *Williamsport*, 475 U.S. 534, 89 L.Ed. 2d 501 (1986). While the Third Circuit Court dealt with the "equal access" question, the Supreme Court did not reach that constitutional issue because one of the parties to the suit in the Circuit Court lacked standing and, therefore, that Court should have dismissed the case for want of jurisdiction. Ibid., 516.

28. *Lemon* v. *Kurtzman*, 403 U.S. 602, 612, 613 (1971).

29. *Bender* v. *Williamsport*, 741 F. 2d 538, 541 (3rd Cir. 1984).

30. In *Wallace* v. *Jaffree*, 105 S. Ct. 2479 (1985), the U.S. Supreme Court held such a law unconstitutional.

31. In *Grand Rapids* v. *Ball*, 473 U.S. 373, 87 L.Ed. 2d 267 (1985) and *Aguilar* v. *Felton*, 473 U.S. 402, 87 L.Ed. 2d 290 (1985), the Supreme Court held similar programs unconstitutional.

POSTSCRIPT

Is Church-State Separation Being Threatened?

If the Constitution is indeed a document that attempts to guarantee the protection of minority opinions from a possibly oppressive majority, can it be applied equally to all parties in any value-laden dispute such as those involving the relationship of church and state? An exhaustive review of historical cases dealing with manifestations of this basic problem may be found in Martha McCarthy's article "Religion and Public Schools," in the August 1985 issue of the *Harvard Educational Review*.

An extremely wide variety of articles is available on this volatile area of concern, including "Stepchildren of the Moral Majority," by Daniel Yankelovich, *Psychology Today* (November 1981); "The Crusade to Ban Books," by Stephen Arons, *Saturday Review* (June 1981); "Textbook Censorship and Secular Humanism in Perspective," by Franklin Parker, *Religion and Public Education* (Summer 1988); Rod Farmer's "Toward a Definition of Secular Humanism," *Contemporary Education* (Spring 1987); Mel and Norma Gabler's "Moral Relativism on the Ropes," *Communication Education* (October 1987); and Donald Vandenberg's "Education and the Religious," *Teachers College Record* (Fall 1987).

Three other provocative sources of insights are these: Thomas W. Goodhue's "What Should Public Schools Say About Religion?" *Education Week* (April 23, 1986); "How Prayer and Public Schooling Can Coexist," Eugene W. Kelly, Jr., *Education Week* (November 12, 1986); and Edward A. Wynne's "The Case for Censorship to Protect the Young," *Issues in Education* (Winter 1985).

Other excellent sources are these: Warren A. Nord, "The Place of Religion in the World of Public School Textbooks," and Mark G. Yudof, "Religion, Textbooks, and the Public Schools," both in *The Educational Forum* (Spring 1990), and James Davison Hunter's "Modern Pluralism and the First Amendment," *The Brookings Review* (Spring 1990).

Four recent books explore aspects of the issue: *The Rights of Religious Persons in Public Education* (1991) by John W. Whitehead; *Religious Fundamentalism and American Education: The Battle for the Public Schools* (1990) by Eugene F. Provenzo, Jr.; *A Standard for Repair: The Establishment of Religion Clause of the U.S. Constitution* (1992) by Jeremy Gunn; and *Why We Still Need Public Schools: Church/State Relations and Visions of Democracy* (1992) edited by Art Must, Jr.

In the end, the main problem is one of finding an appropriate balance between the two First Amendment clauses within the context of public schooling and making that balance palatable and realizable at the local school level.

ISSUE 6

Should Multiculturalism Permeate the Curriculum?

YES: James A. Banks, from "Multicultural Education: Development, Dimensions, and Challenges," *Phi Delta Kappan* (September 1993)

NO: Linda Chavez, from "Demystifying Multiculturalism," *National Review* (February 21, 1994)

ISSUE SUMMARY

YES: Education professor James A. Banks, a leading advocate of multicultural education, identifies what he feels are some of the current misconceptions about multicultural education, details its accomplishments, and promotes its further implementation in the schools.

NO: Linda Chavez, director of the Center for the New American Community, attacks the basic assumptions of multiculturalists and accuses them of following a political agenda designed to culturally divide America.

During the past 20 years or so, American public schools have been encouraged to embrace multiculturalism as a curricular focus. The "No One American" statement, issued by the American Association of Colleges of Teacher Education in 1972, set the tone for the movement by calling for an effort to support cultural diversity and global understanding. In the 1980s a number of influential writers, such as Allan Bloom, E. D. Hirsch, Jr., Arthur M. Schlesinger, Jr., William J. Bennett, and Nathan Glazer, warned of the divisive nature of multiculturalism and called for a renewed curricular focus on cultural commonalities shaped by the Western tradition.

Thus was launched the so-called culture wars, which have persisted on an educational battlefield that extends from kindergarten to graduate school. Several books, including Bennett's *To Reclaim a Legacy*, Lynne Cheney's *American Memory: A Report on the Humanities in the Nation's Public Schools* (1988), and Dinesh D'Souza's *Illiberal Education: The Politics of Race and Sex on Campus* (1991), stirred much of the public's concern over what many felt was an encroachment by the multiculturalists upon the traditional canon and the subsequent diminishment of cultural literacy. In defense of multiculturalism, Ira Shor, in his book *Culture Wars: School and Society in the Conservative Restoration* (1987), claims that the underlying motivation of the cultural literacy "backlash" was to restore conservative themes and "right words" that establish "raw authority at the top" while discrediting the liberalism of the

1960s. Also supportive of a multicultural curriculum is Asa G. Hilliard III, who contends that the traditional Eurocentric curriculum is warped and restrictive; that the primary goal of multiculturalism is to present a truthful and meaningful rendition of the whole of human experience; and that a pluralistic curriculum is not a matter of ethnic quotas for "balance," as some conservatives contend.

Two social realities undergird the multiculturalist effort to reform the curriculum at all levels: the traditional curriculum has neglected the contributions made by minority groups to the American culture, and the economy is becoming more and more globalized. Given these conditions, the multicultural approach may be seen as serving to give a new and expanded definition to the "American experience." What effect a multicultural curriculum will have on American traditions and social institutions remains to be seen. Serious questions continue to be debated—questions involving the future path of cultural development in American society, and sociological questions about the relationships between the institutionally dominant majority culture and the minority cultures, the populations of which are increasing.

In the opposing selections offered here, James A. Banks argues that multiculturalism is helping to develop more positive attitudes among students of different cultural backgrounds and that it will eventually reshape the American identity in a positive way. Linda Chavez maintains that the multiculturalists confuse race and national origin (which are immutable traits) with cultural attributes (which are learned) and wrongly dismiss the idea of one common American culture. On the contrary, she contends, most minorities and immigrants strive for assimilation into the mainstream culture; therefore, multiculturalism is not a grassroots movement but a political strategy for keeping the country culturally divided.

YES

James A. Banks

MULTICULTURAL EDUCATION: DEVELOPMENT, DIMENSIONS, AND CHALLENGES

The bitter debate over the literary and historical canon that has been carried on in the popular press and in several widely reviewed books has overshadowed the progress that has been made in multicultural education during the last two decades. The debate has also perpetuated harmful misconceptions about theory and practice in multicultural education. Consequently, it has heightened racial and ethnic tension and trivialized the field's remarkable accomplishments in theory, research, and curriculum development. The truth about the development and attainments of multicultural education needs to be told for the sake of balance, scholarly integrity, and accuracy. But if I am to reveal the truth about multicultural education, I must first identify and debunk some of the widespread myths and misconceptions about it.

Multicultural Education Is for the Others.

One misconception about multicultural education is that it is an entitlement program and curriculum movement for African Americans, Hispanics, the poor, women, and other victimized groups.[1] The major theorists and researchers in multicultural education agree that the movement is designed to restructure educational institutions so that all students, including middle-class white males, will acquire the knowledge, skills, and attitudes needed to function effectively in a culturally and ethnically diverse nation and world.[2] Multicultural education, as its major architects have conceived it during the last decade, is not an ethnic- or gender-specific movement. It is a movement designed to empower all students to become knowledgeable, caring, and active citizens in a deeply troubled and ethnically polarized nation and world.

The claim that multicultural education is only for people of color and for the disenfranchised is one of the most pernicious and damaging misconceptions with which the movement has had to cope. It has caused intractable problems and has haunted multicultural education since its inception. Despite all that has been written and spoken about multicultural education being for all students, the image of multicultural education as an entitlement program for the "others" remains strong and vivid in the public imagination, as well as in the hearts and minds of many teachers and administrators. Teachers who teach in predominantly white schools and districts often state that they don't have a program or plan for multicultural education because they have few African American, Hispanic, or Asian American students.

When educators view multicultural education as the study of the "others," it is marginalized and held apart from mainstream education reform. Several critics of multicultural education, such as Arthur Schlesinger, John Leo, and Paul Gray, have perpetuated the idea that multicultural education is the study of the "other" by defining it as synonymous with Afrocentric education.[3] The history of intergroup education teaches us that only when education reform related to diversity is viewed as essential for all students—and as promoting the broad public interest—will it have a reasonable chance of becoming institutionalized in the nation's schools, colleges, and universities.[4] The intergroup education movement of the 1940s and 1950s failed in large part because intergroup educators were never able to persuade mainstream educators to believe that the approach was needed by and designed for all students. To its bitter but quiet end, mainstream educators viewed intergroup education as something for schools with racial problems and as something for "them" and not for "us."

Multicultural Education Is Opposed to the Western Tradition.

Another harmful misconception about multicultural education has been repeated so often by its critics that many people take it as self-evident. This is the claim that multicultural education is a movement that is opposed to the West and to Western civilization. Multicultural education is not anti-West, because most writers of color—such as Rudolfo Anaya, Paula Gunn Allen, Maxine Hong Kingston, Maya Angelou, and Toni Morrison—are Western writers. Multicultural education itself is a thoroughly Western movement. It grew out of a civil rights movement grounded in such democratic ideals of the West as freedom, justice, and equality. Multicultural education seeks to extend to all people the ideals that were meant only for an elite few at the nation's birth.

Although multicultural education is not opposed to the West, its advocates do demand that the truth about the West be told, that its debt to people of color and women be recognized and included in the curriculum, and that the discrepancies between the ideals of freedom and equality and the realities of racism and sexism be taught to students. Reflective action by citizens is also an integral part of multicultural theory. Multicultural education views citizen action to improve society as an integral part of education in a democracy; it links knowledge, values, empowerment, and action. Multicultural education is also postmodern in its assumptions about knowledge and knowledge construction; it challenges positivist assumptions about the relationships between human values, knowledge, and action.

Positivists, who are the intellectual heirs of the Enlightenment, believe that it is possible to structure knowledge that is objective and beyond the influence of human values and interests. Multicultural theorists maintain that knowledge is positional, that it relates to the knower's values and experiences, and that knowledge implies action. Consequently, different concepts, theories, and paradigms imply different kinds of actions. Multiculturalists believe that, in order to have valid knowledge, information about the social condition and experiences of the knower are essential.

A few critics of multicultural education, such as John Leo and Dinesh D'Souza, claim that multicultural education has reduced or displaced the study of Western civilization in the nation's schools and colleges. However, as Gerald Graff points out in his welcome book *Beyond the Culture Wars*, this claim is simply not true. Graff cites his own research at the college level and that of Arthur Applebee at the high school level to substantiate his conclusion that European and American male authors—such as Shakespeare, Dante, Chaucer, Twain, and Hemingway—still dominate the required reading lists in the nation's high schools and colleges.[5] Graff found that, in the cases he examined, most of the books by authors of color were optional rather than required reading. Applebee found that, of the 10 book-length works most frequently required in the high school grades, only one title was by a female author (Harper Lee's *To Kill a Mockingbird*), and not a single work was by a writer of color. Works by Shakespeare, Steinbeck, and Dickens headed the list.

Multicultural Education Will Divide the Nation.

Many of its critics claim that multicultural education will divide the nation and undercut its unity. Schlesinger underscores this view in the title of his book, *The Disuniting of America: Reflections on a Multicultural Society*. This misconception is based partly on questionable assumptions about the nature of U.S. society and partly on a mistaken understanding of multicultural education. The claim that multicultural education will divide the nation assumes that the nation is already united. While we are one nation politically, sociologically our nation is deeply divided along lines of race, gender, and class. The current debate about admitting gays into the military underscores another deep division in our society.

Multicultural education is designed to help unify a deeply divided nation rather than to divide a highly cohesive one. Multicultural education supports the notion of *e pluribus unum*—out of many, one. The multiculturalists and the Western traditionalists, however, often differ about how the *unum* can best be attained. Traditionally, the larger U.S. society and the schools tried to create unity by assimilating students from diverse racial and ethnic groups into a mythical Anglo American culture that required them to experience a process of self-alienation. However, even when students of color became culturally assimilated, they were often structurally excluded from mainstream institutions.

The multiculturalists view *e pluribus unum* as an appropriate national goal, but they believe that the *unum* must be negotiated, discussed, and restructured to reflect the nation's ethnic and cultural diversity. The reformulation of what it means to be united must be a process that involves the participation of diverse groups within the nation, such as people of color, women, straights, gays, the powerful, the powerless, the young, and the old. The reformulation must also involve power sharing and participation by people from many different cultures who must reach beyond their cultural and ethnic borders in order to create a common civic culture that reflects and contributes to the well-being of all. This common civic culture will extend beyond the cultural borders of any single group and constitute a civic "borderland" culture.

In *Borderlands*, Gloria Anzaldúa contrasts cultural borders and borderlands and calls for a weakening of the former in order to create a shared borderland culture in which people from many different cultures can interact, relate, and engage in civic talk and action. Anzaldúa states that "borders are set up to define the places that are safe and unsafe, to distinguish us from them. A border is a dividing line, a narrow strip along a steep edge. A borderland is a vague and undetermined place created by the residue of an unnatural boundary. It is in a constant state of transition."[6]

MULTICULTURAL EDUCATION HAS MADE PROGRESS

While it is still on the margins rather than in the center of the curriculum in most schools and colleges, multicultural content has made significant inroads into both the school and the college curricula within the last two decades. The truth lies somewhere between the claim that no progress has been made in infusing the school and college curricula with multiethnic content and the claim that such content has replaced the European and American classics.

In the elementary and high schools, much more ethnic content appears in social studies and language arts textbooks today than was the case 20 years ago. In addition, some teachers assign works written by authors of color along with the more standard American classics. In his study of book-length works used in the high schools, Applebee concluded that his most striking finding was how similar present reading lists are to past ones and how little change has occurred. However, he did note that many teachers use anthologies as a mainstay of their literature programs and that 21% of the anthology selections were written by women and 14% by authors of color.[7]

More classroom teachers today have studied the concepts of multicultural education than at any previous point in our history. A significant percentage of today's classroom teachers took a required teacher education course in multicultural education when they were in college. The multicultural education standard adopted by the National Council for Accreditation of Teacher Education in 1977, which became effective in 1979, was a major factor that stimulated the growth of multicultural education in teacher education programs. The standard stated: "The institution gives evidence of planning for multicultural education in its teacher education curricula including both the general and professional studies components."[8] . . .

Textbooks have always reflected the myths, hopes, and dreams of people with money and power. As African Americans, Hispanics, Asians, and women become more influential, textbooks will increasingly reflect their hopes, dreams, and disappointments. Textbooks will have to survive in the marketplace of a browner America. Because textbooks still carry the curriculum in the nation's public schools, they will remain an important focus for multicultural curriculum reformers.

THE DIMENSIONS OF MULTICULTURAL EDUCATION

One of the problems that continues to plague the multicultural education movement, both from within and without, is the tendency of teachers, administrators, policy makers, and the public to oversimplify the concept. Multicultural education is a complex and multidimensional concept, yet media commentators and educators alike often focus on only one of its many dimensions. Some teachers view it only as the inclusion of content about ethnic groups into the curriculum; others view it as an effort to reduce prejudice; still others view it as the celebration of ethnic holidays and events. After I made a presentation in a school in which I described the major goals of multicultural education, a math teacher told me that what I said was fine and appropriate for language arts and social studies teachers but that it had nothing to do with him. After all, he said, math was math, regardless of the color of the kids.

This reaction on the part of a respected teacher caused me to think more deeply about the images of multicultural education that had been created by the key actors in the field. I wondered whether we were partly responsible for this teacher's narrow conception of multicultural education as merely content integration. It was in response to such statements by classroom teachers that I conceptualized the dimensions of multicultural education. I will use the following five dimensions to describe the field's major components and to highlight important developments within the last two decades: 1) content integration, 2) the knowledge construction process, 3) prejudice reduction, 4) an equity pedagogy, and 5) an empowering school culture and social structure.[9] I will devote most of the rest of this article to the second of these dimensions.

CONTENT INTEGRATION

Content integration deals with the extent to which teachers use examples, data, and information from a variety of cultures and groups to illustrate the key concepts principles, generalizations, and theories in their subject area or discipline. In many school districts as well as in popular writing, multicultural education is viewed almost solely as content integration. This narrow conception of multicultural education is a major reason why many teachers in such subjects as biology, physics, and mathematics reject multicultural education as irrelevant to them and their students....

KNOWLEDGE CONSTRUCTION

The knowledge construction process encompasses the procedures by which social, behavioral, and natural scientists create knowledge in their disciplines. A multicultural focus on knowledge construction includes discussion of the ways in which the implicit cultural assumptions, frames of reference, perspectives, and biases within a discipline influence the construction of knowledge. An examination of the knowledge construction process is an important part of multicultural teaching. Teachers help students to understand how knowledge is created and how it is influenced by factors of race, ethnicity, gender, and social class.

Within the last decade, landmark work related to the construction of knowledge has been done by feminist social scientists and epistemologists, as well as by scholars in ethnic studies. Working in philosophy and sociology, Sandra Harding, Lorraine Code, and Patricia Hill Collins have done some of the most important work related to knowledge construction.[10] This ground-breaking work, although influential among scholars and curriculum developers, has been overshadowed in the popular media by the heated debates about the canon. These writers and researchers have seriously challenged the claims made by the positivists that knowledge can be value-free, and they have described the ways in which knowledge claims are influenced by the gender and ethnic characteristics of the knower. These scholars argue that the human interests and value assumptions of those who create knowledge should be identified, discussed, and examined.

Code states that the sex of the knower is epistemologically significant because knowledge is both subjective and objective. She maintains that both aspects should be recognized and discussed. Collins, an African American sociologist, extends and enriches the works of writers such as Code and Harding by describing the ways in which race and gender interact to influence knowledge construction. Collins calls the perspective of African American women the perspective of "the outsider within." She writes, "As outsiders within, Black women have a distinct view of the contradictions between the dominant group's actions and ideologies."[11] ...

I have identified five types of knowledge and described their implications for multicultural teaching.[12] Teachers need to be aware of the various types of knowledge so that they can structure a curriculum that helps students to understand each type. Teachers also need to use their own cultural knowledge and that of their students to enrich teaching and learning. The types of knowledge I have identified and described are: 1) personal/cultural, 2) popular, 3) mainstream academic, 4) transformative, and 5) school. (I will not discuss school knowledge in this article.)

Personal/cultural knowledge consists of the concepts, explanations, and interpretations that students derive from personal experiences in their homes, families, and community cultures. Cultural conflict occurs in the classroom because much of the personal/cultural knowledge that students from diverse cultural groups bring to the classroom is inconsistent with school knowledge and with the teacher's personal and cultural knowledge. For example, research indicates that many African American and Mexican American students are more likely to experience academic success in cooperative rather than in competitive learning environments.[13] Yet the typical school culture is highly competitive, and children of color may experience failure if they do not figure out the implicit rules of the school culture.[14]

The popular knowledge that is institutionalized by the mass media and other forces that shape the popular culture has a strong influence on the values, perceptions, and behavior of children and young people. The messages and images carried by the media, which Carlos Cortés calls the societal curriculum,[15] often reinforce the stereotypes and misconceptions about racial and ethnic groups that are institutionalized within the larger society. ...

The concepts, theories, and explanations that constitute traditional Western-centric knowledge in history and in the social and behavioral sciences constitute mainstream academic knowledge. Traditional interpretations of U.S. history—embodied in such headings as "The European Discovery of America" and "The Westward Movement"—are central concepts in mainstream academic knowledge. Mainstream academic knowledge is established within mainstream professional associations, such as the American Historical Association and the American Psychological Association. It provides the interpretations that are taught in U.S. colleges and universities.

The literary legacy of mainstream academic knowledge includes such writers as Shakespeare, Dante, Chaucer, and Aristotle. Critics of multicultural education, such as Schlesinger, D'Souza, and Leo, believe that mainstream academic knowledge in the curriculum is being displaced by the new knowledge and interpretations that have been created by scholars working in women's studies and in ethnic studies. However, mainstream academic knowledge is not only threatened from without but also from within. Postmodern scholars in organizations such as the American Historical Association, the American Sociological Association, and the American Political Science Association are challenging the dominant positivist interpretations and paradigms within their disciplines and creating alternative explanations and perspectives.

Transformative academic knowledge challenges the facts, concepts, paradigms, themes, and explanations routinely accepted in mainstream academic knowledge. Those who pursue transformative academic knowledge seek to expand and substantially revise established canons, theories, explanations, and research methods. The transformative research methods and theory that have been developed in women's studies and in ethnic studies since the 1970s constitute, in my view, the most important developments in social science theory and research in the last 20 years.

It is important for teachers and students to realize, however, that transformative academic scholarship has a long history in the United States and that the current ethnic studies movement is directly linked to an earlier ethnic studies movement that emerged in the late 1800s.[16] George Washington Williams published volume 1 of the first history of African Americans in 1882 and the second volume in 1883. Other important works published by African American transformative scholars in times past included works by W. E. B. Du Bois, Carter Woodson, Horace Mann Bond, and Charles Wesley.

The works of these early scholars in African American studies, which formed the academic roots of the current multicultural education movement when it emerged in the 1960s and 1970s, were linked by several important characteristics. Their works were transformative because they created data, interpretations, and perspectives that challenged those that were established by white, mainstream scholarship. The work of the transformative scholars presented positive images of African Americans and refuted stereotypes that were pervasive within the established scholarship of their time....

THE OTHER DIMENSIONS

The "prejudice reduction" dimension of multicultural education focuses on the characteristics of children's racial attitudes and on strategies that can be used to help students develop more positive racial and ethnic attitudes. Since the 1960s, social scientists have learned a great deal about how racial attitudes in children develop and about ways in which educators can design interventions to help children acquire more positive feelings toward other racial groups. I have reviewed that research in two recent publications and refer *Kappan* readers to them for a comprehensive discussion of this topic.[17]

This research tells us that by age 4 African American, white, and Mexican American children are aware of racial differences and show racial preferences favoring whites. Students can be helped to develop more positive racial attitudes if realistic images of ethnic and racial groups are included in teaching materials in a consistent, natural, and integrated fashion. Involving students in vicarious experiences and in cooperative learning activities with students of other racial groups will also help them to develop more positive racial attitudes and behaviors.

An *equity pedagogy* exists when teachers use techniques and teaching methods that facilitate the academic achievement of students from diverse racial and ethnic groups and from all social classes. Using teaching techniques that cater to the learning and cultural styles of diverse groups and using the techniques of cooperative learning are some of the ways that teachers have found effective with students from diverse racial, ethnic, and language groups.[18]

An *empowering school culture and social structure* will require the restructuring of the culture and organization of the school so that students from diverse racial, ethnic, and social-class groups will experience educational equality and a sense of empowerment. This dimension of multicultural education involves conceptualizing the school as the unit of change and making structural changes within the school environment. Adopting assessment techniques that are fair to all groups, doing away with tracking, and creating the belief among the staff members that all students can learn are important goals for schools that wish to create a school culture and social structure that are empowering and enhancing for a diverse student body.

MULTICULTURAL EDUCATION AND THE FUTURE

The achievements of multicultural education since the late Sixties and early Seventies are noteworthy and should be acknowledged. Those who have shaped the movement during the intervening decades have been able to obtain wide agreement on the goals of and approaches to multicultural education. Most multiculturalists agree that the major goal of multicultural education is to restructure schools so that all students will acquire the knowledge, attitudes, and skills needed to function in an ethnically and racially diverse nation and world. As is the case with other interdisciplinary areas of study, debates within the field continue. These debates are consistent with the philosophy of a field that values democracy and diversity. They are also a source of strength.

Multicultural education is being implemented widely in the nation's schools, colleges, and universities. The large number of national conferences, school district workshops, and teacher education courses in multicultural education are evidence of its success and perceived importance. Although the process of integration of content is slow and often contentious, multicultural content is increasingly becoming a part of core courses in schools and colleges. Textbook publishers are also integrating ethnic and cultural content into their books, and the pace of such integration is increasing.

Despite its impressive successes, however, multicultural education faces serious challenges as we move toward the next century. One of the most serious of these challenges is the highly organized, well-financed attack by the Western traditionalists who fear that multicultural education will transform America in ways that will result in their own disempowerment. Ironically, the successes that multicultural education has experienced during the last decade have played a major role in provoking the attacks.

The debate over the canon and the well-orchestrated attack on multicultural education reflect an identity crisis in American society. The American identity is being reshaped, as groups on the margins of society begin to participate in the mainstream and to demand that their visions be reflected in a transformed America. In the future, the sharing of power and the transformation of identity required to achieve lasting racial peace in America may be valued rather than feared, for only in this way will we achieve national salvation.

NOTES

1. Nathan Glazer, "In Defense of Multiculturalism," *New Republic*, 2 September 1991, pp. 18–22; and Dinesh D'Souza, "Illiberal Education," *Atlantic*, March 1991, pp. 51–79.

2. James A. Banks, *Multiethnic Education: Theory and Practice*, 3rd ed. (Boston: Allyn and Bacon, 1994); James A. Banks and Cherry A. McGee Banks, eds., *Multicultural Education: Issues and Perspectives*, 2nd ed. (Boston: Allyn and Bacon, 1993); and Christine E. Sleeter and Carl A. Grant, *Making Choices for Multicultural Education: Five Approaches to Race, Class, and Gender* (Columbus, Ohio: Merrill, 1988).

3. Arthur M. Schlesinger, Jr., *The Disuniting of America: Reflections on a Multicultural Society* (Knoxville, Tenn.: Whittle Direct Books, 1991); John Leo, "A Fringe History of the World," *U.S. News & World Report*, 12 November 1990, pp. 25–26; and Paul Gray, "Whose America?," *Time*, 8 July 1991, pp. 13–17.

4. Hilda Taba et al., *Intergroup Education in Public Schools* (Washington, D.C.: American Council on Education, 1952).

5. Gerald Graff, *Beyond the Culture Wars: How Teaching the Conflicts Can Revitalize American Education* (New York: Norton, 1992); and Arthur N. Applebee, "Stability and Change in the High School Canon," *English Journal*, September 1992, pp. 27–32.

6. Gloria Anzaldúa, *Borderlands: La Frontera: The New Mestiza* (San Francisco: Spinsters/Aunt Lute, 1987), p. 3.

7. Applebee, p. 30.

8. *Standards for the Accreditation of Teacher Education* (Washington, D.C.: National Council for Accreditation of Teacher Education, 1977), p. 4.

9. James A. Banks, "Multicultural Education: Historical Development, Dimensions, and Practice," in Linda Darling-Hammond, ed., *Review of Research in Education*, vol. 19 (Washington, D.C.: American Educational Research Association, 1993), pp. 3–49.

10. Sandra Harding, *Whose Science, Whose Knowledge? Thinking from Women's Lives* (Ithaca, N.Y.: Cornell University Press, 1991); Lorraine Code, *What Can She Know? Feminist Theory and the Construction of Knowledge* (Ithaca, N.Y.: Cornell University Press, 1991); and Patricia Hill Collins, *Black Feminist Thought: Knowledge, Consciousness, and the Politics of Empowerment* (New York: Routledge, 1990).

11. Collins, p. 11.

12. James A. Banks, "The Canon Debate, Knowledge Construction, and Multicultural Education," *Educational Researcher*, June/July 1993, pp. 4–14.

13. Robert E. Slavin, *Cooperative Learning* (New York: Longman, 1983).

14. Lisa D. Delpit, "The Silenced Dialogue: Power and Pedagogy in Educating Other People's Children," *Harvard Educational Review*, vol. 58, 1988, pp. 280–98.

15. Carlos E. Cortés, "The Societal Curriculum: Implications for Multiethnic Education," in James A. Banks, ed., *Education in the '80s: Multiethnic Ed-*

ucation (Washington, D.C.: National Education Association, 1981), pp. 24–32.

16. James A. Banks, "African American Scholarship and the Evolution of Multicultural Education," *Journal of Negro Education*, Summer 1992, pp. 273–86.

17. James A. Banks, "Multicultural Education: Its Effects on Students' Racial and Gender Role Attitudes," in James P. Shaver, ed., *Handbook of Research on Social Studies Teaching and Learning* (New York: Macmillan, 1991), pp. 459–69; and idem, "Multicultural Education for Young Children: Racial and Ethnic Attitudes and Their Modification," in Bernard Spodek, ed., *Handbook of Research on the Education of Young Children* (New York: Macmillan, 1993), pp. 236–50.

18. Barbara J. R. Shade, ed., *Culture, Style, and the Educative Process* (Springfield, Ill.: Charles C. Thomas, 1989).

NO

Linda Chavez

DEMYSTIFYING MULTICULTURALISM

Multiculturalism is on the advance, everywhere from President Clinton's Cabinet to corporate boardrooms to public-school classrooms. If you believe the multiculturalists' propaganda, whites are on the verge of becoming a minority in the United States. The multiculturalists predict that this demographic shift will fundamentally change American culture—indeed destroy the very idea that America *has* a single, unified culture. They aren't taking any chances, however. They have enlisted the help of government, corporate leaders, the media, and the education establishment in waging a cultural revolution. But has America truly become a multicultural nation? And if not, will those who capitulate to these demands create a self-fulfilling prophecy?

At the heart of the argument is the assumption that the white population is rapidly declining in relation to the non-white population. A 1987 Hudson Institute report helped catapult this claim to national prominence. The study, *Workforce 2000,* estimated that by the turn of the century only 15 per cent of new workers would be white males. The figure was widely interpreted to mean that whites were about to become a minority in the workplace—and in the country.

In fact, white males will still constitute about 45 per cent—a plurality—of the workforce in the year 2000. The proportion of white men in the workforce *is* declining—it was nearly 51 per cent in 1980—but primarily because the proportion of white women is growing. They will make up 39 per cent of the workforce within ten years, according to government projections, up from 36 per cent in 1980. Together, white men and women will account for 84 per cent of all workers by 2000—hardly a minority share.

But the business world is behaving as if a demographic tidal wave is about to hit. A whole new industry of "diversity professionals" has emerged to help managers cope with the expected deluge of non-white workers. These consultants are paid as much as $10,000 a day to train managers to "value diversity," a term so ubiquitous that it has appeared in more than seven hundred articles in major newspapers in the last three years. According to Heather MacDonald in *The New Republic,* about half of Fortune 500 corporations now employ someone responsible for "diversity."

* * *

What precisely does valuing diversity mean? The underlying assumptions seem to be that non-whites are so different from whites that employers must make major changes to accommodate them, and that white workers will be naturally resistant to including non-whites in their ranks. Public-opinion polls don't bear out the latter. They show that support among whites for equal job opportunity for blacks is extraordinarily high, exceeding 90 per cent as early as 1975. As for accommodating different cultures, the problem is not culture—or race, or ethnicity—but education. Many young people, in particular, are poorly prepared for work, and the problem is most severe among those who attended inner-city schools, most of them blacks and Hispanics.

Nevertheless, multiculturalists insist on treating race and ethnicity as if they were synonymous with culture. They presume that skin color and national origin, which are immutable traits, determine values, mores, language, and other cultural attributes, which, of course, are learned. In the multiculturalists' world view, African-Americans, Puerto Ricans, or Chinese-Americans living in New York City have more in common with persons of their ancestral group living in Lagos or San Juan or Hong Kong than they do with other New Yorkers who are white. Culture becomes a fixed entity, transmitted, as it were, in the genes, rather than through experience. Thus, "Afrocentricity," a variant of multiculturalism, is "a way of being," its exponents claim. According to a leader of the Afrocentric education movement, Molefi Kete Asante, there is "one African Cultural System manifested in diversities," whether one speaks of Afro-Brazilians, Cubans, or Nigerians (or, presumably, African-Americans). Exactly how this differs from the traditional racist notion that all blacks (Jews, Mexicans, Chinese, etc.) think alike is unclear. What is clear is that the multiculturalists have abandoned the ideal that all persons should be judged by the content of their character, not the color of their skin. Indeed, the multiculturalists seem to believe that a person's character is *determined* by the color of his skin and by his ancestry.

Such convictions lead multiculturalists to conclude that, again in the words of Asante, "[T]here is no common American culture." The logic is simple, but wrongheaded: Since Americans (or more often, their forebears) hail from many different places, each of which has its own specific culture, the argument goes, America must be multicultural. And it is becoming more so every day as new immigrants bring their cultures with them.

Indeed, multiculturalists hope to ride the immigrant wave to greater power and influence. They have certainly done so in education. Some 2.3 million children who cannot speak English well now attend public school, an increase of 1 million in the last seven years. Multicultural advocates cite the presence of such children to demand bilingual education and other multicultural services. The Los Angeles Unified School District alone currently offers instruction in Spanish, Armenian, Korean, Cantonese, Tagalog, Russian, and Japanese. Federal and state governments now spend literally billions of dollars on these programs.

Ironically, the multiculturalists' emphasis on education undercuts their argument that culture is inextricable from race or national origin. They are acutely aware just how fragile cultural identification is;

why else are they so adamant about re-inforcing it? Multiculturalists insist on teaching immigrant children in their native language, instructing them in the history and customs of their native land and imbuing them with reverence for their ancestral heroes, lest these youngsters be seduced by American culture. Far from losing faith in the power of assimilation, they seem to believe that without a heavy dose of multicultural indoctrination, immigrants won't be able to resist it. And they're right, though it remains to be seen whether anything, including the multiculturalists' ardent movements, will ultimately detour immigrants from the assimilation path.

The urge to assimilate has traditionally been overpowering in the United States, especially among the children of immigrants. Only groups that maintain strict rules against intermarriage with persons outside the group, such as Orthodox Jews and the Amish, have ever succeeded in preserving distinct, full-blown cultures within American society. (It is interesting to note that religion seems to be a more effective deterrent to full assimilation than the secular elements of culture, including language.) Although many Americans worry that Hispanic immigrants, for example, are not learning English and will therefore fail to assimilate into the American mainstream, little evidence supports the case. By the third generation in the United States, a majority of Hispanics, like other ethnic groups, speak only English and are closer to other Americans on most measures of social and economic status than they are to Hispanic immigrants. On one of the most rigorous gauges of assimilation—intermarriage—Hispanics rank high. About one-third of young third-generation Hispanics marry non-Hispanic whites, a pattern similar to that of young Asians. Even for blacks, exogamy rates, which have been quite low historically, are going up; about 3 per cent of blacks now marry outside their group.

* * *

The impetus for multiculturalism is not coming from immigrants, but from their more affluent and assimilated native-born counterparts. The proponents are most often the elite—the best educated and most successful members of their respective racial and ethnic groups. College campuses, where the most radical displays of multiculturalism take place, are fertile recruiting grounds. Last May, for example, a group of Mexican-American students at UCLA, frustrated that the university would not elevate the school's 23-year-old Chicano-studies program to full department status, stormed the faculty center, breaking windows and furniture and causing half a million dollars in damage. The same month, a group of Asian-American students at UC Irvine went on a hunger strike to pressure administrators into hiring more professors of Asian-American studies. These were not immigrants, or even, by and large, disadvantaged students, but middle-class beneficiaries of their parents' or grandparents' successful assimilation to the American mainstream.

The protestors' quest had almost nothing to do with any effort to maintain their ethnic identity. For the most part, such students probably never thought of themselves as anything but American before they entered college. A recent study of minority students at the University of California at Berkeley found that most Hispanic and Asian students "discovered" their ethnic identity after they arrived on campus—when they also discovered that they were victims of systematic discrimination. As one Mexican-American freshman summed it up, she was "unaware of the things that have been going on with our people, all the injustice we've suffered, how the world really is. I thought racism didn't exist and here, you know, it just comes to light." The researchers added that "students of color" had difficulty pinpointing exactly what constituted this "subtle form of the new racism.... There was much talk about certain facial expressions, or the way people look, and how white students 'take over the class' and speak past you."

Whatever their new-found victim status, these students look amazingly like other Americans on most indices. For example, the median family income of Mexican-American students at Berkeley in 1989 was $32,500, slightly above the national median for all Americans that year, $32,191; and 17 per cent of those students came from families that earned more than $75,000 a year, even though they were admitted to the university under affirmative-action programs (presumably because they suffered some educational disadvantage attributed to their ethnicity).

Affirmative-action programs make less and less sense as discrimination diminishes in this society—which it indisputably has—and as minorities improve their economic status. Racial and ethnic identity, too, might wane if there weren't such aggressive efforts to ensure that this not happen. The multiculturalists know they risk losing their constituency if young blacks, Hispanics, Asians, and others don't maintain strong racial and ethnic affiliations. Younger generations must be *trained* to think of themselves as members of oppressed minority groups entitled to special treatment. And the government provides both the incentives and the money to ensure that this happens. Meanwhile, the main beneficiaries are the multicultural professionals, who often earn exorbitant incomes peddling identity.

One particularly egregious example occurred in the District of Columbia last fall. The school system paid $250,000 to a husband-and-wife consultant team to produce an Afrocentric study guide to be used in a single public elementary school. Controversy erupted after the two spent three years and produced only a five-page outline. Although the husband had previously taught at Howard University, the wife's chief credential was a master's degree from an unaccredited "university" which she and her husband had founded. When the *Washington Post* criticized the school superintendent for his handling of the affair, he called a press conference to defend the couple, who promptly claimed they were the victims of a racist vendetta.

D.C. students rank lowest in the nation in math and fourth-lowest in verbal achievement; one can only wonder what $250,000 in tutoring at one school might have done. Instead, the students were treated to bulletin boards in the classrooms proclaiming on their behalf: "We are the sons and daughters of The Most High. We are the princes and princesses of African kings and queens. We are the descendants of our black ancestors. We are black and we are proud." This incident is not unique. Thousands of consultants with little or no real expertise sell feel-good programs to school systems across the nation.

* * *

Multiculturalism is not a grassroots movement. It was created, nurtured, and expanded through government policy. Without the expenditure of vast sums of public money, it would wither away and die. That is not to say that ethnic communities would disappear from the American scene or that groups would not retain some attachment to their ancestral roots. American assimilation has always entailed some give and take, and American culture has been enriched by what individual groups brought to it. The distinguishing characteristic of American culture is its ability to incorporate so many disparate groups, creating a new whole from the many parts. What could be more American, for example, than jazz and film, two distinctive art forms created, respectively, by blacks and immigrant Jews but which all Americans think of as their own? But in the past, government—especially public schools—saw it as a duty to try to bring newcomers into the fold by teaching them English, by introducing them to the great American heroes astheir own, by instilling respect for American institutions. Lately, we have nearly reversed course, treating each group, new and old, as if what is most important is to preserve its separate identity and space.

It is easy to blame the ideologues and radicals who are pushing the disuniting of America, to use Arthur Schlesinger's phrase, but the real culprits are those who provide multiculturalists the money and the access to press their cause. Without the acquiescence of policy-makers and ordinary citizens, multiculturalism would be no threat. Unfortunately, most major institutions have little stomach for resisting the multicultural impulse—and many seem eager to comply with whatever demands the multiculturalists make. Americans should have learned by now that policy matters. We have only to look at the failure of our welfare and crime policies to know that providing perverse incentives can change the way individuals behave—for the worse. Who is to say that if we pour enough money into dividing Americans we won't succeed?

POSTSCRIPT

Should Multiculturalism Permeate the Curriculum?

The issue of multicultural education is complex and difficult to resolve because it reverberates to the core of the American democratic experience. Is the nation strengthened and its minority populations empowered by the process of assimilation into a culture with primarily Western European origins? Or is the United States—which is an immigrant nation—constantly redefined by the cultural influences that come to its shores?

Further research will reveal a wealth of theories and opinions that illuminate the basic problem and its many aspects. Among recommended sources are the following: "Dimensions of Multicultural Education," by Carlos F. Diaz, *National Forum* (Winter 1994); "Why We Must Pluralize the Curriculum," by Asa G. Hilliard III, *Educational Leadership* (December 1991/January 1992); "Where Is Multiculturalism Leading Us?" by Nathan Glazer, *Phi Delta Kappan* (December 1993); "Self-Esteem and Multiculturalism in the Public Schools," by Kay S. Hymowitz, *Dissent* (Winter 1992); and "Multicultural Education: Five Views," by Christine E. Sleeter, *Kappa Delta Pi Record* (Fall 1992).

The political perspective on this topic is examined in Herbert Kohl, "The Politically Correct Bypass: Multiculturalism and the Public Schools," *Social Policy* (Summer 1991); Henry A. Giroux, "Curriculum, Multiculturalism, and the Politics of Identity," *NASSP Bulletin* (December 1992); Christine Canning, "Preparing for Diversity: A Social Technology for Multicultural Community Building," *The Educational Forum* (Summer 1993); and Francis J. Ryan, "Will Multiculturalism Undercut Student Individuality?" *Educational Horizons* (Spring 1993).

Some theme issues of journals to explore are "Polarizing American Culture," *Society* (July/August 1993); "Multicultural Education," *Phi Delta Kappan* (September 1993); "Critical Perspectives on Diversity," *The Educational Forum* (Summer 1993); and two issues of *National Forum* that focus on "Immigration and the Changing Face of America" (Summer 1994) and "Multiculturalism and Diversity" (Winter 1994).

Three books worthy of note are: *Multicultural Literacy: Opening the American Mind* by Simonson and Walker (1988); *Battle of the Books: The Curriculum Debate in America* by James Atlas (1990); and *Affirming Diversity: The Socio-Political Context of Multicultural Education* by Sonia Nieto (1992).

ISSUE 7

Has Court-Mandated School Desegregation Failed?

YES: Jonathan Kozol, from "Giant Steps Backward: Romance of the Ghetto School," *The Nation* (May 23, 1994)

NO: Roger Wilkins, from "Poor Blacks After *Brown*: Dream Deferred But Not Defeated," *The Nation* (May 23, 1994)

ISSUE SUMMARY

YES: Social critic and educator Jonathan Kozol argues that the 1954 Supreme Court decision in *Brown v. Board of Education*, calling for the desegregation of U.S. schools, has been practically invalidated by subsequent rulings and actions.

NO: History professor Roger Wilkins recognizes that there have been some setbacks since the ruling, but he argues that, overall, *Brown* has "destroyed American apartheid" and enriched the whole society.

The 40th anniversary of the U.S. Supreme Court decision in *Brown v. Board of Education of Topeka, Kansas,* has been marked by a number of appraisals of the progress that has been made in the long and arduous process of racial desegregation in public education and in the society as a whole. For example, "The Growth of Segregation in American Schools: Changing Patterns of Separation and Poverty Since 1968," by Gary Orfield et al., in *Equity and Excellence in Education* (April 1994), analyzes recent research by the Harvard Project on School Desegregation. This report's dismal conclusions regarding the level of segregation that still exists in American schools today lend support to Jonathan Kozol's portrayal of schools in poverty-stricken areas in *Savage Inequalities: Children in America's Schools* (1991). In his book, Kozol argues that prevailing school funding practices have ensured that schools in poor, mostly minority districts would remain of the lowest quality, both physically and socially. Similarly, an editorial in the May 23, 1994, issue of *The Nation* titled "*Brown* at 40" describes a Topeka that is still segregated, a situation shaped by racism, classism, local politics, and a lack of political activism. Furthermore, the May 1994 issue of *Emerge* is dedicated to the theme "Separate and Unequal: The Education of Blacks 40 Years After *Brown*."

Has educator and politician Horace Mann's optimistic nineteenth-century promise that the public schools would be "a great equalizer" and a "balance wheel of the social machinery" been realized? Or has the flight of whites and middle-class blacks from U.S. urban centers doomed social integration? Civil rights legislation, the use of federal power to force local jurisdictions to use busing to achieve desegregation, affirmative action campaigns, controlled choice plans, and the establishment of magnet schools (those with a focused theme) to promote integration have certainly produced some positive results. But population shifts and the immigration waves of recent decades—along with some failures within the strategies listed above—have brought about resegregation in and around many major urban centers. In Kansas City, for example, a great sum of money has been spent under federal court pressure to revitalize the public school system by establishing an elaborate magnet school approach. Although some students have benefited, particularly at the elementary school level, the results have been disappointing in terms of desegregation, white retention in the system, and test score improvement for minority students.

In "Rethinking 'Brown,'" *The Executive Educator* (June 1992), David A. Splitt analyzes the recent U.S. Supreme Court ruling in a Georgia case, *Freeman v. Pitts,* which allows lower courts to consider the quality of education that minority students are receiving when deciding whether to modify or dismiss desegregation orders. He notes that this alteration of high court opinion— which, based on the *Brown* decision, previously held that "separate educational facilities are inherently unequal"—seems to be rooted in the contention that "minority students, given the same quality of teaching, staff, and facilities, can achieve the same educational success as white students" whether or not the school is racially integrated. Splitt adds, however, that this new nonintegration approach to equality does not address such social problems as "the racial mistrust and ignorance that arise when children grow up having minimal contact with other races and cultures."

In the following selections, Jonathan Kozol cites a number of Supreme Court decisions since *Brown* that have locked black and Latino children into situations of isolation and abandonment. In his argument, Kozol points to statistics showing that the proportion of black children attending segregated schools is at its highest level since the death of civil rights leader Martin Luther King, Jr. Roger Wilkins, on the other hand, sees *Brown* as the key event in the demolition of "the legal shackles that had bound blacks as closely as possible to slavery." He maintains that in addition to bringing about school desegregation, the decision has led to the desegregation of most other aspects of society and to the emergence of a solid black middle and working class.

YES

Jonathan Kozol

GIANT STEPS BACKWARD:
ROMANCE OF THE GHETTO SCHOOL

Walking into limitless numbers of all-black or black and Latino schools in al-most any Northern city these days, visitors old enough to have lived through the optimistic years of 1954 to 1968 sometimes interpret what they see today as evidence of an abandonment by white America that germinated in the Reagan and Bush eras. In fact, however, the practical invalidation of *Brown v. Board of Education* was assured approximately twenty years ago in two important cases, *San Antonio Independent School District v. Rodriguez* and *Milliken v. Bradley*. In the accolades recently showered upon Justice Harry Blackmun for some of the enlightened votes he cast during his tenure on the Court, I have seen no reference to his damaging, and crucial, role in both of these decisions.

In *Rodriguez*, which began as a class-action suit filed in 1968, parents of children in the impoverished and mostly Latino Edgewood district, which includes a part of San Antonio, sought relief from a school-funding system based on local wealth that afforded their schools less than half as much per pupil as the nearby white and wealthy district known as Alamo Heights. The suit was successful in the federal district court of San Antonio, which found Texas in violation of the equal protection clause of the U.S. Constitution; it was then appealed to the Supreme Court, where it was reversed in 1973.

"The argument here," said Justice Lewis Powell, who wrote the majority decision, is not that poor children "are receiving no public education; rather, it is that they are receiving a poorer quality education" than children in rich districts. In cases where wealth is the issue, he wrote, "the equal protection clause does not require absolute equality."

Powell wrote that the district court had been in error in deciding that the Texas funding system had created a "suspect class" of people who had been unjustly treated. There is, he wrote, "no basis ... for assuming that the poorest people ... are concentrated in the poorest districts." Nor, he added, is there "more than a random chance that racial minorities are concentrated" in such districts.

In his dissent, Justice Thurgood Marshall challenged the distinction made by Powell between "absolute" and "relative" degrees of deprivation, as well as Powell's judgment that because the children in the Edgewood district got a "basic minimal" education, that was all that was required or deserved. "The equal protection clause," wrote Marshall, "is not addressed to... minimal sufficiency" but to equality, and he cited *Brown* to the effect that education, "where the state has undertaken to provide it, is a right which must be made available to all on equal terms."

Nonetheless, the Court's majority thought otherwise and in a single word —"reversed"—Justice Powell ended any expectations of poor people that their children might be given what their wealthy neighbors got in public school.

A year later, in *Milliken*, a U.S. district court in Michigan, finding the schools of metropolitan Detroit both "separate" and "unequal," and observing that racial integration could not be achieved within the borders of Detroit, ordered a metropolitan solution that required integration of the quarter-million children of Detroit with some 500,000 children of surrounding suburbs that included wealthy communities such as Bloomfield Hills and Grosse Pointe.

Again, the Supreme Court overruled the district court, finding the proposed solution punitive to the white suburbs and insisting that Detroit would have to scramble to desegregate as best it could by scattering its rapidly diminishing white student population among larger numbers of black children—a directive that was certain to accelerate white flight out of the city. The majority decision this time was written by Chief Justice Warren Burger.

After "20 years of small, often difficult steps" toward equal justice, Marshall wrote in another of his powerful dissents, "the Court today takes a giant step backwards.... Our nation, I fear, will be ill-served by the Court's refusal to remedy separate and unequal education." The majority's decision, he said, was "a reflection of a perceived public mood that we have gone far enough in enforcing the Constitution's guarantee of equal justice" rather than a product of neutral principles of law. "In the short run, it may seem to be the easier course to allow our great metropolitan areas to be divided up ... into two cities—one white, the other black—but it is a course, I predict, our people will ultimately regret. I dissent."

Justices William Brennan, Byron White and William Douglas cast dissenting votes as well. Justice Blackmun did not dissent. Again, as in *Rodriguez*, Blackmun voted with the 5-to-4 majority. The combined effect of the two decisions—the firt one ruling out equality, the second denying the possibility of metropolitan solutions—was to lock black and Latino children into the isolation and abandonment we see today. One wonders if Blackmun, an enlightened jurist in so many ways, may now regret the role he played in these decisions as much as he regrets his earlier support for the death penalty. Had only his one vote been cast with that of Marshall in these two cases, the destinies of millions of poor children would have been dramatically revised.

Today, after four decades of white flight, the proportion of black children who go to segregated schools is at its highest level since the death of Dr. King. "The civil rights impulse from the 1960s is dead in the water and the ship is floating backward," notes

Gary Orfield, a Harvard professor who has written several studies on school segregation. Schools in the South are the most likely to be integrated. Most "hypersegregated" are the schools of the Northeast. For Latino children, the most segregated schools are in New York. For black children, New York ranks third, following Illinois and Michigan. "Two-thirds of America's black children know few, if any, white people," *The New York Times* observes.

In certain ways, the most notable feature of the present age is that all this is more or less accepted. Black and Latino principals often seem amused or startled if I even bring the matter up. Once, in an all-black school in New York City, I asked a principal, "Do you think of yourself as running a segregated school?" He smiled, touched my arm and said, "That's what it is, of course. This is apartheid. That's the way it is and it's not going to change. Why bang my head against the wall?"

Many, understandably, have learned to make a virtue of necessity and have found a way to draw pride out of scorn, pretending to choose what has in fact been chosen for them by America, and even claiming to find merit in an isolation that may nurture cultural autonomy.

The nation, moreover, has facilitated this romanticized accommodation by providing a lexicon of innovative phrases to adorn apartheid with the trappings of an often inauthentic version of empowerment. Thus, we hear of "site-based" ghetto schools, "restructured" ghetto schools, ghetto schools with "greater input" from parents, ghetto schools with curriculum more relevant to the "special needs" of those we have encaged. But the cage itself, the institution of the ghetto school as permanent disfigurement upon the body of American democracy, goes virtually unquestioned.

This is not intended to demean the genuine effectiveness of many who *have* managed to empower parents and decentralize their schools—important victories in any educational community. Some, such as Bill Ayers in Chicago, have been brilliantly successful. One fears, however, that there is a sense now that we can do nothing more than to "empower within borders"—that the tide of racial and class segregation is in itself unstoppable.

Persistent groups and individuals still fight against the tide. Attorneys like John Brittain in Connecticut, Arthur Benson in Missouri, and dozens of others all over the nation still try to fashion magnet plans, metropolitan arrangements—some voluntary, some mandated—to attempt to make the promise of the *Brown* decision real. Some partially succeed.

In Kansas City, the disparagement of cynical observers notwithstanding, white flight has been substantially arrested and may have begun to be reversed; many of the schools there are spectacular. But it took years of litigation and the spending of $1 billion to create the hopeful Kansas City system that exists today. Will other states and cities be prepared to go that route? Will other black communities still think it worth the cost in pain and faith and years of legal battles? It is hard to say, because the forces now arrayed against them are so vast.

Newspapers that try to take the pulse of black opinion on these questions tend to cite the words of middle-class black people who have often benefited from attendance at good integrated schools but find the emotional costs extremely high. "I think the trend is for people to retreat back into their comfort zone," says a black investment manager at New York's

Bankers Trust. "Nobody wants to subject their children... or themselves to an environment where they're not wanted." But, as he would probably concede, this is a preference voiced by someone who is standing on a plateau of considerable privilege. I don't know many students in the South Bronx who would call their school a "comfort zone."

"I don't have to go somewhere else to get the better things in life," says a middle-class black woman who runs a community-development corporation in Harlem. But the truth is that, with few exceptions, children *do* need to "go somewhere else" outside their economically destitute neighborhoods if they hope to get a shot at schools like those we see in Great Neck, which spends twice as much per pupil as nearby New York City and sends almost all its students on to colleges, where they receive the instruments of economic power now denied to most of those who live in Jersey City or the Bronx.

The romance of the all-black school that fosters black empowerment with black-determined curriculum, black teachers and black principals is often so compelling that white advocates of integration feel disarmed, intimidated and subdued into a watchful silence. But the vast majority of black adults still recognize that separate almost always *means* unequal in America, and that the dynamics of school finance guarantee that there can never be more than a handful of those show-piece segregated schools that press reports sometimes extol. More commonly, as in Jersey City and East St. Louis, the segregated districts, starved of funds, soon resemble pedagogic bantustans in a colonial relationship with state fiscal agencies, which now and then impose "receiverships" upon them, at which point they have no power at all. This may be one reason that, as Andrew Hacker has observed, some 85 percent of black Americans have said when polled that they prefer to live in mixed communities and only "one in eight say they prefer a neighborhood that is all or mostly black."

Nearly thirty years ago, Dr. Kenneth Clark wrote in his book *Dark Ghetto* of the ways in which a segregated population may be induced to satisfy the wishes of the white society by claiming to desire, even to enjoy, a subjugated way of life it has not chosen but knows no way to escape. "A most cruel... consequence of enforced segregation," he wrote, "is that its victims can be made to accommodate to their victimized status and under certain circumstances to state that it is their desire to be set apart, or to agree that subjugation is not really detrimental." The fact remains, he said, that these forms of isolation "are not voluntary states." Segregation, he concluded, "is neither sought nor imposed by healthy... human beings."

Conservative black voices have, however, been receiving the most widespread hearing from white society in recent years. Black television personalities like Tony Brown, with corporate sponsorship on PBS, preach the merits of go-it-alone black education and black enterprise. Other black conservatives openly ridicule the goals of *Brown* before appreciative white business groups that pay them well to be reassured that black kids will do much better on their own and "do not need to sit beside white children" to "get smarter"—a simplistic joke that always wins applause by making a caricature of the idea of integration and depicting integrationists as racist for not adequately valuing the cultural attractions of apartheid.

Corporate think tanks are rapidly building an extensive farm team of such black conservatives to bat for them in public. By the time they get on C-SPAN and PBS, many have their sound-bites honed to perfection. They hit rhetorical home runs while more progressive blacks and liberal whites often sit back and watch the game with sorrow and passivity. No comparable farm team has been nurtured by the left, which has been busy litigating and rethinking while the right has learned to shape public opinion.

Litigation will continue, both in the school arena and, perhaps far more important, in the seldom-mentioned area of residential segregation and enforcement of fair housing legislation; but the battle for the public conscience has to be addressed as well. A new generation of progressive black, Latino and white intellectuals armed with forensic skills may be emerging now, but they cannot thrive and won't prevail without the same resources and access to the media that conservatives still overwhelmingly command. Whether such resources and such access can be made available is by no means clear.

The other prospect, possibly more likely, is that things will go on pretty much unchanged. Segregated schools will continue to decay. Many more black men will go to prison than to college. Clever innovations decorated with new versions of old jargon— ghetto "academies of excellence," schools of "effectiveness" with uniforms and tougher discipline that may sometimes resemble very handsome inner-city boot camps—will continue to be heralded as "signs of hope" in press reports, until at length it all explodes into yet another riot or uprising, next time very possibly in New York City or Chicago. Perhaps only an uprising of that nature will mobilize the forces needed for the next great struggle of our age; but no one who has seen the human costs of such uprisings in the past can look upon this prospect without trepidation.

NO

Roger Wilkins

POOR BLACKS AFTER *BROWN:* DREAM DEFERRED BUT NOT DEFEATED

When the Warren Court handed down the decision in *Brown v. Board of Education of Topeka, Kansas,* it set in motion a train of events that has changed the country and affected every citizen. It destroyed American apartheid and enriched our society. It also brought the nation a sobering dose of racial reality that foreshadows a long, painful and expensive struggle if we are ever to free ourselves of the enduring destruction and anguish flowing from what James Madison called our "original sin."

Brown was ultimately about much more than education. To understand its full impact, we have to remember what this country was like before the decision.

For all its ugliness, there was something almost innocent about the pre-*Brown* time. A few years after the decision had come down and the complexities it spawned had become apparent, Robert Carter, Thurgood Marshall's chief deputy at the NAACP Legal Defense Fund, was asked why more thought hadn't been given to what would happen next. Carter replied that all the forethought had gone into destroying the dual system of education because "we thought segregation was the box we were in."

In fact, segregation was so stifling and humiliating that it was very hard to see other evils. If instead of cardboard the walls of the "box we were in" had been made of glass, we could say that blacks looking out from the suffocating insults of segregation could see nothing wrong with the rest of America except that they weren't in it.

In addition, I think many African-Americans believed that there were millions of "good" white people whose souls were imbued with the spirit of America's highest expressed ideals. It is also fair to say that in the eyes of most sympathetic whites and of most activist blacks the terrible racial wrong was that "worthy" blacks were injured. The great bulk of black poverty was hidden in the rural South or stuck off in barely visible corners of large cities.

But ultimately, the fate of poor blacks is at the heart of America's racial problem. From the beginning, the race question in America was about economics and psychology, and it still is. Blacks weren't brought to the Western

Hemisphere to be civilized or converted to Christianity. They were brought here for economic reasons. Their labor was required to help tame a wild continent and to wrest profits from it. To accomplish that task, they were degraded, brutalized and kept ignorant. That was the state in which the vast majority left slavery in 1865.

The task for America then and now has been to find a way for the economy to absorb the mass of unskilled and degraded workers. Millions of them were penned up on rural Southern plantations until the middle of this century when mechanization pushed them—peasants and semislaves—off the farms and into the cities by the millions.

That exodus was in full swing at the time of the *Brown* decision. The exodus, like the decision, was a part of the breakup of the pre-World War II, post-slavery American world. After the war black soldiers had come home hungering for freedom, and many Americans had become aware of the irony of the country's having fought a war against fascism with a segregated army. The Soviet Union was competing with us throughout the Third World by pointing to our disgraceful treatment of black citizens. In 1947 Jackie Robinson had driven the black man's dignity and ability into the national consciousness with his great rookie season. The next year, President Truman had issued an executive order desegregating the armed forces.

But blacks were still brutally held in place by an economic-legal-police-caste system that was undergirded by violence. A year after *Brown*, a black Chicago teenager was lynched in Mississippi for violating racial mores in greeting a white woman. In the North, blacks were submerged under a thick culture of smug, superior condescension that led to such ironies as blacks being limited to janitorial and elevator operator jobs on newspapers that thundered editorially against Southern racism. And in 1954, the black poverty rate, while heading down, was still close to 70 percent.

In that world, *Brown* proved to be a second Emancipation Day. Blacks read the decision to say: "The Constitution really does apply to me!" It ended seven decades of disgraceful racist jurisprudence by the Supreme Court. And the forces it liberated—from the Montgomery bus boycott and the rest of the civil rights movement to the youth/anti–Vietnam War movement, the antipoverty movement, the women's movement and the lesbian and gay rights movement—exposed fault lines in a society that had previously been obscured by the patriotism deployed to fight World War II.

The societal changes caused by *Brown* were enormous. In the post-*Brown* world, much school desegregation was accomplished and virtually all the public spaces in the rest of society were desegregated as well. The civil rights movement forced the federal government to move both legislatively and administratively in its behalf. Blacks moved into positions undreamed of in the pre-*Brown* world—Chairman of the Joint Chiefs of Staff, President of Planned Parenthood, quarterback in the N.F.L., president of the National Education Association, mayors of major cities, bank tellers, police chiefs and professionals in institutions ranging from newspapers to investment banking firms.

Most of the public and economic aspects of American life continue to be controlled by white men, but the changes wrought by *Brown* widened opportunities—particularly in government at all levels—so that a solid black middle and working class emerged. As the sociologist William Julius Wilson has noted, that working and middle class has used desegregation to escape the confines of the traditional ghetto, leaving the less skilled and poorest blacks behind in decimated Third World sections of cities all over the country.

Successful blacks are still forced to engage in soul-wrenching struggles from the halls of Congress to medical associations to corporate board rooms, where their own aspirations and their visions for the country are often challenged by people who range from out-and-out bigots to those who are well-intentioned but in deep denial about racism. But middle-class problems pale by comparison with those of the blacks left behind and left out. One of the things that hurts the poorest blacks is a conclusion often drawn from that comparison. Many white Americans seem to hold the view that the gates of opportunity were thrown wide open during and after the sixties and that the worthy blacks "moved on up" while the unworthy languished because of their own deficiencies.

In our innocence, we thought that after *Brown* white Americans could be *taught* out of their individual prejudices. Many of us thought the civil rights movement, the strong moral declarations from the White House and the legislative activity by Congress would serve as a great national teach-in about the irrationality and un-Americanness of racial prejudice, and that bigotry would be isolated in a few twisted souls and some unreconstructed regions of the South.

We were yet to learn that more than three centuries of racial subordination had shaped much of American institutional behavior as well as the personal psychology of vast numbers of white people. We had thought of racism as damaging only blacks. We were yet to learn that vast numbers of whites were physically dependent on—addicted to, one might say—their belief in their superiority over blacks.

Moreover, the great migration of peasants from the farms to the cities—as many as 3.5 million by some estimates—had laid the foundation for another kind of lesson. The migrants came in such numbers that they overwhelmed the job-generating capacities of the cities and most of the systems that help make the cities habitable.

Connected to the rest of America as they were by television, these migrants were stirred in their ghetto desperation —as we all were—by the daily scenes of civil rights struggles and triumphs. But as the rest of the country changed, they saw their sorrowful position at the bottom of society as irretrievably static and absolutely untouched by all the *Sturm und Drang* they saw on their television sets. So they revolted in city after city during the mid- and late sixties. The riots sent shock waves through the rest of the country and provided fuel for the racism that smoldered just below the unnatural racial civility of the civil rights years.

Though we had civilized ourselves enough so that politicians had now to refrain from yelling "nigger, nigger, nigger," they could surely shout "law and order" and "forced busing." In his presidential campaigns of 1968 and 1972, George Wallace showed Northern politicians that there was much political gold to be mined in the racial fears and resentments harbored by white Northerners. Subsequently Richard Nixon, Ronald Reagan, George Bush and, finally, Bill Clinton found ways to make exquisite use of that deep American political knowledge.

Rapid economic and cultural change ripped through the country and ravaged the ghettos. America became saturated with sexuality; the streams of drugs and guns coming into the country turned into torrential rivers; and finally, and most devastatingly, the economy hit a wall in 1973.

Part of the optimism of the 1960s flowed from a deep belief in the power of the economy and from the hope that its manufacturing sector would suck the migrants up into the world of work. In fact, the economic changes in the 1970s that forced middle-class wives into the work force to maintain living standards overwhelmed the unskilled portion of the labor force. Unskilled black men who were employed lost 25 to 40 percent of real income. Many fell out of the economy entirely.

The overall black unemployment rate has dipped below 10 percent only once in the past two decades. The black male unemployment rate averaged almost 13 percent during the 1980s after peaking at almost 19 percent during the 1981–82 recession. In fact, the portion of the black community just below the newly enlarged middle and working classes has been in a permanent condition of severe economic depression for twenty years. After dipping a bit in the late sixties, the black poverty rate has risen to about 33 percent. The black unemployment rate seems permanently fixed at about two and a half times the white rate.

Even mild recession brings severe social dislocations among all classes of workers. Newspapers report increases of depression, alcoholism, drug abuse, spouse and child abuse, suicide and family breakup among whites as well as others who have been adversely affected.

The impact of all these trends is evident in the ghettos of America today. In many of them, the drug trade appears to be the only viable economic opportunity. These neighborhoods are filled with would-be workers who are now economically redundant as a result of the deindustrialization and globalization of the American economy. While the nature and the causes of their economic plight are rarely analyzed in the popular media, the human disasters that result from it are the garish daily fare of all our journalism, from low to high.

To undergird the new form its racism has taken, America has reverted to an intellectual exercise that is older than the Republic: to examine in painstaking detail the human results of the damage that has been done to blacks and to conclude that it is proof of their unfitness. In the only book he ever published, *Notes on the State of Virginia*, Thomas Jefferson examined the slaves he was using and degrading and found them inferior to whites in virtually every human respect, from beauty and intellect to odor.

Up to the cataclysm wrought by *Brown*, black *inferiority* was the preferred justification for ignoring black anguish and suppressing black aspirations. Black inferiority is no longer discussed, at least in mixed company. But now, even the most respectable mainstream organs of news and opinion trumpet that it is problems of *behavior* that separate the poorest blacks from the rest of us.

There is no doubt that some behavior in the poorest black precincts is frightening and deeply troubling. There is criminality and irresponsibility. Although it is rarely reported, there is also a great deal of gallantry and grit in the ghetto. While the bad aspects of life in the inner city are portrayed endlessly in the press and discussed exhaustively in policy circles, little time and discussion is devoted to how people got that way and what really keeps them trapped. Just as Jefferson's slaves were, by nature, dumb, ugly and smelly, so now our fellow citizens in the ghetto are, by nature, criminal, licentious and irresponsible.

Our poll-driven politics is the best barometer of the depth of our national racism. After two weeks of saturation coverage of the Los Angeles riots in 1992 and highly publicized visits by both presidential candidates, the subject of urban revitalization vanished from the public eye into political black holes in both parties. Before it did, however, Candidate Clinton, in response to Peter Jennings's question about how he would have responded to the riots had he been President, said, "Well, first I would sign the crime bill."

In office, the President has yet to spend an ounce of political capital on programs directly affecting the black poor. His precipitate dumping of his erstwhile friend Lani Guinier was a graphic demonstration of how skittish he is about appearing in any way to be sympathetic to strong advocacy on behalf of blacks.

Guinier has called for a national conversation about race. In today's environment, that is a radical proposal. There is little honest public dialogue about race. There are political issues, framed by white politicians and designed for white voter consumption, that seek to give the impression of controlling blacks. The welfare debate, for example, ranges from urging that we end the program altogether to plans to train people for the jobs they will be forced to take af-

ter two years. There is no discussion of the scarcity of jobs, despite the fact that our official perpetual undercount of unemployment shows more than 8 million Americans out of work.

Racism thus joins two other enduring strands at the center of American culture, individualism and capitalism. Myths about them are intertwined and mutually reinforcing. Americans are led to believe that capitalism is efficient and just. All *individuals* who are energetic and disciplined can make it in our economy. Those who fail are unworthy. Therefore, there is nothing wrong with the system. Capitalism is just. Individual worthiness and effort are rewarded. Those who have reaped the most rewards are, of course, the most virtuous and worthy citizens of that society.

Those myths obscure many unpleasant truths about America. One of those truths is that we never did really promise forty acres and a mule to freed slaves and surely never tried to deliver them. As a matter of fact, no real effort has ever been made to incorporate the mass of unskilled blacks into the economy. If economic circumstances require their labor, they are tolerated, as during the nation's four big wars of the twentieth century. If not, tough; they, their skin and all of the attributes ascribed to it are blamed for their misfortune.

And so we watch helplessly the slow but sure destruction of our cities, the erosion of our Bill of Rights and the shredding of much of the civility that makes life livable. Our best hope rests on the fact that there have been some dark days in the past and America has then seen some light and has forged racial progress. Our ideals really do count for something. At some levels we really do think we are special and that we live by the ideals of the Declaration of Independence and the Gettysburg Address.

It took us most of the twentieth century to throw off the legal shackles that had bound blacks as closely as possible to slavery during the last half of the nineteenth. *Brown* was the key event in that struggle. Facing up to the enduring racism at the center of our culture and undertaking the substantial and sustained social and economic efforts required to undo the massive damage inflicted on the poorest blacks is an even bigger challenge than the one we have overcome. A strong hundred-year effort would be a modest estimate of the time required. After all, it took us 375 years to get into the hole we now occupy. It's been only forty years since *Brown*.

POSTSCRIPT

Has Court-Mandated School Desegregation Failed?

On the interrelated issues of school segregation, racism, poverty, and urban decline, a number of classic studies can provide valuable information and analysis. Among them are *The Other America* by Michael Harrington (1962); *Equality of Educational Opportunity* by James S. Coleman et al. (1966); *Schooling in Capitalist America* by Samuel Bowles and Herbert Gintis (1976); and *Old and New Ideas About School Desegregation* by Charles V. Willie (1984).

Three articles that bring a wealth of expertise to the understanding of the problem are "Rich Schools, Poor Schools: The Persistence of Unequal Education," by Arthur Wise, *College Board Review* (Spring 1989); "Educating Poor Minority Children," by James P. Comer, *Scientific American* (November 1988); and "The Student Incentive Plan: Mitigating the Legacy of Poverty," by George Richmond, *Phi Delta Kappan* (November 1990).

Among recent books addressing the issue are *Making Schools Work for Underachieving Minority Students* edited by Josie G. Bain and Joan L. Herman (1990); *Schooling Disadvantaged Children: Racing Against Catastrophe* by Gary Natriello, Edward L. McDill, and Aaron M. Pallas (1990); *Issues in African-American Education* by Walter Gill (1991); *The Education of African-Americans* edited by Charles V. Willie, Antoine M. Garibaldi, and Wornie L. Reed (1991); and *The Homeless* by Christopher Jencks (1994).

Pungent descriptions of desegregation and inner-city schools can be found in *The World We Created at Hamilton High* by Gerald Grant (1988); *Warriors Don't Cry: A Searing Memoir of the Battle to Integrate Little Rock's Central High* by Melba Pattillo Beals (1994); and *The Uptown Kids: Struggle and Hope in the Projects* by Terry Williams and William Kornblum (1994).

Among the many recent articles that have been published on racial discrimination in the United States, the following are especially recommended: "Reverse Racism, or How the Pot Got to Call the Kettle Black," by Stanley Fish, *Atlantic Monthly* (November 1993); "Twenty-Five Years After the Coleman Report: What Should We Have Learned?" by James M. Towers, *The Clearing House* (January–February 1992); "Oklahoma City: Separate and Equal," by James Traub, *Atlantic Monthly* (September 1991); Jonathan Kozol, "Inequality and the Will to Change," *Equity and Choice* (Spring 1992); Sharon D. Michalove, "The Educational Crusade of Jonathan Kozol," *The Educational Forum* (Spring 1993); Paul T. Hill, "Reinventing Urban Public Education," *Phi Delta Kappan* (January 1994); and Forrest R. White, "*Brown* Revisited," *Phi Delta Kappan* (September 1994).

ISSUE 8

Will Reforming School Funding Remove "Savage Inequalities"?

YES: Ruth Sidel, from "Separate and Unequal," *The Nation* (November 18, 1991)

NO: Peter Schrag, from "Savage Equalities: The Case Against Jonathan Kozol," *The New Republic* (December 16, 1991)

ISSUE SUMMARY

YES: Sociology professor Ruth Sidel examines Jonathan Kozol's controversial book *Savage Inequalities* and finds his argument for the equalization of funding compelling.

NO: Journalist Peter Schrag argues that Kozol's analysis is sometimes simplistic and often impractical.

Ever since the landmark school desegregation decision of the U.S. Supreme Court in 1954 and the civil rights legislation of the mid-1960s, the issue of equal opportunity has occupied a dominant position in discourse on education. Governmental actions such as redistricting, forced busing, and the establishment of magnet schools have met with some success in equalizing educational opportunities for all school-age children. But it has become increasingly obvious that these efforts have had only a mild impact on the wide disparity in funding between schools in affluent areas as opposed to those in poverty-stricken areas.

About 20 years ago the courts dealt with a number of cases involving inequities in funding, among them *Hobson v. Hansen* (1971), *Serrano v. Priest* (1971), and *San Antonio v. Rodriguez* (1973). In the last of these, the Supreme Court found that inequities did exist but that they did not violate the equal protection clause of the Fourteenth Amendment since no one was *completely* deprived of educational opportunity. This ruling turned the matter back to the individual states, and, indeed, some 16 years later the Texas court ruled that the Rodriguez children were unconstitutionally denied the right to equal educational opportunity by virtue of their residence in a tax-poor district in San Antonio.

Some states have moved to close the gaps among their school districts' per-pupil expenditures, some by providing a guaranteed base for all, others by giving rewards for increased local tax-raising efforts, and one, Hawaii, by providing full state funding for all public schools. Among the states themselves, of course, wide disparities exist. Figures for 1991–1992 show a range in per-pupil spending from New Jersey's high average of $9,246 to Mississippi's low average of $3,183.

In 1991 Jonathan Kozol graphically portrayed the results of prevailing funding practices in his book *Savage Inequalities: Children in America's Schools*. The impact of Kozol's guided tour of dilapidated schools and disheartened students and teachers in East St. Louis, Chicago, New York, Camden, San Antonio, and Washington, D.C., has brought the public to a new level of concern. In addition, two studies, William Julius Wilson's *The Truly Disadvantaged* (1987) and Mike Rose's *Lives on the Boundary* (1989), and two insider's descriptions, Samuel G. Freedman's *Small Victories* (1990) and Emily Sachar's *Shut Up and Let the Lady Teach* (1990), give further evidence of the deterioration of poverty-area schools. As early as 1967 Kozol described his personal experiences in an inner-city school in Boston in another high-impact book, *Death at an Early Age*.

In *Savage Inequalities* Kozol contends that the reforms of the 1980s have had little or no effect on the quality of schools in poor districts. "None of the national reports I saw made even passing reference to inequality or segregation," he states. Efforts to bring about greater equity have been thwarted by taxpayer revolts, the general economic downturn of recent years, and the still-prevailing attitude that putting more money into poor districts will not change anything, that money is not the answer. Kozol contends that policy decisions are often steered by a "conservative anxiety" that equity leads to "leveling," that democratizing opportunity will drag the best schools down to "a sullen norm, a mediocre middle ground of uniformity."

The selections that follow are reactions to Jonathan Kozol's book and its recommendations for action. Ruth Sidel agrees with Kozol's call for an intensive effort to finance the education of every child in America equitably and sees this effort as one step toward developing a just society. Peter Schrag, while acknowledging the emotional impact of Kozol's descriptions, argues that equalization of spending is not the solution. He further suggests that such attempts may even have unintended negative consequences.

YES   Ruth Sidel

SEPARATE AND UNEQUAL

In his latest book, *Savage Inequalities: Children in America's Schools,* Jonathan Kozol describes the city of East St. Louis, Illinois: 98 percent black, with no obstetric services, no regular garbage collection and few jobs. East St. Louis is located in easily flooded lowlands called the Bottoms. Raw sewage flows into basements, playgrounds and backyards all over the city. Lead levels are "astronomical" and fumes from nearby chemical plants poison the air. Premature births and infant mortality rates are extraordinarily high and the majority of children are underimmunized. The U.S. Department of Housing and Urban Development has described East St. Louis, where 75 percent of the population receives some form of public assistance, as "the most distressed small city in America." The *St. Louis Post–Dispatch* describes it as "America's Soweto."

The schools of East St. Louis mirror these horrendous conditions: In 1989 both the Martin Luther King Junior High School and the East St. Louis Senior High School had to be closed after sewage flowed into the kitchen and from the toilets. The same week more than 500 school employees were laid off. The remaining teachers face constant shortages of chalk and paper, the sports facilities are in tatters and the science labs are thirty to fifty years out of date. One teacher states, "I have done without so much for so long that if I were assigned to a suburban school I'm not sure I'd recognize what they were doing. We are utterly cut off."

East St. Louis sets the tone for this moving, often shocking, always heart-breaking book. After his searing depiction of schools there, Kozol goes on to describe inferior, underfinanced, often physically dangerous schools in poor communities and lavish, state-of-the-art, incredibly affluent schools in and around Chicago, New York, the Camden–Cherry Hill area of New Jersey and Washington, D.C. Kozol's special skill is the ability to weave together detailed descriptions of facilities, analyses of the financial situation in each school and district and, above all, interviews with teachers, students and administrators in which he seems to uncover the heart of what they are thinking and feeling. Using these techniques he brings the reader with him during his two-year investigation of schools in some thirty neighborhoods across the country.

From Ruth Sidel, "Separate and Unequal," *The Nation* (November 18, 1991). Copyright © 1991 by The Nation Company, Inc. Reprinted by permission.

What startled Kozol most, and will be indelibly stamped on anyone who reads this important book, is the "remarkable degree of racial segregation that persisted almost everywhere," particularly outside the Deep South. Most of the urban schools he visited were 95 to 99 percent nonwhite and, what is perhaps even more disturbing, few people in positions of power were interested in addressing the issue of segregation. As Kozol states, "The dual society, at least in public education, seems in general to be unquestioned."

* * *

Not only is the U.S. public education system virtually separate but it is grossly unequal. Kozol describes conditions in many of the Chicago schools: a shortage of teachers (on an average morning 5,700 children in 190 classrooms have no teacher); a shortage of supplies (chemistry labs without beakers, water or bunsen burners; playgrounds and gyms without rudimentary equipment; toilets without toilet paper); and a system that long ago gave up on its students ("If a kid comes in not reading," according to one Chicago high school English teacher, "he goes out not reading").

Kozol points out that poor children in some of the worst inner-city schools often start their education with "faith and optimism, and they often seem to thrive during the first few years." But by the third grade their teachers see signs of failure, by the fourth grade the children themselves see failure looming and by fifth or sixth grade many are skipping school; as Kozol states, the route from truanting to dropping out is "direct and swift."

In contrast, the principal of the New Trier High School in Winnetka, Illinois, states confidently, "Our goal is for students to be successful." The school, situated on twenty-seven suburban acres, offers Latin and six other foreign languages; the senior English class is reading Nietzsche, Darwin, Plato, Freud and Goethe. In addition to seven gyms and an Olympic-size swimming pool, New Trier operates a television station. Every freshman is assigned a faculty adviser who counsels roughly two dozen students. At Du Sable, a high school in nearby Chicago, each guidance counselor advises 420 students.

The conditions are duplicated in and around each city Kozol visited. In New York City two schools barely fifteen minutes apart by car reveal the same patterns. Public School 261 in the North Bronx is located in what was once a roller-skating rink. No sign identifies the building as a school; the building has no windows. Four kindergartens and a sixth-grade class of Spanish-speaking children share one room. One full-time and one part-time counselor are available to work with the 1,300 children, 90 percent of whom are black or Latino. Textbooks are scarce and students must often share those that are available.

In the same school district, just a few miles to the west, P.S. 24 is situated in the Riverdale section of the Bronx, a residential area with parks, libraries, large cooperative apartment buildings and many beautiful, expensive homes. The school serves 825 children from kindergarten through the sixth grade. Kozol describes essentially three groupings within the school: one for special classes for the mentally retarded, in which most of the students are poor and black or Latino; one for mainstream students, the vast majority of whom are white and Asian; and a third track for "gifted" students. As

Kozol observes, the fourth-grade gifted class is "humming with excitement." The class, according to the teacher, emphasizes "critical thinking, reasoning and logic." The students were at that time writing a new Bill of Rights, examining a concept their personal experience clearly helps them to understand.

Report after report has shown that the poorest districts in New York receive significantly lower allocations than the wealthier districts and that per-pupil expenditures within the city of New York ($5,500 in 1987) are dramatically lower than comparable expenditures in the affluent suburbs surrounding the city (more than $11,000 in some of the affluent communities on Long Island). The same differentials exist, of course, in all the metropolitan areas Kozol examines. The per-pupil expenditure was, for example, $5,500 in the late 1980s in Chicago secondary schools, compared with $8,500 to $9,000 in the highest-spending northern suburbs. But the ultimate meaning of these savage inequalities is their impact on the lives, feelings and self-image of the children themselves. The children movingly speak of the enormous discrepancies between schools for the affluent and schools for the poor, between schools for white children and schools for children of color. A 14-year-old girl states, "We have a school in East St. Louis named for Dr. King. The school is full of sewer water and the doors are locked with chains. Every student in that school is black. It's like a terrible joke on history." A Latino boy from a high school in the South Bronx says, "People on the outside may think that we don't know what it is like for other students, but we *visit* other schools and we have eyes and we have brains. You cannot hide the differences. You see

it and compare." Or an eleventh grader from Camden, New Jersey: "So long as there are no white children in our school, we're going to be cheated. That's America. That's how it is." The children in these schools may not acquire the skills so necessary for living in a postindustrial society, but they certainly learn the explicit meaning of living in a profoundly racist and classist society. Moreover, the children in affluent neighborhoods also absorb the message of living in a grossly unequal society in which individual success is the highest good. Students in the affluent New York City suburb of Rye for the most part oppose busing, suggest a "separate but equal" solution to the problems of inequity in education and offer a blame-the-victim analysis of differences in educational opportunity. When Kozol asks about the possibility of raising taxes in order to equalize educational opportunities one student succinctly summarizes the ideology of the 1980s and the 1990s: "I don't see how that benefits me."

* * *

Ultimately, Kozol addresses the central issue of educational equity in a country that prides itself on equal opportunity. As he points out, funding education, particularly during a time of federal cutbacks to human services and extreme reluctance to raise taxes, is a zero-sum game. Additional money for Chicago schools is likely to mean less money for Winnetka students. Improved facilities for students in the rest of the Bronx will, in all likelihood, mean fewer resources for students in Riverdale. Since 1989, when the Texas Supreme Court struck down the old school-financing system based primarily on property taxes, Texas political leaders have searched for a method of attaining school equity. Currently, the so-called Robin Hood plan is in effect there, which takes property-tax money from rich districts and distributes it among poorer districts. Predictably, rich districts complain they will be reduced to mediocrity while poor ones claim they still do not have the resources they need. But the Robin Hood plan may appear elsewhere as well, as lawsuits challenging school financing are under way in twenty-two other states.

The issue is not likely to disappear. The publication of *Savage Inequalities* will insure that the injustice and incredible shortsightedness of American educational policy are vividly and compassionately brought to the forefront of the public's consciousness and the agenda of policymakers. As with his earlier books, particularly *Death at an Early Age* and

Rachel and Her Children, Jonathan Kozol movingly and persuasively documents the devastating inequities in American society and provides information and insight that will help move the country toward a more humane educational policy.

But, as Kozol clearly recognizes, a more humane educational policy is not enough. Until the millions of American children who currently live in poverty have an adequate standard of living, until the millions of American children who are hungry have enough to eat, until the millions of homeless children have an adequate place to live, and until all children have first-rate health care, we will not begin to develop a just society. The awareness, discussion and, it is to be hoped, action engendered by *Savage Inequalities* will move us closer to that achievable goal.

NO

Peter Schrag

SAVAGE EQUALITIES

It's almost twenty-five years since the publication of Jonathan Kozol's *Death at an Early Age,* which recounted his eight months as a teacher in a rundown Boston ghetto school. Kozol was fired by the then notorious Boston School Committee for reading Langston Hughes's poem "Ballad of a Landlord" to his fourth-grade class—not part of the syllabus, the school committee said— and instantly became a major voice in the movement for school equity and integration of the late 1960s and early 1970s.

Kozol has never strayed far from that theme and has now returned to it with a book called *Savage Inequalities* that's gotten a respectful, even glowing, reception. Just before it came out, *Publishers Weekly* carried an unprecedented open letter on its cover, where it has never run anything but advertising, to tell George Bush to read this "startling and disturbing" new book. *Savage Inequalities* has made Kozol once again the most visible left-wing critic of American education and the star witness in a movement, now spreading to more than a dozen states—among them Alabama, Alaska, Idaho, Illinois, Indiana, Minnesota, Missouri, New Hampshire, North Dakota, South Dakota, Tennessee—to get court orders to equalize per-pupil spending between public schools in rich and poor communities.

It's a moving book—about filthy schools where roofs leak and halls are flooded each time it rains, where three or four classes have to share a gym or cafeteria because there aren't enough rooms, where teachers have outdated textbooks or none at all. It's also a reminder that a lot of those kids really want to learn, aren't on drugs, and understand that this is a society that treats white suburban children a lot better than it treats black inner-city kids. Given the thin gruel that the Bush administration has served up to deal with the nation's horrendous school problems—roughly equal parts school "choice," testing, and that old conservative favorite "more money's not the answer"— it's not surprising that Kozol is getting attention.

The rationale of the equalizers is simple: unequal spending among schools denies children equal protection of the laws. A poor community with a weak

From Peter Schrag, "Savage Equalities: The Case Against Jonathan Kozol," *The New Republic* (December 16, 1991). Copyright © 1991 by The New Republic, Inc. Reprinted by permission of *The New Republic.*

tax base simply can't spend as much on each child's education as a wealthy one, even if it raises rates to the breaking point, and that's patently unfair.

But is equalization of all spending —which, in addition to increasing the spending in poor districts, means capping the spending of affluent or motivated districts—really the solution? Consider California, the only major state where equalization has been thoroughly tried. (Texas and New Jersey are now starting down the same path but haven't gotten beyond the political acrimony and administrative chaos to be fair tests.) The results have been a wondrous illustration of the law of unintended consequences.

The most obvious of those consequences is that equalization sharply reduced local incentives to raise school taxes. After the California Supreme Court ruled, in *Serrano v. Priest* (1976), that the old funding system was unconstitutional, the legislature agreed to bring per-pupil spending in virtually all of the state's districts to within $100 (later revised to $200) of the state average. It proposed to do that not by requiring the rich districts to spend less, something that would have been academically unseemly and politically impossible, but by directing additional state money to the poor districts. Yet since the funding formula also reduced state funding one dollar for each dollar that districts might have raised in additional local property taxes, it eliminated much of the rationale and motivation for local efforts to improve the schools. (The exceptions to the formula were a few oil-rich districts that get no state aid.)

School equalization might have taken decades to achieve had it not been for the fortuitous passage of Proposition 13 in 1978. By slashing and capping local property tax revenues, Prop 13 shifted the burden of school funding to state income and sales taxes, which made equalization a lot easier to realize. But because of 13, and perhaps because of *Serrano* as well, the state's spending on schools has also slipped precipitately— from sixth or seventh in the nation to twenty-fifth or twenty-sixth. California now spends less per child than any other major industrial state, and less than the national average. As one state education official said recently, it is much harder to motivate people to pay more taxes for education when they can't see the results right down the street.

Kozol has a lot of numbers dramatizing the inequities in spending between, for example, Camden and Princeton, New Jersey; Chicago and suburban New Trier High School; and New York City and suburban Manhasset (Long Island). But he doesn't point out that the $7,299 New York City spent on each child in 1989– 90 was nearly double what most of the fanciest California suburbs got to spend that same year. California now spends roughly $5,100 a year per student. The national average is $5,500. The university town of Davis, where I live, and which sends as many of its graduates to college as New Trier, would kill to get $6,000 per student, let alone $7,000.

With the power to appropriate funds having shifted from local boards to the state government, it is no longer possible to know who is responsible for the financial problems of the local schools— the board that allocates the funds and overspends or mismanages them or the governor and legislature that fail to pony up enough to begin with. The same goes for responsibility for the construction of new schools, now so incomprehensibly divided between state and local agencies that almost no one understands the system.

Moreover, since school boards no longer have anything to do with setting tax rates, the interest of local business groups and taxpayer organizations in the schools—or in running people for the board—has sharply declined, leaving more and more districts in the control of the only well-financed group that's really interested in school affairs: the teachers' union. The Los Angeles school board, which runs the largest system in the state, is now controlled by people who got the lion's share of their election campaign support from UTLA, the United Teachers of Los Angeles. As fiscal control moves to the state, the moderate citizens' groups that once were the backbone of local government and local schools are less and less involved.

It shouldn't be surprising, then, that the union-dominated Los Angeles board awarded huge raises to its teachers three years ago—the average increase was roughly 27 percent over three years—and is now in deep financial trouble. And though it stands out in its generosity to employees, it's hardly alone. Two other large districts, Oakland and Richmond, are in such financial trouble from general mismanagement that they were taken over by state-appointed trustees; two dozen others teeter on the verge of bankruptcy. One-third of all the state's districts, according to state Controller Gray Davis, are spending more money than they take in.

* * *

Many of those problems are attributable to the state's generally dismal fiscal situation, but not all of them. District after district has been overly generous in setting pay scales, counting on state appropriations it didn't get. Most of the extra money that was supposed to go toward improving the inner-city schools also went directly into increasing teacher and administrative salaries even while programs have been cut to the bone. No state in the country has as large a gap between what it pays its school employees and what it spends on everything else. California is fifth in the nation in teachers salaries and dead last—meaning worst—in class size: many classes are now running well over thirty children, even in elementary schools. We also have leaky roofs and rotting buildings, but we have them in the suburbs as well as in the inner cities.

Kozol says, correctly, that poor children are trapped in awful inner-city schools, while the middle class has choices. But he refuses to give poor children the chance to escape to better public schools, through choice. He's also too simplistic in blaming the comparatively poor performance of our schools on money alone. No country has ever done, or even tried, what this country is now trying: to take such a diverse population of children —20 percent of them from below the poverty level, many of them speaking little English, many from one-parent or no-parent families (all problems George Bush's education "program" ignore[d]) —and educate each child at least through the twelfth grade for a high-tech culture. Under the circumstances, our schools are doing better than one might expect—as well at least as we did two decades ago. And given also what we've learned about the schools' external problems—poverty, broken families, teenage pregnancies, drugs, lack of health care, lack of child care—the first place to spend (and equalize) new money on children may not be in the K–12 school program, but on broader social problems.

Although Kozol acknowledges that equalization has been problematic in California, his support for the idea remains undiminished. Of course, Proposition 13 and fiscal mismanagement exacerbated the problems here. But the fact remains that equalization—any way you formulate it—tends to destroy local accountability and erode the supports and sense of mission that make strong schools possible.

POSTSCRIPT

Will Reforming School Funding Remove "Savage Inequalities"?

In a 1992 interview ("On Savage Inequalities: A Conversation With Jonathan Kozol," Marge Scherer, *Educational Leadership,* December 1992/January 1993), Kozol made his priorities very clear: "We've got to distinguish between injustice and inconvenience. Before we deal with an affluent child's existential angst, let's deal with the kid in Chicago who had not had a permanent teacher for the past five years." This gets at the crux of the matter; in a static and unjust economy Robin Hood is elevated from criminal to hero.

A scholar who does not share this view is sociologist Nathan Glazer. In an article in the Winter 1992 issue of *The Public Interest* entitled "The Real World of Urban Education," Glazer contends that research shows that expenditure of money does not seem to correlate well with educational success. He suggests that we had better find out where our money is now going before we demand equalization of its distribution.

Other views on the equalization issue include these: "*Brown v. Board of Education:* Time for a Reassessment," by Donald C. Orlich, *Phi Delta Kappan* (April 1991); "Race and Equality of Opportunity: A School Finance Perspective," by C. Phillip Kearney and Li-Ju Chen, *Journal of Education Finance* (Winter 1990); "Toward Educational Change and Economic Justice: An Interview With Herbert Kohl," by Joe Nathan, *Phi Delta Kappan* (May 1991); and "Ghetto Schools Are Getting Worse: Why Not Give Choice a Chance?" by Bill Bradley, *The Philadelphia Inquirer* (March 12, 1992).

Further information can be obtained in other issues of the *Journal of Education Finance*; in the *Journal of Negro Education* special issue on "Urban Future" (Summer 1989); in the *Phi Delta Kappan* special report on "Children of Poverty" (October 1990); in the National School Boards Association report *A Survey of Public Education in the Nation's Urban School Districts* (1989); in the Committee for Economic Development's *Children in Need: Investment Strategies for the Educationally Disadvantaged* (1987); and in the book *Outside In: Minorities and the Transformation of American Education* (1989) by Paula S. Fass.

Sharon D. Michalove's article "The Educational Crusade of Jonathan Kozol," in the Spring 1993 issue of *The Educational Forum*, is worth reading, as is the Spring 1994 issue of *Theory into Practice*, which is devoted to the theme "Financing Education." The journal contains articles by Keith Geiger, Robert Slavin, Allan Ornstein, and Daniel U. Levine, and it features Martha M. McCarthy's "The Courts and School Finance Reform," which should be of particular interest to students of education law.

ISSUE 9

Should National Goals and Standards Guide School Reform?

YES: Edward M. Kennedy, from "On the Common Core of Learning," *The Educational Forum* (Summer 1994)

NO: Stephen Arons, from "Constitutional Implications of National Curriculum Standards," *The Educational Forum* (Summer 1994)

ISSUE SUMMARY

YES: Senator Edward M. Kennedy (D-Massachusetts) argues that the "Goals 2000" education reform legislation will create a common purpose in America's schools and render them more effective.

NO: Legal studies professor Stephen Arons maintains that the national curriculum standards aspect of the legislation will undermine important freedoms and threaten cultural diversity.

In recent years a large number of national reports appear to have placed economic reconstruction and growth firmly in the driver's seat when it comes to reconsidering educational objectives and making curricular decisions. These reports include the National Commission on Excellence in Education's *A Nation at Risk,* the Education Commission of the States' *Action for Excellence,* the Twentieth Century Fund's *Making the Grade,* and the National Science Foundation's *Educating Americans for the Twenty-First Century.* In 1990 the Bush administration adopted six national goals in its "America 2000" plan, which was designed to build "schools of the 21st century." The plan envisioned all children in the United States starting school prepared to learn, at least 90 percent of students graduating from high school, all students being able to cope with challenging subject matter (particularly math and science), all adults being literate and responsible citizens, and all graduates of the nation's schools being able to compete in a global economy.

To achieve the "America 2000" goals, the administration suggested moving toward more choice and more competition among schools, brought business leaders into the planning process, and emphasized the desirability of national testing and a more unified curriculum. The Clinton administration has adopted the goals established by the Bush administration—renaming the plan "Goals 2000: Educate America"—but it is downplaying the role of the private sector. Secretary of Education Richard W. Riley has actively promoted the goals, but he has also stressed that it is critical for individual states to have a choice in assessing student progress toward the goals.

The goal-setting strategy itself has been broadly criticized. In "Countdown —The Goals 2000: Educate America Act," *National Forum* (Fall 1993), Martha W. Young contends that because terms are undefined and policies are based on vague and sometimes fuzzy thinking, the national education goals raise issues rather than resolve them. In "What Standards Can't Solve: Death in the Everyday Classroom," *The Nation* (May 24, 1993), Stephen O'Connor asserts that the goals simply do not deal with important matters such as violence, family disintegration, poverty, teenage pregnancy, and drugs. From another viewpoint, James Moffett, in *The Universal Schoolhouse* (1994), decries the government's conviction that business can show how to set the public schools' house in order, arguing that political and economic considerations are obscuring practical knowledge about how to improve learning. (Moffett's ideas are excerpted in the April 1994 issue of *Phi Delta Kappan* in an article titled "On to the Past: Wrong-Headed School Reform.")

Behind the arguments over the proposed goals and standards lies the basic question of how to achieve balance among federal, state, and local power in shaping school policy. Does "top-down" planning produce solid results? The national educational reforms initiated in the 1980s have brought about, at best, mixed evidence of success. One skeptic of national reform, Deborah W. Meier, in "Myths, Lies, and Public Schools," *The Nation* (September 21, 1992), asserts that "the debate over education reform belongs in local communities. Only such a community-centered debate will restore the public's sense that it has a stake in public schools." Another critical aspect is pointed to by Keith Geiger, president of the National Education Association, in "Schools, Society, and the Economy," *Vital Speeches of the Day* (July 1, 1991). He says, "Our national leaders *say* education is a priority. But the investment that would make that priority a reality has not been forthcoming."

In the following selections, Edward M. Kennedy offers support to the federal government's campaign for national goals and standards as an important mechanism for ensuring a more consistent level of high quality in U.S. public schools. Stephen Arons expresses grave concerns about the survival of individual and cultural freedom under a political imposition of centralized curriculum standards.

YES

Edward M. Kennedy

ON THE COMMON CORE OF LEARNING

Few topics are more important than academic content standards for what we want graduates to know and be able to do. These standards will represent our vision of the future, a vision we can achieve only by effective coordination at every level—federal, state, and local.

Although academic standards are critically important, standards alone will not ensure that students reach them. How subjects are taught makes all the difference in whether or not the content is learned, retained, and used. The key to success will lie in the implementation and in well-trained and knowledgeable teachers. As we address the question of standards, therefore, we must invest more in teachers and place them closer to the center of the effort to have all children meet higher standards. Teachers are the ones who educate children—not school districts, or state legislatures, or federal laws.

We must help reorganize schools to give teachers and students more time to acquire skills and knowledge, more time to help each other and work together, more time to plan and share effective strategies, more time to involve parents, and most of all, more time for teachers to develop closer ties with students.

The U.S. Senate Labor Committee has recognized the pre-eminence of teachers in achieving the National Education Goals by adding an eighth goal:

> By the year 2000, the nations' teaching force will have access to programs for the continued improvement of their professional skills and the opportunity to acquire the knowledge and skills needed to instruct and prepare all American students for the next century.

We intend to back up this commitment as we reauthorize the Elementary and Secondary Education Act.

The federal government can help meet this challenge through increased set-asides for professional development in programs such as Chapter I and Chapter II. This may seem like taking funds from children to give to teachers. However, few reforms will do more for pupils than well-prepared, engaged, and energetic teachers.

To overcome the inertia of long-standing and ingrained teaching methods, we must not resort to the old techniques of sending teachers back to school themselves or imposing new requirements from Washington. The changes that teachers need to make must be worked out by the teachers themselves.

Well-prepared teachers alone, however, won't create a common purpose in schools. We must set high academic standards for all students to which all members of the education community—students, teachers, parents, and citizens—commit.

The task of designing a core curriculum based on clear, shared concepts is obviously complex. We must be aware of the diverse cultures in the United States and other lands that have made important contributions to civilization. We must consider a wide range of disciplines, including new fields such as biotechnology and environmental studies, that are increasingly important in today's world. We must recognize the value of acquiring a second language, and the great resource our bilingual citizens bring to this country. We must include the arts, which offer students access to alternative means of self-expression and communication that they can share with others.

In addition to these critical considerations, we must ensure that our goals for our students are visionary:

- Our students should have the basic analytical skills and confidence to realize that a combination of hard work, research, and disciplined thinking can help them deal with the challenges they face in life.

- Students should be able to read at a level that will enable them to function effectively and acquire information needed to make informed judgments.

- They should be able to communicate effectively in spoken and written English, and be able to write in a logical and informative way.

- They should have the math skills to accomplish everyday commercial transactions with ease, accuracy, and understanding, and should be able to perceive relationships.

- They should understand the basics of science and the scientific method.

- They should have a fundamental respect and understanding for others, especially for the diversity of our culture that is our strength. We must help our students learn more about one another and about the rest of the world.

- They should understand the difference between primary and secondary sources, and have the skills and motivation to seek primary sources on things that matter to them.

- They should understand the basic values and history of our democratic society, including informed participation, dealing in good faith, the ability to understand opposing viewpoints, and empathy for one's fellow human beings.

- Finally, students should understand that education is a process that is never finished, so that they will look for learning opportunities in every situation.

These are ambitious goals, and the federal government has a role to play in helping Massachusetts and all other states, students, teachers, and schools meet them. Through President Bill Clinton's education reform legislation called Goals 2000, we will help states and local school districts raise standards for all students, and help all students meet them. We are also working to create networks for teachers and schools through technology. We are learning that Washington must let go, and reduce the bureaucracy that we have helped create.

In the decade since we have been talking about school reform in earnest, overall spending on education has increased by 40 percent. Nearly every state has adopted more rigorous curriculum and attendance requirements for a high-school diploma. The results, however, have been discouraging.

There are many reasons, but a significant one is that we lack a clear vision of what students should know. The course requirements that have been added rest on weak foundations. In many cases, we have been reinforcing an outdated and inadequate structure. Many school practices are ineffective and even counterproductive. We must design a new blueprint for education, a plan for the future that specifies what students need to know, when they need to learn it, and what we need to do to help them.

Despite funding increases, many school districts are still struggling to carry out their existing tasks. Frequently they lack the financial and human resources to review their practices and reform their schools. The federal government and state governments can help by offering leadership, by developing new models, and by providing financial and technical assistance to schools willing to adopt these new models.

The purpose of the Goals 2000 legislation is to do just that—to give "top-down" support for "bottom-up" reform. Goals 2000 authorizes $400 million this year and additional sums in future years for grants to states to enter into partnerships with local schools to help them train their teachers, organize their programs, and focus their budgets to answer a fundamental question: How do we make sure that every student in a school learns the challenging material set out in the school's standards?

Goals 2000 codifies the six education goals adopted by President George Bush and the National Governors' Association in 1989. In pursuit of these ends, Goals 2000 creates a National Education Standards and Improvement Council that will be responsible for certifying voluntary content standards in nine key areas—English, math, science, foreign languages, the arts, history, geography, economics, and civics and government. The result will be a set of outlines describing the ideas, skills, and facts that students should know to be competent in these fields.

In addition, the bill will also create a National Skill Standards Board, to develop voluntary standards for occupational training. These standards will give clearer guidance to educators and students about the training necessary for different fields and will provide the basis for a voluntary system of vocational certification. These standards will make it easier for workers to change jobs and will help to coordinate many different job training programs currently funded by the federal government.

These education and skill standards are not intended to create a national curriculum. Such a step would run the risk of stifling experimentation and regional diversity. Rather, these standards are intended to offer states and districts a strictly voluntary model and to serve as an example for states to consider as they formulate their own standards.

Such a model will be of little use, however, without guidance on teaching and on the tools that students need to attain these standards. To succeed, students must have access to well-trained teachers and effective teaching materials.

The Secretary of Education will oversee development of a set of voluntary standards for determining whether schools are giving students an adequate opportunity to learn. These "opportunity-to-learn" standards will provide states, parents, teachers, and administrators with a measuring stick to gauge their resources and determine which areas need more support.

Unless every state addresses the question of whether or not each student has a fair chance to master challenging content, there is a danger that the poorest schools will be unfairly penalized for failure to achieve unrealistic goals. Obviously, it would be wrong, for instance, to make knowledge of a foreign language a graduation requirement in schools where foreign languages are never taught.

Besides offering guidance and support, however, the federal government must also give states and schools wider discretion in the spending of federal dollars. Here, the federal government is clearly part of the problem. A patchwork of individual federal programs has been targeted at special student populations or high-priority areas such as science and math. Though well-intentioned, these ad hoc programs often hinder real reform. Categorical funding and regulations increase bureaucracy and fragment the curriculum, making it harder for schools to devise creative, comprehensive plans for reform.

Our goal here is less micromanagement and greater flexibility. Teachers and schools should be free to use federal funding more flexibly as long as they achieve positive results. Goals 2000 takes a first step in this direction by offering funding to state and local jurisdictions to develop and implement their own school improvement plans.

Congress must also do a better job of concentrating federal resources where they are most needed. When the Elementary and Secondary Education Act comes up for reauthorization this year, a major test will be the effort to create more flexible rules for Chapter I.

In large part, our schools are unfairly overburdened today. Too often, too many teachers and educators are obliged to perform the work of health and welfare and other social service agencies for too many pupils because these other agencies are failing in this mission. As a result, too many children come to school hungry, sick, homeless, neglected, abused—and unable to learn.

As we take steps to raise academic expectations for students, we must do more to help schools meet these other challenges. In the past Congress, I introduced a comprehensive services bill to address these issues, and we will work this year to incorporate health services for children into health care reform.

The next key element in federal support for education reform must be technology. At a forum in January 1994 at West Roxbury High School to discuss technology in the future of American education, Patty Knox, a teacher in the Lawrence public schools, told us how bringing technology into the classroom had transformed the behavior and performance of many of her students. One student, Martin, came to class last year with low grades, little motivation, and poor attendance. But he became so intrigued by the new technology that his performance improved dramatically. This year he has moved on to a new class without technology. He is losing interest in school again, and his performance has fallen back.

Technology in the classroom is not a luxury. It is central to education reform.

Through interactive computer software, students can have a more effective and independent role in the learning process. Distance-learning networks can reach into urban or rural communities or even reach across the nation and the world electronically. They enable students and teachers to pool resources and tap new sources of information. Teachers approach their work with renewed enthusiasm, and students find learning more appealing.

Technology in the classroom is also essential to prepare students for the modern workplace. Computers are transforming virtually every sector of the economy, from manufacturing to health care to retailing. Without training in new technology, students will be at a disadvantage in the job market, and the United States will fall behind in the world economy.

Too few teachers and students have access to adequate technology. Many classrooms lack even a telephone, let alone a computer. Much of the available equipment and software is outdated. Even in schools with up-to-date equipment, adequate technical support and training for teachers are often unavailable.

Technology must not be limited to a few privileged schools. To give students the skills they need to find a good job, to bring schools to excellence, to give parents confidence that children are getting a solid education, wherever they go to school—we must work to bring good technology into every classroom.

The Technology for Education Act, the bipartisan bill that Senator Bingaman of New Mexico, Senator Cochran of Mississippi, and I have introduced in the Senate, is designed to support educators in moving toward this goal. By providing grants and low-interest loans to purchase new hardware and software, by funding teacher training and technical assistance, by making funds available to states to develop technology plans, and by coordinating these efforts through the U.S. Department of Education, the bill will help integrate technology into learning.

These elements—voluntary standards, bottom-up reform, more flexible use of federal funds, and improved access to technology—are essential to education reform. Without them, whatever progress is made will be piecemeal at best, limited to individual schools and individual school districts.

The federal government can't do the job alone. But it can provide greater leadership, support, and resources for the communities, schools, and teachers throughout the country that are striving for reform. I intend to do all I can to see that Congress is a responsible and productive partner in this essential effort.

NO
Stephen Arons

CONSTITUTIONAL IMPLICATIONS OF NATIONAL CURRICULUM STANDARDS

It is the essence of constitutional democracy in the United States—and a paradox that many people do not fully appreciate—that, in order for the majoritarian politics of self-government to work, freedoms of belief and expression must be protected from majority control. The First Amendment, which is the lynchpin of this system of freedoms (Emerson 1966), requires that every agency of government remain neutral as to the content of virtually all communication and belief. The Constitution of the United States embodies the view that unless the wellspring of intellectual and cultural diversity is thus protected, the just consent of the governed will be rendered hollow, and a "despotism over the mind" (Mill 1859, 191) established.

This essay suggests that the creation of national curriculum standards, as part of the Goals 2000: Educate America Act (1994), is inconsistent with the fundamental structure of constitutional democracy and will undermine our most important freedoms. There has been very little scholarly debate or public discourse about the effect of a national curriculum on individual liberty. Neither has there been much discussion about the alternative means available for attaining the student achievement goals to which the nation subscribed in the act. As a result, Goals 2000 may be regarded as a serious, but largely unperceived, threat to intellectual vitality, cultural diversity, and liberties that the Supreme Court has called the "sphere of intellect and spirit which it is the purpose of the First Amendment to our Constitution to reserve from all official control" (*West Virginia State Board of Education v. Barnette*, 319 U.S. 642 [1943]).

The Goals 2000 (1994) legislation requires the creation and federal approval of substantive content standards in nine subject-matter areas: English, mathematics, science, foreign languages, civics and government, economics, the arts, history, and geography. These national standards, which may be too limited or distorted to match the diversity of American lives, will prescribe the knowledge and the skills that every student in the United States will be

From Stephen Arons, "Constitutional Implications of National Curriculum Standards," *The Educational Forum*, vol. 58 (Summer 1994). Copyright © 1994 by Kappa Delta Pi, an international honor society in education. Reprinted by permission. References omitted.

expected to master; and the success of both standards and students will be measured by performance tests approved by the federal government.

It is expected that teacher training and certification will be made consistent with these standards, that privately published textbooks will reflect the substance of these standards, and that, eventually, certificates of employability, the content of some higher education, and even the availability of federal and state education funds will come to revolve around these standards. The idea, according to Undersecretary of Education Marshall Smith, is to improve the quality of output of the nation's schools by a systemic, standards-driven reform of every school in the United States (O'Neil 1993b, 8).

Some have called this effort a "nationalization of education policy" (Wise and Leibbrand 1993, 134) and its product a "national curriculum" (O'Neil 1993a, 6). Only 2 of the goals in the act deal with substantive curriculum standards and performance testing. Goal 3 calls for students to demonstrate "competency over challenging subject matters" in 9 categories, while Goal 5 states that "by the year 2000, United States students will be first in the world in mathematics and science achievement" (Goals 2000 1994, sec. 102 [3 and 5]). The specific content over which students are to be tested—and the assessment instruments—are to be approved by two politically appointed federal panels, the National Education Goals Panel and the National Education Standards and Improvement Council (Goals 2000 1994, Title II, Parts A and B). The act describes the standards as voluntary and includes a clause stating that federal funds may not be made conditional upon state adoption of the standards (Goals 2000 1994, sec. 213 [h]), but the momen-

tum behind the national standards movement, its pervasiveness in virtually every sector of education, and the bureaucracy created by the act suggest that its voluntary nature will be short-lived. Among the act's purposes is to provide "a framework for the reauthorization of all Federal education programs" (Goals 2000 1994, sec. 2 [6])....

THE RECONSTITUTION OF U.S. SCHOOLING

Several protections built into the Goals 2000 act are designed to allay the fear that a national curriculum will be imposed upon every school, teacher, and student in the United States, but these protections are weak and could easily be repealed in an intolerant atmosphere. More to the point, these protections could be rendered inoperative by federal administrative discretion, by self-censorship of state education leaders eager to please the U.S. Department of Education, or by local educators who wish to avoid accountability to diverse education constituents by claiming that national curriculum standards tie their hands.

When the U.S. Constitution transferred power from the newly independent states to the federal government in 1789, many Federalists claimed that a constitution designed around checks and balances and based upon a limited grant of specific powers would keep the federal government from infringing on individual freedoms. This response was viewed with skepticism; the result was the adoption of the Bill of Rights in 1791 (Bernstein 1987). The assurances built into Goals 2000 national curriculum standards should be viewed with the same skepticism—especially given the difficulty the courts have had in applying the existing Bill of Rights to a system of education the Framers did not even imagine.

A national curriculum would be more than simply a set of state curriculum requirements writ large. Because of the scope, it would necessarily be less sensitive, not only to variations among geographical communities but to nongeographical communities of belief, cultural and religious subgroups, families, and individuals, as well. The standards to be created will be outcome-based. Their power to impose uniformity over an existing pluralism of beliefs would be far greater than most state curriculum requirements, which historically have required only that certain courses be taken by students. Unlike state curriculum requirements, a national curriculum will be at the center of a systemic overhaul of U.S. schooling, reaching into all aspects of education, from teacher training and certification to student testing, state textbook approval (DeCastell, Luke, and Luke 1989), and even the distribution of federal aid. There are five reasons why the eventual creation of a national curriculum is a restructuring of education so fundamental that it is likely to undermine U.S. education, reduce cultural and intellectual diversity, and weaken the central principle of constitutional democracy.

National Curriculum and Principles of Constitutional Democracy

First, the idea of a government-imposed national curriculum is inconsistent with the principles upon which the Constitution is based. In order for a system of popular sovereignty to work, each citizen must be free to participate in the conflict of "government by discussion" (Sunstein 1993). This participation hinges on the freedom each participant has to form,

hold, and express opinions and beliefs, and to communicate freely in the marketplace of ideas. Openly derived public policy is vital to democratic life; but so, too, is the voluntary formation and maintenance of communities—communities based on common interests, heritage, geography, language, and religion. The diversity of these communities depends upon the security of the basic freedoms of belief and communication (Cobb 1992).

Emerson (1966, 3) argued succinctly that protecting freedom of expression is necessary:

(1) as a method of assuring individual self-fulfillment, (2) as a means of attaining the truth, (3) as a method of securing participation by the members of the society in social, including political, decision-making, and (4) as a means of maintaining the balance between stability and change in the society.

First Amendment freedoms protect constitutional principles and philosophical commitments grounded in the sanctity of each mind and in the voluntary nature of social cohesion. If the national government is empowered to create a curriculum that defines student success through a series of national performance tests, the relationship of individuals to government envisioned by the Constitution will be eroded.

Virtually no schooling is value-neutral. Much of it touches upon conscience, worldview, and the basic beliefs that are central to each person's definition of reality. To the extent that a national curriculum is successful, therefore, it creates a kind of political perpetual-motion machine. When the beliefs transmitted by schooling are heavily influenced by government, the intellectual basis for citizen participation in shaping policy and culture is also heavily influenced by government. The consent of the governed touted by the Declaration of Independence then becomes a mere form of words. The elitism of Plato's Republic replaces the democracy of Franklin's. "Laws that cast a pall of orthodoxy over the classroom" (*Keyishian v. Board of Regents*, 385 U.S. 603 [1967]) threaten critical thinking; and a bland and passionless curriculum becomes the best that can be hoped for by committed teachers seeking room to practice their profession. If a federal council of political appointees were to deliberate the content of a required catechism instead of the content of nine performance-tested school subjects, the second American revolution would not be long in coming.

The Public's Conception of Schooling
Second, the adoption of a national curriculum is likely to transform the idea of education in the public mind. As the nationalization process develops, the public's conception of schooling will shift still further from the already weakened Enlightenment ideal of individual self-development and freedom to determine one's own relationship to the culture. Individual conscience will be marginalized. Deep, personal engagement with learning—and the interactive communication between individual and culture—will be reduced to a banking theory of learning (Freire 1970). More and more, teaching will be viewed as a bureaucratic task, rather than as a profession requiring informed, independent judgment (National Foundation for the Improvement of Education 1994). Eventually, schooling may be seen as a narrow form of technical training geared to the centrally planned production of that knowledge and those skills and beliefs that the national government views as necessary for global economic and technological competition in the twenty-first century.

In the idea of creating national standards that specify what every child must know, there is a hidden curriculum for the nation—and the schools (Apple 1979; 1982; 1992; Gatto 1992). Shifting the balance of power over learning and teaching to the federal government will push public consciousness about schooling in a direction neither desired nor anticipated by most advocates of national standards. With virtually no debate, the government will have changed the public's perception of the nature and expansive possibilities of schooling. The complex connection between democracy and education will become further attenuated; and the image of teaching as a subversive activity will fade. This change in public consciousness will affect citizen expectations and, in turn, the understandings and votes of legislators and judges passing upon education freedoms dissenters claim.

Government Opposition to Claims
Third, the coupling of federal power with curriculum policy may substantially decrease the ability of dissenting individuals and communities to protect their existing, constitutionally based school freedoms in court. The balancing that is conducted by the courts in most school cases involving freedom of belief and intellect places a heavy burden upon those who would deny or infringe upon those freedoms (Emerson 1966). To carry this burden, a government agency usually must show that its justification for the contested policy is of overwhelming importance to the well-being of society. In its absence, those asserting their fundamental freedoms will prevail.

The problem with a national, performance-tested curriculum, established pursuant to an act of Congress, is that it is likely to be more convincing to the courts as a compelling justification for infringing upon individual and cultural freedoms than would arguments grounded in state or local curriculum standards. Since much of the freedom of belief and intellect recognized by the courts in school cases is already compromised and tenuous, the result may be the further weakening of these freedoms. The point may appear to be a narrow legal one, but having the federal government weigh in on one side of a schooling case could have profound effects on the way in which the courts balance individual freedoms and government interests.

Recall, for example, that the State of Wisconsin tried to override the Amish right to free exercise of religion in *Wisconsin v. Yoder.* Had the argument against the Amish included a claim that the future health of the American economy required that all children adhere to national curriculum standards in order to become technologically proficient and economically productive adults, the result might have been different.

Political Conflict Over Curriculum
Fourth, the adoption of national curriculum standards will shift the focus of political conflict over curriculum from the local to the state and national levels. At first this might appear to be positive development, since it could reduce the effectiveness of various extremist groups that are presently targeting local school districts for takeovers, conducting campaigns of intolerance against beliefs with which they disagree, or promoting a brand of vouchers that would weaken public school funding without a mean-

ingful increase in real choice among those students most in need. But this is a shortsighted view. Before long, local and state curriculum wars will resurface on the national level, perhaps as part of an extremist presidential campaign. Polarizing politics, based on superficial discourse and ideological posturing, will then substantially increase the intensity and destructiveness of conflicts over curriculum as they become abstract issues useful to politicians and groups with national aspirations. The struggle in the legislature and courts of Florida, over whether Lake County teachers will be required to teach that U.S. culture is superior to all others in the world, is but the smallest indication of the conflicts likely to occur as higher levels of government acquire increased power over school content (West 1994).

The history of struggles over schooling suggests that to make individual learning a subject for political conflict weakens the participation of individuals in their own education, reduces the professionalism of teaching, and undermines intellectual and cultural diversity (Tyack 1974; Spring 1975; Nasaw 1979). The past two decades have seen enormous growth in conflicts over curriculum content, textbooks, and school libraries (Nelkin 1977; Davis 1979; Arons 1986; DelFattore 1992). These ideological battles have often engaged the intense passions that most people reserve for issues of conscience and basic belief, and which the First Amendment reserves from majority coercion. Issues in contention have included contests between Genesis and evolution; the presentation of gender roles in reading texts; the roles of authority, patriotism, spirituality, and critical thinking in civics courses; and the basic value decisions that give significance to schooling and meaning to life.

As these conflicts demonstrate, it is a weakness in the present structure of schooling that local majorities are empowered to use the political process to impose fundamental beliefs upon minorities through controlling the content of curriculum. That weakness is increased exponentially by the creation of a national curriculum. At base, the issue is not which political, cultural, or religious group correctly understands reality, or which group advocates the true morality. The issue is whether empowering the government to decide such issues and to impose them upon schools and students can foster anything but unnecessary and unmanageable conflict over matters best left to individuals. The compromised freedoms discussed earlier are testament to the problems that arise when individuals do not have power to choose the education that reflects their own beliefs and life goals or to select schooling that advances what Einstein (1954, 61) called "that divine curiosity which every healthy child possesses."

One of the main principles underlying the constitutional command that the freedoms of belief, intellect, and expression be preserved from government control is the need to keep conflicts of conscience from destroying individual liberty. By removing these conflicts from the purview of government, the First Amendment also protects the political process from being rendered ineffective by conflicts over individual conscience. The U.S. Supreme Court saw the danger of ignoring these truths when it struck down the compulsory pledge of allegiance in public schools in 1943 (*West Virginia v. Barnette*, 319 U.S. 641, 637):

Probably no deeper division of our people could proceed from any provocation than from finding it necessary to choose what doctrine and whose program public educational officials shall compel youth to unite in embracing.

If [public education] is to impose any ideological discipline, however, each party or denomination must seek to control, or failing that, to weaken the influence of the educational system.

Need for an Education Bill of Rights

Fifth, the magnitude of the change in U.S. education that national curriculum standards will eventually bring about amounts to a virtual reconstitution of American schooling. Under this new constitution of education, prospects of protecting freedom and diversity remain uncertain; and virtually no reliable protections have been written into the Goals 2000 act. With the anticipated shift of the balance of power over curriculum content to the federal government, the problem of protecting the individual "sphere of intellect and spirit" from official control will become still more difficult; and the likelihood of honoring pluralism will diminish even as the nation becomes more diverse. With regard to education, U.S. citizens in 1994 find themselves in a position similar to those who contemplated a new constitution in 1789—in need of a bill of rights.

What should an education bill of rights contain? Broadly, it ought to guarantee to every child the right to an education, and secure in schools the rights of conscience, of belief, of intellect, of dissent, and of expression against the pressures of political majorities and governmental coercion. In particular, it should:

• Guarantee to every child an appropriate education regardless of race, ethnic or linguistic background, religion, gender, sexual orientation, physical or mental disability, or family economic status.

- Secure the right of students and families to choose other than a government-run school, and of those of subcultures to receive schooling consistent with their deeply held beliefs; neither right to be conditional upon family economic status.
- Secure the right of nongovernment schools to be free of governmental content regulation, and to adopt curriculum goals and standards of their own choosing.
- Protect public school students and teachers from having to confess a belief in any ideological point of view and from, in any other way, having imposed on them an orthodoxy of beliefs that contradicts their conscience, cultural heritage, or spiritual values.
- Secure the status of teachers as professionals by enhancing academic freedom and due process protections against job loss, discrimination, textbook and library censorship, or other penalties arising from political pressures or content-based government requirements.
- Protect the rights of expression, inquiry, press, and privacy of public school students.

AN ALTERNATIVE TO A NATIONAL CURRICULUM

As the Goals 2000 legislation makes clear, the creation and enforcement of national curriculum content standards has been justified as a means of increasing students' performance and their preparation for competition in a global economy (Goals 2000 1994). It has also been justified by the need to reduce the "savage inequalities" that plague Amer-

ican schooling (Kozol 1991). These inequalities are nowhere more destructive than in the widely varying expectations that schools and school personnel hold for their students. Such disparate expectations, which often become self-fulfilling prophecies, are especially pernicious when based on the socioeconomic status, race, or linguistic background of students, and when institutionalized in practices such as tracking (Wheelock 1992) and school segregation (Orfield 1988).

The question is whether creation of enforceable national curriculum standards—which arguably will threaten individual liberty, cultural diversity, and freedom of the mind—are necessary to attain the goals of economic competitiveness and equity, or whether there are means available for attaining these goals without the severe costs predicted in this article. Such a less restrictive—and more effective—alternative to a national curriculum can be envisioned. In fact, the alternative is simple, practical, and consistent with the new law's fourth goal addressing teacher education and professional development (Goals 2000 1994). It would require that the federal government allocate funds sufficient to support the creation of a 10-year revolving program of continuing education for all school teachers in each of the 9 academic fields. By the end of the 10 years, every teacher in the United States, whether teaching reading to 6-year-olds or advanced physics to 17-year-olds, would have participated. At no cost to the teacher, each would attend 2 summers of continuing education relevant to a field of specialization and in the pedagogy needed to teach successfully students of any background.

The program would be decentralized, diverse, and unrestricted by government content requirements beyond the mere naming of subject matters. Each project would be organized by a different consortium of college or university faculty, professional educators, and teachers in localities around the country. The content of the continuing education would be determined by the independent judgment of the participants about the state of knowledge in each subject area. Teachers would have choices as to which program they attended but would be required to attend a minimum number of months within 10 years. The cost of attendance would be borne by the federal government through the issuance of scholarships to all teachers. In the early years, preference would be given to teachers working at schools where the quality of education is poorest, as measured by the attainment of students under existing practices. Federal and state governments would ensure the availability of resources such as lab equipment, library holdings, teaching materials, and adequate classrooms necessary to make enhanced teaching possible.

The program would be entirely one of professional self-development aided by college and university scholars and funded by a federal commitment to increasing the quality of teaching in the nation's schools. The focus on teaching quality—and teachers' ability to enhance equity as well as excellence—is based on the view that teachers are the primary asset of the education enterprise, and that teaching quality is at present one of the most unequally distributed factors in every state. Moreover, the direct enhancement of teaching quality—of knowledge, skills, and commitment to all students—does not require that any

governmental entity or political majority be empowered to control the content of the teacher's relationship with his or her students; and the national curriculum provisions of Goals 2000 could, therefore, be repealed.

The practicability of this alternative means for achieving equity and excellence is a fact of legal as well as educational and political significance; and it suggests one avenue that constitutional challenges to a national curriculum might take in the future. In constitutional law, a fundamental liberty such as the freedom of belief and expression may not be abridged by a legislative enactment unless a compelling justification for doing so exists. Part of a court's decision as to whether a government has advanced such a compelling justification rests on an inquiry as to whether the goals of the challenged legislation could be achieved by a legislative program less restrictive of the fundamental liberties at stake. If such a "less restrictive alternative" is practical, the challenged legislation will be judged unconstitutional even if there is an otherwise compelling justification for it.

Rebuilding the instructional infrastructure of U.S. schools could do much more to improve the quality of learning than would a top-down prescription of content by political bodies—without the damage to liberty, diversity, independence of mind, and teacher professionalism. Reinvigorating teaching, further educating all teachers, and trusting them to do their work at the highest professional level, would hardly be a panacea for the enormous problems confronting the nation's schools. In the long run, though, a teacher-based substitute for national curriculum standards would more effectively accomplish the goal of reducing inequality of opportunity and educating students for global competitiveness. Equally important, it would preserve the rights of individuals, families, and communities to judge for themselves—free of government manipulation—what constitutes useful schooling, acceptable personal goals, and a meaningful life in a pluralistic society. The First Amendment —and the principles of constitutional democracy—should entitle each of us to no less.

POSTSCRIPT

Should National Goals and Standards Guide School Reform?

Ernest Boyer, president of the Carnegie Foundation for the Advancement of Teaching, in "Educational Goals: An Action Plan," *Vital Speeches of the Day* (June 1, 1990), states, "We are moving in this country from a local to a national view of education and we need better arrangements to guide the way.... The challenge is to develop a *national* agenda for school renewal while retaining leadership at the state and local levels." But Allen C. Ornstein, in "A Message to the President," *The Educational Forum* (Fall 1993), asserts that a new and ominous consensus is developing—one that promotes national needs and goals above local or pluralistic needs and goals, and that seeks a common core of subjects, content, and values to be imposed.

These and other aspects of the issue are discussed from a variety of viewpoints in the following articles: Evan Clinchy, "Needed: A Clinton Crusade for Quality and Equality," *Phi Delta Kappan* (April 1993); Elliot W. Eisner, "Should America Have a National Curriculum?" *Educational Leadership* (October 1991); "National Priorities for Education: A Conversation With U.S. Secretary of Education Richard W. Riley," *National Forum* (Fall 1993); Diane Ravitch, "National Standards and Curriculum Reform," *NASSP Bulletin* (December 1992); Larry Cuban, "How Can a 'National Strategy' Miss a Third of Our Schools?" *Principal* (September 1993); and "The Six National Goals: A Road to Disappointment," *Phi Delta Kappan* (May 1994).

Additional insight into the politics of school reform can be found in New York senator Daniel Patrick Moynihan's "Educational Goals and Political Plans," *The Public Interest* (Winter 1991), and in the books of education scholar Joel Spring, particularly his 1988 work *Conflict of Interest: The Politics of American Education*.

For information about the process of school reform and for specific ideas for bringing reform, see *Making Schools Better* by Larry Martz (1992), especially chapter 1, "Revolution in Small Bites"; *Educational Renaissance: Our Schools at the Turn of the Twenty-First Century* by Marvin Cetron and Margaret Gayle (1991); *We Must Take Charge: Our Schools and Our Future* by Chester E. Finn, Jr. (1991); *Smart Schools, Smart Kids: Why Do Some Schools Work?* by Edward B. Fiske (1991); George H. Wood, *Schools That Work: America's Most Innovative Public Educational Programs* (1992); and Theodore Sizer, *Horace's School: Redesigning the American High School* (1992).

PART 2

Specific Issues

In this section, the issues debated probe concerns that currently face educators and policymakers. How these debates are resolved will affect the future direction of education in our society.

- Can "Choice" Lead the Way to Educational Reform?

- Are Religious Fundamentalists Damaging Public Education?

- Are Major Policy Changes Needed to Fight Gender Bias in the Schools?

- Is Full Inclusion of Disabled Students Desirable?

- Do Black Students Need an Afrocentric Curriculum?

- Should Bilingual Education Programs Be Abandoned?

- Does Tracking Create Educational Inequality?

- Do "Discipline Programs" Promote Ethical Behavior?

- Are Current Sex Education Programs Lacking in Moral Guidance?

- Should Schools Offer Condoms to Students?

- Can Outcome-Based Education Transform America's Schools?

- Is Mandatory Community Service Desirable and Legal?

ISSUE 10

Can "Choice" Lead the Way to Educational Reform?

YES: John E. Chubb and Terry M. Moe, from "America's Public Schools: Choice *Is* a Panacea," *The Brookings Review* (Summer 1990)

NO: Frances C. Fowler, from "The Shocking Ideological Integrity of Chubb and Moe," *Journal of Education* (Spring 1991)

ISSUE SUMMARY

YES: Political science researchers John E. Chubb and Terry M. Moe, authors of the much-discussed *Politics, Markets, and America's Schools*, make the case for choice as a means of true reform.

NO: Frances C. Fowler of Miami University in Oxford, Ohio, analyzes the premises underlying the proposals of Chubb and Moe and finds an antidemocratic tone.

One of the more heated educational debates in recent years has been the one concerned with finding ways to provide parents and learners with a greater range of choices in schooling. Some people see the public school system as a monolithic structure that runs roughshod over individual inclinations and imposes a rigid social philosophy on its constituents. Others feel that the reduced quality of public education, particularly in large urban areas, demands that parents be given support in their quest for better learning environments. Still others agree with sociologist James S. Coleman's contention that "the greater the constraints imposed on school attendance—short of dictating place of residence and prohibiting attendance at private schools—the greater the educational gap between those who have the money to escape the constraints and those who do not."

Measures that emphasize freedom of choice abound and are often connected with desegregation and school reform goals. Some jurisdictions have developed a system of magnet schools to serve the dual purposes of equality and quality; some districts now allow parents to send their children to any public school under their control; and a few urban districts (notably Milwaukee and Kansas City) are experimenting with funding plans to allow private school alternatives.

Two of the much-discussed ideas of dealing with this last possibility are tuition tax credits and voucher plans. The first, provided by the federal, state, or local government, would expand the number of families able to send their children to the school of their choice and would, according to advocates, improve the quality of public schooling by encouraging competition. Voucher plans, first suggested in 1955 by conservative economist Milton Friedman, are designed to return tax monies to parents of school-aged children for use in a variety of authorized public and private educational settings. Opponents of either approach take the position that such moves will turn the public schools into an enclave of the poor and will lead to further racial, socioeconomic class, and religious isolation. The question of church-state separation looms large in the minds of those who oppose these measures.

In the Brookings Institution study *Politics, Markets, and America's Schools*, John E. Chubb and Terry M. Moe contend that market-driven choice is the most potent means of bringing about true school reform. This research has given rise to a number of entrepreneurial efforts, among them entrepreneur Christopher Whittle's "Edison Project" (a proposed nationwide system of private schools) and Educational Alternatives, Inc. (a private enterprise that attempts to rescue poor-quality public schools). The "choice" ideology has also bolstered parental desires to engage in home schooling. In many ways, the nation seems to be moving toward a blending of the private and public domains in the field of education.

In the selections that follow, Chubb and Moe present the basic assumptions that undergird their analysis of the ills of the public schools and offer a set of recommendations to rejuvenate the process of education in the United States. Frances C. Fowler offers a point-by-point critique of the suggestions made by Chubb and Moe and an incisive interpretation of their ideological bias.

YES

John E. Chubb and
Terry M. Moe

AMERICA'S PUBLIC SCHOOLS: CHOICE *IS* A PANACEA

For America's public schools, the last decade has been the worst of times and the best of times. Never before have the public schools been subjected to such savage criticism for failing to meet the nation's educational needs—yet never before have governments been so aggressively dedicated to studying the schools' problems and finding the resources for solving them.

The signs of poor performance were there for all to see during the 1970s. Test scores headed downward year after year. Large numbers of teenagers continued to drop out of school. Drugs and violence poisoned the learning environment. In math and science, two areas crucial to the nation's success in the world economy, American students fell far behind their counterparts in virtually every other industrialized country. Something was clearly wrong.

During the 1980s a growing sense of crisis fueled a powerful movement for educational change, and the nation's political institutions responded with aggressive reforms. State after state increased spending on schools, imposed tougher requirements, introduced more rigorous testing, and strengthened teacher certification and training. And, as the decade came to an end, creative experiments of various forms—from school-based management to magnet schools—were being launched around the nation.

We think these reforms are destined to fail. They simply do not get to the root of the problem. The fundamental causes of poor academic performance are not to be found in the schools, but rather in the institutions by which the schools have traditionally been governed. Reformers fail by automatically relying on these institutions to solve the problem—when the institutions are the problem.

The key to better schools, therefore, is institutional reform. What we propose is a new system of public education that eliminates most political and bureaucratic control over the schools and relies instead on indirect control through markets and parental choice. These new institutions naturally function to promote and nurture the kinds of effective schools that reformers have wanted all along.

SCHOOLS AND INSTITUTIONS

Three basic questions lie at the heart of our analysis. What is the relationship between school organization and student achievement? What are the conditions that promote or inhibit desirable forms of organization? And how are these conditions affected by their institutional settings?

Our perspective on school organization and student achievement is in agreement with the most basic claims and findings of the "effective schools" literature, which served as the analytical base of the education reform movement throughout the 1980s. We believe, as most others do, that how much students learn is not determined simply by their aptitude or family background—although, as we show, these are certainly influential—but also by how effectively schools are organized. By our estimates, the typical high school student tends to learn considerably more, comparable to at least an extra year's worth of study, when he or she attends a high school that is effectively organized rather than one that is not.

Generally speaking, effective schools— be they public or private—have the kinds of organizational characteristics that the mainstream literature would lead one to expect: strong leadership, clear and ambitious goals, strong academic programs, teacher professionalism, shared influence, and staff harmony, among other things. These are best understood as integral parts of a coherent syndrome of organization. When this syndrome is viewed as a functioning whole, moreover, it seems to capture the essential features of what people normally mean by a team—principals and teachers working together, cooperatively and informally, in pursuit of a common mission.

How do these kinds of schools develop and take root? Here again, our own perspective dovetails with a central theme of educational analysis and criticism: the dysfunctions of bureaucracy, the value of autonomy, and the inherent tension between the two in American public education. Bureaucracy vitiates the most basic requirements of effective organization. It imposes goals, structures, and requirements that tell principals and teachers what to do and how to do it—denying them not only the discretion they need to exercise their expertise and professional judgment but also the flexibility they need to develop and operate as teams. The key to effective education rests with unleashing the productive potential already present in the schools and their personnel. It rests with granting them the autonomy to do what they do best. As our study of American high schools documents, the freer schools are from external control the more likely they are to have effective organizations.

Only at this late stage of the game do we begin to part company with the mainstream. While most observers can agree that the public schools have become too bureaucratic and would benefit from substantial grants of autonomy, it is also the standard view that this transformation can be achieved within the prevailing framework of democratic control. The implicit assumption is that, although political institutions have acted in the past to bureaucratize, they can now be counted upon to reverse course, grant the schools autonomy, and support and nurture this new population of autonomous schools. Such an assumption, however, is not based on a systematic understanding of how these institutions operate and what their consequences are for schools.

POLITICAL INSTITUTIONS

Democratic governance of the schools is built around the imposition of higher-order values through public authority. As long as that authority exists and is available for use, public officials will come under intense pressure from social groups of all political stripes to use it. And when they do use it, they cannot blithely assume that their favored policies will be faithfully implemented by the heterogeneous population of principals and teachers below—whose own values and professional views may be quite different from those being imposed. Public officials have little choice but to rely on formal rules and regulations that tell these people what to do and hold them accountable for doing it.

These pressures for bureaucracy are so substantial in themselves that real school autonomy has little chance to take root throughout the system. But they are not the only pressures for bureaucracy. They are compounded by the political uncertainty inherent in all democratic politics: those who exercise public authority know that other actors with different interests may gain authority in the future and subvert the policies they worked so hard to put in place. This knowledge gives them additional incentive to embed their policies in protective bureaucratic arrangements—arrangements that reduce the discretion of schools and formally insulate them from the dangers of politics.

These pressures, arising from the basic properties of democratic control, are compounded yet again by another special feature of the public sector. Its institutions provide a regulated, politically sensitive setting conducive to the power of unions, and unions protect the interests of their members through formal constraints on the governance and operation of schools—constraints that strike directly at the schools' capacity to build well-functioning teams based on informal cooperation.

The major participants in democratic governance—including the unions—complain that the schools are too bureaucratic. And they mean what they say. But they are the ones who bureaucratized the schools in the past, and they will continue to do so, even as they tout the great advantages of autonomy and professionalism. The incentives to bureaucratize the schools are built into the system.

MARKET INSTITUTIONS

This kind of behavior is not something that Americans simply have to accept, like death and taxes. People who make decisions about education would behave differently if their institutions were different. The most relevant and telling comparison is to markets, since it is through democratic control and markets that American society makes most of its choices on matters of public importance, including education. Public schools are subject to direct control through politics. But not all schools are controlled in this way. Private schools—representing about a fourth of all schools—are subject to indirect control through markets.

What difference does it make? Our analysis suggests that the difference is considerable and that it arises from the most fundamental properties that distinguish the two systems. A market system is not built to enable the imposition of higher-order values on the schools, nor is it driven by a democratic struggle to exercise public authority. Instead, the authority to make educational choices is radically decentralized to those most immediately involved. Schools compete for the support of parents and students, and parents and students are free to choose among schools. The system is built on decentralization, competition, and choice.

Although schools operating under a market system are free to organize any way they want, bureaucratization tends to be an unattractive way to go. Part of the reason is that virtually everything about good education—from the knowledge and talents necessary to produce it, to what it looks like when it is produced—defies formal measurement through the standardized categories of bureaucracy.

The more basic point, however, is that bureaucratic control and its clumsy efforts to measure the unmeasurable are simply *unnecessary* for schools whose primary concern is to please their clients. To do this, they need to perform as effectively as possible, which leads them, given the bottom-heavy technology of education, to favor decentralized forms of organization that take full advantage of strong leadership, teacher professionalism, discretionary judgment, informal cooperation, and teams. They also need to ensure that they provide the kinds of services parents and students want and that they have the capacity to cater and adjust to their clients' specialized needs and interests, which this same syndrome of effective organization allows them to do exceedingly well.

Schools that operate in an environment of competition and choice thus have strong incentives to move toward the kinds of "effective-school" organizations that academics and reformers would like to impose on the public schools. Of course, not all schools in the market will respond equally well to these incentives. But those that falter will find it more difficult to attract support, and they will tend to be weeded out in favor of schools that are better organized. This process of natural selection complements the incentives of the marketplace in propelling and supporting a population of autonomous, effectively organized schools. . . .

INSTITUTIONAL CONSEQUENCES

No institutional system can be expected to work perfectly under real-world conditions. Just as democratic institutions cannot offer perfect representation or perfect implementation of public policy, so markets cannot offer perfect competition or perfect choice. But these imperfections, which are invariably the favorite targets of each system's critics, tend to divert attention from what is most crucial to an understanding of schools: as institutional systems, democratic control and market control are strikingly different in their fundamental properties. As a result, each system structures individual and social choices about education very differently, and each has very different consequences for the organization and performance of schools. Each system puts its own indelible stamp on the schools that emerge and operate within it.

What the analysis in our book suggests, in the most practical terms, is that American society offers two basic paths to the emergence of effective schools. The first is through markets, which scarcely operate in the public sector, but which act on private schools to discourage bureaucracy and promote desirable forms of organization through the natural dynamics of competition and choice.

The second path is through "special circumstances,"—homogeneous environments free of problems—which, in minimizing the three types of political pressures just discussed, prompt democratic governing institutions to impose less bureaucracy than they otherwise would. Private schools therefore tend to be effectively organized because of the way their system naturally works. When public schools happen to be effectively organized, it is in spite of their system— they are the lucky ones with peculiarly nice environments.

As we show in our book, the power of these institutional forces is graphically reflected in our sample of American high schools. Having cast our net widely to allow for a full range of noninstitutional factors that might reasonably be suspected of influencing school autonomy, we found that virtually all of them fall by the wayside. The extent to which a school is granted the autonomy it needs to develop a more effective organization is overwhelmingly determined by its sectoral location and the niceness of its institutional environment.

Viewed as a whole, then, our effort to take institutions into account builds systematically on mainstream ideas and findings but, in the end, puts a very different slant on things. We agree that effective organization is a major determinant of student achievement. We also agree that schools perform better the more autonomous they are and the less encumbered they are by bureaucracy. But we do not agree that this knowledge about the proximate causes of effective performance can be used to engineer better schools through democratic control. Reformers are right about where they want to go, but their institutions cannot get them there.

The way to get schools with effective organizations is not to insist that democratic institutions should do what they are incapable of doing. Nor is it to assume that the better public schools, the lucky ones with the nice environments, can serve as organizational models for the rest. Their luck is not transferable. The way to get effective schools is to recognize that the problem of ineffective performance is really a deep-seated institutional problem that arises from the most fundamental properties of democratic control.

The most sensible approach to genuine education reform is therefore to move toward a true institutional solution a different set of institutional arrangements that actively promotes and nurtures the kinds of schools people want. The market alternative then becomes particularly attractive, for it provides a setting in which these organizations take root and flourish. That is where "choice" comes in.

EDUCATIONAL CHOICE

It is fashionable these days to say that choice is "not a panacea." Taken literally, that is obviously true. There are no panaceas in social policy. But the message this aphorism really means to get across is that choice is just one of many reforms with something to contribute. School-based management is another. So are teacher empowerment and professionalism, better training programs, stricter accountability, and bigger budgets. These and other types of reforms all bolster school effectiveness in their own distinctive ways—so the reasoning goes— and the best, most aggressive, most comprehensive approach to transforming the public school system is therefore one that wisely combines them into a multifaceted reformist package.

Without being too literal about it, we think reformers would do well to entertain the notion that choice *is* a panacea. Of all the sundry education reforms that attract attention, only choice has the capacity to address the basic institutional problem plaguing America's schools. The other reforms are all system-preserving. The schools remain subordinates in the structure of public authority—and they remain bureaucratic.

In principle, choice offers a clear, sharp break from the institutional past. In practice, however, it has been forced into the same mold with all the other reforms. It has been embraced half-heartedly and in bits and pieces— for example, through magnet schools and limited open enrollment plans. It has served as a means of granting parents and students a few additional options or of giving schools modest incentives to compete. These are popular moves that can be accomplished without changing the existing system in any fundamental way. But by treating choice like other system-preserving reforms that presumably make democratic control work better, reformers completely miss what choice is all about.

Choice is not like the other reforms and should not be combined with them. Choice is a self-contained reform with its own rationale and justification. It has the capacity *all by itself* to bring about the kind of transformation that reformers have been seeking to engineer for years in myriad other ways. Indeed, if choice is to work to greatest advantage, it must be adopted *without* these other reforms, since they are predicated on democratic control and are implemented by bureaucratic means. The whole point of a thoroughgoing system of choice is to free the schools from these disabling constraints by sweeping away the old institutions and replacing them with new ones. Taken seriously, choice is not a system-preserving reform. It is a revolutionary reform that introduces a new system of public education.

A PROPOSAL FOR REAL REFORM

The following outline describes a choice system that we think is equipped to do the job. Offering our own proposal allows us to illustrate in some detail what a full-blown choice system might look like, as well as to note some of the policy decisions that must be made in building one. More important, it allows us to suggest what our institutional theory of schools actually entails for educational reform.

Our guiding principle in the design of a choice system is this: public authority must be put to use in creating a system that is almost entirely beyond the reach of public authority. Because states have primary responsibility for American public education, we think the best way to achieve significant, enduring reform is for states to take the initiative in withdrawing authority from existing institutions and vesting it directly in the schools, parents, and students. This restructuring cannot be construed as an exercise in delegation. As long as authority remains "available" at higher levels within state government, it will eventually be used to control the schools. As far as possible, all higher-level authority must be eliminated.

What we propose, more specifically, is that state leaders create a new system of public education with the following properties.

The Supply of Schools

The state will be responsible for setting criteria that define what constitutes a "public school" under the new system. These criteria should be minimal, roughly corresponding to the criteria many states now use in accrediting private schools—graduation requirements, health and safety requirements, and teacher certification requirements. Any educational group or organization that applies to the state and meets these minimal criteria must then be chartered as a public school and granted the right to accept students and receive public money.

Existing private schools will be among those eligible to participate. Their participation should be encouraged, because they constitute a supply of already effective schools. Our own preference would be to include religious schools too, as long as their sectarian functions can be kept clearly separate from their educational functions. Private schools that do participate will thereby become public schools, as such schools are defined under the new choice system.

School districts can continue running their present schools, assuming those schools meet state criteria. But districts will have authority over only their own schools and not over any of the others that may be chartered by the state.

Funding

The state will set up a Choice Office in each district, which, among other things, will maintain a record of all school-age children and the level of funding— the "scholarship" amounts—associated with each child. This office will directly compensate schools based on the specific children they enroll. Public money will flow from funding sources (federal, state, and district governments) to the Choice Office and then to schools. At no point will it go to parents or students.

The state must pay to support its own Choice Office in each district. Districts may retain as much of their current governing apparatus as they wish— superintendents, school boards, central offices, and all their staff. But they have to pay for them entirely out of the revenue they derive from the scholarships of those children who voluntarily choose to attend district-run schools. Aside from the governance of these schools, which no one need attend, districts will be little more than taxing jurisdictions that allow citizens to make a collective determination about how large their children's scholarships will be.

As it does now, the state will have the right to specify how much, or by what formula, each district must contribute for each child. Our preference is for an equalization approach that requires wealthier districts to contribute more per child than poor districts do and that guarantees an adequate financial foundation to students in all districts. The state's contribution can then be calibrated to bring total spending per child up to whatever dollar amount seems desirable; under an equalization scheme, that would mean a larger state contribution in poor districts than in wealthy ones.

While parents and students should be given as much flexibility as possible, we think it is unwise to allow them to supplement their scholarship amounts with personal funds. Such "add-ons" threaten to produce too many disparities and inequalities within the public system, and many citizens would regard them as unfair and burdensome.

Complete equalization, on the other hand, strikes us as too stifling and restrictive. A reasonable trade-off is to allow collective add-ons, much as the current system does. The citizens of each district can be given the freedom to decide whether they want to spend more per child than the state requires them to spend. They can then determine how important education is to them and how much they are willing to tax themselves for it. As a result, children from different districts may have different-sized scholarships.

Scholarships may also vary within any given district, and we strongly think that they should. Some students have very special educational needs—arising from economic deprivation, physical handicaps, language difficulties, emotional problems, and other disadvantages—that can be met effectively only through costly specialized programs. State and federal programs already appropriate public money to address these problems. Our suggestion is that these funds should take the form of add-ons to student scholarships. At-risk students would then be empowered with bigger scholarships than the others, making them attractive clients to all schools—and stimulating the emergence of new specialty schools.

Choice Among Schools
Each student will be free to attend any public school in the state, regardless of district, with the student's scholarship —consisting of federal, state, and local contributions—flowing to the school of choice. In practice most students will probably choose schools in reasonable proximity to their homes. But districts will have no claim on their own residents.

To the extent that tax revenues allow, every effort will be made to provide transportation for students who need it. This provision is important to help open up as many alternatives as possible to all students, especially the poor and those in rural areas.

To assist parents and students in choosing among schools, the state will provide a Parent Information Center within its local Choice Office. This center will collect comprehensive information on each school in the district, and its parent liaisons will meet personally with parents in helping them judge which schools best meet their children's needs. The emphasis here will be on personal contact and involvement. Parents will be required to visit the center at least once, and encouraged to do so often. Meetings will be arranged at all schools so that parents can see firsthand what their choices are.

The Parent Information Center will handle the applications process in a simple fashion. Once parents and students decide which schools they prefer, they will fill out applications to each, with parent liaisons available to give advice and assistance and to fill out the applications themselves (if necessary). All applications will be submitted to the Center, which in turn will send them out to the schools.

Schools will make their own admissions decisions, subject only to nondiscrimination requirements. This step is absolutely crucial. Schools must be able to define their own missions and build their own programs in their own ways, and they cannot do that if their student population is thrust on them by outsiders.

Schools must be free to admit as many or as few students as they want, based on whatever criteria they think relevant— intelligence, interest, motivation, special needs—and they must be free to exercise their own, informal judgments about individual applicants. Schools will set their own "tuitions." They may choose to do so explicitly, say, by publicly announcing the minimum scholarship they are willing to accept. They may also do it implicitly by allowing anyone to apply for admission and simply making selections, knowing in advance what each applicant's scholarship amount is. In either case, schools are free to admit students with different-sized scholarships, and they are free to keep the entire scholarship that accompanies each student they have admitted. That gives all schools incentives to attract students with special needs, since these children will have the largest scholarships. It also gives schools incentives to attract students from districts with high base-level scholarships. But no school need restrict itself to students with special needs, nor to students from a single district.

The application process must take place within a framework that guarantees each student a school, as well as a fair shot at getting into the school he or she most wants. That framework, however, should impose only the most minimal restrictions on the schools.

We suggest something like the following. The Parent Information Center will be responsible for seeing that parents and students are informed, that they have visited the schools that interest them, and that all applications are submitted by a given date. Schools will then be required to make their admissions decisions within a set time, and students who are accepted into more than one school will be required to select one as their final choice. Students who are not accepted anywhere, as well as schools that have yet to attract as many students as they want, will participate in a second round of applications, which will work the same way.

After this second round, some students may remain without schools. At this point, parent liaisons will take informal action to try to match up these students with appropriate schools. If any students still remain unassigned, a special safety-net procedure—a lottery, for example—will be invoked to ensure that each is assigned to a specific school.

As long as they are not "arbitrary and capricious," schools must also be free to expel students or deny them readmission when, based on their own experience and standards, they believe the situation warrants it. This authority is essential if schools are to define and control their own organizations, and it gives students a strong incentive to live up to their side of the educational "contract."

Governance and Organization

Each school must be granted sole authority to determine its own governing structure. A school may be run entirely by teachers or even a union. It may vest all power in a principal. It may be built around committees that guarantee representation to the principal, teachers, parents, students, and members of the community. Or it may do something completely different.

The state must refrain from imposing *any* structures or requirements that specify how authority is to be exercised within individual schools. This includes the district-run schools: the state must not impose any governing apparatus on them either. These schools, however, are subordinate units within district government—they are already embedded in a larger organization—and it is the district authorities, not the schools, that have the legal right to determine how they will be governed.

More generally, the state will do nothing to tell the schools how they must be internally organized to do their work. The state will not set requirements for career ladders, advisory committees, textbook selection, in-service training, preparation time, homework, or anything else. Each school will be organized and operated as it sees fit.

Statewide tenure laws will be eliminated, allowing each school to decide for itself whether or not to adopt a tenure policy and what the specifics of that policy will be. This change is essential if schools are to have the flexibility they need to build well-functioning teams. Some schools may not offer tenure at all, relying on pay and working conditions to attract the kinds of teachers they want, while others may offer tenure as a supplementary means of compensating and retaining their best teachers.

Teachers, meantime, may demand tenure in their negotiations (individual or collective) with schools. And, as in private colleges and universities, the best teachers are well positioned to get it, since their services will be valued by any number of other schools. School districts may continue to offer districtwide tenure, along with transfer rights, seniority preference, and whatever other personnel policies they have offered in the past. But these policies apply only to district-run schools and the teachers who work in them.

Teachers will continue to have a right to join unions and engage in collective bargaining, but the legally prescribed bargaining unit will be the individual school or, as in the case of the district government, the larger organization that runs the school. If teachers in a given school want to join a union or, having done so, want to

exact financial or structural concessions, that is up to them. But they cannot commit teachers in other schools, unless they are in other district-run schools, to the same things, and they must suffer the consequences if their victories put them at a competitive disadvantage in supplying quality education.

The state will continue to certify teachers, but requirements will be minimal, corresponding to those that many states have historically applied to private schools. In our view, individuals should be certified to teach if they have a bachelor's degree and if their personal history reveals no obvious problems. Whether they are truly good teachers will be determined in practice, as schools decide whom to hire, observe their own teachers in action over an extended period of time, and make decisions regarding merit, promotion, and dismissal.

The schools may, as a matter of strategy, choose to pay attention to certain formal indicators of past or future performance, among them: a master's degree, completion of a voluntary teacher certification program at an education school, or voluntary certification by a national board. Some schools may choose to require one or more of these, or perhaps to reward them in various ways. But that is up to the schools, which will be able to look anywhere for good teachers in a now much larger and more dynamic market.

The state will hold the schools accountable for meeting certain procedural requirements. It will ensure that schools continue to meet the criteria set out in their charters, that they adhere to nondiscrimination laws in admissions and other matters, and that they collect and make available to the public, through the Parent Information Center, information on their mission, their staff and course offerings, standardized test scores (which we would make optional), parent and student satisfaction, staff opinions, and anything else that would promote informed choice among parents and students.

The state will not hold the schools accountable for student achievement or other dimensions that call for assessments of the quality of school performance. When it comes to performance, schools will be held accountable from below, by parents and students who directly experience their services and are free to choose. The state will play a crucial supporting role here in monitoring the full and honest disclosure of information by the schools—but it will be only a supporting role.

CHOICE AS A PUBLIC SYSTEM

This proposal calls for fundamental changes in the structure of American public education. Stereotypes aside, however, these changes have nothing to do with "privatizing" the nation's schools. The choice system we outline would be a truly public system—and a democratic one.

We are proposing that the state put its democratic authority to use in creating a new institutional framework. The design and legitimation of this framework would be a democratic act of the most basic sort. It would be a social decision, made through the usual processes of democratic governance, by which the people and their representatives specify the structure of a new system of public education.

This framework, as we set it out, is quite flexible and admits of substantial variation on important issues, all of them matters of public policy to be decided by representative government. Public officials and their constituents would be free to take their own approaches to taxation, equalization, treatment of religious schools, additional funding for disadvantaged students, parent add-ons, and other controversial issues of public concern, thus designing choice systems to reflect the unique conditions, preferences, and political forces of their own states.

Once this structural framework is democratically determined, moreover, governments would continue to play important roles within it. State officials and agencies would remain pivotal to the success of public education and to its ongoing operation. They would provide funding, approve applications for new schools, orchestrate and oversee the choice process, elicit full information about schools, provide transportation to students, monitor schools for adherence to the law, and (if they want) design and administer tests of student performance. School districts, meantime, would continue as local taxing jurisdictions, and they would have the option of continuing to operate their own system of schools.

The crucial difference is that direct democratic control of the schools—the very *capacity* for control, not simply its exercise—would essentially be eliminated. Most of those who previously held authority over the schools would have their authority permanently withdrawn, and that authority would be vested in schools, parents, and students. Schools would be legally autonomous: free to govern themselves as they want, specify their own goals and programs and methods, design their own organizations, select their own student bodies, and make their own personnel decisions. Parents and students would be legally empowered to choose among alternative schools, aided by institutions designed to promote active involvement, well-informed decisions, and fair treatment.

DEMOCRACY AND EDUCATIONAL PROGRESS

We do not expect everyone to accept the argument we have made here. In fact, we expect most of those who speak with authority on educational matters, leaders and academics within the educational community, to reject it. But we will regard our effort as a success if it directs attention to America's institutions of democratic control and provokes serious debate about their consequences for the nation's public schools. Whether or not our own conclusions are right, the fact is that these issues are truly basic to an understanding of schools, and they have so far played no part in the national debate. If educational reform is to have any chance at all of succeeding, that has to change.

In the meantime, we can only believe that the current "revolution" in public education will prove a disappointment. It might have succeeded had it actually been a revolution, but it was not and was never intended to be, despite the lofty rhetoric. Revolutions replace old institutions with new ones. The 1980s reform movement never seriously thought about the old institutions and certainly never considered them part of the problem. They were, as they had always been, part of the solution—and, for that matter, part of the definition of what democracy and public education are all about.

This identification has never been valid. Nothing in the concept of democracy requires that schools be subject to direct control by school boards, superintendents, central offices, departments of education, and other arms of government. Nor does anything in the concept of public education require that schools be governed in this way. There are many paths to democracy and public education. The path America has been trodding for the past half-century is exacting a heavy price—one the nation and its children can ill afford to bear, and need not. It is time, we think, to get to the root of the problem.

NO

Frances C. Fowler

THE SHOCKING IDEOLOGICAL
INTEGRITY OF CHUBB AND MOE

In the fall of 1990, John Chubb and Terry Moe's book—still called by what was apparently its pre-publication title of *What Price Democracy? Politics, Markets, and America's Schools*—was debated at a national education conference. The debate itself was tame. A carefully neutral moderator introduced the speakers and provided smooth transitions between them. The first speaker, an education professor at a prestigious private university, praised the book and announced his agreement with its policy proposals. The second, an education professor at a less prestigious private university, called it the most important book on education in a decade. He regretted only that the authors "bashed democracy over the head." The third was less positive: he criticized Chubb and Moe's statistics and found them wanting. Only the fourth suggested that both Chubb and Moe's premises and their conclusions were questionable.

After the debate, the floor was opened to audience participation. The room became hot, both physically and emotionally. One man blurted that he considered the book "a conclusion in search of an analysis." Several others raised questions about desegregation, education of the handicapped, and the selectivity of private schools. Yet the anger in the room remained largely inchoate and inarticulate. Afterward, muttered arguing could be heard in the halls and elevators.

At the end of this review I will seek to explain the reactions of both the panel and the audience. But first I will have to explain what is really going on in Chubb and Moe's book. In doing so, I will not analyze their statistics; others have done that. Nor will I discuss how the implementation of their proposal would affect equity in American education although that is important. Rather, I will focus on their ideology. I will describe how it shapes and misshapes their book. I will also discuss its meaning for American education. First, however, I will summarize their major argument.

THE ARGUMENT OF THE BOOK

Chubb and Moe begin *Politics, Markets, and America's Schools* with a discussion of the current education reform movement. Uncritically accepting the premise

From Frances C. Fowler, "The Shocking Ideological Integrity of Chubb and Moe," *Journal of Education*, vol. 173, no. 3 (Summer 1991). Copyright © 1991 by the Trustees of Boston University. Reprinted by permission.

that it is the poor quality of public education which has caused the United States to become uncompetitive in the international economy, they announce that all reforms proposed to date will fail because they do not attack the root problem. The *real* problem, as they see it, is the institutions which govern public education. In their words:

> Our analysis shows that the system's familiar arrangements for direct democratic control do indeed impose a distinctive structure on the educational choices of all the various participants—and that this structure tends to promote organizational characteristics that are ill-suited to the effective performance of American public schools. (p. 21)

In Chapter 2 Chubb and Moe elaborate on their theory. As public institutions, public schools are naturally political, bureaucratic, coercive, hierarchical, and filled with conflict. Pulled in many directions by interest groups and labor unions, they cannot possibly educate children well. In contrast, private schools are subject to market forces which encourage responsiveness to their "clientele." Their decentralized autonomy, "social homogeneity," and strong principals permit them to organize effectively. Thus, they successfully educate their students.

The next three chapters describe Chubb and Moe's research. Using data from the High School and Beyond survey of the early 1980s and their own Administrator and Teacher Survey, they ran a series of regression analyses and other statistical tests. Their findings are displayed in 49 tables. On the strength of this analysis, they conclude that private schools perform better than public ones and that their superiority is related to their organizational characteristics.

The last chapter contains Chubb and Moe's policy proposal. They advocate abolishing the democratic governance of public schools. In its place a choice program should be established. Although the authors do not use the word "voucher," in essence they propose an unregulated voucher plan. All schools— public and private—which met "minimal criteria" would participate. Parents would receive "scholarships" for their children. These could be used at any school willing to accept their children as students. Schools would be free to develop their own admissions criteria (subject to nondiscrimination rules), establish their own tuition fees, and expel students. Meanwhile, tenure laws would be repealed, and each school would be free to devise its own system of internal governance. Teacher certification requirements would be minimal, and the state would not hold schools accountable for student achievement or any other performance measures. Chubb and Moe are not optimistic that their proposal will be adopted, but they believe that their book will be successful if it "directs attention to America's institutions of democratic control" (p. 228).

THE IDEOLOGICAL CHARACTER OF THE BOOK

In form, *Politics, Markets, and America's Schools* appears to be a scholarly work which has been popularized to appeal to a general, but educated, audience. In the foreword, the president of the Brookings Institution writes that it "is the culmination of a large study" (p. x) and lists five funding agencies. The book contains 49 statistical tables, and its four appendices provide detailed information about technical aspects of the study's methodology. The 254 footnotes cite most of the major relevant works in the areas of politics of education, effective schools, and political science.

Like most scholarly works this book includes a theoretical framework. The authors never identify their theory by name. Among political scientists, however, Moe is considered a "peripheral member of the rational choice school" (Almond, 1990, p. 127). Rational choice theorists, assuming that political institutions function like markets and that individuals seek to maximize their material interests, use economic models to analyze politics. They distrust political processes and consider markets more efficient (Almond, 1990).

These beliefs are evident in Chubb and Moe's development of their theory. They argue that democratic control of education leads to bureaucracy, hierarchy, and inefficiency. In contrast, markets encourage autonomy, discretion, diversity, and responsiveness. They are therefore more efficient than politically controlled systems. Chubb and Moe elaborate upon their theory by adding to it some elements of Social Darwinism. Market systems perform a type of "natural selection," so that only the best organizations "survive," (p. 33). They also "promote desirable forms of organization through the natural dynamics of competition and choice" (p. 190). Of course, this theory closely resembles what Bruce Cooper (1988) labels neoconservative ideology.

Genuine scholars use theoretical frameworks to give coherence and meaning to their inquiry, but they do not allow their theories to become intellectual blinders. Rather, they test them by bringing them into contact with real phenomena. When the evidence disconfirms their theories, they modify or abandon them. In *Politics, Markets, and America's Schools*, however, Chubb and Moe repeatedly evade evidence which might raise doubts about the validity of their theory. Numerous examples could be cited, but this discussion will be limited to three: their handling of the nature of private education, their handling of international comparisons, and their handling of the social context of schools.

The authors never define "public" or "private" (the lack of careful definitions is a pervasive problem in the book), but their theory leads them to assume that public and private schools are very different. Because public institutions seek to "impose" "higher-order values" (p. 62) upon society, they inevitably become bureaucratic and hierarchical. In contrast, private institutions are free "to find their niche—a specialized segment of the market to which they can appeal" (p. 55). Since much of the book extols private schools and their organizational strengths, one would expect to find some details about private education in it. At the very least, one would expect some discussion of its demographic characteristics. Such information is lacking. The most detailed descriptions are provided in two brief passages:

> About half of all private schools are Catholic, and the rest are a diverse lot of religious schools, college preparatory schools, military academies, schools for children with special problems or talents, and many other types of schools as well. (p. 27)

> The authority to control each private school is vested in the school's owner —which may be an individual, a partnership, a church, a corporation, a nonprofit agency, or some other form of organization. (p. 32)

These descriptions suggest considerable diversity among American private schools, an idea consistent with the demands of the authors' theory. These descriptions are, however, inaccurate. When Chubb and Moe's data were collected in the early 1980s, American private education was dominated by religious organizations. Fully 70% of private school students attended Catholic schools; another 22.2% attended Lutheran, Jewish, and Evangelical schools. Other types of schools enrolled a mere 7.8% of the private school population (Erickson, 1985).

American private education is almost exclusively a religious enterprise. One question which Chubb and Moe should therefore have addressed is this one: In what sense are churches "private" institutions? Like "public" institutions, churches hold "higher-order values" which they often seek to impose upon others. Like "public" institutions, their organization is often bureaucratic and hierarchical. Is it possible that the terms "public" and "private" are not as sharply dichotomous as Chubb and Moe believe, but rather points on a continuum? If so, where do churches fall on that continuum? It is arguable that, in comparing public and private schools, the authors actually compared similar organizations. It is also arguable that the slightly higher achievement scores of private school students result, not from the natural dynamics of market forces, but from the strong religious commitment of private school teachers, administrators, parents, and students. Chubb and Moe do not address these issues. Their theory blinds them to such possibilities—and also to the real nature of American private education.

In their handling of international comparisons, Chubb and Moe also avoid dealing with facts which might disconfirm their theory. Like many who are concerned about the quality of American public education, they refer to the superior educational performance of such countries as Japan, Germany, and France. They also mention the current inability of the United States to compete effectively in international markets. Such comments seem strangely out of place in this book, for Japan, Germany, and France operate large public school systems which are democratically controlled. Not until page 66 do the authors hint that this fact might pose a problem for their argument. There a number discreetly refers readers to a long footnote, printed on page 289, which reads in part:

> In principle, one should be able to learn... by taking advantage of institutional variation across nations—by comparing, for instance, the American system of public education with the educational systems of Japan or France. This is not our purpose here... an enormous amount of new research would have to be carried out.... American public bureaucracies tend to be far more constraining and formally complex than bureaucracies in parliamentary systems.... Nations are different—and appearances can be deceiving.

Of course, Chubb and Moe cannot have it both ways. If nations are too different to permit comparisons, then they should have refrained from making cross-national comparisons of student achievement and economic performance, in the first place. Once again, they have evaded evidence which would disconfirm their theory that democratically controlled institutions are inherently inefficient. I cannot speak to the Japanese situation, but I have spent considerable time in both French and German schools. A close examination of public education in those countries would reveal organizational structures which combine centralized bureaucracy with participatory democracy at the building level. It would also reveal powerful teachers unions which "co-manage" the school system with administrators. Finally, it would reveal a general belief that public education is more prestigious than private education.

These findings would not fit well within Chubb and Moe's theoretical framework. Instead, they would raise questions such as these: Is the problem in American schools too little democracy rather than too much? Do French and German teachers work better than their American colleagues because their strong unions make them feel empowered and secure? Does the American tendency to denigrate everything public make it difficult for our public schools to command the respect which they need in order to accomplish their mission? Such questions move far beyond the narrow constraints of Chubb and Moe's theory. It is not surprising that they chose not to look at education in other countries.

The real nature of their theory becomes clearest at the end of their discussion of the social context of American public schools. In a 14-page analysis of the causes of student achievement, Chubb and Moe make some important admissions. They acknowledge the importance of family background and of family economic resources. They also admit that causality can be reciprocal—that although school organization can affect student achievement, student characteristics may also cause certain types of school organizations to develop. Possibly they

realized that they would lose credibility if they completely ignored these issues. Then, having made these concessions, they write in a revealing paragraph:

> *We do believe* we have a workable method of analysis.... Despite all we have said about the problem of reciprocal causality, *we believe* that the key influences on student achievement tend to run in one direction. *We believe* that school control affects school organization more than the other way around.... *We also believe* that this causal chain is firmly anchored at the front end by institutions. (p. 114; my italics)

No evidence is provided for these "beliefs." Nor is a logical argument offered in their support. Nothing could be clearer: Chubb and Moe's "theory" is actually a matter of belief. It functions in their book, not as a theory subject to confirmation or disconfirmation by evidence, but as an ideology. In short, their book is not a scholarly work. It is a sophisticated piece of propaganda written to support a policy proposal.

THE ANTIDEMOCRATIC CHARACTER OF THE BOOK

The most disturbing fact about *Politics, Markets, and America's Schools* is neither that it is ideological nor that it is propaganda. The most disturbing fact about it is that it is openly antidemocratic. In all fairness to Chubb and Moe, it must be said that they do not directly attack democracy itself. Rather, they carefully qualify their arguments in order to limit their attack to the democratic control of public education. However, anyone who accepts the premises underlying their attack on the democratic control of public schools can easily extend their argument to all public institutions.

Chubb and Moe's first premise is that the "direct democratic control" of American education causes it to be inefficient. Of course, a major inaccuracy lies at the heart of this premise—American public education is *not* governed by a system of "direct democratic control." Its governance system employs indirect, or representative, democratic structures such as school boards, superintendents, and state legislatures. Chubb and Moe never mention the possibility that more elements of truly *direct* democratic control might solve some of the problems of American schools. Presumably they believe that both direct and representative democratic control share the same weakness: because they impose "higher-order values" on schools they are inefficient.

Unfortunately, Chubb and Moe never identify these "higher-order values." However, a close reading of the book and a careful analysis of what is and is not said suggests that these "higher-order values" include the core democratic values of freedom, equality, and fraternity. For example, the authors advocate the repeal of teacher tenure. Historically, one reason for the passage of tenure laws was to ease political pressures on teachers to teach and live only in those ways which suited their school boards. Since Chubb and Moe never explain how the intellectual and personal freedom of teachers will be protected under their system, it is fair to conclude that such freedoms are probably included among their "higher-order values."

They seem somewhat more concerned about student equality than about teacher freedom; they express some concern about equal educational opportunity. Yet they qualify it with statements like:

"Complete equalization... strikes us as too stifling and restrictive" (p. 220). They also fail to address the problem of unequal resources and how it might affect the ability of parents to choose schools for their children. Because of such qualifications and omissions, one wonders if such policies as desegregation and education of the handicapped fall within the scope of their "higher-order values." Certainly, they say very little about those issues.

The suspicion that their commitment to equality is weak is reinforced by their rejection of the idea that democratic fraternity means learning to live with people different from oneself. Instead, they argue that "social homogeneity" is important to schools' performance because it reduces conflict about goals (pp. 62–63). Again, "social homogeneity" is never clearly defined. Nonetheless, in the total context of the book, one is justified in thinking that it almost certainly includes homogeneity of social class and religious affiliation. It may also include homogeneity of race, ethnicity, and language. In any event, Chubb and Moe seem to understand fraternity as living among one's own kind rather than led to value cultural differences by encountering them during one's formative years.

Although Chubb and Moe never clearly define the "higher-order values" which public education "imposes," they are sure that those values have a negative impact upon the schools. To be precise, the imposition of these values causes undesirable organizational characteristics to develop. These include bureaucracy, unresponsiveness, and goal displacement. The result is inefficiency. They directly link these negative qualities to "democratic control." Nothing can convey the flavor of their critique as well as their own words:

> In this sense, democracy is essentially coercive. The winners get to use public authority to impose their policies on the losers. (p. 28)

> Democracy cannot remedy the mismatch between what parents and students want and what the public schools provide. Conflict and disharmony are built into the system. (p. 34)

> In sum, the politics of democratic control promotes the piece-by-piece construction of a peculiar set of organizational arrangements that are highly bureaucratic. (p. 44)

> The key to understanding why America's public schools are failing is to be found in a deeper understanding of how its traditional institutions of democratic control actually work. The nation is experiencing a crisis in public education not because these democratic institutions have functioned perversely or improperly or unwisely, but because they have functioned quite normally. Democratic control normally produces ineffective schools. This is how it works. (p. 227)

Chubb and Moe could hardly be clearer. The problem is not the way that Americans have understood democracy or the particular set of democratic institutions which Americans have developed. The problem is democracy itself. Democracy is political; it is difficult; it is also inefficient. Clearly, if democratic control "normally produces ineffective schools" (p. 227), one is justified in concluding that Chubb and Moe probably believe that it also produces ineffective cities, states, and nations. In short, democracy is just ineffective.

The second basic premise of the book is that market control systems can remedy most of the flaws in democratic institutions. Although the authors concede that market systems have imperfections, they do not discuss these flaws in depth. Instead, they propose changing the governance of American schools from a political control system to a market control system. The "guiding principle" of this reform would be that "public authority must be put to use in creating a system that is almost entirely beyond the reach of public authority" (p. 218). They recommend doing this by amending state constitutions, because "the legal foundation of the new system would then be very difficult to change or violate once put in place" (p. 309). Under their proposal, the authority to govern schools would devolve to the building level and autonomous schools would compete for students. This competition would supposedly promote effective school organizations and higher academic performance.

A key element in their proposal is the role of the school principal. Since a market system depends on the responsiveness of those who operate enterprises to their "clients," principals would have to be empowered to lead. Chubb and Moe believe that principals should be given "concentrated authority" (p. 52) so that they can shape their schools. In particular, the principal should be completely in control of personnel decisions in his (the feminine pronoun is never used) school. He should have the authority "to build a hand-picked team of 'right-thinking' teachers" (p. 52). Such a team could work smoothly together to attract "a specialized clientele" (p. 60). Teachers who ceased to be effective team players would be "eliminated" (p. 50).

In their last paragraph, Chubb and Moe write that "there are many paths to democracy" (p. 229). Given their casual attitude toward definitions, they might argue that their proposal is, in fact, democratic. It is simply another "path to democracy." But the broad outlines of their proposal suggest a different conclusion. Authority over education is to be removed from the public; the new system is to be made very difficult to change; managers exercising "concentrated authority" are to play a major role in it. Such systems are not unheard of in the history of governance structures. They are not, however, usually called "democratic." They have other names.

THE REACTIONS OF THE
DEBATERS AND THEIR AUDIENCE

Returning to the debate of Chubb and Moe's book at the 1990 education conference, it is easy to understand why the members of the audience became angry. Almost all were university professors; almost all were Americans. They had come to the conference consciously expecting to hear reports of research which conformed to their conception of the nature of scholarship. Unconsciously, they had come expecting that all policy proposals would be expressed in traditional American political discourse. Neither expectation was fulfilled.

It is not quite so easy to understand why only one person—the last panelist —challenged Chubb and Moe's ideas. The others took easier ways out. They maintained neutrality; or they criticized the methodology of the study; or, at most, they raised obvious equity issues. Yet the inchoate anger in the room suggested that these responses were felt as inadequate even as they were offered. Why? I would

like to suggest that by revealing the real implications of Chubb and Moe's ideology the debate also revealed the contradiction that lies at the heart of traditional American political discourse. It was that revelation which left the audience emotional.

Robert Dahl, one of the grand old men of American political science, has argued that in the late 19th century an "ideological transfer" occurred in the United States (Dahl, 1977, p. 7). At that time the "agrarian order that... was extraordinarily congenial to democracy was... displaced by a new socioeconomic order of corporate capitalism that was much less compatible" (p. 7). Yet supporters of the new order continued to speak in the ideological terms of the order which had been displaced. The old democratic terminology of the early nineteenth century was simply applied to the new economic institutions. For example, arguments against government regulation of individuals were "transferred" to corporations. As a result, American political thinking and discourse contain inner contradictions.

Of course, the same inner contradictions occur in the politics of American education. Public schools are an inheritance from the early 19th century. Later education movements, such as the cult of efficiency, contained ideological elements which conflicted with the basic premises of public education (Callahan, 1962). Yet, for generations the sacred aura around public schools prevented people from thinking such ideological concepts through to their logical conclusions. The democratic ideas of Thomas Jefferson and others were simply juxtaposed with ideas drawn from Social Darwinism and Scientific Management. They sounded good together, and few people noticed that they contradicted each other. This contradictory political discourse was the discourse which those attending the education conference expected to hear.

But Chubb and Moe have ideological integrity. They elevate efficiency above all other values; they idealize market control systems; they believe that "nature" causes the dynamics of competition and selection in human societies. Moreover, they are willing to let "nature" have its way, unchallenged by "higher-order values" such as human concepts of social justice or political freedom. Of course, these ideas have nothing whatever to do with democracy—*but, unlike most Americans of the last century, Chubb and Moe follow them through to their logical conclusion.* They attack democracy. Given their ideological premises, this attack makes perfect sense.

Only one person in the audience that day was able to answer Chubb and Moe adequately—that is to say, at the level of theory. He was a critical theorist. Had Dahl been in the audience, he too could have responded adequately. So could anyone else who was well grounded in social or political theory. But most of the panel and the audience were unable to respond. Accustomed to the old, contradictory discourse, they were caught short. As Dahl says, it "distorts our understanding of ourselves and of our possibilities" (p. 1).

The panelist who called *Politics, Markets, and America's Schools* one of the most important books of the decade was, however, correct. This is an important book for three reasons. First, it clearly reveals the conflict between the historic democratic ideals of the United States and neo-conservative ideology. Second, it clearly reveals the central educational issue of the 1990s. That issue is not school choice, or restructuring, or accountability, or even international competitiveness. It is whether the United States will continue to have a school system which is, in any meaningful sense, public. Finally, it reveals the level at which the debate over the future of American education must be enjoined. Chubb and Moe's ideology is consistent with their conclusions and policy recommendations. In *Politics, Markets, and America's Schools* they move beyond the contradiction identified by Dahl. It is time for other Americans to move beyond that contradiction as well. Chubb and Moe should be answered in clear, consistent, and theoretical terms by those American scholars who are not willing to discard democracy. It is time for more ideological integrity.

REFERENCES

Almond, G. A. (1990). *A discipline divided: Schools and sects in political science.* Newbury Park, CA: SAGE Publications.

Callahan, R. E. (1962). *Education and the cult of efficiency.* Chicago: University of Chicago Press.

Cooper, B. S. (1988). School reform in the 1980s: The New Right's legacy. *Educational Administration Quarterly, 24,* 282–298.

Dahl, R. A. (1977). On removing certain impediments to democracy in the United States. *Political Science Quarterly, 92,* 1–20.

Erickson, D. A. (1985). Choice and private schools: Dynamics of supply and demand. In D. C. Levy (Ed.), *Private education: Studies in choice and public policy* (pp. 82–109). New York: Oxford University Press.

POSTSCRIPT

Can "Choice" Lead the Way to Educational Reform?

Legislation designed to increase parental choice was debated a number of times in the past two years in the U.S. Congress. A typical Republican position was that the country desperately needs choices in education but that the powerful special interest groups (such as teachers' unions) are not interested in the feelings of the majority of the American people but are interested only in more money for pet projects. A typical Democratic stance was that vouchers provide encouragement and a publicly funded mechanism to abandon neighborhood public schools and leave them with less support.

Two factors weighed heavily in the legislative consideration of choice: the effect on equalization of opportunity and the implications for separation of religion and education. The first of these is treated by Stanley C. Trent in "School Choice for African-American Children Who Live in Poverty: A Commitment to Equity or More of the Same?" *Urban Education* (October 1992) and by Charles V. Willie in "Controlled Choice: An Alternative Desegregation Plan for Minorities Who Feel Betrayed," *Education and Urban Society* (February 1991). The second is discussed by Americans for Religious Liberty in "School Choice: Panacea or Scam?" *Voice of Reason* (Winter 1991); by David Bernstein in "Religion in School: A Role for Vouchers," *Current* (May 1992); by John E. Coons in " 'Choice' Plans Should Include Private Option," *Education Week* (January 17, 1990); and by Dennis L. Evans in "The Risks of Inclusive 'Choice' Plans," *Education Week* (February 14, 1990).

Two works that cover the topic rather comprehensively are *Choice in Public Education* (1990) edited by Boyd H. Walberg and *School Choice: Issues and Answers* (1991) by Ruth Randall and Keith Geiger. Other journal articles include these: William Bainbridge and Steven Sundre, "School Choice: The Education Issue of the 1990s," *Children Today* (January/February 1991); John G. Boswell, "Improving Our Schools: Parental Choice Is Not Enough," *The World & I* (February 1990); Deborah Meier, "Choice Can *Save* Public Education," *The Nation* (March 4, 1991); and Lois D. Whealey, "Choice or Elitism?" *The American School Board Journal* (April 1991).

Also see James R. Rinehart's "Choice and the Public Schools," *The Educational Forum* (Spring 1992); David L. Kirp's "What School Choice Really Means," *The Atlantic Monthly* (November 1992), which appraises the much-lauded East Harlem school choice system; Myron Lieberman's "The School Choice Fiasco," *The Public Interest* (Winter 1994); and Daniel McGroarty's "School Choice Slandered," *The Public Interest* (Fall 1994).

ISSUE 11

Are Religious Fundamentalists Damaging Public Education?

YES: Zita Arocha, from "The Religious Right's March into Public School Governance," *The School Administrator* (October 1993)

NO: Ralph E. Reed, Jr., and Robert L. Simonds, from "The Agenda of the Religious Right," *The School Administrator* (October 1993)

ISSUE SUMMARY

YES: Zita Arocha, a freelance writer who specializes in education and social issues, examines some of the recent political successes of various ultraconservative groups, and she argues that these groups have hidden agendas to redefine school curricula.

NO: Christian Coalition leader Ralph E. Reed, Jr., and Robert L. Simonds, president of Citizens for Excellence in Education, maintain that the educational goals of the religious right represent mainstream ideology and the concerns of many parents.

The religious grounding of early schooling in America certainly cannot be denied, nor can the history of religious influences on the conduct of governmental functions. For example, U.S. Supreme Court decisions in the early decades of the twentieth century allowed certain cooperative practices between public school systems and community religious groups. However, it must also be recognized that many students, parents, and taxpayer organizations were distressed by some of these accommodating policies. Legal action taken by or on behalf of some of the offended parties led to Supreme Court restrictions on prayer and on Bible reading in the public schools in the 1960s. Particularly notable are the decisions of *Murray v. Curlett, School District of Abington Township v. Schempp,* and *Engle v. Vitale.* These decisions curtailed the use of public school time and facilities for ceremonial and devotional religious purposes; but they did not outlaw the discussion of religion or the use of religious materials in appropriate academic contexts.

During the 1970s and 1980s religious activists, led by the Reverend Jerry Falwell's conservative group, the Moral Majority, campaigned against what they perceived to be the tyranny of an educational establishment dominated by the philosophy of secular humanism. On the legal front and in local school board meetings, this increasingly vocal faction pressed for tighter censorship of school materials, the inclusion of creation science in the curriculum, a voucher system that would include private school options, and the legalization of voluntary organized prayer in the public schools. The Supreme Court, despite its moving toward the ideological right because of judicial appointments made by Presidents Ronald Reagan and George Bush during the 1980s, has held the line against efforts to weaken the wall of separation between church and state in school matters. As a result, the teaching of creationism in school has been disallowed, organized moments of "silent meditation" have been vetoed, textbook censorship has been curtailed, and, most recently, in *Lee v. Weisman* (1992), graduation prayers have been declared unconstitutional.

The rightward swing in the 1994 elections seems to have set the stage for stronger action from members of the religious right, which includes such conservative organizations as Pat Robertson's Christian Coalition, James C. Dobson's Focus on the Family, Phyllis Schlafly's Eagle Forum, the Traditional Values Coalition, Citizens for Excellence in Education, and Concerned Women for America. In the political arena, the ideas of the these groups receive support from the Heritage Foundation; commentator Pat Buchanan; Representative Newt Gingrich (R-Georgia), Speaker of the House; William J. Bennett, codirector of Empower America; and talk show host Rush Limbaugh.

In "Shotgun Wedding: Notes on Public Education's Encounter With the New Christian Right," *Phi Delta Kappan* (May 1994), George Kaplan describes the groups that compose the religious right as becoming the "self-appointed conscience of American society." He suggests that these groups have met with some success, claiming that "the attitudes of the larger culture and its opinion shapers are showing signs of merging with some of the Christian Right's longtime preoccupations with clean living, solid academic grounding, and respect for family." This may explain the recent successes of conservative candidates in local and state elections. In light of the changing political climate, liberal organizations, such as the National Education Association and People for the American Way, are preparing for anticipated battles over school policies during the remaining years of the twentieth century.

Zita Arocha, in the first of the two selections that follow, warns of the campaign by ultraconservatives to gain control of local and state boards of education. She advises school officials to become more proactive in bringing to the public's attention the exact nature of the policies and programs of these groups. Ralph E. Reed, Jr., and Robert L. Simonds, leaders of two powerful Christian organizations, detail the educational agenda of religious conservatives, which they maintain involves positive reforms that will produce academic excellence and good citizenship in America's students.

YES

Zita Arocha

THE RELIGIOUS RIGHT'S MARCH INTO PUBLIC SCHOOL GOVERNANCE

A run-off school board race in Klein, Texas, a suburb of Houston, last February drew so many voters that poll workers ran out of ballots and had to use note-book paper. An acrimonious, media-intense election between Steven Blount, a liberal school board member who is a Unitarian, and his challenger, David Strawn, a Christian fundamentalist, sparked the unusually heavy turnout.

"You would have thought we were running for governor," says Blount, 45, a training specialist for Exxon, of the race that drew 10,800 voters—three times the number in any previous school board election—and active participation by local churches and political leaders.

The election was Strawn's third unsuccessful try for the school board in the last three years. This time around, he came within 100 votes of winning a seat on the seven-member school board, but later was defeated by Blount in the run-off election.

The main issues stressed during the campaign by Strawn, a 46-year-old sales representative, were restoring "academic excellence, Godly morale, and traditional American values to the classroom."

GAINING CONTROL

The same ideological battle that pitted Blount against Strawn in Klein is taking place in hundreds of communities across the country as religious con-servatives try to influence educational policies by taking their philosophies from the pulpit to the soapbox.

Where there are no definitive figures, officials with the Christian funda-mentalist organization, Citizens for Excellence in Education, claim more than 4,500 "parents with conservative family values" have been elected to school boards since 1989. Nationwide there are 96,000 school board members.

The liberal advocacy group, People For the American Way, which monitors the activity of the religious right across the country, has identified 243 religious conservatives who ran for local school boards in primaries or general elections in 1992–93, and about one-third were successful in their campaigns.

According to a report issued by People For the American Way in July, religious right members are a majority on five school boards—Vista, Calif.; Round Rock, Texas; Duval County, Fla.; Lake County, Fla., and New Berlin, Wis.

This may be a holy war, but it often looks more like guerrilla warfare. The concerted opposition to "liberalism" in public education does not always stand publicly shoulder to shoulder with the known organizations of the religious right. But the issues are usually the same ones attacked by organized national conservative groups like Citizens for Excellence in Education and the Christian Coalition, frequently focusing on sex education, self-esteem, and programs that emphasize independent thinking.

DEMOCRATIC EXERCISE

The bottom line is this: religious fundamentalists are using the democratic process effectively, sometimes joining forces with taxpayers, senior citizens, and other conservative religious groups that share their agenda. They are winning seats on local and state school boards and they are using hard-won power to reshape educational policy.

The school board elections are an easy target because they draw few voters and little attention from the news media.

"School boards are the easiest way for them to enter the political system," says Skipp Porteous, a former fundamentalist minister turned critic who heads the Institute for First Amendment Studies, a liberal advocacy group. "In the next few years we will see thousands of school boards facing a situation where local Christian right groups, backed by national groups, will be trying to take over school boards."

Thomas Shannon, executive director of the National School Boards Association, says attempts by religious right candidates to win school boards seats are "not an evil threat at all but... simply a situation where a group of people want to make their impact in a democratic way."

He says the solution is for more citizens to get involved in the school election process. "If anything, this could stimulate people to get out the vote across the whole political spectrum because that's the essence of democracy."

The enemies of the religious right take many forms, from condoms to literature. In school districts across the country, Christian fundamentalists target multicultural curricula, performance-based education that stresses independent thinking, sex and AIDS education, puppets that are used to teach children self-esteem, free lunch programs for poor children, and some books they consider offensive.

"What they are saying is 'let's water down the teaching of evolution, let's stop discussing sex education, let's get rid of classes on self-esteem, and let's remove these books from the library,'" says Robert Boston, a spokesperson for the liberal advocacy organization, Americans United for the Separation of Church and State.

In Vista, Calif., a suburb of San Diego, after two religious fundamentalists joined another conservative on the five-member school board in 1992, one of the first issues they tackled was whether to open their meetings with an invocation and hire four attorneys who have conservative Christian views. The board approved a pre-meeting prayer, but did not hire the new attorneys.

Vista board members in a 3–2 vote in August ordered that discussions of creationism be included in history and language arts classes. The policy also requires discussion of scientific evidence that disputes the theory of evolution.

This spring, three conservatives were elected to the seven-member school board in Round Rock, Texas, a racially diverse bedroom community near Austin. The board has voted 5 to 1 (one member was not present) to allow prayer at graduation ceremonies if they are initiated by students. Later this year, the board is expected to consider whether to allow counselors to continue using a puppet called Pumsy that teaches self-esteem to students. Some parents have complained the puppet teaches children secular values.

STATE INCURSIONS

The religious conservatives also have been active in trying to elect members to state boards of education, which set policies on public school curriculum and funding, says Brenda Welburn, deputy director of the National Association of State Boards of Education.

Last year, several hundred bills were introduced in state legislatures, usually by conservatives, to change the governing structure of state school boards, according to Welburn. Some bills sought to abolish the boards, curtail their authority, or change them from appointed to elected bodies, thereby creating opportunities for conservatives to win seats. Voters in Virginia will decide a referendum in November whether to begin electing local school board members.

As a result of legislative changes, the Ohio state board of education was reduced last year in size from 21 to 9. At least two new board members who were elected are religious conservatives,

Welburn says. "I have met them and they told me their agenda... that the public school system needs to have morals and values and teach about God and prayer in the schools."

INFLUENCING VOTERS

Religious conservatives say they do not have a hidden agenda but only seek a return to family values and back-to-basics education.

"Our goal is to get parents who have kids in the public schools to serve on school boards so that school board run reflect their views," says Robert Simonds, president of Citizens for Excellence in Education [CEE].

The 10-year-old organization also wants to make sure school programs and curriculum do not "damage or destroy" children's faith in God, he adds.

Simonds insists the group does not "endorse" candidates and instead educates voters on the issues.

In California, the CEE successfully collected signatures to place a referendum on school choice on the November ballot. The plan would allow parents to use public money to send their children to public or private schools.

Christian Coalition, founded by television evangelist Pat Robertson, also has been active in school board races nationally, most recently in New York City where it joined with Catholics, Orthodox Jews, and Latinos to help religious conservatives win 56 of 288 school boards seats this spring.

The group says "pro-family and religious conservative" candidates now control six of the city's 32 districts.

Before the election, Christian Coalition, with backing from the Catholic Archdiocese of New York, distributed more than 1,000 voter guides in churches explaining where candidates stood on issues such as voluntary school prayer, AIDS awareness education, and a curriculum that "included segments that described and encouraged acceptance of homosexual behavior and practices."

Ralph Reed, executive director of the Christian Coalition, says the organization's "mainstream agenda" includes support for parental rights, freeing schools from crime and drugs, a back-to-basics curriculum, and school choice.

JOB INSECURITY

As conservatives win seats and, in a few cases, form majorities on school boards, some school administrators' education initiatives—and sometimes their jobs—are on the line.

"There's no doubt in my mind that I'm one of the casualties of the battle" by religious fundamentalists, says former New York City School Chancellor Joseph Fernandez, who lost his job in June after conservative religious groups and others criticized liberal policies he established. They focused their ire on a program to distribute condoms in high schools and a plan to implement a new curriculum that taught tolerance toward gays.

Another former school superintendent, Carolyn Trohoski, resigned from her job in 1992 as head of the Phoenixville Area School District near Valley Forge, Pa., after tiring of several years of challenges by a local taxpayers' group. While not defining itself as "the religious right," the group presented the same agenda that usually is advocated by religious conservatives.

"The reason I left was I had a heart attack the previous year . . . and it became very apparent that the stress of the situation wouldn't improve my heart condition," she says.

She says the taxpayers' organization, which was thought to have ties to religious right groups, constantly demanded to see purchase records, teacher contracts, and lots of other budget materials. At the end of her tenure, the group also challenged a portion of the school district's curriculum that teaches decision-making skills.

Trohoski says the group's criticisms were similar to those raised by Citizens for Excellence in Education against Pennsylvania's new state educational curriculum, called Outcome Based Education, which stresses critical thinking skills.

Richard Swantz, superintendent in La Crosse, Wis., says he feared he would lose his job after a local citizens' group mounted an aggressive attack against a busing plan designed to integrate Hmong children and other disadvantaged students with more affluent students.

After two recall elections and two regular elections during the last year, the plan has been upheld by the current school board.

"I remember thinking 'I'm at the end of my career. I'm probably three, maybe five years away from retirement and I've never been canned from a job,'" says Swantz. "Then I thought, 'Hey, this is a hell of a way to go out.'"

Swantz says some local residents suspected religious conservatives were behind the recall of school board members who supported the busing plan.

"I can't say there was definitely any religious right movement," he says. "But what I have seen is that in terms of the questions they ask and the issues they raise there are similarities."

HIDDEN AGENDAS

In La Crosse and Phoenixville, as in other parts of the country, religious right activity at the school district level in some places is difficult to pin down.

Critics of the religious conservatives say that in the past they have used "stealth" tactics to win school board seats by failing to disclose their affiliation with fundamentalist groups and not showing up at candidate forums or speaking before parent-teacher groups. Lately, though, news media attention and citizen organizing efforts are making it more difficult for candidates to hide agendas.

One reason is that opponents of the religious conservatives are getting savvier—checking into the background of challengers, using the media to publicize issues, sponsoring more public candidate forums, forming liaisons with teacher groups, and disseminating fact sheets.

"We get calls all the time from people who want to start groups to counter efforts by the religious right," says Boston, of Americans United for the Separation of Church and State, a group based in Washington, D.C. "They ask us what they can do to make sure who these people are who are running or what they can do now that these people are seated."

Liberal organizations are even combating the religious conservatives' literature (one book published by Citizens for Excellence in Education is titled *How to Elect Christians to Public Office*) with their own publications. Proteous is co-author of *Challenging The Christian Right: The Activist's Handbook*, which includes state-by-state listings of religious right groups and information on how to do research on religious right organizations.

UNMASKED IDENTITY

In the Klein, Texas, election, Blount's first plan of attack against religious fundamentalists was to invite more than 40 local movers and shakers including the Republican and Democratic precinct chairmen to a breakfast meeting. Armed with newspaper articles and publications from Citizens for Excellence in Education, Blount revealed that Strawn was a past president of the local CEE chapter in Houston.

"I blew his cover," Blount says. "I let them know what his agenda was."

Blount also used the news media and a fact sheet he distributed to counteract erroneous information.

A week before the election, Blount went to the local newspaper with an anonymous flyer from a non-existent gay and lesbian organization endorsing him and another candidate for the school board. Although never proven, he suspects the flyer had been distributed by supporters of his opponent.

A subsequent newspaper article revealed that the gay group didn't exist.

Two days before the election, dozens of supporters stayed home from work to telephone friends and neighbors and ask them to vote for Blount and another like-minded candidate.

Martin Kaplan, a resident of Newton, Mass., and chair of the state board of education, used written material from the religious right to show that a local group fighting a sex and health education plan had ties to national right-wing Christian organizations.

"They were quite angry," says Kaplan, who made the revelation in a speech before the Newton school board at a jam-packed meeting in May.

Later the conservative opponents threatened to submit a slate of candidates for the school board election in November. After Kaplan's presentation, the Newton school board voted 9–0 to adopt the sex education program.

After three conservatives won election to the Round Rock, Texas, school board in May, Karen Apperson says she and more than a dozen other parents formed an informal group to monitor school board meetings and stay on top of school issues.

"This is not about conservatives against liberals," says the 36-year-old mother and former PTA president. "This is about what kind of things we want taught in our schools... we are a vehicle for parents when certain issues are attacked or programs are changed."

So far, the most successful organizing effort by parents who disagree with the objectives of religious conservatives occurred in San Diego County after an anti-abortion group endorsed slates of conservative candidates to run for seats on the county's 42 school boards in 1990.

A coalition of PTA members, teacher union activists, and administrators attended school board meetings, issued press releases, wrote letters to the editors of newspapers, organized candidate forums, and endorsed slates of moderate candidates. The awareness-raising efforts partially paid off. Of some 90 religious right candidates who ran for school board seats in San Diego County in 1990 and 1992, about half won, says People For the American Way.

BETTER COMMUNICATION

By and large, as religious right activity has intensified in communities across the country, school officials have moved cautiously, adopting low-key, wait-and-see approaches.

In the few cases where religious conservatives compose a majority on a school board, administrators keep attention focused on the larger issues like the quality of instruction, and budget priorities —knowing they may have to implement policies they do not agree with or back away from education reforms they hold dear.

Sometimes, school officials successfully rely on legal opinions or established procedures to deal with religious right challenges, for example, letting a committee of parents and school officials make recommendations on whether to ban a book or do away with a self-esteem program.

Often it's a matter of explaining to concerned citizens what education programs are all about.

In Pennsylvania where religious conservatives, senior citizens, and taxpayer groups have challenged the new statewide school curriculum, Trohoski, associate director of the Pennsylvania Association of School Administrators, spends much of her time giving seminars to educators on how to "communicate with parents and reduce the level of animosity."

Generally, school officials haven't done a good job of selling the curriculum reform program to citizens. "We need to talk in 7-Eleven language instead of alphabet jargon," she says.

KEEPING COOL

Swantz, the superintendent in La Crosse, says it was hard for him to stay focused on his job of running the 8,000-student school system when his busing plan to mainstream Hmong children was under heavy fire. After members of the board that approved the plan lost their seats, new board members opposed the integration initiative and asked Swantz to resign.

Before the new board was able to undo the plan, some of those board members lost their seats. A majority on the current board favors the plan and supports Swantz.

He says he kept his composure during the tumultuous year by "maintaining as much professional behavior as I could" and by working hard to make sure the busing plan, implemented in the fall of 1992, went off without a glitch.

But it still was hard.

"When you are up to your behind in alligators," he says, "it's difficult to remember that the primary thing is to drain the swamp."

NO

Ralph E. Reed, Jr., and
Robert L. Simonds

THE AGENDA OF THE RELIGIOUS RIGHT

THE CHRISTIAN COALITION

An enormous amount of disinformation has been disseminated by the radical left in recent years about the supposed "agenda" of religious conservatives for America's public schools.

Left-wing organizations like People For the American Way have alleged that religious conservatives want to ban books, impose mandatory prayer, and eliminate school breakfast programs. Because the truth does not serve their political agenda, they engage in distortion.

Happily, the facts are otherwise. The Christian Coalition strongly supports our public school system. An educated citizenry is essential to democracy because it requires citizens to take an active and informed role in their government. As Thomas Jefferson once said, "If a nation expects to be ignorant and free, in a state of civilization, it expects what never was and never will be."

A strong and effective public school system is essential to good citizenship. While we support innovative alternatives to the public schools, such as private schools or home schools, the vast majority of students (about 87 percent today) will attend public schools. We cannot neglect or abandon them because they will be the cornerstone of education for millions of young people, the future leaders and innovators of tomorrow.

Our Beliefs

Accordingly, the Christian Coalition has a mainstream agenda for public education that includes four basic principles:

No. 1: We favor parental rights.
A growing body of data suggests that active participation of parents is more important to educational attainment than race, income, or socio-economic status. Good education involves parents; poor education precludes it. We need to restore parental rights and parental involvement in the public schools,

From Ralph E. Reed, Jr., and Robert L. Simonds, "The Agenda of the Religious Right," *The School Administrator* (October 1993). Copyright © 1993 by The American Association of School Administrators. Reprinted by permission.

something we hear encouraged in PTA meetings and school board sessions throughout the country.

The Christian Coalition wants to promote good citizenship among parents and students by informing them of how school boards work and ways of effectively communicating with elected officials. Yet groups like People For the American Way seek to limit the access of churchgoers and parents by branding them intolerant or even dangerous.

A parental rights movement is building across the nation. In Chicago a group of parents recent filed suit against the city for failing to provide their children, many of whom cannot read and write, with an adequate education. In Wisconsin earlier this year, Linda Cross, a parent and school teacher, narrowly lost her campaign for state superintendent of schools after being outspent 10-to-1 by a union-backed candidate who opposed school choice.

The parental rights movement found its most dramatic expression recently in New York City. School board elections in New York historically have been sedate affairs. But the 1993 campaign read like a subplot from Tom Wolfe's *Bonfire of the Vanities*, complete with the histrionics, bombast, and larger-than-life politics unique to the Big Apple.

The controversy began with the Rainbow Curriculum, a multicultural curriculum that included instruction about the homosexual lifestyle to first graders. Mary Cummins, a brassy Irish grandmother and school board member in the Queens borough, refused to implement the program. She and other Queens school board members were fired summarily by Chancellor Joseph Fernandez, who later was fired by the New York City Board of Education for his role in the controversy.

Crisis Declared

The ongoing battle spilled over into the campaign for school board seats in the city's five boroughs and 32 districts. Parents groups and pro-family organization distributed 500,000 nonpartisan voter guides informing voters where 540 candidates stood on a broad range of issues, including school choice and more parental involvement in curriculum decisions.

The American Civil Liberties Union hysterically called the involvement of churchgoing voters "the greatest civil liberties crisis in the history of New York City." The Rev. Al Sharpton denounced parents' efforts as "racist."

But when the dust cleared, *The New York Times* estimated that 56 of 89 pro-family candidates won board seats, a stunning 63 percent success rate in one of the most liberal cities in the nation. Even in Manhattan's Lower East Side, openly pro-family and religious conservative candidates won in liberal districts. Six of New York's 32 school districts now are controlled by parental rights advocates.

The New York City experience also debunked the myth of so-called "stealth candidates," which radical left organizations argue is the chosen tactic of religious conservatives. More than a million newspaper ads, broadsides, voter guides, and voter cards listed all the candidates and where they stood on key issues.

The pro-family candidates won because of their stands on the issues, not in spite of them. They ran openly and proudly on the issues—and won stunning upsets. The real stealth candidates are liberal incumbents, who talk one way to get elected and then vote the opposite.

Christian Coalition voter guides told the truth about their radical voting records, and dozens of candidates were rejected at the polls as a result.

The New York City voter education effort created a multi-ethnic, ecumenical coalition for common sense. The Roman Catholic Archdiocese, the Congress of Racial Equality led by Democratic civil rights leader Roy Innis, the National Committee for the Furtherance of Jewish Education, and the Family Defense Council all assisted in the non-partisan voter education effort. The pro-family movement's inroads into the African-American, Hispanic, Catholic, and Jewish communities may be the most significant development since its emergence in the late 1970s.

Guarantee Safety

*No. 2: We believe schools must
be free from crime and drugs.*
No students can learn unless they first feel safe. The sad fact is too many of our schools are not safe. According to the Department of Justice, 100,000 children bring firearms to school every day and 160,000 students stay home each day because they fear for their safety.

Little wonder. An estimated 200,000 crimes are committed on school property every month and 942 teachers are assaulted or threatened with assault by students or delinquents. Earlier this year in Lorain, Ohio, a young female student brought a knife to school and planned to stab her teacher in exchange for a bounty of lunch money pooled by her classmates. Only the last-minute intervention by a principal prevented the murder.

In Columbus, Ga., last spring a dozen sixth graders plotted to kill their teacher for disciplining them and requiring them to do their homework. One boy brought a pistol to school, while another attempted to push the teacher down a flight of stairs. These children were 12 years old.

We must expel delinquents and violent criminals from our schools. Where necessary, violent and disruptive students should be separated from students who are serious about learning.

Emphasize Skills

*No. 3: We believe curriculum must
return to the basics.*
The three Rs that once dominated the curriculum in public schools have been whittled away by values clarification, multiculturalism, human sexuality courses, and outcome-based education.

According to the U.S. Department of Education, only 25 percent of eighth graders in the United States are proficient in mathematics. Two-thirds of high school seniors cannot name the decade in which the Civil War was fought or the half-century in which Columbus discovered America.

This knowledge is essential to good citizenship and to a future work force that can compete in an international economy. The one simple standard that should govern curriculum decisions is: will it help students learn to read, write, and perform basic math skills?

The real dispute over human sexuality courses is the frightening extent to which these curricula violate parental rights and take time away from basic skills. Children who know everything they ever wanted to know about sex but cannot read or write are ill-prepared for the job market and civic life.

Healthy Competition

No. 4: We believe school choice will improve public education by introducing healthy competition.

Surveys show 70 percent of the American people favor the right to choose the best schools for their child. Those who know the public schools best know the effectiveness of choice. An estimated 22 percent of public school teachers send their children to private schools—twice the national average. Among schoolteachers in Chicago, more than 40 percent opt for private or parochial schools.

A school choice initiative will be on the ballot in California next month. As with the tax limitation movement and the success of Proposition 13, a victory in California could sweep across the country like a prairie fire.

Even without legislation, the grassroots school choice movement is gaining ground. In San Antonio, Texas, the Children's Educational Opportunity Foundation, a non-profit group, is providing scholarships to 934 inner-city children for half their tuition. To qualify, students' families must be below the poverty level and must raise half the funds for their tuition, giving parents a genuine stake in their education. Applications are flooding the foundation's offices. The Golden Rule Insurance Company began a similar program in Indianapolis in 1991.

Competition will improve rather than threaten the public schools. School choice has prevailed in higher education for decades. The G.I. Bill has given government scholarships to millions of veterans. These can be used at any college or university. Whether Stanford, Notre Dame, or the University of Texas, all colleges compete based on their ability to meet the needs of students. The result is the finest system of higher education in the world.

Mainstream Demands

This is the mainstream agenda of the Christian Coalition for the public schools. Parental rights, safe schools, a basics curriculum, and school choice will give us an educational system that is unrivaled in the world.

We must reform our schools not only for the sake of our children, but for the sake of our democracy. For as Thomas Jefferson wisely noted, an educated citizenry is a necessary condition for freedom.

CITIZENS FOR EXCELLENCE IN EDUCATION

Everyone loses in a cultural war. Look at Bosnia and other world scenes. Or look at the New York City schools' fallen schools chancellor (who promoted the idea that young children should learn about homosexuality) or at Los Angeles, where another top school chief went down in ignominy in 1991 because of "Mission SOAR," a new age, occultic curriculum.

What causes these mid-career debacles by otherwise intelligent educational leaders? The answer is, of course, both simple and complex.

It's simple in that a good dose of higher-order thinking skills, more commonly known as common sense, would help. It's complex because of the often irrational influence of left-wing educational radicals whose agenda is a socialist, anti-Christian diatribe designed to denigrate all religions, but especially Christianity.

Complaints Ignored

For most Americans, and certainly for me, forcing the left-wing educational extremists' agenda upon our innocent school children is unacceptable. I believe that agenda soon will be history.

Parents in many communities literally have begged their local superintendents and school boards to listen honestly (i.e., to consider a mutually acceptable solution) to their complaints. Some do, but only a few. The rest tell parents: "We have a model school—you are the only one who has complained"; "We can't change our curriculum every time a parent comes in here with a complaint, we would be changing it a dozen times a week" (sometimes these two mutually opposite postulates are given in the same breath); or "Trust us, we know what's best for your child. We are trained professionals" (implying parents are uneducated, untrained, and ignorant about what's best for their child).

Superintendents who are trained never to give in to parents' complaints because of the "if you give an inch, they'll take a mile" theory are as likely to succeed as the old secular scientists' flat earth theory.

School districts that send teachers and administrators to seminars on "How to Stop Fundamentalists in Education" or "How to Deal with Right-Wing Parents Complaints" are going to be targeted by secular and conservative parent groups through tax-rebellion and lawsuits. Why not? Wouldn't that rightly happen if the seminar focused on "How to Stop African-American Influence on Education"? Should we conclude that the National Education Association, People For the American Way, and school districts that send representatives to these bigoted Christophobic gatherings are as bad as the Ku Klux Klan?

In Denver, Colo., these organizations and others collaborated at just such an anti-Christian, anti-religious-right seminar for teachers and administrators. Christians were described as "narrow-minded," "rigid," "a threat," "evangelical bigots," "homophobics," and the "enemy." The two Christian groups most under attack were Citizens for Excellence in Education and Focus on the Family.

School districts couldn't write seminar enrollment checks fast enough. One Colorado district sent seven representatives costing nearly $3,000 of taxpayers' money on tuition alone. One participating superintendent said, "What's at issue ... is who's going to control the schools. It's us versus them," he said, referring to "us" as his board of education and "them" as the local Christian community that supports the local schools.

Offensive Actions

Citizens for Excellence in Education [CEE] has some questions about this hate-mongering activity:

1. Are those who attend these sessions the same school people who espouse pluralism, cultural diversity, religious freedom, and parental inclusion?
2. Are children being taught that Christians are dangerous?
3. Are Christians acting illegally or undemocratically by electing parents to school boards?
4. What's all this talk about balancing our school boards? Is there a Christian balance on your district's board?

A recent editorial in the Greeley, Colo., *Tribune* asked: " ... is there no one at any level of the administration and/or school board who can see the ramifications of participating in a conference like this, in a community of over 100 churches? Does it occur to no one that this sizable minority pays taxes and votes on bond issues; that they elect school boards and volunteer their time in classrooms and for fundraising? Did no one think that many of the parents within this district would be offended by this conference? Hello?"

The *Tribune* editorial concluded: "Any moment now we expect a school administrator to come riding through the center of town on a government issue mount, waving a publicly-funded lantern, reining up in a cloud of dust... crying, 'The Christians are coming, the Christians are coming!'"

If this were an isolated incident, it would hardly be noticeable nationally, but it is happening right now in all 50 states. If public schools think there is opposition now, wait until this backlash builds. There will be a lot of new people running our schools—and you can be sure they will be listening sincerely, to parents' concerns.

True Minority?

Approximately 235,000 churches operate in the United States. Of those, 155,000 are the much larger congregations of Bible-believing evangelicals, meaning there are roughly 10 evangelical churches for every U.S. school district.

Consider also the Gallup Poll findings of the 1980s that 98 percent of all Americans believe in God; 85 percent of all homes below the Mason/Dixon line are Christian homes; 75 percent of all homes above the Mason/Dixon line are Christian homes; and 190 million Americans are Christians who believe the Bible. It becomes very obvious who are the majority in America!

The National Education Association is proud of its political voting clout with teachers. Realize, though, there are about 60 parents for every teacher in the public schools. It's rather obvious where the voting power is, just between parents and teachers.

In 1989, Citizens for Excellence in Education began encouraging the election of parents with conservative family values to local and state school boards. That year, about 250 were elected across the country. In 1990, CEE parents helped elect 454, a year later 1,257, and last year 3,611.

We have observed that the more name-calling there is against Christians, the more likely we are to succeed in school board elections. Although CEE does not endorse any candidates, we educate the community on the issues involved.

CEE now has 1,350 chapters and 185,000 active parents with a little more than a million "stand-by" parents. CEE also has more than 800 churches operating Public School Awareness Committees to keep parents informed. Our goal is 10 churches (and committees) in every school district and one local CEE parent chapter in every school district.

Our Beliefs

CEE has a simple agenda:

- To return academic excellence to our schools;
- To return moral sanity and family values to our schools;
- To elect parents to community and statewide school boards who will hire parent-sensitive superintendents when these boards don't listen.

CEE wants an academic schedule with goals similar to the National Commission on Excellence in Education's "A Nation at Risk." Billions have been spent on school reform nationally—only to see more affective (psychological, new age, homosexual) agendas take precedence over academics. Parents want to keep the SAT as our national assessment test.

Outcome-based education is doomed to failure not because it's a bad idea, but because the name is a smokescreen for an even more liberal agenda of undefined outcomes, opening a Pandora's box. Deceit just won't wash anymore.

Parents with Citizens for Excellence in Education want public schools to:

- Be honest in everything they do, maintain local control and traditional American values, focus on an academic environment in which teachers teach and not just facilitate, develop a racial multicultural American melting pot theory, and maintain school discipline and character development courses.
- Stop following the advice of "Christian bashers," such as the American Civil Liberties Union, People For the American Way, and the National Education Association, and to permit parental choice.

CEE along with Christian Coalition, Concerned Women for America, EXCEL, and others, got 960,000 signatures to put the school choice initiative on next month's California ballot. If we win, school leaders also will be winners. You will be set free from the bondage of the NEA monopoly on education.

History's Lesson

Parents are doing what any intelligent, highly educated people would do in a democracy—voting for individuals committed to our children and to the viewpoints of parents. Parents today are becoming better informed than the so-called "professionals" in education. Besides CEE, we know of more than 200 other parent organizations, with the number growing dramatically.

A wake-up call for district superintendents may be in order. Will blind arrogance lead to public education's downfall? Parents want peace and cooperation. But it take two to tango or two to war. Rational people should be able to negotiate in peace.

He who will not learn from history (what has worked in the past and can work today) will learn too late that ignorance can be destructive. We have watched curriculum specialists and administrators fall prey to special interest groups and university eggheads who live and thrive on publishing wild ideas.

America's children are the losers. Is that what anyone wants? Parents have had to say no! Please work with us or you will force us to abandon you. We want to trust you. Right now, we can't afford that luxury.

POSTSCRIPT

Are Religious Fundamentalists Damaging Public Education?

Religious groups gained at least one victory in the 1980s with the passage of the Equal Access Act, federal legislation that guarantees access to public school facilities for students wishing to engage in religious activities during nonschool hours. The legislation, which has been challenged in some localities, has been upheld by the U.S. Supreme Court. A more conservative Congress may be expected to fashion new laws in coming years to further accommodate the wishes of the religious right.

Evidence of the growing warfare over educational philosophy and policies can be found in "Targets of the Right," by Janet L. Jones, *American School Board Journal* (April 1993); Matthew Freeman, *The San Diego Model: A Community Battles the Religious Right* (1993); Stephen Bates, *Battleground: One Mother's Crusade, the Religious Right, and the Struggle for Control of Our Classrooms* (1993); "The Legal Cost of Challenging the Far Right," by Leon F. Szeptycki and Harold W. Dodge, *The School Administrator* (October 1993); and "Keeping Calm When Church Meets State," by Randy Hitz and Paula Butterfield, *American School Board Journal* (January 1994).

At the local level, censorship of school and library materials has been much in the news during the past decade. Censorship conflicts are explored and analyzed in James Moffett's "Varieties of Censorship," *Journal of Thought* (December 1990); Kerwin Swint's "Another Look at the Textbook Wars," *Georgia Social Science Journal* (Spring 1991); "Book Battles," by Donna Harrington-Lueker, *American School Board Journal* (February 1991); Nat Hentoff's "Saving Kids from Satan's Books," *The Progressive* (May 1991); Joan Delfattore's *What Johnny Shouldn't Read: Textbook Censorship in America* (1992); "Curriculum Challenge from the Religious Right," by Louise Adler and Kip Tellez, *Urban Education* (July 1992); Allan C. Ornstein's "The Censored Curriculum: The Problem With Textbooks Today," *NASSP Bulletin* (November 1992); and Martha M. McCarthy's "Challenges to the Public School Curriculum: New Targets and Strategies," *Phi Delta Kappan* (September 1993).

The recent Supreme Court ruling on graduation prayers is analyzed in "Much Ado Over Graduation Prayers," by Martha M. McCarthy, *Phi Delta Kappan* (October 1993), and in "*Lee v. Weisman*: The Supreme Court Pronounces the Benediction on Public School Graduation Prayers," by Ralph D. Mawdsley and Charles J. Russo, *West's Education Law Quarterly* (January 1993).

ISSUE 12

Are Major Policy Changes Needed to Fight Gender Bias in the Schools?

YES: American Association of University Women, from *How Schools Short-change Girls: A Study of Major Findings on Girls and Education* (American Association of University Women, 1992)

NO: Rita Kramer, from "Are Girls Shortchanged in School?" *Commentary* (June 1992)

ISSUE SUMMARY

YES: The American Association of University Women (AAUW), an organization of college and university graduates that works for the advancement of women, offers a wide variety of policy changes designed to balance the educational inequities that the organization has found exist between boys and girls in the American school system.

NO: Rita Kramer, a writer who specializes in education issues, finds the charges made in the AAUW report to be unfounded and misleading, and she argues that the recommendations for change made by the association are self-serving and anti-intellectual.

Have societal values and mores discriminated against females in American culture, thereby limiting the development of their human potential? If so, should this discrimination be reversed by governmental action? A 1992 report released by the American Association of University Women (AAUW), *How Schools Shortchange Girls*, answers a resounding "Yes!" to both questions with regard to women's educational experiences.

Two books that were published after the AAUW's report came out, Myra Sadker and David Sadker's *Failing at Fairness: How America's Schools Cheat Girls* and Judy Mann's *The Difference: Growing Up Female in America*, provide research-based and ideological support for the AAUW's position. According to Mann, "Some classroom sexism is subtle, but it is constant and pervasive. Some of it is so blatant, so ruthlessly destructive of our daughters' ambitions, that it ought to be indicted as malicious wounding." Say the Sadkers, "Sitting in the same classroom, reading the same textbook, listening to the same teacher, boys and girls receive very different educations." During their career-long research, the Sadkers found that most teachers expect boys to be active, aggressive, and independent, and to excel in math and science, while girls are expected to be quiet, cooperative, and dependent, and to perform well in reading and the language arts. These expectations, the Sadkers conclude, lead to great differences in how teachers interact with male and female students.

In the arena of governmental action, some legislation has addressed gender discrimination in the schools. For example, Title IX of the 1972 Education Amendments to the Civil Rights Act declared that gender discrimination in educational programs receiving federal subsidies is illegal. The law covered such areas as athletics, physical education, vocational education, and financial aid. One challenge to the application of this law, *Grove City College v. Bell,* was defeated by the Supreme Court, and in 1987 the law gained strength with the passage of the Civil Rights Restoration Act. Additionally, the Women's Educational Equity Act of 1974 reduced gender stereotyping and improved career opportunities for females, and a Gender Equity in Education Act, prompted by the AAUW report, has recently come under consideration.

Although these legislative efforts are applauded by many women's organizations, such as the National Organization for Women, the National Council for Research on Women, and the Women's Equity Action League, there are those who deem them much ado about little. Christina Hoff Sommers, author of *Who Stole Feminism?* sees the current effort as a "do a study, declare a crisis, get a bill" approach to policy making. If the AAUW report is accurate, she asks, why do girls consistently outperform boys with regard to grades, attendance, and participation in extracurricular activities? And why do more females than males go on to higher education? Similarly, Diane Ravitch, an assistant secretary of education for the Bush administration, finds gender equity legislation to be an unnecessary waste of federal funds. She concedes that a gender bias is embedded in the popular culture and that it often persists in the home. However, the place one is least likely to encounter it, she contends, is in the schools, where great strides have been made in the past quarter-century to redress patterns of historical discrimination that have squelched female opportunity.

The findings of the AAUW are translated into specific suggestions for school reforms and legislative action in the following excerpt from the executive summary of the association's report *How Schools Shortchange Girls.* In order to alleviate disparities in how males and females are treated, the AAUW says that schools need to do a better job for girls in the areas of vocational and professional aspirations, self-esteem, and performance in mathematics and the sciences. Rita Kramer, in upholding the conclusions of Sommers and Ravitch, argues that the AAUW report is supported by faulty research and cites contrary findings that she feels sap the reform agenda of its strength.

YES

American Association of University Women

CHANGING SCHOOLS THAT SHORTCHANGE GIRLS

Few people understand the inequities that occur daily in classrooms across the country. We addressed that problem in Title IX of the 1972 Education Amendments, which prohibits discrimination in educational institutions receiving federal funds. Many of us worked hard to ensure this legislation passed. But its passage did not solve the problem.

This report synthesized all available research on girls in school and found compelling evidence that girls are not receiving the same quality, or even quantity, of education as their brothers. Girls do not receive equitable amounts of teacher attention, are less apt than boys to see themselves reflected in the materials they study, and often are not expected or encouraged to pursue higher-level math and science.

Presented here are recommendations to form a base for a new and enlightened education policy that will ensure that this nation will provide the best possible education for all its children:

Strengthened reinforcement of Title IX is essential.

1. Require school districts to assess and report on a regular basis to the Office for Civil Rights in the U.S. Department of Education on their own Title IX compliance measures.

2. Fund the Office for Civil Rights at a level that permits increased compliance reviews and full and prompt investigation of Title IX complaints.

3. In assessing the status of Title IX compliance, school districts must include a review of the treatment of pregnant teens and teen parents. Evidence indicates these students are still the victims of discriminatory treatment in many schools.

Teachers, administrators, and counselors must be prepared and encouraged to bring gender equity and awareness to every aspect of schooling.

4. State certification standards for teachers and administrators should require course work on gender issues, including new research on women, bias

in classroom-interaction patterns, and how schools can develop and implement gender-fair multicultural curricula.

5. If a national teacher examination is developed, it should include items on methods for achieving gender equity in the classroom and in curricula.

6. Teachers, administrators, and counselors should be evaluated on the degree to which they promote and encourage gender-equitable and multicultural education.

7. Support and released time must be provided by school districts for teacher-initiated research on curricula and classroom variables that affect student learning. Gender equity should be a focus of this research and a criterion for awarding funds.

8. School improvement efforts must include a focus on the ongoing professional development of teachers and administrators, including those working in specialized areas such as bilingual, compensatory, special, and vocational education.

9. Teacher training courses must not perpetuate assumptions about the superiority of traits and activities traditionally ascribed to males in our society. Assertive and affiliative skills as well as verbal and math skills must be fostered in both girls and boys.

10. Teachers must help girls develop positive views of themselves and their futures, as well as an understanding of the obstacles women must overcome in a society where their options and opportunities are still limited by gender stereotypes and assumptions.

The formal school curriculum must include the experiences of women and men from all walks of life. Girls and boys must see women and girls reflected and valued in the materials they study.

11. Federal and state funding must be used to support research, development, and follow-up study of gender-fair multicultural curricular models.

12. The Women's Educational Equity Act Program (WEEAP), in the U.S. Department of Education, must receive increased funding to continue developing curricular materials and models and to assist school districts in Title IX compliance.

13. School curricula should deal directly with issues of power, gender politics, and violence against women. Better-informed girls are better equipped to make decisions about their futures. Girls and young women who have a strong sense of themselves are better able to confront violence and abuse in their lives.

14. Educational organizations must support, via conferences, meetings, budget deliberations, and policy decisions, the development of gender-fair multicultural curricula in all areas of instruction.

15. Curricula for young children must not perpetuate gender stereotypes and should reflect sensitivity to different learning styles.

Girls must be educated and encouraged to understand that mathematics and the sciences are important and relevant to their lives. Girls must be actively supported in pursuing education and employment in these areas.

16. Existing equity guidelines should be effectively implemented in all programs supported by local, state, and federal governments. Specific attention must be directed toward including women on planning committees and focusing on girls and women in the goals, instructional strategies, teacher training, and research components of these programs.

17. The federal government must fund and encourage research on the effect

on girls and boys of new curricula in the sciences and mathematics. Research is needed particularly in science areas where boys appear to be improving their performance while girls are not.

18. Educational institutions, professional organizations, and the business community must work together to dispel myths about math and science as "inappropriate" fields for women.

19. Local schools and communities must encourage and support girls studying science and math by showcasing women role models in scientific and technological fields, disseminating career information, and offering "hands-on" experiences and work groups in science and math classes.

20. Local schools should seek strong links with youth-serving organizations that have developed successful out-of-school programs for girls in math and science and with those girls' schools that have developed effective programs in these areas.

Continued attention to gender equity in vocational education programs must be a high priority at every level of educational governance and administration.

21. Linkages must be developed with the private sector to help ensure that girls with training in nontraditional areas find appropriate employment.

22. The use of a discretionary process for awarding vocational education funds should be encouraged to prompt innovative efforts.

23. All states should be required to make support services (such as child care and transportation) available to both vocational and prevocational students.

24. There must be continuing research on the effectiveness of vocational education for girls and the extent to which the 1990 Vocational Education Amendments benefit girls.

Testing and assessment must serve as stepping stones, not stop signs. New tests and testing techniques must accurately reflect abilities of both girls and boys.

25. Test scores should not be the only factor considered in admissions or awarding scholarships.

26. General aptitude and achievement tests should balance sex differences in item types and contexts. Tests should favor neither females nor males.

27. Tests that relate to "real-life situations" should reflect the experiences of both girls and boys.

Girls and women must play a central role in educational reform. The experiences, strengths, and needs of girls from every race and social class must be considered in order to provide excellence and equity for all our students.

28. National, state, and local governing bodies should ensure that women of diverse backgrounds are equitably represented on committees and commissions on educational reform.

29. Receipt of government funding for inservice and professional development programs should be conditioned on evidence of efforts to increase the number of women in positions in which they are underrepresented. All levels of government have a role to play in increasing the numbers of women, especially women of color, in education management and policy positions.

30. The U.S. Department of Education's Office of Educational Research and Improvement (OERI) should establish an advisory panel of gender-equity experts to work with OERI to develop a re-

search and dissemination agenda to foster gender-equitable education in the nation's classrooms.

31. Federal and state agencies must collect, analyze, and report data broken down by race/ethnicity, sex, and some measure of socioeconomic status, such as parental income or education. National standards for use by all school districts should be developed so that data is comparable across district and state lines.

32. National standards for computing dropout rates should be developed for use by all school districts.

33. Professional organizations should ensure that women serve on education-focused committees. Organizations should utilize the expertise of their female membership when developing educational initiatives.

34. Local schools must call on the expertise of teachers, a majority of whom are women, in their restructuring efforts.

35. Women teachers must be encouraged and supported to seek administrative positions and elected office, where they can bring the insights gained in the classroom to formulation of education policies.

A critical goal of education reform must be to enable students to deal effectively with the realities of their lives, particularly in areas such as sexuality and health.

36. Strong policies against sexual harassment must be developed. All school personnel must take responsibility for enforcing these policies.

37. Federal and state funding should be used to promote partnerships between schools and community groups, including social service agencies, youth-serving organizations, medical facilities, and local businesses. The needs of students, particularly as highlighted by pregnant teens and teen mothers, require a multi-institutional response.

38. Comprehensive school-based health- and sex-education programs must begin in the early grades and continue sequentially through grade 12. These courses must address the topics of reproduction and reproductive health, sexual abuse, drug and alcohol use, and general mental and physical health issues. There must be a special focus on AIDS prevention.

39. State and local school board policies should enable and encourage young mothers to complete school, without compromising the quality of education these students receive.

40. Child care for the children of teen mothers must be an integral part of all programs designed to encourage young women to pursue or complete educational programs.

NO

Rita Kramer

ARE GIRLS SHORTCHANGED
IN SCHOOL?

In America today, more girls graduate from high school than boys and more of
them go on to college, where they make up 55 percent of the total enrollment.
Yet according to a report recently released by the American Association of
University Women (AAUW), "girls are invisible" in classrooms which "day
in, day out, deliver the message that women's lives count for less than men's."

This report, *How Schools Shortchange Girls*, has been enthusiastically greeted
by the media. With almost no attempt to evaluate the evidence on which it
purports to be based, front-page articles in most of the nation's leading newspapers have simply passed on the report's conclusions: that standardized
tests are biased against girls; that curricula and textbooks ignore or stereo-
type women; that teachers demonstrate bias by paying less attention to girls;
and that because of discrimination girls lag behind boys in math and science
and tend not to pursue careers in those fields.

All these charges are either false or misleading. And no wonder, since *How
Schools Shortchange Girls* is based on a body of research some of which is
outdated, much of which is trivial (unpublished doctoral dissertations and
obscure publications), and some of which was done under the auspices of the
organization issuing the report—a little like quoting yourself as an authority
for your own opinions. The report ignores any published evidence—of which
there is quite a bit—that does not support its conclusions and overlooks any
inconvenient facts that contradict or even tend to modify those conclusions or
suggest explanations other than bias for any statistical discrepancy in favor
of boys (though not when the numbers favor girls).

Take, for example, the charge that the Scholastic Aptitude Test (SAT) is
biased against girls. True, girls do somewhat less well than boys on the SAT,
which is used to help determine admission to college; it is also true that girls
get higher grades in college than boys. Since the SAT thus "underpredicts"
the performance of girls in college, it must, says the AAUW report, be biased
against them. But this could just as well be turned around and used as
evidence that boys are the victims of grading bias. After all, scholars not
quoted in the report have pointed out that girls tend to take more courses in

which grading is easier (art, music, literature), and which involve the verbal skills in which girls do better, than the tougher math and science courses more boys tend to take.

The charge that textbooks are biased against women is even more bizarre. Thus, a quantitative analysis of the content of three leading high-school texts in American history carried out at the Center for the Study of Social and Political Change at Smith College (and not cited by the AAUW report) found that women are portrayed more favorably than men; that there are proportionately more pictures of women, largely in untraditional roles; that even minor achievements by women are given extensive treatment compared to the achievements of men; that women are never represented unflatteringly, although men may be; that most accounts of historical events such as wars are considered primarily in terms of the contributions made by women (and minorities).

Students who read nothing but these textbooks (and that means most students in American high schools) wind up knowing more about minor female characters in the American past than about men who have had a significant influence on world and national affairs. The 1987 National Assessment of Educational Progress test of history and literature found that more high-school students could identify Harriet Tubman than Winston Churchill or Joseph Stalin and more knew that the Seneca Falls Declaration concerned women's rights than when Lincoln was President. In *American Voices*, a new Scott, Foresman entry into the lucrative textbook market, the index entries under "Women" and "Women's" are more than twice as long

as those under World War I and World War II together.

* * *

As for the observation that teachers pay more attention to boys, this is one of those ambiguous findings that the authors of the AAUW report automatically ascribe to bias. It has long been common knowledge that boys are more aggressive and harder to control in the traditional classroom. Calling on them more frequently may be a strategy for keeping them in line, focusing them on the academic task at hand. But even so, there is no evidence to indicate that this kind of attention translates into their learning more, earning better grades, or getting into college more easily (which, as we have seen, they do not).

Nor is there any evidence that, as the AAUW report charges, girls "are systematically discouraged from" and "are being steered away from" science, mathematics, and technology. The report—ignoring the possibility that biological, developmental, or cultural factors may well have something to do with the relative disinclination of girls to study these subjects—once again simply assumes that bias is at work. Accordingly, it suggests special programs for girls in math and science.

But encouraging girls to go into previously avoided fields, and then to work hard at excelling in them, is not exactly what the authors of the AAUW report have in mind here. We get some notion of what they do have in mind from a talk given by one of them, Dr. Peggy McIntosh, an associate director at the Wellesley College Center for Research on Women, to teachers in Brookline, Massachusetts, in the fall of 1990.

McIntosh begins by describing a little girl who is unable to solve the problems on a worksheet that asks her to add a series of three numbers such as 1 + 3 + 5. McIntosh objects to the assignment as an example of "the right/wrong, win/lose/kill or be killed system" that defines learning as mastery—"vertical thinking," as she calls it.

Vertical thinking involves "competition, exact thinking, decisiveness, being able to make an argument that will persuade others or to turn in the perfect paper." To avoid such evils, McIntosh recommends revising the assignment in terms of "lateral thinking," which instead of asking, "How am I doing?" asks, "What is it to be alive?" One way of doing this is just to give the child the answers. Another is to let the children solve all problems in a group. (Incidentally, McIntosh's program for curricular innovation involves putting "not just math, but biology and chemistry off the right/wrong axis.")

* * *

The AAUW report, then, reflects the increasingly widespread attitude in American life that sees everything in terms of bias and group entitlements and ignores all the subtle and complex aspects of human nature that differentiate individuals —including women—from one another. As usual, the bottom line is a call for remedial legislation—in this case for a reactivation of the Women's Educational Equity Act Program (WEEAP).

It was under WEEAP that federal funding was made available in 1974 for the development of "nonsexist" textbooks and other curricular materials. But since the Department of Education's publication in 1983 of the report of the National Committee on Excellence in Education, *A Nation at Risk*, programs for school reform have concentrated on issues other than gender bias—most notably on why American children of both sexes do so poorly on all measures of academic ability compared to children in other countries, whom they manage to outdo only on measures of self-esteem. Under the present Secretary, Lamar Alexander, the focus of the Department of Education is on raising academic standards throughout the system from kindergarten to college. Along the way, requests for continued funding for WEEAP have been dropped.

It is this process that the AAUW seeks to reverse by persuading us that the problem with our schools is gender bias rather than a bias against academic achievement. But sharing this latter bias to the full, the AAUW report could not be expected to fight it. And indeed, accepting its shoddy analysis and carrying out the predictably anti-intellectual recommendations that follow from it would only make our schools worse—for girls and boys alike.

POSTSCRIPT

Are Major Policy Changes Needed to Fight Gender Bias in the Schools?

Substantial progress has undeniably been made in the area of gender equity in recent decades as regards progress in curricular materials, in the encouragement of female aspirations, and in the financial support of women's athletics. Statistics show how women have progressed academically over the past quarter-century: In 1970 women earned only 6 percent of all first professional degrees; by 1991 that figure was up to 39 percent. In 1970 only 14 percent of all doctoral degrees went to women; that figure is now nearly 40 percent. In roughly the same period the percentage of medical degrees that were earned by women increased from 8 percent to 36 percent. In 1993 women composed 42 percent of first-year medical students. The proportion of females earning law degrees has leaped from 5 percent in 1970 to over 40 percent now. The percentage of dental degrees in the same period has jumped from 1 percent to 32 percent. And women now earn the majority of degrees awarded in the pharmaceutical and veterinary sciences.

A combination of public awareness, advocacy groups, and federal and state legislation have produced these positive results. But some people maintain that there still lingers a persistent undercurrent of sexism in the everyday lives of students, sustained by outdated textbooks and unconscious teacher behavior. This situation is discussed in Myra Sadker and David Sadker's "Sexism in the Classroom: From Grade School to Graduate School," *Phi Delta Kappan* (March 1986); Jacquelynne S. Eccles's "Gender Roles and Women's Achievement," *Educational Researcher* (June–July 1986); and A. O. Carelli's edited book *Sex Equity in Education* (1988).

Among the best of the more recent works on gender inequalities in the schools are *Gender Play: Girls and Boys in School* by Barrie Thorne (1993); Susan J. Scollay's "The Forgotten Half," *The American School Board Journal* (April 1994); Gilbert T. Sewall's review of the AAUW report in *Society* (May–June 1993); and Marie C. Wilson's review of the Sadkers' book *Failing at Fairness* in *The Washington Post Education Review* (April 3, 1994).

Three noteworthy books are *Gender and Schools* by Lynda Measor and Patricia J. Sikes (1992); *Beyond Silenced Voices* by Lois Weis and Michelle Fine (1993); and *School Girls* by Peggy Orenstein (1993), which contains a model for a nonsexist classroom. Also worth reading are Sherrie L. Gradin's "What's Gender Got to Do With It?" *National Forum* (Winter 1994); "The Road Less Traveled by Girls," by Natalie Carter Holms, *The School Administrator* (December 1991); and Sandra Acker's "Gender and Education: Into the 1990s," *Journal of Education Policy* (January–March 1994).

ISSUE 13

Is Full Inclusion of Disabled Students Desirable?

YES: Jean B. Arnold and Harold W. Dodge, from "Room for All," *The American School Board Journal* (October 1994)

NO: Albert Shanker, from "Where We Stand on the Rush to Inclusion," *Vital Speeches of the Day* (March 1, 1994)

ISSUE SUMMARY

YES: Attorney Jean B. Arnold and school superintendent Harold W. Dodge discuss the federal Individuals with Disabilities Education Act and argue that its implementation can benefit all students.

NO: Teachers' union president Albert Shanker maintains that the full inclusion ideology, although well intentioned, is not the best way to educate students with disabilities and may, in fact, be harmful in many cases.

The Education for All Handicapped Children Act of 1975 (Public Law 94–142), which mandated that schools provide free public education to all students with disabilities, is an excellent example of how federal influence can translate social policy into practical alterations of public school procedures at the local level. With this act, the general social policy of equalizing educational opportunity and the specific social policy of ensuring that young people with various physical, mental, and emotional disabilities are constructively served by tax dollars were brought together in a law designed to provide persons with disabilities the same services and opportunities as nondisabled individuals. Legislation of such delicate matters does not ensure success, however. Although most people applaud the intentions of the act, some people find the expense ill-proportioned, and others feel that the federal mandate is unnecessary and heavy-handed.

Some of the main elements of the 1975 legislation were that all learners between the ages of 3 and 21 with handicaps—defined as students who are hearing impaired, visually impaired, physically disabled, emotionally disturbed, mentally retarded, or who have special learning disabilities—would be provided a free public education, that each of these students would have an individualized education program jointly developed by the school and the parents, that each student would be placed in the least restrictive learning environment appropriate to him or her, and that parents would have approval rights in placement decisions.

The 1990 version of the original law, the Individuals with Disabilities Education Act (IDEA), has spawned an "inclusive schools" movement, whose supporters recommend that *no* students be assigned to special classrooms or segregated wings of public schools. According to advocates of the act, "The inclusion option signifies the end of labeling and separate classes but not the end of necessary supports and services" for all students needing them.

The primary justification for inclusion, or "mainstreaming," has traditionally resided in the belief that disabled children have a right to and can benefit from inclusion in a regular educational environment whenever possible. French sociologist Emile Durkheim felt that attachment and belonging were essential to human development. If this is the case, then integration of young people with disabilities into regular classrooms and into other areas of social intercourse—as opposed to keeping them isolated in special classrooms—would seem to be highly desirable.

But practical concerns sometimes clash with governmental desires. Under IDEA, for example, students with disabilities who are placed in regular classroom settings must be provided with appropriate supplemental resources and services. In a period of economic restriction, however, how much money can a locality afford to spend on the special needs of certain students? The Supreme Court decision in the 1982 *Rowley* case drew some limits by denying continuous sign language interpretation for a deaf student in a public school. Justice William H. Rehnquist, in stating the majority position, contended that the schools are not obliged to provide services "sufficient to maximize each child's potential." In many decisions since *Rowley*, the lower courts have been generally supportive of parents who seek expanded services for their disabled children. In a recent Virginia case, however, the public school system was allowed to remove an autistic boy from a regular classroom over his parents' objections.

Douglas Fuchs and Lynn S. Fuchs, in "Inclusive Schools Movement and the Radicalization of Special Education Reform," *Exceptional Children* (February 1994), pose this question: How likely is the "inclusive schools" movement to bring special education and general education into synergistic alignment? One viewpoint comes from a five-year government study released in 1994, which found that special-needs students who spend all their time in regular classrooms fail more frequently than those who spend only some. This report, along with the American Federation of Teachers' call for an end to the practice of seeking all-day inclusion for every child, no matter how medically fragile or emotionally disturbed, have helped to keep the issue boiling.

In the selections that follow, Jean B. Arnold and Harold W. Dodge direct specific suggestions toward school board policymakers for complying with the requirements and intentions of the current law regarding full inclusion, and they argue that quality inclusion programs and services for students with disabilities will be beneficial to all students. Union leader Albert Shanker asserts that the "moral crusade" for inclusion may be well intentioned but that it is fraught with dangers for all concerned.

YES
Jean B. Arnold and Harold W. Dodge

ROOM FOR ALL

Few topics ignite more controversy among educators these days than full inclusion of disabled youngsters in regular classrooms. Part of the reason is that many people don't understand—or wrongly understand—what's required under the law.

One of the greatest myths is that full inclusion obligates a public school district to educate *every* student with a disability in a regular classroom for the *entire* school day. Full inclusion doesn't mean that. It means students with disabilities might be placed in a regular education classroom on a full-time basis, but, if appropriate and necessary, they still can be "pulled out" for special instruction or related services.

That is what Congress originally intended in adopting the statutory provision of the Individuals with Disabilities Education Act (IDEA) concerning placement in the "least restrictive environment appropriate." But many educators have been implementing the concept backward.

Here's what we mean: School officials might decide to place Johnny, a 6-year-old Down's syndrome child with an IQ of 45, in a classroom for the trainable mentally retarded as soon as his parents enroll him in school. They might later determine Johnny can be "mainstreamed" with regular education students for art, music, and lunch.

Actually, the way the law reads, Johnny should be placed in a regular classroom first, along with appropriate supplemental aids and services to assist him in that setting. If Johnny isn't benefiting from the education he receives in that setting, then the district should consider more restrictive and segregated options or settings that would enable him to get a good education, but still remain in his regular classroom as much as possible.

In some cases, even this scenario is not appropriate, and the student needs a more segregated environment, but the determination must be made on a case-by-case basis for each child. And it should begin with the idea of placement in a regular classroom and only then move to the more restricted setting—not vice versa.

PLACEMENT

For school boards, understanding inclusion—and what's legally required of your schools in educating disabled students—begins with understanding certain key legal concepts surrounding inclusion, as well as the findings in significant court cases.

The first legal concept to be familiar with is *placement*. Simply defined, placement is the setting in which the disabled child receives instruction. It is *not* the curriculum or program provided the student.

Both IDEA and case law indicate that you should heed certain points when deciding a child's placement:

- If possible, you should place a disabled child in a regular education classroom in the public school the child would attend if he or she had no disability. The deciding factor: whether, given the nature or severity of the child's disability, appropriate goals and objectives for the child can be achieved in a regular classroom, with or without the use of supplemental aids and services. The child's individualized education program, or IEP, determines the appropriate goals and objectives for that child.

- If you rule out the regular classroom for a specific child, you must select an alternative placement from a continuum of settings and arrangements (arrayed from least restrictive to most restrictive) maintained by the school system. The continuum might include, for example, resource-room instruction, a self-contained classroom, or even a private placement. You must select the placement in which the appropriate education goals for the child can

be achieved with the fewest restrictions possible.

- Even when you rule out primary placement in the regular education environment, the disabled child must be educated with, and allowed to interact with, other children to the maximum extent appropriate to the needs of the disabled child.

- Placement decisions must be made at least annually by a group of people who consider broad-based, documented information about the child. These people must know the child and understand the evaluation data and the placement alternatives. At a minimum, the school representatives on the committee should include an educator who is knowledgeable about the student's disability, the student's teacher, and a special education supervisor.

LEAST-RESTRICTIVE ENVIRONMENT

Another essential item for you and your school board colleagues to understand is *least restrictive environment*, or LRE. According to IDEA, "Each public agency shall insure: (1) That to the maximum extent appropriate, handicapped children, including children in public or private institutions or other care facilities, are educated with children who are not handicapped, and (2) That special classes, separate schooling, or other removal of handicapped children from the regular educational environment occurs only when the nature or severity of the handicap is such that education in regular classes with the use of supplementary aids and services cannot be achieved satisfactorily." (34 C.F.R. 300.550 [b].)

Note that the law doesn't prohibit separate classes and separate schools; it merely requires they be filled on the basis of student need—not administrative convenience.

The leading court case in defining least restrictive environment is *Daniel R.R. v. State Board of Education* (1989). This case established several questions your district can use to decide whether a disabled child can be educated satisfactorily in the regular classroom. Before removing any child from the regular education classroom, your district should weigh its answers to each of these questions:

1. Have you taken steps to accommodate children with disabilities in regular education? IDEA requires school districts to provide supplementary aids and services and to modify the regular education program in an effort to mainstream children with disabilities. Examples of these modifications include shortened assignments, note-taking assistance, visual aids, oral tests, and frequent breaks. The modifications should be geared to each disabled child's individual needs. If you make no effort to accommodate children with disabilities in the regular education classroom, you violate the law.

2. Are your district's efforts to accommodate the child in regular education sufficient or token? A school district's efforts to supplement and modify regular education so disabled children can participate must amount to more than "mere token gestures," according to the ruling in *Daniel R.R.* The IDEA requirement for accommodating disabled children in regular education is broad. But, the ruling says, a school district need not provide "every conceivable supplementary aid or service" to assist disabled children in regular education. Furthermore, regular education instructors are not required to de-

vote all or even most of their time to one disabled child to the detriment of the entire class.

A district also is not required to modify the regular education program beyond recognition. As the court held in *Daniel R.R.*: "[M]ainstreaming would be pointless if we forced instructors to modify the regular education curriculum to the extent that the handicapped child is not required to learn any of the skills normally taught in regular education." Such extensive modifications would result in special education being taught in a regular education classroom.

3. Will the child benefit educationally from regular education? Another factor to consider is whether the child is capable of benefiting from regular education. Central to this question is whether the child can achieve the "essential elements" of the regular education curriculum.

You must consider both the nature and severity of the child's handicap as well as the curriculum and goals of the regular education class in determining educational benefit. However, a disabled child cannot be expected to achieve on a par with children who don't have disabilities before being permitted to attend the regular education classroom. Furthermore, you must remember that academic achievement is not the only purpose of mainstreaming. Allowing the child to be with children who aren't disabled can be beneficial in itself.

4. What will be the child's overall educational experience in the mainstreamed environment? Just because a child can receive only minimal academic benefit from regular education doesn't mean the child automatically should be excluded from regular education. You must consider the child's overall educational experience in the mainstreamed environment, balancing the benefits of regular and special education. Children who can't comprehend many of the essential elements of a lesson might still receive great benefit from their nondisabled peers, who serve as language and behavior models.

On the other hand, some children might become frustrated by their inability to succeed in the regular education classroom. If this frustration outweighs any benefit received from regular education, mainstreaming might prove detrimental to the child. Similarly, other children might need more structure than is available in the regular education setting. Your district must determine whether mainstreaming would be more beneficial or detrimental to the disabled child, considering both academic and social benefit.

5. What effect does the disabled child's presence have on the regular classroom environment? In determining the LRE, consider whether the child's presence in a regular education classroom adversely affects the education other children are receiving. First, determine whether the child engages in disruptive behavior that negatively affects the other children. Second, determine whether the disabled child requires so much of the teacher's attention that the teacher is forced to ignore the other children. If the teacher spends so much time with the disabled child that the rest of the class suffers, then the child should be educated in a special education classroom.

If you determine the child cannot be educated full time in the regular education classroom, you still have a duty to mainstream the child to the maximum

extent appropriate. For instance, if regular academic classes are not appropriate for a given disabled child, the district could mainstream the child for nonacademic classes and activities, such as gym, recess, music, art, or lunch.

In short, placement in regular education is not an "all-or-nothing" proposition. Rather, school districts are required to offer a continuum of services for disabled children. A disabled child should be mainstreamed in regular education for as much of the time as is appropriate. Rarely will total exclusion from children without disabilities be deemed appropriate.

BEYOND THE LEGAL REQUIREMENTS

Regardless of what IDEA says, the issue of whether students with disabilities can or should be served in regular education settings will continue to be debated and decided in the legal arena. Even so, the real issues are not legal; they are based in tradition, values, and beliefs. An increased understanding of how inclusion works, when implemented under the law, will help shape those traditions, values, and beliefs and will help school boards like yours design and put into practice high-quality inclusive programs and educational services for their students with disabilities.

Such services, however, can't be mandated or created without the contributions of teachers, administrators, and parents. Your board can try to reduce the number of potential problems or pitfalls by providing technical assistance for teachers and by finding activities that build consensus between staff and parents and provide information and education for everyone. Also, your district can attempt to learn from the successful experiences of other school districts.

A compelling case for inclusion does exist, supported by research, school statistics, and informal observations about inclusive programs presently in place. The biggest benefit will come when disabled students feel they "belong" with the regular-education chil- dren, rather than being segregated in separate classes or separate schools. As Sen. Robert T. Stafford, the Republican senator from Vermont and one of the bill's primary sponsors, said on the final days of passage of the Education of All Handicapped Children Act, the precursor of IDEA, these extraordinary children want only to lead ordinary lives.

NO

Albert Shanker

WHERE WE STAND ON THE RUSH
TO INCLUSION

United States education is in trouble and there are a lot of reasons for it. One of them is the tendency of American education to be moved—massively moved—by fads and ideologies. We can think back to the 1950s when I started teaching and something swept the country called the New Math. The overwhelming majority of teachers said it doesn't work; the kids don't get it; we don't get it. But it took 25 to 30 years before there was recognition of its weaknesses and a movement away from it. And New Math is not the only example of this phenomenon.

If we think of a field like medicine, we see that in the medical and pharmaceutical worlds, there are all sorts of cautions taken before new medicine is placed on the market. When something is discovered and you read about it in the newspapers, you know that you can't go out the next day and buy it at the drugstore because it has to be thoroughly tested before it becomes available. You know that there will be many additional experiments before this new remedy is marketed. When it finally becomes available, there are always all sorts of warnings attached.

Unfortunately, in education we tend to operate in such a way that one or two or a handful of people or advocacy groups grab on to some new idea, present it as a panacea, and "sell" it to an educational community that is hungry for answers. And once a fad is adopted, it takes a long, long period of time after the damage is done to undo it.

Now we have a rush towards something called inclusion. We don't know what the long-term effects are. We have had mainstreaming for more than 15 years, but in mainstreaming disabled students' progress was always being monitored by special education teachers. Inclusion was tried in only a few small places and immediately was viewed as the panacea, the only moral answer, the only way to educate students with disabilities. In addition, some people now claim that anybody who's against inclusion is immoral, a new segregationist, or antieducation. That kind of rhetoric is quite effective in shutting off discussion. There may be a lot of people who are intimidated or afraid to say anything, even though they don't like what's happening.

The inclusion that is being advocated is the placement of all students with disabilities into general education classrooms *without regard to the nature or severity of the students' disabilities, without regard to their ability to behave and function appropriately in a regular classroom, without regard to the educational benefits they derive, and without regard to the impact that that inclusion has on the other students in the class.* In other words, it's basically a view that this is the right thing to do, and it's the right thing under all circumstances. And there is a tremendous push on the part of some U.S. government officials, state boards of education, and a number of advocacy groups to implement that brand of inclusion.

Before we go any further with our discussion of inclusion, it's important to start with what schools are about. Schools have three functions: the development of knowledge and skills, the development of adults who are economically viable, and the development of social and interpersonal relations. Looked at another way, there are intellectual benefits, there are economic benefits, and there are political and social benefits in terms of developing the ability to function within a democracy. The argument on the part of the full inclusionists rests on the social benefits of education. Some have even stated that they don't care if other children don't learn to read and write, if they have learned to "get along."

Any new policy in American education that will affect what students learn and their interpersonal and social development should not be implemented hastily and certainly should not be implemented before there is full discussion and scrutiny of the issues. New programs should not be implemented without some periods of experimentation where we have an opportunity to see and judge the effects of actual implementation.

Large numbers of books are written about well-intentioned programs, things that the government tried to do in the '50s and '60s and '70s that didn't work out quite the way they were supposed to. I think many of these programs were worthwhile, even if they had some unintended consequences. But the fact is that we now know that we often get something that's quite different from what was envisioned in the first place. And, therefore, it's important to engage in some trial, some experimentation, before deciding that everybody has to do it in this particular way.

There is no doubt that every child, regardless of abilities, disabilities, problems, or status, has a right to a free public education. But that does not mean that any particular child has a right to a particular placement in a particular class or a particular school.

I believe that large numbers of students who are now separated in special education could undoubtedly be included and integrated in regular classrooms. I believe that it would be profitable for many students with disabilities and for the rest of the class if many disabled students not now being educated in regular classrooms were placed there. Therefore, I agree with those who say that we probably have too many youngsters separated out and many who could be integrated. Many of our members who are very concerned about this movement toward inclusion feel that way, too.

The AFT's [American Federation of Teachers'] position is not a movement to label and to separate and to create two systems. It is a position that says that we cannot make blanket decisions about every student. We cannot say that all students should be in regular classrooms whatever their disability, whatever their ability to function in a classroom and profit from it, and whatever the impact on the other youngsters.

We offer an alternative to the full inclusionists' point of view, and that alternative is that placement ought to depend on those very things. It ought to depend on the nature of the disability. It ought to depend on the ability of that child to function within a regular classroom. It ought to depend upon the impact of such a placement on that child and on all the other children.

In other words, we are staying away from ideology, away from the notion that the same thing fits all kids, that all kids have to be treated the same even though they're different. We need to treat youngsters in terms of what's best for them and not according to some ideological theory.

In each case, we need to ask what is the impact of a particular placement on the child who has a disability, and we also have to ask what is the impact on all the others in the class. We are especially concerned with children who are very emotionally disturbed and with children who are medically fragile and need medical attention throughout the day. Very little good is done by including children in a regular class if the entire academic mission of that class, the entire focus, becomes "How do we adjust to this child?" When the teacher and the paraprofessional and everybody else in the class focus on how to handle one particular child, what is the effect on the rest of the class?

If parents see that their kids are not getting out of school what they're supposed to be getting, that the entire class is focused on adjusting to one very disruptive child or on a child whose many medical needs must be met by the teacher, those parents are going to start pressing for vouchers. They're going to start pressing for the privatization of education, and instead of a public school system which includes many children of many different races, religions, nationalities, we're going to end up with highly separated and segregated schools. So that in the name of inclusion, we may end up getting the most separated and segregated school system that we can possibly have in this country. That is one of the central dangers of this movement.

One argument for inclusion is a civil rights argument. But this is based on a faulty analogy. Once upon a time, we used to segregate black youngsters and send them to separate schools. The Supreme Court of the United States ruled that even if you tried to provide equal facilities in those schools, separate can never be equal. The view in the full inclusion movement is that once you separate kids out, you label them, and there is a stigma attached to the label. Therefore, the argument goes, a judgment that was true for black youngsters during the period of segregation is also true for youngsters today who suffer from some disability. Therefore, it follows, we must end all separation.

The problem with the analogy is that it's not very accurate. Black youngsters were being kept out for one reason, because they were black, because of the color of their skin. There is the same range of learning abilities among black youngsters as among white youngsters, and the black students were kept out for a reason that was totally irrelevant and totally racist. It was race and not their ability to function within normal classrooms that kept them out. But if a youngster is kept out of the classroom because that youngster needs instruction in Braille or if a youngster is kept out of a classroom because his or her medical problems are not likely to be attended to in a regular classroom, we have something that's very different.

In one case, youngsters were separated out for a reason that was totally irrelevant to their education. As a matter of fact, it was destructive of their education. In another case, youngsters are being separated out because of special needs and special problems that they have. Two very, very different motivations and two very, very different attitudes.

We are saying that some children need separate classrooms not to harm them or because anyone desires that the youngsters be separated, but to meet their different and special educational needs. If a youngster is constantly violent and constantly noisy and disruptive, so the class can't function when that youngster is there, we need to separate that youngster out so that he or she can learn and so that the rest of the class can function.

I see no basis for the civil rights analogy. Black youngsters then were so eager to learn that, when the civil rights movement reached its height, they were willing to risk a great deal walking through lines of hostile people protected by troops, they were so eager to learn. This is very different from a youngster who is yelling and screaming

and fighting and throwing things. The analogy just does not stand.

I would very strongly suggest that the way we should behave as educators and the way we should behave as individuals would be very much the way a caring and intelligent parent would act. What was very interesting about my appearance on a number of radio shows on this issue was that a number of parents who called in and talked about the fact that they had four or five children and they were very, very different. And parents who had an extremely disturbed youngster who was violent would not insist that that youngster be at all the other activities with all the other children. One youngster might be taking piano lessons; another might be athletically inclined; a third might be doing something else. Many of these parents were very concerned that one of the youngsters would disturb and disrupt and destroy the work of the other youngsters. It seems to me that the same kind of judgment that an intelligent parent would exercise ought to be exercised by all of us as a society.

Not very long ago, a film came out called "Educating Peter." I saw it last year at the AFT QuEST Conference [July, 1993, Washington, D.C.] where we had a session on this issue. It is a very moving film, which was really put together to be an argument in favor of inclusion. What the film did not tell you was that inclusion there was really done right. That is, the teacher involved was given time off and given special training. There were additional personnel assigned to the class. All of the supports that are frequently missing were there.

But as I watched that film, I saw that Peter was very unpredictable and very disruptive, and on occasion violent. At the end of the film, he was less disruptive and able to relate to the teacher and the other youngsters a little bit more. The other youngsters had learned to accept him and live with him, and my heart went out. It is a tear-jerker and you see that something very good was accomplished there because the kids were a little closer together. My emotional reactions were the same as everybody else who watched the film.

But I had another reaction, too. I wondered whether the youngsters in that class had spent a whole year in adjusting to how to live with Peter and whether they did any reading, whether they did any writing, whether they did any mathematics, whether they did any history, whether they did any geography. And it seems to me that it's a terrible shame that we don't ask that question. Is the only function of the schools to get kids to learn to live with each other? Would we be satisfied if that's what we did and if all the youngsters came out not knowing any of the things that they're supposed to learn academically? Will any of them, disabled or non-disabled, be able to function as adults?

We now have legislation, Goals 2000, that President Clinton is supporting and the governors are supporting. We have a National Educational Goals Panel. We have an attempt to lift the nation very quickly from a low level of performance to a high level of performance. There's great doubt as to whether we can do it, because it will be very difficult. We need coordination of three levels of government. We need substantial retraining of teachers. We need different attitudes on the part of students towards their work.

Do we really believe that we can simultaneously accomplish that mission and at the same time do something that no other country in the world has ever done? Do we really believe that we can take youngsters with very, very severe disabilities and, at the same time we're trying to get world-class education, include youngsters who need extensive medical attention and youngsters who are extremely disturbed and deal with all of their problems?

The advocates hope that by mixing all children, children with disabilities will gain the respect of children who are not disabled. I think the underlying motive is undeniably excellent—we're all going to be living together as adults; we're going to be working together as adults; and therefore, if we can live with each other as much as possible as youngsters in school, that will be the beginning of learning to live and work with each other as grownups. But if extremely disturbed, violent youngsters are put in the regular classrooms, do we really think that the other youngsters are going to learn respect—or are they going to learn contempt? Are they going to develop hostility? This rush to inclusion has created a situation where placements of students with disabilities are being made incorrectly in many cases. Because this is so, we may develop exactly the opposite values that we say that we want to develop.

One of the reasons for the push to inclusion is that taking youngsters with special needs out of small classrooms, not giving them special teachers, psychologists, social workers, therapists and other professionals, and including them with everybody else saves money. And during a period of time like this when school budgets are under attack, many of these youngsters are likely to lose their special help when they are placed in regular classrooms. Part of the thrust of the inclusion movement is saving money.

Some school districts see that special education is more expensive and reason that if they could push all disabled youngsters into regular education, they can squeeze some of the money out of their special education budgets and have special education go away. In theory, youngsters with special problems who are integrated into a regular class are supposed to have special services follow them. But given the financial situation of our states and school districts, and given the fact that the federal government has never met its commitment to fund its share of education for the disabled, does anybody really believe that the large amount of money that's necessary to provide these services in individual classrooms is going to be made available?

What we are doing here is very difficult to do. There are other organizations out there. There are people in those organizations who have thought the same thoughts and felt the same things and had the same experiences and had letters and telephone calls from teachers and from parents and from administrators and from different constituents. Many have made public statements about their concerns. But it didn't seem that anyone who is pushing this movement would listen. In this climate, the AFT could not sit back and remain silent. We have joined them.

I want to conclude by saying that I think that we can turn this around. There are many, many advocacy groups in the special education field who are unhappy and uneasy with this policy. In the radio shows that I was on, there were parents whose youngsters were included who said they agreed with us because they weren't sure that their kids would be able to adjust, and they wanted the option of being able to move their kids back if it didn't work out. They liked the idea that they could try this out and if it worked, of course, they wanted it that way. But they didn't want it that way as a matter of policy. And they didn't want it that way as a matter of ideology.

I have a copy of a letter that appeared in the Eugene, Oregon newspaper called *The Register-Guard.* It's a short letter, but it's one that really shows that somebody out there understands the issues and the politics of it very clearly. The headline is "Challenge and Inclusion." The letter says,

"Albert Shanker, President of the American Federation of Teachers, spoke the unspeakable when he suggested that not all special needs children should be fully mainstreamed or included in the regular classroom. The inclusion movement is both politically correct, namely satisfying the liberals, and cost-effective, namely satisfying the conservatives. By challenging it, Shanker has guaranteed himself attacks from both camps.

"I applaud his willingness to accept such attacks. I hope his comments will remind us that placement of special needs students should be based not on political correctness or economic expediency, but on careful consideration of the physical, emotional, educational and social welfare of all the students involved. I have taught special needs students in special programs for 28 years. My goal and the goal of every special needs teacher I have known has always been to help students develop those skills, behaviors and attitudes that would allow them to return to and succeed in the regular classroom, or upon leaving school, to succeed on the job and in their personal lives.

"Every special needs teacher I've ever known is dedicated to each student's placement in the least restrictive appropriate educational setting. However, in this era of cutbacks, special needs programs are being dismantled and special needs students are being included in regular classes. Classes that are increasing in size by five to ten students and wherein teacher's aides are being eliminated as further cost-saving measures. Certainly the inclusion movement is politically correct and certainly it's cost-effective. But please don't try to tell me it's good for the kids."

That's our view.

POSTSCRIPT

Is Full Inclusion of Disabled Students Desirable?

One wit has claimed that P.L. 94–142 was really a "full employment act for lawyers." Indeed, there has been much litigation regarding the identification, classification, placement, and specialized treatment of disabled children since the introduction of the 1975 act.

Some important cases that came to light around the time of P.L. 94–142's implementation include *Diana v. State Board of Education*, which dealt with the misclassification of mental retardation for Mexican American students; *Armstrong v. Kline*, which considered extended-year programming for a severely handicapped student; *Department of Education v. Katherine D.*, which debated regular classroom placement of a child with multiple disabilities; and *Irving Independent School District v. Tatro*, which dealt with the provision of catheterization services.

More recently, the ruling in *Greer v. Rome City School District* (1992) permitted the parents to place their child, who has Down's syndrome, in a regular classroom with supplementary services. Also, the decision in *Sacramento City Unified School District v. Holland* (1994) allowed a girl with an IQ of 44 to be placed in a regular classroom full time, in accordance with her parents' wishes (the school system had wanted the student to split her time equally between regular and special education classes). These cases demonstrate that although the aspect of the law stipulating parental involvement in the development of individual education programs can invite cooperation, it can also lead to conflict. Who knows best about a child's educational needs, the parents or the professionals?

Teacher attitude becomes a crucial component in the success or failure of placements of disabled students in regular classrooms. Some articles addressing this and related matters are Martin Diebold, "A School-Level Investigation of Predictions of Attitudes About Mainstreaming," *Journal of Special Education* (Fall 1986); "Willingness of Regular and Special Educators to Teach Students With Handicaps," by Karen Derk Gans, *Exceptional Children* (October 1987); W. N. Bender, "The Case Against Mainstreaming," *Education* (Spring 1985); and Lynn Miller, "The Regular Education Initiative and School Reform: Lessons from the Mainstream," *Remedial and Special Education* (May–June 1990).

An interview with an authority on this issue can be found in "David Hornbeck on the Changing Face of Special Education," *The School Administrator* (February 1992). Also, interesting personal accounts are offered in Susan Ohanian, "P.L. 94–142: Mainstream or Quicksand?" *Phi Delta Kappan* (November

1990); Pete Idstein, "Swimming Against the Mainstream(ing)," *Phi Delta Kappan* (December 1993); and Tina Vaughn, "Inclusion Can Succeed," *Equity and Excellence in Education* (April 1994).

Other noteworthy articles are "Inclusive Education: An Issue of Social Justice," by Linda Couture Gerrard, *Equity and Excellence in Education* (April 1994); "Disruptive Disabled Kids: Inclusion Confusion," by Diane Brockett, *School Board News* (October 1994); and two pieces in the September 1994 *Phi Delta Kappan*, "Mainstreaming: One School's Reality" and "Thinking of Inclusion for All Special Needs Students? Better Think Again."

ISSUE 14

Do Black Students Need an Afrocentric Curriculum?

YES: Molefi Kete Asante, from "The Afrocentric Idea in Education," *Journal of Negro Education* (Spring 1991)

NO: Arthur M. Schlesinger, Jr., from "The Disuniting of America," *American Educator* (Winter 1991)

ISSUE SUMMARY

YES: Black studies professor Molefi Kete Asante puts forth his argument for providing black students with an Afrocentric frame of reference, which he feels would enhance their self-esteem and learning.

NO: Noted historian Arthur M. Schlesinger, Jr., documents his concerns about the recent spread of Afrocentric programs, the multiculturalization of the curriculum, and the use of history as therapy.

A more specific manifestation of the argument over multicultural emphases in the curriculum of the public schools can be seen in the recent experimentation with Afrocentric frameworks in predominantly black neighborhood schools and in the attempts to create all-black male classes and schools. Although many school districts are revising the curriculum to embrace a more multicultural perspective, some (such as Atlanta, Georgia) are developing and using an African-centered curricular base. Movement in this direction has been inspired, at least in part, by the work of Temple University scholar Molefi Kete Asante, framer of the Afrocentric idea in his 1980 book *Afrocentricity.*

The Afrocentrists feel that the traditional emphasis on white European history and culture, and the disregard of African history and culture, alienates black schoolchildren who are unable to feel an attachment to the content being offered. Many who support the Afrocentrists would agree with Asa G. Hilliard III, a professor of educational psychology, who has stated that there is a vast amount of important information about African people that *everyone*, not only black schoolchildren, should be aware of.

In his much-discussed book, *The Disuniting of America: Reflections on a Multicultural Society* (1991), historian Arthur M. Schlesinger, Jr., denounces this movement as an extreme example of a "cult of ethnicity." Agreeing with Schlesinger, David Nicholson (in " 'Afrocentrism' and the Tribalization of America: The Misguided Logic of Ethnic Education Schemes," *The Washing-*

ton Post, September 23, 1990) argues that "the sweeping call for 'curricula of inclusion' is based on untested, unproven premises. Worse, because it intentionally exaggerates differences, it seems likely to exacerbate racial and ethnic tensions."

To which Kariamu Welsh, a proponent of Asante's position, would reply:

> The eyes of the African-American must be on his own center, one that reflects and resembles him and speaks to him in his own language.... If one understands properly African history, an assumption can never be made that Afrocentricity is a back to 'anything' movement. It is an uncovering of one's true self, it is the pinpointing of one's center, and it is the clarity and focus through which black people must see the world in order to escalate. [From the foreword to Asante's book.—Ed.]

Lending support to Welsh's position, a study by a North Carolina University researcher showed that studying Africa and African American history and culture leads to improved overall academic performance by black students.

A different slant emerges from the insights of Richard Cohen, a *Washington Post* columnist writing in an October 7, 1990, column: "Changing the curriculum in school districts where blacks predominate would tend only to put these students further outside the mainstream. They would know what others do not, which is all right. But they would not know what most others do—and that's been the problem in the first place."

A subissue of the basic controversy involves providing not only an Afrocentric curriculum for black students but all-male classes or even all-male schools. Some commentators claim that the federal inattention to poor urban families in the 1980s provided the impetus for proposing such classes and schools. As Larry Cuban states in "Desperate Remedies for Desperate Times," *Education Week*, November 20, 1991, "To advocate a single-sex school, an Afrocentric curriculum taught by black male teachers who enforce strict rules is, indeed, a strong response to a desperate situation." The effort attempts to combat the present epidemic of academic failure and male-on-male violence.

In the articles that follow, Molefi Kete Asante establishes the necessity of Afrocentric programs, examines theoretical and philosophical underpinnings of his view, and charts a path for implementation at all levels of education. Arthur M. Schlesinger, Jr., questions the basic assumptions from which Asante's argument flows and expresses fears about divisive strategies and historical manipulation.

YES

Molefi Kete Asante

THE AFROCENTRIC IDEA IN EDUCATION

INTRODUCTION

Many of the principles that govern the development of the Afrocentric idea in education were first established by Carter G. Woodson in *The Mis-education of the Negro* (1933). Indeed, Woodson's classic reveals the fundamental problems pertaining to the education of the African person in America. As Woodson contends, African Americans have been educated away from their own culture and traditions and attached to the fringes of European culture; thus dislocated from themselves, Woodson asserts that African Americans often valorize European culture to the detriment of their own heritage (p. 7). Although Woodson does not advocate rejection of American citizenship or nationality, he believed that assuming African Americans hold the same position as European Americans vis-à-vis the realities of America would lead to the psychological and cultural death of the African American population. Furthermore, if education is ever to be substantive and meaningful within the context of American society, Woodson argues, it must first address the African's historical experiences, both in Africa and America (p. 7). That is why he places on education, and particularly on the traditionally African American colleges, the burden of teaching the African American to be responsive to the long traditions and history of Africa as well as America. Woodson's alert recognition, more than 50 years ago, that something is severely wrong with the way African Americans are educated provides the principal impetus for the Afrocentric approach to American education.

In this article I will examine the nature and scope of this approach, establish its necessity, and suggest ways to develop and disseminate it throughout all levels of education. Two propositions stand in the background of the theoretical and philosophical issues I will present. These ideas represent the core presuppositions on which I have based most of my work in the field of education, and they suggest the direction of my own thinking about what education is capable of doing to and for an already politically and economically marginalized people—African Americans:

1. Education is fundamentally a social phenomenon whose ultimate purpose is to socialize the learner; to send a child to school is to prepare that child to become part of a social group.
2. Schools are reflective of the societies that develop them (i.e., a White supremacist-dominated society will develop a White supremacist educational system).

DEFINITIONS

An alternative framework suggests that other definitional assumptions can provide a new paradigm for the examination of education within the American society. For example, in education, *centricity* refers to a perspective that involves locating students within the context of their own cultural references so that they can relate socially and psychologically to other cultural perspectives. Centricity is a concept that can be applied to any culture. The centrist paradigm is supported by research showing that the most productive method of teaching any student is to place his or her group within the center of the context of knowledge (Asante, 1990). For White students in America this is easy because almost all the experiences discussed in American classrooms are approached from the standpoint of White perspectives and history. American education, however, is not centric; it is Eurocentric. Consequently, non-White students are also made to see themselves and their groups as the "acted upon." Only rarely do they read or hear of non-White people as active participants in history. This is as true for a discussion of the American Revolution as it is for a discussion of Dante's *Inferno;* for instance, most classroom discussions of the European slave trade concentrate on the activities of Whites rather than on the resistance efforts of Africans. A person educated in a truly centric fashion comes to view all groups' contributions as significant and useful. Even a White person educated in such a system does not assume superiority based upon racist notions. Thus, a truly centric education is different from a Eurocentric, racist (that is, White supremacist) education.

Afrocentricity is a frame of reference wherein phenomena are viewed from the perspective of the African person. The Afrocentric approach seeks in every situation the appropriate centrality of the African person (Asante, 1987). In education this means that teachers provide students the opportunity to study the world and its people, concepts, and history from an African world view. In most classrooms, whatever the subject, Whites are located in the center perspective position. How alien the African American child must feel, how like an outsider! The little African American child who sits in a classroom and is taught to accept as heroes and heroines individuals who defamed African people is being actively de-centered, dislocated, and made into a nonperson, one whose aim in life might be to one day shed that "badge of inferiority": his or her Blackness. In Afrocentric educational settings, however, teachers do not marginalize African American children by causing them to question their own self-worth because their people's story is seldom told. By seeing themselves as the subjects rather than the objects of education—be the discipline biology, medicine, literature, or social studies—African American students come to see themselves not merely as seekers of knowledge but as integral participants in it. Because all content areas are adaptable to an Afrocentric approach, African American students can be made to see themselves as centered in the reality of any discipline.

It must be emphasized that Afrocentricity is *not* a Black version of Eurocentricity (Asante, 1987). Eurocentricity is based on White supremacist notions whose purposes are to protect White privilege and advantage in education, economics, politics, and so forth. Unlike Eurocentricity, Afrocentricity does not condone ethnocentric valorization at the expense of degrading other groups' perspectives. Moreover, Eurocentricity presents the particular historical reality of Europeans as the sum total of the human experience (Asante, 1987). It imposes Eurocentric realities as "universal"; i.e., that which is White is presented as applying to the human condition in general, while that which is non-White is viewed as group-specific and therefore not "human." This explains why some scholars and artists of African descent rush to deny their Blackness; they believe that to exist as a Black person is not to exist as a universal human being. They are the individuals Woodson identified as preferring European art, language, and culture over African art, language, and culture; they believe that anything of European origin is inherently better than anything produced by or issuing from their own people. Naturally, the person of African descent should be centered in his or her historical experiences as an African, but Eurocentric curricula produce such aberrations of perspective among persons of color.

Multiculturalism in education is a nonhierarchical approach that respects and celebrates a variety of cultural perspectives on world phenomena (Asante, 1991). The multicultural approach holds that although European culture is the majority culture in the United States, that is not sufficient reason for it to be imposed on diverse student populations as "universal." Multiculturalists assert that education, to have integrity, must begin with the proposition that all humans have contributed to world development and the flow of knowledge and information, and that most human achievements are the result of mutually interactive, international effort. Without a multicultural education, students remain essentially ignorant of the contributions of a major portion of the world's people. A multicultural education is thus a fundamental necessity for anyone who wishes to achieve competency in almost any subject.

The Afrocentric idea must be the stepping-stone from which the multicultural idea is launched. A truly authentic multicultural education, therefore, must be based upon the Afrocentric initiative. If this step is skipped, multicultural curricula, as they are increasingly being defined by White "resisters" (to be discussed below) will evolve without any substantive infusion of African American content, and the African American child will continue to be lost in the Eurocentric framework of education. In other words, the African American child will neither be confirmed nor affirmed in his or her own cultural information. For the mutual benefit of all Americans, this tragedy, which leads to the psychological and cultural dislocation of African American children, can and should be avoided.

THE REVOLUTIONARY
CHALLENGE

Because it centers African American students inside history, culture, science, and so forth rather than outside these subjects, the Afrocentric idea presents the most revolutionary challenge to the ideology of White supremacy in education during the past decade. No other theoretical position stated by African Americans has ever captured the imagination of such a wide range of scholars and students of history, sociology, communications, anthropology, and psychology. The Afrocentric challenge has been posed in three critical ways:

1. It questions the imposition of the White supremacist view as universal and/or classical (Asante, 1990).
2. It demonstrates the indefensibility of racist theories that assault multiculturalism and pluralism.
3. It projects a humanistic and pluralistic viewpoint by articulating Afrocentricity as a valid, nonhegemonic perspective.

SUPPRESSION AND DISTORTION:
SYMBOLS OF RESISTANCE

The forces of resistance to the Afrocentric, multicultural transformation of the curriculum and teaching practices began to assemble their wagons almost as quickly as word got out about the need for equality in education (Ravitch, 1990). Recently, the renowned historian Arthur Schlesinger and others formed a group called the Committee for the Defense of History. This is a paradoxical development because only lies, untruths, and inaccurate information need defending. In their arguments against

the Afrocentric perspective, these proponents of Eurocentrism often clothe their arguments in false categories and fake terms (i.e., "pluralistic" and "particularistic" multiculturalism) (Keto, 1990; Asante, 1991). Besides, as the late African scholar Cheikh Anta Diop (1980) maintained: "African history and Africa need no defense." Afrocentric education is not against history. It is *for* history—correct, accurate history—and if it is against anything, it is against the marginalization of African American, Hispanic American, Asian American, Native American, and other non-White children. The Committee for the Defense of History is nothing more than a futile attempt to buttress the crumbling pillars of a White supremacist system that conceals its true motives behind the cloak of American liberalism. It was created in the same spirit that generated Bloom's *The Closing of the American Mind* (1987) and Hirsch's *Cultural Literacy: What Every American Needs to Know* (1987), both of which were placed at the service of the White hegemony in education, particularly its curricular hegemony. This committee and other evidences of White backlash are a predictable challenge to the contemporary thrust for an Afrocentric, multicultural approach to education.

Naturally, different adherents to a theory will have different views on its meaning. While two discourses presently are circulating about multiculturalism, only one is relevant to the liberation of the minds of African and White people in the United States. That discourse is Afrocentricity: the acceptance of Africa as central to African people. Yet, rather than getting on board with Afrocentrists to fight against White hegemonic education, some Whites (and some Blacks as well) have opted to plead for a return to the educational plantation. Unfortunately for them, however, those days are gone, and such misinformation can never be packaged as accurate, correct education again.

Ravitch (1990), who argues that there are two kinds of multiculturalism— *pluralist multiculturalism* and *particularist multiculturalism*—is the leader of those professors whom I call "resisters" or opponents to Afrocentricity and multiculturalism. Indeed, Ravitch advances the imaginary divisions in multicultural perspectives to conceal her true identity as a defender of White supremacy. Her tactics are the tactics of those who prefer Africans and other non-Whites to remain on the mental and psychological plantation of Western civilization. In their arrogance the resisters accuse Afrocentrists and multiculturalists of creating "fantasy history" and "bizarre theories" of non-White people's contributions to civilization. What they prove, however, is their own ignorance. Additionally, Ravitch and others (Nicholson, 1990) assert that multiculturalism will bring about the "tribalization" of America, but in reality America has always been a nation of ethnic diversity. When one reads their works on multiculturalism, one realizes that they are really advocating the imposition of a White perspective on everybody else's culture. Believing that the Eurocentric position is indisputable, they attempt to resist and impede the progressive transformation of the monoethnic curriculum. Indeed, the closets of bigotry have opened to reveal various attempts by White scholars (joined by some Blacks) to defend White privilege in the curriculum in much the same way as it has been so staunchly defended in the larger society. It was perhaps inevitable that the introduction of the Afrocentric idea would open up the discussion of the American school curriculum in a profound way.

Why has Afrocentricity created so much of a controversy in educational circles? The idea that an African American child is placed in a stronger position to learn if he or she is centered—that is, if the child sees himself or herself within the content of the curriculum rather than at its margins—is not novel (Asante, 1980). What is revolutionary is the movement from the idea (conceptual stage) to its implementation in practice, when we begin to teach teachers how to put African American youth at the center of instruction. In effect, students are shown how to see with new eyes and hear with new ears. African American children learn to interpret and center phenomena in the context of African heritage, while White students are taught to see that their own centers are not threatened by the presence or contributions of African Americans and others.

THE CONDITION OF EUROCENTRIC EDUCATION

Institutions such as schools are conditioned by the character of the nation in which they are developed. Just as crime and politics are different in different nations, so, too, is education. In the United States a "Whites-only" orientation has predominated in education. This has had a profound impact on the quality of education for children of all races and ethnic groups. The African American child has suffered disproportionately, but White children are also the victims of monoculturally diseased curricula.

The Tragedy of Ignorance
During the past five years many White students and parents have approached

me after presentations with tears in their eyes or expressing their anger about the absence of information about African Americans in the schools. A recent comment from a young White man at a major university in the Northeast was especially striking. As he said to me: "My teacher told us that Martin Luther King was a commie and went on with the class." Because this student's teacher made no effort to discuss King's ideas, the student maliciously had been kept ignorant. The vast majority of White Americans are likewise ignorant about the bountiful reservoirs of African and African American history, culture, and contributions. For example, few Americans of any color have heard the names of Cheikh Anta Diop, Anna Julia Cooper, C. L. R. James, or J. A. Rogers. All were historians who contributed greatly to our understanding of the African world. Indeed, very few teachers have ever taken a course in African American Studies; therefore, most are unable to provide systematic information about African Americans.

Afrocentricity and History

Most of America's teaching force are victims of the same system that victimizes today's young. Thus, American children are not taught the names of the African ethnic groups from which the majority of the African American population are derived; few are taught the names of any of the sacred sites in Africa. Few teachers can discuss with their students the significance of the Middle Passage or describe what it meant or means to Africans. Little mention is made in American classrooms of either the brutality of slavery or the ex-slaves' celebration of freedom. American children have little or no understanding of the nature of the capture, transport, and enslavement of Africans. Few have been taught the true horrors of being taken, shipped naked across 25 days of ocean, broken by abuse and indignities of all kinds, and dehumanized into a beast of burden, a thing without a name. If our students only knew the truth, if they were taught the Afrocentric perspective on the Great Enslavement, and if they knew the full story about the events since slavery that have served to constantly dislocate African Americans, their behavior would perhaps be different. Among these events are: the infamous constitutional compromise of 1787, which decreed that African Americans were, by law, the equivalent of but three-fifths of a person (see Franklin, 1974); the 1857 Dred Scott decision in which the Supreme Court avowed that African Americans had no rights Whites were obliged to respect (Howard, 1857); the complete dismissal and nonenforcement of Section 2 of the Fourteenth Amendment to the Constitution (this amendment, passed in 1868, stipulated as one of its provisions a penalty against any state that denied African Americans the right to vote, and called for the reduction of a state's delegates to the House of Representatives in proportion to the number of disenfranchised African American males therein); and the much-mentioned, as-yet-unreceived 40 acres and a mule, reparation for enslavement, promised to each African American family after the Civil War by Union General William T. Sherman and Secretary of War Edwin Stanton (Oubre, 1978, pp. 18–19, 182–183; see also Smith, 1987, pp. 106–107). If the curriculum were enhanced to include readings from the slave narratives; the diaries of slave ship captains; the journals of slaveowners; the abolitionist newspapers; the writings of the freedmen and freedwomen; the accounts of African American civil rights, civic, and social organizations; and numerous others, African American children would be different, White children would be different—indeed, America would be a different nation today.

America's classrooms should resound with the story of the barbaric treatment of the Africans, of how their dignity was stolen and their cultures destroyed. The recorded experiences of escaped slaves provide the substance for such learning units. For example, the narrative of Jacob and Ruth Weldon presents a detailed account of the Middle Passage (Feldstein, 1971). The Weldons noted that Africans, having been captured and brought onto the slave ships, were chained to the deck, made to bend over, and "branded with a red hot iron in the form of letters or signs dipped in an oily preparation and pressed against the naked flesh till it burnt a deep and ineffaceable scar, to show who was the owner" (pp. 33–37). They also recalled that those who screamed were lashed on the face, breast, thighs, and backs with a "cat-o'-nine tails" wielded by White sailors: "Every blow brought the returning lash pieces of grieving flesh" (p. 44). They saw mothers with babies at their breasts basely branded and lashed, hewed and scarred, till it would seem as if the very heavens must smite the infernal tormentors with the doom they so richly merited" (p. 44). Children and infants were not spared from this terror. The Weldons tell of a nine-month-old baby on board a slave ship being flogged because it would not eat. The ship's captain ordered the child's feet placed in boiling water, which dissolved the skin and nails, then ordered the child whipped again; still the child refused to eat. Eventually the captain killed the baby with his own hands and commanded the child's mother to throw the dead baby overboard. When the mother refused, she, too, was beaten, then forced to the ship's side, where "with her head averted so she might not see it, she dropped the body into the sea" (p. 44). In a similar vein a captain of a ship with 440 Africans on board noted that 132 had to be thrown overboard to save water (Feldstein, 1971, p. 47). As another wrote, the "groans and soffocating [sic] cries for air and water coming from below the deck sickened the soul of humanity" (Feldstein, 1971, p. 11).

Upon landing in America the situation was often worse. The brutality of the slavocracy is unequalled for the psychological and spiritual destruction it wrought upon African Americans. Slave mothers were often forced to leave their children unattended while they worked in the fields. Unable to nurse their children or to properly care for them, they often returned from work at night to find their children dead (Feldstein, 1971 p. 49). The testimony of Henry Bibb also sheds light on the bleakness of the slave experience:

> I was born May 1815, of a slave mother ... and was claimed as the property of David White, Esq.... I was flogged up; for where I should have received moral, mental, and religious instructions, I received stripes without number, the object of which was to degrade and keep me in subordination. I can truly say that I drank deeply of the bitter cup of suffering and woe. I have been dragged down to the lowest depths of human degradation and wretchedness, by slaveholders. (Feldstein, 1971, p. 60)

Enslavement was truly a living death. While the ontological onslaught caused some Africans to opt for suicide, the most widespread results were dislocation, disorientation, and misorientation —all of which are the consequences of the African person being actively de-centered. The "Jim Crow" period of second-class citizenship, from 1877 to 1954, saw only slight improvement in the lot of African Americans. This era was characterized by the sharecropper sys-tem, disenfranchisement, enforced segre-gation, internal migration, lynchings, un-employment, poor housing conditions, and separate and unequal educational fa-cilities. Inequitable policies and practices veritably plagued the race.

No wonder many persons of African descent attempt to shed their race and become "raceless." One's basic identity is one's self-identity, which is ultimately one's cultural identity; without a strong cultural identity, one is lost. Black children do not know their people's story and White children do not know the story, but remembrance is a vital requisite for understanding and humility. This is why the Jews have campaigned (and rightly so) to have the story of the European Holocaust taught in schools and colleges. Teaching about such a monstrous human brutality should forever remind the world of the ways in which humans have often violated each other. Teaching about the African Holocaust is just as important for many of the same reasons. Additionally, it underscores the enormity of the effects of physical, psychological, and economic dislocation on the African population in America and throughout the African diaspora. Without an understanding of the historical experiences of African people, American children cannot make any real headway in addressing the problems of the present.

Certainly, if African American chil-dren were taught to be fully aware of the struggles of our African forebears they would find a renewed sense of pur-pose and vision in their own lives. They would cease acting as if they have no past and no future. For instance, if they were taught about the historical relation-ship of Africans to the cotton industry—how African American men, women, and children were forced to pick cotton from "can't see in the morning 'til can't see at night," until the blood ran from the tips of their fingers where they were pricked by the hard boll; or if they were made to visualize their ancestors in the burning sun, bent double with constant stooping, and dragging rough, heavy croaker sacks behind them—or picture them bringing those sacks trembling to the scale, fear-ful of a sure flogging if they did not pick enough, perhaps our African Amer-ican youth would develop a stronger entrepreneurial spirit. If White children were taught the same information rather than that normally fed them about Amer-ican slavery, they would probably view our society differently and work to trans-form it into a better place.

CORRECTING DISTORTED INFORMATION

Hegemonic education can exist only so long as true and accurate informa-tion is withheld. Hegemonic Eurocen-tric education can exist only so long as Whites maintain that Africans and other non-Whites have never contributed to world civilization. It is largely upon such false ideas that invidious distinc-tions are made. The truth, however, gives one insight into the real reasons behind human actions, whether one chooses to follow the paths of others or not. For ex-ample, one cannot remain comfortable teaching that art and philosophy originated in Greece if one learns that the Greeks themselves taught that the study of these subjects originated in Africa, specifically ancient Kemet (Herodotus, 1987). The first philosophers were the Egyptians Kagemni, Khun-anup, Ptah-hotep, Kete, and Seti; but Eurocentric education is so disjointed that students have no way of discovering this and other knowledge of the organic relationship of Africa to the rest of human history. Not only did Africa contribute to human history, African civilizations pre-date all other civilizations. Indeed, the human species originated on the continent of Africa—this is true whether one looks at either archaeological or biological evidence.

Two other notions must be refuted. There are those who say that African American history should begin with the arrival of Africans as slaves in 1619, but it has been shown that Africans visited and inhabited North and South America long before European settlers "discovered" the "New World" (Van Sertima, 1976). Secondly, although America became something of a home for those Africans who survived the horrors of the Middle Passage, their experiences on the slave ships and during slavery resulted in their having an entirely different (and often tainted) perspective about America from that of the Europeans and others who came, for the most part, of their own free will seeking opportunities not available to them in their native lands. Afrocentricity therefore seeks to recognize this divergence in perspective and create centeredness for African American students.

CONCLUSION

The reigning initiative for total curricular change is the movement that is being proposed and led by Africans, namely, the Afrocentric idea. When I wrote the first book on Afrocentricity (Asante, 1980), now in its fifth printing, I had no idea that in 10 years the idea would both shake up and shape discussions in education, art, fashion, and politics. Since the publication of my subsequent works, *The Afrocentric Idea* (Asante, 1987) and *Kemet, Afrocentricity, and Knowledge* (Asante, 1990), the debate has been joined in earnest. Still, for many White Americans (and some African Americans) the most unsettling aspect of the discussion about Afrocentricity is that its intellectual source lies in the research and writings of African American scholars. Whites are accustomed to being in charge of the major ideas circulating in the American academy. Deconstructionism, Gestalt psychology, Marxism, structuralism, Piagetian theory, and so forth have all been developed, articulated, and elaborated upon at length, generally by White scholars. On the other hand, Afrocentricity is the product of scholars such as Nobles (1986), Hilliard (1978), Karenga (1986), Keto (1990), Richards (1991), and Myers (1989). There are also increasing numbers of young, impressively credentialled African American scholars who have begun to write in the Afrocentric vein (Jean, 1991). They, and even some young White scholars, have emerged with ideas about how to change the curriculum Afrocentrically.

Afrocentricity provides all Americans an opportunity to examine the perspective of the African person in this society and the world. The resisters claim that Afrocentricity is anti-White; yet, if Afrocentricity as a theory is against anything it is against racism, ignorance, and monoethnic hegemony in the curriculum. Afrocentricity is not anti-White; it is, however, pro-human. Further, the aim of the Afrocentric curriculum is not to divide America, it is to make America flourish as it ought to flourish. This nation has long been divided with regard to the educational opportunities afforded to children. By virtue of the protection provided by society and reinforced by the Eurocentric curriculum, the White child is already ahead of the African American child by first grade. Our efforts thus must concentrate on giving the African American child greater opportunities for learning at the kindergarten level. However, the kind of assistance the African American child needs is as much cultural as it is academic. If the proper cultural information is provided, the academic performance will surely follow suit.

When it comes to educating African American children, the American educational system does not need a tune-up, it needs an overhaul. Black children have been maligned by this system. Black teachers have been maligned. Black history has been maligned. Africa has been maligned. Nonetheless, two truisms can be stated about education in America. First, some teachers *can and do* effectively teach African American children; secondly, if some teachers can do it, others can, too. We must learn all we can about what makes these teachers' attitudes and approaches successful, and then work diligently to see that their successes are replicated on a broad scale. By raising the same questions that Woodson posed more than 50 years ago, Afrocentric education, along with a significant reorientation of the American educational enterprise, seeks to respond to the African person's psychological and cultural dislocation. By providing philosophical and theoretical guidelines and criteria that are centered in an African perception of re-

ality and by placing the African American child in his or her proper historical context and setting, Afrocentricity may be just the "escape hatch" African Americans so desperately need to facilitate academic success and "steal away" from the cycle of miseducation and dislocation.

REFERENCES

Asante, M. K. (1980). *Afrocentricity: The theory of social change.* Buffalo, NY: Amulefi.

Asante, M. K. (1987). *The Afrocentric idea.* Philadelphia: Temple University Press.

Asante, M. K. (1990). *Kemet, Afrocentricity, and knowledge.* Trenton, NJ: Africa World Press.

Bloom, A. (1987). *The closing of the American mind.* New York: Simon & Schuster.

Feldstein, S. (1971). *Once a slave: The slave's view of slavery.* New York: William Morrow.

Franklin, J. H. (1974). *From slavery to freedom.* New York: Knopf.

Herodotus. (1987). *The history.* Chicago: University of Illinois Press.

Hilliard, A. G., III. (1978, June 20). *Anatomy and dynamics of oppression.* Speech delivered at the National Conference on Human Relations in Education, Minneapolis, MN.

Hirsch, E. D. (1987). *Cultural literacy: What every American needs to know.* New York: Houghton Mifflin.

Howard, B. C. (1857). *Report of the decision of the Supreme Court of the United States and the opinions of the justices thereof in the case of Dred Scott versus John F. A. Sandford, December term, 1856.* New York: D. Appleton & Co.

Jean, C. (1991). *Beyond the Eurocentric veils.* Amherst, MA: University of Massachusetts Press.

Karenga, M. R. (1986). *Introduction to Black studies.* Los Angeles: University of Sankore Press.

Keto, C. T. (1990). *Africa-centered perspective of history.* Blackwood, NJ: C. A. Associates.

Nicholson, D. (1990, September 23). Afrocentrism and the tribalization of America. *The Washington Post,* p. B-1.

Nobles, W. (1986). *African psychology.* Oakland, CA: Black Family Institute.

Oubre, C. F. (1978). *Forty acres and a mule: The Freedman's Bureau and Black land ownership.* Baton Rouge, LA: Louisiana State University Press.

Ravitch, D. (1990, Summer). Multiculturalism: E pluribus plures. *The American Scholar,* pp. 337–354.

Richards, D. (1991). *Let the circle be unbroken.* Trenton, NJ: Africa World Press.

Smith, J. O. (1987). *The politics of racial inequality: A systematic comparative macro-analysis from the colonial period to 1970.* New York: Greenwood Press.

Van Sertima, I. (1976). *They came before Columbus.* New York: Random House.

Woodson, C. G. (1915). *The education of the Negro prior to 1861: A history of the education of the colored people of the U.S. from the beginning of slavery.* New York: G. P. Putnam's Sons.

Woodson, C. G. (1933). *The Mis-education of the Negro.* Washington, DC: Associated Publishers.

Woodson, C. G. (1936). *African background outlined.* Washington, DC: Association for the Study of Afro-American Life and History.

NO
Arthur M. Schlesinger, Jr.

THE DISUNITING OF AMERICA

Most white Americans through most of American history simply considered colored Americans inferior and unassimilable. Not until the 1960s did integration become a widely accepted national objective. Even then, even after legal obstacles to integration fell, social, economic, and psychological obstacles remained. Both black Americans and red Americans have every reason to seek redressing of the historical balance. And indeed the cruelty with which white Americans have dealt with black Americans has been compounded by the callousness with which white historians have dealt with black history.

Even the best historians: Frederick Jackson Turner, dismissing the slavery question as a mere "incident" when American history is "rightly viewed"; Charles and Mary Beard in their famous *The Rise of American Civilization*, describing blacks as passive in slavery and ludicrous in Reconstruction and acknowledging only one black achievement—the invention of ragtime; Samuel Eliot Morison and Henry Steele Commager, writing about childlike and improvident Sambo on the old plantation. One can sympathize with W. E. B. Du Bois's rage after reading white histories of slavery and Reconstruction; he was, he wrote, "literally aghast at what American historians have done to this field ... one of the most stupendous efforts the world ever saw to discredit human beings. ..."

The job of redressing the balance has been splendidly undertaken in recent years by both white and black historians. Meticulous and convincing scholarship has reversed conventional judgments on slavery, on Reconstruction, on the role of blacks in American life.

* * *

But scholarly responsibility was only one factor behind the campaign of historical correction. History remains a weapon. "History's potency is mighty," Herbert Aptheker, the polemical chronicler of slave rebellions, has written. "The oppressed need it for identity and inspiration." (Aptheker, a faithful Stalinist, was an old hand at the manipulation of history.)

For blacks the American dream has been pretty much of a nightmare, and, far more than white ethnics, they are driven by a desperate need to vindicate

From Arthur M. Schlesinger, Jr., "The Disuniting of America," *American Educator* (Winter 1991). Adapted from Arthur M. Schlesinger, Jr., *The Disuniting of America: Reflections on a Multicultural Society* (W. W. Norton, 1992). Copyright © 1992 by Arthur M. Schlesinger, Jr. This book was first published by Whittle Books as part of the Larger Agenda Series. Reprinted by permission of Whittle Communications, L.P.

their own identity. "The academic and social rescue and reconstruction of Black history," as Maulana Karenga put it in his influential *Introduction to Black Studies* ("a landmark in the intellectual history of African Americans," according to Molefi Kete Asante of Temple University), "is ... [an] indispensable part of the rescue and reconstruction of Black humanity. For history is the substance and mirror of a people's humanity in others' eyes as well as in their own eyes ... not only what they have done, but also a reflection of who they are, what they can do, and equally important what they can become...."

One can hardly be surprised at the emergence of a there's-always-a-black-man-at-the-bottom-of-it-doing-the-real-work approach to American history. "The extent to which the past of a people is regarded as praiseworthy," the white anthropologist Melville J. Herskovits wrote in his study of the African antecedents of American blacks, "their own self-esteem would be high and the opinion of others will be favorable."

White domination of American schools and colleges, some black academics say, results in Eurocentric, racist, elitist, imperialist indoctrination and in systematic denigration of black values and achievements. "In the public school system," writes Felix Boateng of Eastern Washington University, "the orientation is so Eurocentric that white students take their identity for granted, and African-American students are totally deculturalized"—deculturalization being the "process by which the individual is deprived of his or her culture and then conditioned to other cultural values." "In a sense," says Molefi Kete Asante, the Eurocentric curriculum is "killing our children, killing their minds."

In history, Western-civilization courses are seen as cultural imperialism designed to disparage non-Western traditions and to impress the Western stamp on people of all races. In literature, the "canon," the accepted list of essential books, is seen as an instrumentality of the white power structure. Nowhere can blacks discover adequate reflection or representation of the black self.

Some black educators even argue ultimate biological and mental differences, asserting that black students do not learn the way white students do and that the black mind works in a genetically distinctive way. Black children are said, in the jargon of the educationist, to "process information differently." "There are scientific studies that show, at early ages, the difference between Caucasian infants and African infants," says Clare Jacobs, a teacher in Washington, D.C. "Our African children are very expressive. Every thought we have has an emotional dimension to it, and Western education has historically subordinated the feelings." Charles Willie of Harvard finds several distinct "intelligences" of which the "communication and calculation" valued by whites constitute only two. Other kinds of "intelligence" are singing and dancing, in both of which blacks excel.

Salvation thus lies, the argument goes, in breaking the white, Eurocentric, racist grip on the curriculum and providing education that responds to colored races, colored histories, colored ways of learning and behaving. Europe has reigned long enough; it is the source of most of the evil in the world anyway; and the time is overdue to honor the African contributions to civilization so purposefully suppressed in Eurocentric curricula. Children from nonwhite minorities, so long persuaded of their inferiority by the white hegemons, need the support and inspiration that identification with role models of the same color will give them.

The answer, for some at least, is "Afro-centricity," described by Asante in his book of that title as "the centerpiece of human regeneration." There is, Asante contends, a single "African Cultural System." Wherever people of African descent are, we respond to the same rhythms of the universe, the same cosmological sensibilities. . . . Our Africanity is our ultimate reality."

* * *

The belated recognition of the pluralistic character of American society has had a bracing impact on the teaching and writing of history. Scholars now explore such long-neglected fields as the history of women, of immigration, of blacks, Indians, Hispanics, and other minorities. Voices long silent ring out of the darkness of history.

The result has been a reconstruction of American history, partly on the merits and partly in response to ethnic pressures. In 1987, the two states with both the greatest and the most diversified populations—California and New York —adopted new curricula for grades one to twelve. Both state curricula materially increased the time allotted to non-European cultures.

The New York curriculum went further in minimizing Western traditions. A two-year global-studies course divided the world into seven regions—Africa, South Asia, East Asia, Latin America, the Middle East, Western Europe, and Eastern Europe—with each region given equal time. The history of Western Europe was cut back from a full year to one quarter of the second year. American

history was reduced to a section on the Constitution; then a leap across Jefferson, Jackson, the Civil War, and Reconstruction to 1877.

In spite of the multiculturalization of the New York state history curriculum in 1987—a revision approved by such scholars as Eric Foner of Columbia and Christopher Lasch of Rochester—a newly appointed commissioner of education yielded to pressures from minority interests to consider still further revision. In 1989, the Task Force on Minorities: Equity and Excellence (not one historian among its seventeen members) brought in a report that argued: the "systematic bias toward European culture and its derivatives" has "a terribly damaging effect on the psyche of young people of African, Asian, Latino, and Native American descent." The dominance of "the European-American monocultural perspective" explains why "large numbers of children of non-European descent are not doing as well as expected."

Dr. Leonard Jeffries, the task force's consultant on African-American culture and a leading author of the report, discerns "deep-seated pathologies of racial hatred" even in the 1987 curriculum. The consultant on Asian-American culture called for more pictures of Asian-Americans. The consultant on Latino culture found damning evidence of ethnocentric bias in such usages as the "Mexican War" and the "Spanish-American War." The ethnically correct designations should be the "American-Mexican War" and the "Spanish-Cuban-American War." The consultant on Native American culture wanted more space for Indians and for bilingual education in Iroquois.

A new curriculum giving the four other cultures equitable treatment, the report concluded, would provide "children from Native American, Puerto Rican/Latino, Asian-American, and African-American cultures... higher self-esteem and self-respect, while children from European cultures will have a less arrogant perspective."

The report views division into racial groups as the basic analytical framework for an understanding of American history. Its interest in history is not as an intellectual discipline but rather as social and psychological therapy whose primary function is to raise the self-esteem of children from minority groups. Nor does the report regard the Constitution or the American Creed as means of improvement.

Jeffries scorns the Constitution, finding "something vulgar and revolting in glorifying a process that heaped undeserved rewards on a segment of the population while oppressing the majority." The belief in the unifying force of democratic ideals finds no echo in the report. Indeed, the report takes no interest in the problem of holding a diverse republic together. Its impact is rather to sanction and deepen racial tensions.

* * *

The recent spread of Afrocentric programs to public schools represents an extension of the New York task force ideology. These programs are, in most cases, based on a series of "African-American Baseline Essays" conceived by the educational psychologist Asa Hilliard.

Hilliard's narration for the slide show "Free Your Mind, Return to the Source: The African Origin of Civilization" suggests his approach. "Africa," he writes, "is the mother of Western civilization"—an argument turning on the contention that Egypt was a black African country

and the real source of the science and philosophy Western historians attribute to Greece. Africans, Hilliard continues, also invented birth control and carbon steel. They brought science, medicine, and the arts to Europe; indeed, many European artists, such as Browning and Beethoven, were, in fact, "Afro-European." They also discovered America long before Columbus, and the original name of the Atlantic Ocean was the Ethiopian Ocean.

Hilliard's African-American Baseline Essays were introduced into the school system of Portland, Oregon, in 1987. They have subsequently been the inspiration for Afrocentric curricula in Milwaukee, Indianapolis, Pittsburgh, Washington, D.C., Richmond, Atlanta, Philadelphia, Detroit, Baltimore, Camden, and other cities and continue at this writing to be urged on school boards and administrators anxious to do the right thing.

John Henrik Clarke's Baseline Essay on Social Studies begins with the proposition that "African scholars are the final authority on Africa." Egypt, he continues, "gave birth to what later became known as Western civilization, long before the greatness of Greece and Rome." "Great civilizations" existed throughout Africa, where "great kings" ruled "in might and wisdom over vast empires." After Egypt declined, magnificent empires arose in West Africa, in Ghana, Mali, Songhay—all marked by the brilliance and enlightenment of their administrations and the high quality of their libraries and universities.

Other Baseline Essays argue in a similar vein that Africa was the birthplace of science, mathematics, philosophy, medicine, and art and that Europe stole its civilization from Africa and then engaged in "malicious misrepresentation of African society and people... to support the enormous profitability of slavery." The coordinator of multicultural/multi-ethnic education in Portland even says that Napoleon deliberately shot off the nose of the Sphinx so that the Sphinx would not be recognized as African.

Like other excluded groups before them, black Americans invoke supposed past glories to compensate for real past and present injustices. Because their exclusion has been more tragic and terrible than that of white immigrants, their quest for self-affirmation is more intense and passionate. In seeking to impose Afrocentric curricula on public schools, for example, they go further than their white predecessors. And belated recognition by white America of the wrongs so viciously inflicted on black Americans has created the phenomenon of white guilt—not a bad thing in many respects, but still a vulnerability that invites cynical exploitation and manipulation.

* * *

I am constrained to feel that the cult of ethnicity in general and the Afrocentric campaign in particular do not bode well either for American education or for the future of the republic. Cultural pluralism is not the issue. Nor is the teaching of Afro-American or African history the issue; of course these are legitimate subjects. The issue is the kind of history that the New York task force, the Portland Baseline essayists, and other Afrocentric ideologues propose for American children. The issue is the teaching of *bad* history under whatever ethnic banner.

One argument for organizing a school curriculum around Africa is that black Africa is the birthplace of science, philosophy, religion, medicine, technology, of the great achievements that have been wrongly ascribed to Western civilization. But is this, in fact, true? Many historians and anthropologists regard Mesopotamia as the cradle of civilization; for a recent discussion, see Charles Keith Maisels' *The Emergence of Civilization.*

The Afrocentrist case rests largely on the proposition that ancient Egypt was essentially a black African country. I am far from being an expert on Egyptian history, but neither, one must add, are the educators and psychologists who push Afrocentrism. A book they often cite is Martin Bernal's *Black Athena,* a vigorous effort by a Cornell professor to document Egyptian influence on ancient Greece. In fact, Bernal makes no very strong claims about Egyptian pigmentation; but, citing Herodotus, he does argue that several Egyptian dynasties "were made up of pharaohs whom one can usefully call black."

Frank M. Snowden Jr., the distinguished black classicist at Howard University and author of *Blacks in Antiquity,* is most doubtful about painting ancient Egypt black. Bernal's assumption that Herodotus meant black in the 20th-century sense is contradicted, Snowden demonstrates, "by Herodotus himself and the copious evidence of other classical authors."

Frank J. Yurco, an Egyptologist at Chicago's Field Museum of Natural History, after examining the evidence derivable from mummies, paintings, statues, and reliefs, concludes in the *Biblical Archaeological Review* that ancient Egyptians, like their modern descendants, varied in color from the light Mediterranean type to the darker brown of upper Egypt to the still darker shade of the Nubians around Aswan. He adds that ancient Egyptians would have found the question meaningless and wonders at our presumption in assigning "our primitive racial labels" to so impressive a culture.

After Egypt, Afrocentrists teach children about the glorious West African emperors, the vast lands they ruled, the civilization they achieved; not, however, about the tyrannous authority they exercised, the ferocity of their wars, the tribal massacres, the squalid lot of the common people, the captives sold into slavery, the complicity with the Atlantic slave trade, the persistence of slavery in Africa after it was abolished in the West. As for tribalism, the word *tribe* hardly occurs in the Afrocentric lexicon; but who can hope to understand African history without understanding it.

The Baseline Essay on science and technology contains biographies of black American scientists, among them Charles R. Drew, who first developed the process for the preservation of blood plasma. In 1950 Drew, grievously injured in an automobile accident in North Carolina, lost quantities of blood. *"Not one* of several nearby white hospitals," according to the Baseline Essay, "would provide the blood transfusions he so desperately [sic] needed, and on the way to a hospital that treated Black people, he died." It is a hell of a story—the inventor of blood-plasma storage dead because racist whites denied him his own invention. Only it is not true. According to the biographical entry for Drew written by the eminent black scholar Rayford Logan of Howard for the *Dictionary of American Negro Biography*, "Conflicting versions to the contrary, Drew received prompt medical attention."

Is it really a good idea to teach minority children myths—at least to teach myths as facts?

* * *

The deeper reason for the Afrocentric campaign lies in the theory that the purpose of history in the schools is essentially therapeutic: to build a sense of self-worth among minority children. Eurocentrism, by denying nonwhite children any past in which they can take pride, is held to be the cause of poor academic performance. Race consciousness and group pride are supposed to strengthen a sense of identity and self-respect among nonwhite students.

Why does anyone suppose that pride and inspiration are available only from people of the same ethnicity? Plainly this is not the case. At the age of twelve, Frederick Douglass encountered a book entitled *The Columbian Orator* containing speeches by Burke, Sheridan, Pitt, and Fox. "Every opportunity I got," Douglass later said, "I used to read this book." The orations "gave tongue to interesting thoughts of my own soul, which had frequently flashed through my mind, and died away for want of utterance.... What I got from Sheridan was a bold denunciation of slavery and a powerful vindication of human rights. The reading of these documents enabled me to utter my thoughts." Douglass did not find the fact that the orators were white an insuperable obstacle.

Or hear Ralph Ellison: "In Macon County, Alabama, I read Marx, Freud, T. S. Eliot, Pound, Gertrude Stein, and Hemingway. Books that seldom, if ever, mentioned Negroes were to release me from whatever 'segregated' idea I might have had of my human possibilities." He was freed, Ellison continued, not by the example of Richard Wright and other black writers but by artists who offered a broader sense of life and possibility. "It requires real poverty of the imagination to think that this can come to a Negro only through the example of other Negroes."

Martin Luther King, Jr. did pretty well with Thoreau, Gandhi, and Reinhold Niebuhr as models—and remember, after all, whom King (and his father) were named for. Is Lincoln to be a hero only for those of English ancestry? Jackson only for Scotch-Irish? Douglass only for blacks? Great artists, thinkers, leaders are the possession not just of their own racial clan but of all humanity.

As for self-esteem, is this really the product of ethnic role models and fantasies of a glorious past? Or does it not result from the belief in oneself that springs from achievement, from personal rather than from racial pride?

Columnist William Raspberry notes that Afrocentric education will make black children "less competent in the culture in which they have to compete." After all, what good will it do young black Americans to hear that, because their minds work differently, a first-class education is not for them? Will such training help them to understand democracy better? Help them to fit better into American life?

Will it increase their self-esteem when black children grow up and learn that many of the things the Afrocentrists taught them are not true? Black scholars have tried for years to rescue black history from chauvinistic hyperbole. A. A. Schomburg, the noted archivist of black history, expressed his scorn long ago for those who "glibly tried to prove that half of the world's geniuses have been Negroes and to trace the pedigree of nineteenth-century Americans from the Queen of Sheba."

The dean of black historians in America today is John Hope Franklin. "While a black scholar," Franklin writes, "has a clear responsibility to join in improving the society in which he lives, he must understand the difference between hard-hitting advocacy on the one hand and the highest standards of scholarship on the other."

* * *

The use of history as therapy means the corruption of history as history. All major races, cultures, nations have committed crimes, atrocities, horrors at one time or another. Every civilization has skeletons in its closet. Honest history calls for the unexpurgated record. How much would a full account of African despotism, massacre, and slavery increase the self-esteem of black students? Yet what kind of history do you have if you leave out all the bad things?

"Once ethnic pride and self-esteem become the criterion for teaching history," historian Diane Ravitch points out, "certain things cannot be taught." Skeletons must stay in the closet lest outing displease descendants.

No history curriculum in the country is more carefully wrought and better balanced in its cultural pluralism than California's. But hearings before the State Board of Education show what happens when ethnicity is unleashed at the expense of scholarship. At issue were textbooks responsive to the new curriculum. Polish-Americans demanded that any reference to Hitler's Holocaust be accompanied by accounts of equivalent genocide suffered by Polish Christians. Armenian-Americans sought coverage of Turkish massacres; Turkish-Americans objected. Though black historians testified that the treatment of black history was exemplary, Afrocentrists said the schoolbooks would lead to "textbook genocide." Moslems complained that an illustration of an Islamic warrior with a raised scimitar stereotyped Moslems as "terrorists."

"The single theme that persistently ran through the hearings," Ravitch writes, "was that the critics did not want anything taught if it offended members of their group."

In New York the curriculum guide for eleventh-grade American history tells students that there were three "foundations" for the Constitution: the European Enlightenment, the "Haudenosaunee political system," and the antecedent colonial experience. Only the Haudenosaunee political system receives explanatory sub-headings: "a. Influence upon colonial leadership and European intellectuals (Locke, Montesquieu, Voltaire, Rousseau); b. Impact on Albany Plan of Union, Articles of Confederation, and U.S. Constitution."

How many experts on the American Constitution would endorse this stirring tribute to the "Haudenosaunee political system"? How many have heard of that system? Whatever influence the Iroquois confederation may have had on the framers of the Constitution was marginal; on European intellectuals it was marginal to the point of invisibility. No other state curriculum offers this analysis of the making of the Constitution. But then no other state has so effective an Iroquois lobby.

President Franklin Jenifer of Howard University, while saying that "historical black institutions" like his own have a responsibility to teach young people about their particular history and culture, adds, "One has to be very careful when one is talking about public schools.... There should be no creation of nonexistent history."

Let us by all means teach black history, African history, women's history, Hispanic history, Asian history. But let us teach them as history, not as filiopietistic commemoration. When every ethnic and religious group claims a right to approve or veto anything that is taught in public schools, the fatal line is crossed between cultural pluralism and ethnocentrism. An evident casualty is the old idea that whatever our ethnic base, we are all Americans together.

* * *

The ethnicity rage in general and Afrocentricity in particular not only divert attention from the real needs but exacerbate the problems. The cult of ethnicity exaggerates differences, intensifies resentments and antagonisms, drives ever deeper the awful wedges between races and nationalities. The end game is self-pity and self-ghettoization. Afrocentricity as expounded by ethnic ideologues implies Europhobia, separatism, emotions of alienation, victimization, paranoia.

If any educational institution should bring people together as individuals in friendly and civil association, it should be the university. But the fragmentation of campuses in recent years into a multitude of ethnic organizations is spectacular—and disconcerting.

Stanford University, writer Dinesh D'Souza reports in his book *Illiberal Education*, has "ethnic theme houses." The University of Pennsylvania gives blacks —6 percent of the enrollment—their own yearbook. Campuses today, according to one University of Pennsylvania professor, have "the cultural diversity of Beirut. There are separate armed camps. The black kids don't mix with the white kids.

The Asians are off by themselves. Oppression is the great status symbol."

Oberlin was for a century and a half the model of a racially integrated college. "Increasingly" Jacob Weisberg, an editor at *The New Republic*, reports, "Oberlin students think, act, study, and live apart." Asians live in Asia House, Jews in "J" House, Latinos in Spanish House, blacks in African-Heritage House, foreign students in Third World House. Even the Lesbian, Gay, and Bisexual Union has broken up into racial and gender factions. "The result is separate worlds."

Huddling is an understandable reaction for any minority group faced with new and scary challenges. But institutionalized separatism only crystallizes racial differences and magnifies racial tensions. "Certain activities are labeled white and black," says a black student at Central Michigan University. "If you don't just participate in black activities, you are shunned."

Militants further argue that because only blacks can comprehend the black experience, only blacks should teach black history and literature, as, in the view of some feminists, only women should teach women's history and literature. "True diversity," according to the faculty's Budget Committee at the University of California at Berkeley, requires that courses match the ethnic and gender identities of the professors.

The doctrine that *only* blacks can teach and write black history leads inexorably to the doctrine that blacks can teach and write *only* black history as well as to inescapable corollaries: Chinese must be restricted to Chinese history, women to women's history, and so on. Henry Louis Gates of Duke University criticizes "ghettoized programs where students and members of the faculty sit around and argue about whether a white person can think a black thought?" As for the notion that there is a "mystique" about black studies that requires a person to have black skin in order to pursue them—that, John Hope Franklin observes succinctly, is "voodoo."

The separatist impulse is by no means confined to the black community. Another salient expression is the bilingualism movement. The presumed purpose of bilingualism is transitional: to move non-English-speaking children as quickly as possible from bilingual into all-English classes.

Alas, bilingualism has not worked out as planned: rather the contrary. Testimony is mixed, but indications are that bilingual education retards rather than expedites the movement of Hispanic children into the English-speaking world and that it promotes segregation more than it does integration. Bilingualism "encourages concentrations of Hispanics to stay together and not be integrated," says Alfredo Mathew Jr., a Hispanic civic leader, and it may well foster "a type of apartheid that will generate animosities with others, such as Blacks, in the competition for scarce resources and further alienate the Hispanic from the larger society."

"The era that began with the dream of integration," author Richard Rodriguez has observed, "ended up with scorn for assimilation." The cult of ethnicity has reversed the movement of American history, producing a nation of minorities —or at least of minority spokesmen—less interested in joining with the majority in common endeavor than in declaring their alienation from an oppressive, white, patriarchal, racist, sexist, classist society. The ethnic ideology inculcates the illusion that membership in one or another ethnic group is the basic American experience.

The contemporary sanctification of the group puts the old idea of a coherent society at stake. Multicultural zealots reject as hegemonic the notion of a shared commitment to common ideals. How far the discourse has come from Crevecoeur's "new race," from Tocqueville's civic participation, from Bryce's "amazing solvent" from Myrdal's "American Creed"!

Yet what has held the American people together in the absence of a common eth-nic origin has been precisely a common adherence to ideals of democracy and human rights that, too often transgressed in practice, forever goad us to narrow the gap between practice and principle.

America is an experiment in creating a common identity for people of diverse races, religions, languages, cultures. If the republic now turns away from its old goal of "one people," what is its future? —disintegration of the national community, apartheid, Balkanization, tribalization?

POSTSCRIPT

Do Black Students Need an Afrocentric Curriculum?

How can equal educational opportunities be ensured? What are the current realities of the U.S. educational system, and how should inequalities be addressed? Can opportunities for educational success for black schoolchildren be improved by making the changes Asante recommends? Or is there merit to Schlesinger's contention that Afrocentric programs have the potential to teach myths as facts and do not bode well for addressing the problems of race and inequality in the schools or in U.S. society?

Sources for further exploration of this issue are multiple. For additional insight into the thinking of the opponents presented here, see Asante's "Afrocentric Curriculum" in *Educational Leadership* (December 1991) and Schlesinger's "The American Creed: From Dilemma to Decomposition" in *New Perspectives Quarterly* (Summer 1991). An interesting appraisal of the situation may be found in James Comer's "Racism and the Education of Young Children," *Teachers College Record* (Spring 1989).

Special collections of articles on Afrocentrism may be found in the *Journal of Negro Education* (Summer 1992), which features the thoughts of James A. Banks, Asa G. Hilliard III, Maxine Greene, and Lisa Delpit; *Counseling Psychologist* (April 1989); and *Time* magazine (July 8, 1991). Another good source is the *Journal of Black Studies*, whose December 1990 issue contains two especially interesting pieces: "Afrocentric Cultural Consciousness and African-American Male-Female Relationships," by Yvonne R. Bell et al., and Bayo Oyebade's "African Studies and the Afrocentric Paradigm: A Critique."

Also see these probing articles: Midge Decter's "E Pluribus Nihil: Multiculturalism and Black Children," *Commentary* (Fall 1991); Diane Ravitch's "Multiculturalism: E Pluribus Plures," *American Scholar* (Summer 1990); and C. Vann Woodward's "Equal But Separate," *The New Republic* (July 15 & 22, 1991), which reviews Schlesinger's *The Disuniting of America*.

The Fall 1992 issue of *Western Journal of Black Studies* contains two excellent pieces: Terry Kershaw's "Afrocentrism and the Afrocentric Method" and Norman Harris's "A Philosophical Basis for an Afrocentric Orientation." The Autumn 1992 issue of *Theory into Practice* is devoted to the theme "Literacy and the African-American Learner: The Struggle Between Access and Denial." Two other noteworthy articles are "The Importance of an Afrocentric, Multicultural Curriculum," by Kimberly R. Vann and Jawanza Kunjufu, *Phi Delta Kappan* (February 1993) and "Black Curriculum Orientations: A Preliminary Inquiry," by William H. Watkins, *Harvard Educational Review* (Fall 1993); the latter offers a fine historical treatment.

ISSUE 15

Should Bilingual Education Programs Be Abandoned?

YES: Diane Ravitch, from "Politicization and the Schools: The Case of Bilingual Education," *Proceedings of the American Philosophical Society* (June 1985)

NO: Donaldo Macedo, from "English Only: The Tongue-Tying of America," *Journal of Education* (Spring 1991)

ISSUE SUMMARY

YES: History of education professor Diane Ravitch finds inadequate evidence of success in bilingual education programs and expresses concern over the effort's politicization.

NO: Donaldo Macedo, an associate professor of linguistics, deplores the incessant attack on bilingual education by Ravitch and other conservatives and explores the pedagogical and political implications of abandoning such programs.

The issue of accommodating non-English-speaking immigrants by means of a bilingual education program has been controversial since the late 1960s. Events of the past decades have brought about one of the largest influxes of immigrants to the United States in the nation's history. And the disadvantages that non-English-speaking children and their parents experience during the childrens' years of formal schooling has received considerable attention from educators, policymakers, and the popular press.

Efforts to modify this type of social and developmental disadvantage have appeared in the form of bilingual education programs initiated at the local level and supported by federal funding. Approaches implemented include direct academic instruction in the primary language and the provision of language tutors under the English for Speakers of Other Languages (ESOL) program. Research evaluation of these efforts has produced varied results and has given rise to controversy over the efficacy of the programs themselves and the social and political intentions served by them.

A political movement at the national and state levels to establish English as the official language of the United States has gained support in recent years. Supporters of this movement feel that the bilingual approach will lead to the kind of linguistic division that has torn Canada apart.

Perhaps sharing some of the concerns of the "official English" advocates, increasing numbers of educators seem to be tilting in the direction of the immersion approach. In a recent book, *Forked Tongue: The Politics of Bilingual Education* (1990), Rosalie Pedalineo Porter, a teacher and researcher in the field of bilingual education for over 15 years, issues an indictment of the policies and programs that have been prevalent. One of her central recommendations is that "limited-English children must be placed with specially trained teachers in a program in which these students will be immersed in the English language, in which they have as much contact as possible with English speakers, and in which school subjects, not just social conversations, are the focus of the English-language lessons from kindergarten through twelfth grade."

Amado M. Padilla of Stanford University has examined the rationale behind "official English" and has also reviewed the effectiveness of bilingual education programs (see "English Only vs. Bilingual Education: Ensuring a Language-Competent Society," *Journal of Education,* Spring 1991). Padilla concludes that "the debate about how to assist linguistic minority children should focus on new educational technologies and *not* just on the effectiveness of bilingual education or whether bilingualism detracts from loyalty to this country."

In the first of the articles that follow, Diane Ravitch finds the effort to continue the policy of bilingual education to be overpoliticized. She contends that the program "exemplifies a campaign on behalf of social and political goals that are only tangentially related to education." She claims that "the aim is to use the public schools to promote the maintenance of distinct ethnic communities, each with its own cultural heritage and language." Donaldo Macedo, arguing from an opposing point of view, claims that the conservative ideology that propels the antibilingual education forces ignores the evidence supporting it and fails to recognize the need for preparing students for the ever-changing, multilingual, and multicultural world of the twenty-first century. An "English only" approach, he states, relegates the immigrant population to the margins of society.

YES

Diane Ravitch

POLITICIZATION AND THE SCHOOLS: THE CASE OF BILINGUAL EDUCATION

There has always been a politics of schools, and no doubt there always will be. Like any other organization populated by human beings, schools have their internal politics; for as long as there have been public schools, there have been political battles over their budget, their personnel policies, their curricula, and their purposes. Anyone who believes that there was once a time in which schools were untouched by political controversy is uninformed about the history of education. The decision-making processes that determine who will be chosen as principal or how the school board will be selected or whether to pass a school bond issue are simply political facts of life that are part and parcel of the administration, financing, and governance of schools. There is also a politics of the curriculum and of the profession, in which contending forces argue about programs and policies. It is hard to imagine a school, a school system, a university, a state board of education, or a national department of education in which these kinds of political conflicts do not exist. They are an intrinsic aspect of complex organizations in which people disagree about how to achieve their goals and about which goals to pursue; to the extent that we operate in a democratic manner, conflict over important and even unimportant issues is inevitable.

There is another kind of politics, however, in which educational institutions become entangled in crusades marked by passionate advocacy, intolerance of criticism, and unyielding dogmatism, and in which the education of children is a secondary rather than a primary consideration. Such crusades go beyond politics-as-usual; they represent the politicization of education. Schools and universities become targets for politicization for several reasons: First, they offer a large captive audience of presumably impressionable minds; second, they are expected to shape the opinions, knowledge, and values of the rising generation, which makes them attractive to those who want to influence the future; and third, since Americans have no strong educational philosophy or educational tradition, almost any claim—properly clothed in rhetorical appeals about the needs of children or of American society—can make its way into the course catalogue or the educational agenda.

From Diane Ravitch, "Politicization and the Schools: The Case of Bilingual Education," *Proceedings of the American Philosophical Society*, vol. 129, no. 2 (June 1985). Copyright © 1985 by The American Philosophical Society. Reprinted by permission.

Ever since Americans created public schools, financed by tax dollars and controlled by boards of laymen, the schools have been at the center of intermittent struggles over the values that they represent. The founders of the common school, and in particular Horace Mann, believed that the schools could be kept aloof from the religious and political controversies beyond their door, but it has not been easy to keep the crusaders outside the schoolhouse. In the nineteenth century, heated battles were fought over such issues as which Bible would be read in the classroom and whether public dollars might be used to subsidize religious schools. After the onset of World War I, anti-German hostility caused the German language to be routed from American schools, even though nearly a quarter of the high school population studied the language in 1915. Some of this same fervor, strengthened by zeal to hasten the process of assimilation, caused several states to outlaw parochial and private schools and to prohibit the teaching of foreign language in the first eight years of school. Such laws, obviously products of nationalism and xenophobia, were struck down as unconstitutional by the United States Supreme Court in the 1920s. The legislative efforts to abolish nonpublic schools and to bar the teaching of foreign languages were examples of politicization; their purpose was not to improve the education of any child, but to achieve certain social and political goals that the sponsors of these laws believed were of overwhelming importance.

Another example of politicization in education was the crusade to cleanse the schools of teachers and other employees who were suspected of being disloyal, subversive, or controversial. This crusade began in the years after World War I, gathered momentum during the 1930s, and came to full fruition during the loyalty investigations by state and national legislative committees in the 1950s. Fears for national security led to intrusive surveillance of the beliefs, friends, past associations, and political activities of teachers and professors. These inquiries did not improve anyone's education; they used the educational institutions as vehicles toward political goals that were extraneous to education.

A more recent example of politicization occurred on the campuses during the war in Vietnam. Those who had fought political intrusions into educational institutions during the McCarthy era did so on the ground of academic freedom. Academic freedom, they argued, protected the right of students and teachers to express their views, regardless of their content; because of academic freedom, the university served as a sanctuary for dissidents, heretics, and skeptics of all persuasions. During the war in Vietnam, those who tried to maintain the university as a privileged haven for conflicting views, an open marketplace of ideas, found themselves the object of attack by student radicals. Student (and sometimes faculty) radicals believed that opposition to the war was so important that those who did not agree with them should be harassed and even silenced.

Faced with a moral issue, the activist argued, the university could not stand above the battle, nor could it tolerate the expression of "immoral" views. In this spirit, young radicals tried to prevent those with whom they disagreed from speaking and teaching; towards this end, they heckled speakers, disrupted classes, and even planted bombs on campus. These actions were intended to politicize schools and campuses and, in some instances, they succeeded. They were advocated by sincere and zealous individuals who earnestly believed that education could not take place within a context of political neutrality. Their efforts at politicization stemmed not from any desire to improve education as such, but from the pursuit of political goals.

As significant as the student movement and the McCarthy era were as examples of the dangers of politicization, they were short-lived in comparison to the policy of racial segregation. Segregation of public school children by their race and ancestry was established by law in seventeen states and by custom in many communities beyond those states. The practice of assigning public school children and teachers on the basis of their race had no educational justification; it was not intended to improve anyone's education. It was premised on the belief in the innate inferiority of people whose skin was of dark color. Racial segregation as policy and practice politicized the schools; it used them to buttress a racist social and political order. It limited the educational opportunities available to blacks. Racial segregation was socially and politically so effective in isolating blacks from opportunity or economic advancement and educationally so devastating in retarding their learning that our society continues to pay a heavy price to redress the cumulative deficits of generations of poor education.

The United States Supreme Court's 1954 decision, *Brown v. Board of Education*, started the process of ending state-imposed racial segregation. In those southern states where segregation was the cornerstone of a way of life, white resistance to desegregation was prolonged and intense. The drive to disestablish racial segregation and to uproot every last vestige of its effects was unquestionably necessary. The practice of assigning children to school by their race and of segregating other public facilities by race was a national disgrace. However, the process through which desegregation came about dramatically altered the politics of schools; courts and regulatory agencies at the federal and state level became accustomed to intervening in the internal affairs of educational institutions, and the potential for politicization of the schools was significantly enlarged.

The slow pace of desegregation in the decade after the *Brown* decision, concurrent with a period of rising expectations, contributed to a dramatic buildup of frustration and rage among blacks, culminating in the protests, civil disorders, and riots of the mid-1960s. In response, Congress enacted major civil rights laws in 1964 and 1965, and the federal courts became aggressive in telling school boards what to do to remedy their constitutional violations. Initially, these orders consisted of commands to produce racially mixed schools. However, some courts went beyond questions of racial mix. In Washington, D.C., a federal district judge in 1967 directed the school administration to abandon ability grouping, which he believed discriminated against black children. This was the first time that a federal court found a common pedagogical practice to be unconstitutional.[1]

In the nearly two decades since that decision, the active intervention of the federal judiciary into school affairs has ceased to be unusual. In Ann Arbor, Michigan, a federal judge ordered the school board to train teachers in "black English," a program subsequently found to be ineffectual in improving the education of black students. In California, a federal judge barred the use of intelligence tests for placement of students in special education classes, even though reputable psychologists defend their validity. In Boston, where the school board was found guilty of intentionally segregating children by race, the federal judge assumed full control over the school system for more than a decade; even reform superintendents who were committed to carrying out the judge's program for desegregation complained of the hundreds of court orders regulating every aspect of schooling, hiring, promotion, curriculum, and financing. In 1982, in a case unrelated to desegregation, a state judge in West Virginia ordered the state education department to do "no less than completely reconstruct the entire system of education in West Virginia," and the judge started the process of reconstruction by setting down his own standards for facilities, administration, and curriculum, including what was to be taught and for how many minutes each week.[2]

Perhaps this is as good a way of bringing about school reform as any other. No doubt school officials are delighted when a judge orders the state legislature to raise taxes on behalf of the schools. But it does seem to be a repudiation of our democratic political structure when judges go beyond issues of constitutional rights, don the mantle of school superintendent, and use their authority to change promotional standards, to reconstruct the curriculum, or to impose their own pedagogical prescriptions.

Now, by the definition of politicization that I earlier offered—that is, when educational institutions become the focus of dogmatic crusaders whose purposes are primarily political and only incidentally related to children's education—these ex-amples may not qualify as politicization, although they do suggest how thin is the line between politics and politicization. After all, the judges were doing what they thought would produce better education. The court decisions in places like Ann Arbor, Boston, California, and West Virginia may be thought of as a shift in the politics of schools, a shift that has brought the judiciary into the decision-making process as a full-fledged partner in shaping educational disputes, even those involving questions of pedagogy and curriculum.

The long struggle to desegregate American schools put them at the center of political battles for more than a generation and virtually destroyed the belief that schools could remain above politics. Having lost their apolitical shield, the schools also lost their capacity to resist efforts to politicize them. In the absence of resistance, demands by interest groups of varying ideologies escalated, each trying to impose its own agenda on the curriculum, the textbooks, the school library, or the teachers. Based on the activities of single-issue groups, any number of contemporary educational policies would serve equally well as examples of politicization. The example that I have chosen as illustrative of politicization is bilingual education. The history of this program exemplifies a campaign on behalf of social and political goals that are only tangentially related to education. I would like to sketch briefly the bilingual controversy, which provides an overview of the new politics of education and demonstrates the tendency within this new politics to use educational programs for noneducational ends.

Demands for bilingual education arose as an outgrowth of the civil rights movement. As it evolved, that movement contained complex, and occasionally contradictory, elements. One facet of the movement appealed for racial integration and assimilation, which led to court orders for busing and racial balance; but the dynamics of the movement also inspired appeals to racial solidarity, which led to demands for black studies, black control of black schools, and other race-conscious policies. Whether the plea was for integration or for separatism, advocates could always point to a body of social science as evidence for their goals.

Race consciousness became a necessary part of the remedies that courts fashioned, but its presence legitimized ethnocentrism as a force in American politics. In the late 1960s, the courts, Congress, and policymakers—having been told for years by spokesmen for the civil rights movement that all children should be treated equally without regard to their race or ancestry—frequently heard compelling testimony by political activists and social scientists about the value of ethnic particularism in the curriculum.

Congress first endorsed funding for bilingual education in 1968, at a time when ethnocentrism had become a powerful political current. In hearings on this legislation, proponents of bilingual education argued that non-English-speaking children did poorly in school because they had low self-esteem, and that this low self-esteem was caused by the absence of their native language from the classroom. They claimed that if the children were taught in their native tongue and about their native culture, they would have higher self-esteem, better attitudes toward school, and higher educational achievement. Bilingual educators also insisted that children would learn English more readily if they already knew another language.

In the congressional hearings, both advocates and congressmen seemed to agree that the purpose of bilingual education was to help non-English speakers succeed in school and in society. But the differences between them were not then obvious. The congressmen believed that bilingual education would serve as a temporary transition into the regular English language program. But the bilingual educators saw the program as an opportunity to maintain the language and culture of the non-English-speaking student, while he was learning English.[3]

What was extraordinary about the Bilingual Education Act of 1968, which has since been renewed several times, is that it was the first time that the Congress had ever legislated a given pedagogical method. In practice, bilingual education means a program in which children study the major school subjects in a language other than English. Funding of the program, although small within the context of the federal education budget, created strong constituencies for its continuation, both within the federal government and among recipient agencies. No different from other interest groups, these constituencies pressed for expansion and strengthening of their program. Just as lifelong vocational educators are unlikely to ask whether their program works, so career bilingual educators are committed to their method as a philosophy, not as a technique for language instruction. The difference is this: techniques are subject to evaluation, which may cause them to be revised or discarded; philosophies are not.

In 1974, the Supreme Court's *Lau v. Nichols* decision reinforced demands for bilingual education. The Court ruled against the San Francisco public schools for their failure to provide English language instruction for 1,800 non-English-speaking Chinese students. The Court's decision was reasonable and appropriate. The Court said, "There is no equality of treatment merely by providing students with the same facilities, textbooks, teachers, and curriculum; for students who do not understand English are effectively foreclosed from any meaningful education." The decision did not endorse any particular remedy. It said "Teaching English to the students of Chinese ancestry who do not speak the language is one choice. Giving instruction to the group in Chinese is another. There may be others."[4]

Despite the Court's prudent refusal to endorse any particular method of instruction, the bilingual educators interpreted the *Lau* decision as a mandate for bilingual programs. In the year after the decision, the United States Office of Education established a task force to fashion guidelines for the implementation of the *Lau* decision; the task force was composed of bilingual educators and representatives of language minority groups. The task force fashioned regulations that prescribed in exhaustive detail how school districts should prepare and carry out bilingual programs for non-English-speaking students. The districts were directed to identify the student's primary language, not by his proficiency in English, but by determining which language was most often spoken in the student's home, which language he had learned first, and which language he used most often. Thus a student would be eligible for a bilingual program even if he was entirely fluent in English.[5]

Furthermore, while the Supreme Court refused to endorse any given method, the task force directed that non-English-speaking students should receive bilin-gual education that emphasized instruction in their native language and culture. Districts were discouraged from using the "English as a Second Language" approach, which consists of intensive, supplemental English-only instruction, or immersion techniques, in which students are instructed in English within an English-only context.

Since the establishment of the bilingual education program, many millions of dollars have been spent to support bilingual programs in more than sixty different languages. Among those receiving funding to administer and staff such programs, bilingual education is obviously popular, but there are critics who think that it is educationally unsound. Proponents of desegregation have complained that bilingual education needlessly segregates non-English speakers from others of their age. At a congressional hearing in 1977, one desegregation specialist complained that bilingual programs had been funded "without any significant proof that they would work.... There is nothing in the research to suggest that children can effectively learn English without continuous interaction with other children who are native English speakers."[6]

The research on bilingual education has been contradictory, and studies that favor or criticize the bilingual approach have been attacked as biased. Researchers connected to bilingual institutes claim that their programs resulted in significant gains for non-English-speaking children. But a four-year study commissioned by the United States Office of Education concluded that students who learned bilingually did not achieve at a higher level than those in regular classes, nor were their attitudes toward school significantly different. What they seemed to learn best, the study found, was the language in which they were instructed.[7]

One of the few evidently unbiased, nonpolitical assessments of bilingual research was published in 1982 in the *Harvard Educational Review*. A survey of international findings, it concluded that "bilingual programs are neither better nor worse than other instructional methods." The author found that in the absence of compelling experimental support for this method, there was "no legal necessity or research basis for the federal government to advocate or require a specific educational approach."[8]

If the research is in fact inconclusive, then there is no justification for mandating the use of bilingual education or any other single pedagogy. The bilingual method may or may not be the best way to learn English. Language instruction programs that are generally regarded as outstanding, such as those provided for Foreign Service officers or by the nationally acclaimed center at Middlebury College, are immersion programs, in which students embark on a systematic program of intensive language learning without depending on their native tongue. Immersion programs may not be appropriate for all children, but then neither is any single pedagogical method. The method to be used should be determined by the school authorities and the professional staff, based on their resources and competence.

Despite the fact that the Supreme Court did not endorse bilingual education, the lower federal courts have tended to treat this pedagogy as a civil right, and more than a dozen states have mandated its use in their public schools. The path by which bilingual education came to be viewed as a civil right, rather than as one method of teaching language, demonstrates the politicization of the language issue in American education. The United States Commission on Civil Rights endorsed bilingual education as a civil right nearly a decade ago. Public interest lawyers and civil rights lawyers have also regarded bilingual education as a basic civil right. An article in 1983 in the *Columbia Journal of Law and Social Problems* contended that bilingual education "may be the most effective method of compensatory language instruction currently used to educate language-minority students."[9] It based this conclusion not on a review of educational research but on statements made by various political agencies.

The article states, for example, as a matter of fact rather than opinion: " ... by offering subject matter instruction in a language understood by language-minority students, the bilingual-bicultural method maximizes achievement, and thus minimizes feelings of inferiority that might accompany a poor academic performance. By ridding the school environment of those features which may damage a language-minority child's self-image and thereby interfere with the educative process, bilingual-bicultural education creates the atmosphere most conducive to successful learning."[10]

If there were indeed conclusive evidence for these statements, then bilingual-bicultural education *should* be imposed on school districts throughout the country. However, the picture is complicated; there are good bilingual programs, and there are ineffective bilingual programs. In and of itself, bilingualism is one pedagogical method, as subject to variation and misuse as any other single method. To date, no school district has claimed that the bilingual method succeeded in sharply decreasing the dropout rate of Hispanic children or markedly raising their achievement scores in English and other subjects. The bilingual method is not necessarily inferior to other methods; its use should not be barred. There simply is no conclusive evidence that bilingualism should be preferred to all other ways of instructing non-English-speaking students. This being the case, there are no valid reasons for courts or federal agencies to impose this method on school districts for all non-English speakers, to the exclusion of other methods of language instruction.

Bilingual education exemplifies politicization because its advocates press its adoption regardless of its educational effectiveness, and they insist that it must be made mandatory regardless of the wishes of the parents and children who are its presumed beneficiaries. It is a political program whose goals are implicit in the term "biculturalism." The aim is to use the public schools to promote the maintenance of distinct ethnic communities, each with its own cultural heritage and language. This in itself is a valid goal for a democratic nation as diverse and pluralistic as ours, but it is questionable whether this goal is appropriately pursued by the public schools, rather than by the freely chosen activities of individuals and groups.

Then there is the larger question of whether bilingual education actually promotes equality of educational opportunity. Unless it enables non-English-speaking children to learn English and to enter into the mainstream of American society, it may hinder equality of educational opportunity. The child who spends most of his instructional time learning in Croatian or Greek or Spanish is likely to learn Croatian, Greek, or Spanish. Fluency in these languages will be of little help to those who want to apply to American colleges, universities, graduate schools, or employers, unless they are also fluent in English.

Of course, our nation needs much more foreign language instruction. But we should not confuse our desire to promote foreign languages in general with the special educational needs of children who do not know how to speak and read English in an English-language society.

Will our educational institutions ever be insulated from the extremes of politicization? It seems highly unlikely, in view of the fact that our schools and colleges are deeply embedded in the social and political mainstream. What is notably different today is the vastly increased power of the federal government and the courts to intervene in educational institutions, because of the expansion of the laws and the dependence of almost all educational institutions on public funding. To avoid unwise and dangerous politicization, government agencies should strive to distinguish between their proper role as protectors of fundamental constitutional rights and inappropriate intrusion into complex issues of curriculum and pedagogy.

This kind of institutional restraint would be strongly abetted if judges and policymakers exercised caution and skepticism in their use of social science testimony. Before making social research the basis for constitutional edicts, judges and policymakers should understand that social science findings are usually divergent, limited, tentative, and partial.

We need the courts as vigilant guardians of our rights; we need federal agencies that respond promptly to any violations of those rights. But we also need educational institutions that are free to exercise their responsibilities without fear of pressure groups and political lobbies. Decisions about which textbooks to use, which theories to teach, which books to place in the school library, how to teach, and what to teach are educational issues. They should be made by appropriate lay and professional authorities on educational grounds. In a democratic society, all of us share the responsibility to protect schools, colleges, and universities against unwarranted political intrusion into educational affairs.

REFERENCES

1. *Hobson v. Hansen*, 269 F. Supp. 401 (D.D.C., 1967); Alexander Bickel, "Skelly Wright's Sweeping Decision," *New Republic*, July 8, 1967, pp. 11–12.
2. Nathan Glazer, "Black English and Reluctant Judges," *Public Interest*, vol. 62, Winter 1980, pp. 40–54; *Larry P. v. Wilson Riles*, 495 F. Supp. 1926 (N.D. Calif., 1979); Nathan Glazer, "IQ on Trial," *Commentary*, June 1981, pp. 51–59; *Morgan v. Hennigan*, 379 F. Supp. 410 (D. Mass., 1974); Robert Wood, "The Disassembling of American Education," *Daedalus*, vol. 109, no. 3, Summer 1980, pp. 99–113; *Education Week*, May 12, 1982, p. 5.
3. U.S. Congress, Senate, Committee on Labor and Public Welfare, Special Subcommittee on Bilingual Education, 90th Cong., 1st sess., 1967.
4. *Lau v. Nichols*, 414 U.S. 563 (1974).
5. U.S. Department of Health, Education, and Welfare, "Task Force Findings Specifying Remedies Available for Eliminating Past Educational Practices Ruled Unlawful under *Lau v. Nichols*" (Washington, D.C., Summer 1975).
6. U.S. Congress, House, Subcommittee on Elementary, Secondary, and Vocational Education of the Committee on Education and Labor, Bilingual Education, 95th Cong., 1st sess., 1977, pp. 335–336. The speaker was Gary Orfield.
7. Malcolm N. Danoff, "Evaluation of the Impact of ESEA Title VII Spanish/English Bilingual Education Programs" (Palo Alto, Calif.: American Institutes for Research, 1978).
8. Iris Rotberg, "Some Legal and Research Considerations in Establishing Federal Policy in Bilingual Education," *Harvard Educational Review*, vol. 52, May 1982, pp. 148–168.
9. Jonathan D. Haft, "Assuring Equal Educational Opportunity for Language-Minority Students: Bilingual Education and the Equal Educational Opportunity Act of 1974." *Columbia Journal of Law and Social Problems*, vol. 18, no. 2, 1983, pp. 209–293.
10. Ibid., p. 253.

NO
Donaldo Macedo

ENGLISH ONLY: THE TONGUE-TYING
OF AMERICA

During the past decade conservative educators such as ex-secretary of education William Bennett and Diane Ravitch have mounted an unrelenting attack on bilingual and multicultural education. These conservative educators tend to recycle old assumptions about the "melting pot theory" and our "common culture," assumptions designed primarily to maintain the status quo. Maintained is a status quo that functions as a cultural reproduction mechanism which systematically does not allow other cultural subjects, who are considered outside of the mainstream, to be present in history. These cultural subjects who are profiled as the "other" are but palely represented in history within our purportedly democratic society in the form of Black History Month, Puerto Rican Day, and so forth. This historical constriction was elegantly captured by an 11th-grade Vietnamese student in California:

> I was so excited when my history teacher talked about the Vietnam War. Now at last, I thought, now we will study about my country. We didn't really study it. Just for one day, though, my country was real again. (Olsen, 1988, p. 68)

The incessant attack on bilingual education which claims that it serves to tongue-tie students in their native language not only negates the multilingual and multicultural nature of U.S. society, but blindly ignores the empirical evidence that has been amply documented in support of bilingual education.... [T]he present overdose of monolingualism and Anglocentrism that dominates the current educational debate not only contributes to a type of mind-tied America, but also is incapable of producing educators and leaders who can rethink what it means to prepare students to enter the ever-changing, multilingual, and multicultural world of the 21st century.

It is both academically dishonest and misleading to simply point to some failures of bilingual education without examining the lack of success of linguistic minority students within a larger context of a general failure of public education in major urban centers. Furthermore, the English Only position points to a pedagogy of exclusion that views the learning of English as education itself. English Only advocates fail to question under what conditions

English will be taught and by whom. For example, immersing non-English-speaking students in English as a Second Language [ESL] programs taught by untrained music, art and social science teachers (as is the case in Massachusetts with the grandfather clause in ESL Certification) will hardly accomplish the avowed goals of the English Only Movement. The proponents of English Only also fail to raise two other fundamental questions. First, if English is the most effective educational language, how can we explain that over 60 million Americans are illiterate or functionally illiterate (Kozol, 1985, p. 4)? Second, if education solely in English can guarantee linguistic minorities a better future, as educators like William Bennett promise, why do the majority of Black Americans, whose ancestors have been speaking English for over 200 years, find themselves still relegated to ghettos?

I want to argue in this paper that the answer lies not in technical questions of whether English is a more viable language of instruction or the repetitive promise that it offers non-English-speaking students "full participation first in their school and later in American society" (Silber, 1991, p. 7). This position assumes that English is in fact a superior language and that we live in a classless, race-blind society. I want to propose that decisions about how to educate non-English-speaking students cannot be reduced to issues of language, but rest in a full understanding of the ideological elements that generate and sustain linguistic, racial, and sex discrimination. That is, educators need to develop, as Henry Giroux has suggested, "a politics and pedagogy around a new language capable of acknowledging the multiple, contradictory, and complex subject positions people occupy within different social, cultural, and economic locations" (1992, p. 27). By shifting the linguistic issue to an ideological terrain we will challenge conservative educators to confront the Berlin Wall of racism, classism, and economic deprivation which characterizes the lived experiences of minorities in U.S. public schools. For example, J. Anthony Lukas succinctly captures the ideological elements that promote racism and segregation in schools in his analysis of desegregation in the Boston Public Schools. Lukas cites a trip to Charlestown High School, where a group of Black parents experienced firsthand the stark reality their children were destined to endure. Although the headmaster assured them that "violence, intimidation, or racial slurs would not be tolerated," they could not avoid the racial epithets on the walls: "Welcome Niggers," "Niggers Suck," "White Power," "KKK," "Bus is for Zulu," and "Be illiterate, fight busing." As those parents were boarding the bus, "they were met with jeers and catcalls 'go home niggers. Keep going all the way to Africa!'" This racial intolerance led one parent to reflect, "My god, what kind of hell am I sending my children into?" (Lukas, 1985, p. 282). What could her children learn at a school like that except to hate? Even though forced integration of schools in Boston exacerbated the racial tensions in the Boston Public Schools, one should not overlook the deep-seated racism that permeates all levels of the school structure....

Against this landscape of violent racism perpetrated against racial minorities, and also against linguistic minorities, one can understand the reasons for the high dropout rate in the Boston public schools (approximately 50%). Perhaps racism and other ideological elements are part of a school reality which forces a high percentage of students to leave school, only later to be profiled by the very system as dropouts or "poor and unmotivated students." One could argue that the above incidents occurred during a tumultuous time of racial division in Boston's history, but I do not believe that we have learned a great deal from historically dangerous memories to the degree that our leaders continue to invite racial tensions as evidenced in the Willie Horton presidential campaign issue and the present quota for jobs as an invitation once again to racial divisiveness.

It is very curious that this new-found concern of English Only advocates for limited English proficiency students does not interrogate those very ideological elements that psychologically and emotionally harm these students far more than the mere fact that English may present itself as a temporary barrier to an effective education. It would be more socially constructive and beneficial if the zeal that propels the English Only movement were diverted toward social struggles designed to end violent racism and structures of poverty, homelessness, and family breakdown, among other social ills that characterize the lived experiences of minorities in the United States. If these social issues are not dealt with appropriately, it is naive to think that the acquisition of the English language alone will, somehow, magically eclipse the raw and cruel injustices and oppression perpetrated against the dispossessed class of minorities in the United States. According to Peter McLaren, these dispossessed minority students who

> populate urban settings in places such as Howard Beach, Ozone Park, El Barrio, are more likely to be forced to learn

about Eastern Europe in ways set forth by neo-conservative multiculturists than they are to learn about the Harlem Renaissance, Mexico, Africa, the Caribbean, or Aztec or Zulu culture. (McLaren, 1991, p. 7)

While arguing for the use of the students' native language in their educational development, I would like to make it very clear that the bilingual education goal should never be to restrict students to their own vernacular. This linguistic constriction inevitably leads to a linguistic ghetto. Educators must understand fully the broader meaning of the use of students' language as a requisite for their empowerment. That is, empowerment should never be limited to what Stanley Aronowitz describes as "the process of appreciating and loving oneself" (1985). In addition to this process, empowerment should also be a means that enables students "to interrogate and selectively appropriate those aspects of the dominant culture that will provide them with the basis for defining and transforming, rather than merely serving, the wider social order" (Giroux & McLaren, 1986, p. 17). This means that educators should understand the value of mastering the standard English language of the wider society. It is through the full appropriation of the standard English language that linguistic minority students find themselves linguistically empowered to engage in dialogue with various sectors of the wider society. What I must reiterate is that educators should never allow the limited proficient students' native language to be silenced by a distorted legitimation of the standard English language. Linguistic minority students' language should never be sacrificed, since it is the only means through which they make sense of their own experience in the world.

Given the importance of the standard English language in the education of linguistic minority students, I must agree with the members of the Institute for Research in English Acquisition and Development when they quote Antonio Gramsci in their brochure:

> Without the mastery of the common standard version of the national language, one is inevitably destined to function only at the periphery of national life and, especially, outside the national and political mainstream (READ, 1990)

But these English Only advocates fail to tell the other side of Antonio Gramsci's argument, which warns us:

> Each time that in one way or another, the question of language comes to the fore, that signifies that a series of other problems is about to emerge, the formation and enlarging of the ruling class, the necessity to establish more "intimate" and sure relations between the ruling groups and the popular masses, that is, the reorganization of cultural hegemony. (Gramsci, 1971, p. 16)

This selective selection of Gramsci's position on language points to the hidden curriculum with which the English Only movement seeks to promote a monolithic ideology. It is also part and parcel of an ongoing attempt at "reorganization of cultural hegemony" as evidenced by the unrelenting attack by conservative educators on multicultural education and curriculum diversity....

In contrast to the zeal for a common culture and English only, these conservative educators have remained ominously silent about forms of racism, inequality, subjugation, and exploitation that daily serve to wage symbolic and real violence against those children who by virtue of their language, race, ethnicity, class, or gender are not treated in schools with the dignity and respect all children warrant in a democracy. Instead of reconstituting education around an urban and cultural studies approach which takes the social, cultural, political, and economic divisions of education and everyday life as the primary categories for understanding contemporary schooling, conservative educators have recoiled in an attempt to salvage the status quo. That is, they try to keep the present unchanged even though, as Renato Constantino points out:

> Within the living present there are imperceptible changes which make the status quo a moving reality.... Thus a new policy based on the present as past and not on the present as future is backward for it is premised not on evolving conditions but on conditions that are already dying away. (1978, p. 201)

One such not so imperceptible change is the rapid growth of minority representation in the labor force. As such, the conservative leaders and educators are digging this country's economic grave by their continued failure to educate minorities. As Lew Ferlerger and Jay Mandle convincingly argue, "Unless the educational attainment of minority populations in the United States improves, the country's hopes for resuming high rates of growth and an increasing standard of living look increasingly dubious" (1991, p. 12).

In addition to the real threat to the economic fabric of the United States, the persistent call for English language only in education smacks of backwardness in the present conjuncture of our ever-changing multicultural and multi-lingual society. Furthermore, these conservative educators base their language policy argument on the premise that English education in this country is highly effective. On the contrary. As Patrick Courts clearly argues in his book *Literacy for Empowerment* (1991), English education is failing even middle-class and upper-class students. He argues that English reading and writing classes are mostly based on workbooks and grammar lessons, lessons which force students to "bark at print" or fill in the blanks. Students engage in grudgingly banal exercises such as practicing correct punctuation and writing sample business letters. Books used in their classes are, Courts points out, too often in the service of commercially prepared ditto sheets and workbooks. Courts's account suggests that most school programs do not take advantage of the language experiences that the majority of students have had before they reach school. These teachers become the victims of their own professional ideology when they delegitimize the language experiences that students bring with them into the classroom.

Courts's study is basically concerned with middle-class and upper-middle-class students unburdened by racial discrimination and poverty, students who have done well in elementary and high school settings and are now populating the university lecture halls and seminar rooms. If schools are failing these students, the situation does not bode well for those students less economically, socially, and politically advantaged. It is toward the linguistic minority students that I would like to turn my discussion now.

THE ROLE OF LANGUAGE IN THE EDUCATION OF LINGUISTIC MINORITY STUDENTS

Within the last two decades, the issue of bilingual education has taken on a heated importance among educators. Unfortunately, the debate that has emerged tends to recycle old assumptions and values regarding the meaning and usefulness of the students' native language in education. The notion that education of linguistic minority students is a matter of learning the standard English language still informs the vast majority of bilingual programs and manifests its logic in the renewed emphasis on technical reading and writing skills.

I want to reiterate in this paper that the education of linguistic minority students cannot be viewed as simply the development of skills aimed at acquiring the standard English language. English Only proponents seldom discuss the pedagogical structures that will enable these students to access other bodies of knowledge. Nor do they interrogate the quality of ESL instruction provided to the linguistic minority students and the adverse material conditions under which these students learn English. The view that teaching English constitutes education sustains a notion of ideology that systematically negates rather than makes meaningful the cultural experiences of the subordinate linguistic groups who are, by and large, the objects of its policies. For the education of linguistic minority students to become meaningful it has to be situated within a theory of cultural production and viewed as an integral part of the way in which people produce, transform, and reproduce meaning. Bilingual education, in this sense, must be seen as a medium that constitutes and affirms the historical and existential moments of lived culture. Hence, it is an eminently political phenomenon, and it must be analyzed within the context of a theory of power relations and an understanding of social and cultural reproduction and production. By "cultural reproduction" I refer to collective experiences that function in the interest of the dominant groups rather than in the interest of the oppressed groups that are objects of its policies. Bilingual education programs in the United States have been developed and implemented under the cultural reproduction model leading to a de facto neocolonial educational model. I use "cultural production" to refer to specific groups of people producing, mediating, and confirming the mutual ideological elements that merge from and reaffirm their daily lived experiences. In this case, such experiences are rooted in the interest of individual and collective self-determination. It is only through a cultural production model that we can achieve a truly democratic and liberatory educational experience. I will return to this issue later.

While the various debates in the past two decades may differ in their basic assumptions about the education of linguistic minority students, they all share one common feature: they all ignore the role of language as a major force in the construction of human subjectivities. That is, they ignore the way language may either confirm or deny the life histories and experiences of the people who use it.

The pedagogical and political implications in education programs for linguistic minority students are far-reaching and yet largely ignored. These programs, for example, often contradict a fundamental principle of reading, namely that stu-

dents learn to read faster and with better comprehension when taught in their native tongue. The immediate recognition of familiar words and experiences enhances the development of a positive self-concept in children who are somewhat insecure about the status of their language and culture. For this reason, and to be consistent with the plan to construct a democratic society free from vestiges of oppression, a minority literacy program must be rooted in the cultural capital of subordinate groups and have as its point of departure their own language.

Educators must develop radical pedagogical structures which provide students with the opportunity to use their own reality as a basis of literacy. This includes, obviously, the language they bring to the classroom. To do otherwise is to deny minority students the rights that lie at the core of a democratic education. The failure to base a literacy program on the minority students' language means that oppositional forces can neutralize the efforts of educators and political leaders to achieve decolonization of schooling. It is of tantamount importance that the incorporation of the minority language as the primary language of instruction in education of linguistic minority students be given top priority. It is through their own language that linguistic minority students will be able to reconstruct their history and their culture.

I want to argue that the minority language has to be understood within the theoretical framework that generates it. Put another way, the ultimate meaning and value of the minority language is not to be found by determining how systematic and rule-governed it is. We know that already. Its real meaning has to be understood through the assumptions that govern it, and it has to be understood via the social, political, and ideological relations to which it points. Generally speaking, this issue of effectiveness and validity often hides the true role of language in the maintenance of the values and interests of the dominant class. In other words, the issue of effectiveness and validity becomes a mask that obfuscates questions about the social, political, and ideological order within which the minority language exists.

If an emancipatory and critical education program is to be developed in the United States for linguistic minority students in which they become "subjects" rather than "objects," educators must understand the productive quality of language. James Donald puts it this way:

> I take language to be productive rather than reflective of social reality. This means calling into question the assumption that we, as speaking subjects, simply use language to organize and express our ideas and experiences. On the contrary, language is one of the most important social practices through which we come to experience ourselves as subjects.... My point here is that once we get beyond the idea of language as no more than a medium of communication, as a tool equally and neutrally available to all parties in cultural exchanges, then we can begin to examine language both as a practice of signification and also as a site for culture struggle and as a mechanism which produces antagonistic relations between different social groups. (Donald, 1982, p. 44)

It is to the antagonistic relationship between the minority and dominant speakers that I want to turn now. The antagonistic nature of the minority language has never been fully explored. In order to more clearly discuss this issue of antago-nism, I will use Donald's distinction between oppressed language and repressed language. Using Donald's categories, the "negative" way of posing the minority language question is to view it in terms of oppression—that is, seeing the minority language as "lacking" the dominant standard features which usually serve as a point of reference for the minority language. By far the most common questions concerning the minority language in the United States are posed from the oppression perspective. The alternative view of the minority language is that it is repressed in the standard dominant language. In this view, minority language as a repressed language could, if spoken, challenge the privileged standard linguistic dominance. Educators have failed to recognize the "positive" promise and antagonistic nature of the minority language. It is precisely on these dimensions that educators must demystify the standard dominant language and the old assumptions about its inherent superiority. Educators must develop liberatory and critical bilingual programs informed by a radical pedagogy so that the minority language will cease to provide its speakers the experience of subordination and, moreover, may be brandished as a weapon of resistance to the dominance of the dominant standard language of the curriculum.

In this sense, the students' language is the only means by which they can develop their own voice, a prerequisite to the development of a positive sense of self-worth. As Giroux elegantly states, the students' voice "is the discursive means to make themselves 'heard' and to define themselves as active authors of their worlds" (Giroux & McLaren, 1986, p. 235). The authorship of one's own world also implies the use of one's own language, and relates to what Mikhail Bakhtin describes as "retelling a story in one's own words" (Giroux & McLaren, 1986, p. 235).

A DEMOCRATIC AND LIBERATORY EDUCATION FOR LINGUISTIC MINORITY STUDENTS

In maintaining a certain coherence with the educational plan to reconstruct new and more democratic educational programs for linguistic minority students, educators and political leaders need to create a new school grounded in a new educational praxis, expressing different concepts of education consonant with the principles of a democratic, multicultural, and multilingual society. In order for this to happen, the first step is to identify the objectives of the inherent colonial education that informs the majority of bilingual programs in the United States. Next, it is necessary to analyze how colonialist methods used by the dominant schools function, legitimize the Anglocentric values and meaning, and at the same time negate the history, culture, and language practices of the majority of linguistic minority students. The new school, so it is argued, must also be informed by a radical bilingual pedagogy, which would make concrete such values as solidarity, social responsibility, and creativity. In the democratic development of bilingual programs rooted in a liberatory ideology, linguistic minority students become "subjects" rather than mere "objects" to be assimilated blindly into an often hostile dominant "common" culture. A democratic and liberatory education needs to move away from traditional approaches, which emphasize the acquisition of mechanical basic skills while divorcing education from its ideological

and historical contexts. In attempting to meet this goal, it purposely must reject the conservative principles embedded in the English Only movement I have discussed earlier. Unfortunately, many bilingual programs sometimes unknowingly reproduce one common feature of the traditional approaches to education by ignoring the important relationship between language and the cultural capital of the students at whom bilingual education is aimed. The result is the development of bilingual programs whose basic assumptions are at odds with the democratic spirit that launched them.

Bilingual program development must be largely based on the notion of a democratic and liberatory education, in which education is viewed "as one of the major vehicles by which 'oppressed' people are able to participate in the sociohistorical transformation of their society" (Walmsley, 1981, p. 74). Bilingual education, in this sense, is grounded in a critical reflection of the cultural capital of the oppressed. It becomes a vehicle by which linguistic minority students are equipped with the necessary tools to reappropriate their history, culture, and language practices. It is, thus, a way to enable the linguistic minority students to reclaim "those historical and existential experiences that are devalued in everyday life by the dominant culture in order to be both validated and critically understood" (Giroux, 1983, p. 226). To do otherwise is to deny these students their very democratic rights. In fact, the criticism that bilingual and multicultural education unwisely question the traditions and values of our so-called "common culture" as suggested by Kenneth T. Jackson (1991) is both antidemocratic and academically dishonest. Multicultural education and curriculum diversity did not create the

S & L scandal, the Iran-Contra debacle, or the extortion of minority properties by banks, the stewards of the "common culture," who charged minorities exorbitant loan-sharking interest rates. Multicultural education and curriculum diversity did not force Joachim Maitre, dean of the College of Communication at Boston University, to choose the hypocritical moral high ground to excoriate the popular culture's "bleak moral content," all the while plagiarizing 15 paragraphs of a conservative comrade's text.

The learning of English language skills alone will not enable linguistic minority students to acquire the critical tools "to awaken and liberate them from their mystified and distorted views of themselves and their world" (Giroux, 1983, p. 226). For example, speaking English has not enabled African-Americans to change this society's practice of jailing more Blacks than even South Africa, and this society spending over 7 billion dollars to keep African-American men in jail while spending only 1 billion dollars educating Black males (Black, 1991).

Educators must understand the all-encompassing role the dominant ideology has played in this mystification and distortion of our so-called "common culture" and our "common language." They must also recognize the antagonistic relationship between the "common culture" and those who, by virtue of their race, language, ethnicity, and gender, have been relegated to the margins. Finally, educators must develop bilingual programs based on the theory of cultural production. In other words, linguistic minority students must be provided the opportunity to become actors in the reconstruction of a more democratic and just society. In short, education conducted in English only is alienating to linguistic minority students, since it denies them the fundamental tools for reflection, critical thinking, and social interaction. Without the cultivation of their native language, and robbed of the opportunity for reflection and critical thinking, linguistic minority students find themselves unable to re-create their culture and history. Without the reappropriation of their culture, the valorization of their lived experiences, English Only supporters' vacuous promise that the English language will guarantee students "full participation first in their school and later in American society" (Silber, 1991, p. 7) can hardly be a reality.

REFERENCES

Aronowitz, S. (1985, May). "Why should Johnny read." *Village Voice Literary Supplement*, p. 13.

Black, C. (1991, January 13). Paying the high price for being the world's no. 1 jailor. *Boston Sunday Globe*, p. 67.

Constantino, R. (1928). *Neocolonial identity and counter consciousness*. London: Merlin Press.

Courts, P. (1991). *Literacy for empowerment*. South Hadley, MA: Bergin & Garvey.

Donald, J. (1982). Language, literacy, and schooling. In *The state and popular culture*. Milton Keynes: Open University Culture Unit.

Ferlerger, L., & Mandle, J. (1991). *African-Americans and the future of the U.S. economy*. Unpublished manuscript.

Giroux, H. A. (1983). *Theory and resistance: A pedagogy for the opposition*. South Hadley, MA: Bergin & Garvey.

Giroux, H. (1991). *Border crossings: Cultural workers and the politics of education*. New York: Routledge.

Giroux, H. A., & McLaren, P. (1986). Teacher education and the politics of engagement: The case for democratic schooling. *Harvard Educational Review*, 56(3), 213–238.

Gramsci, A. (1971). *Selections from Prison Notebooks*, (Ed. and Trans. Quinten Hoare & Geoffrey Smith). New York: International Publishers.

Jackson, D. (1991, December 8). The end of the second Reconstruction. *Boston Globe*, p. 27.

Jackson, K. T. (1991, July 7). Cited in a *Boston Sunday Globe* editorial.

Kozol, J. (1985). *Illiterate America*. New York: Doubleday Anchor.

Lukas, J. A. (1985). *Common ground*. New York: Alfred A. Knopf.

McLaren, P. (1991). Critical pedagogy: Constructing an arch of social dreaming and a doorway to hope. *Journal of Education, 173*(1), 9–34.

Olsen, L. (1988). *Crossing the schoolhouse border: Immigrant students and the California public schools*. San Francisco: California Tomorrow.

Silber, J. (1991, May). *Boston University Commencement Catalogue*.

Walmsley, S. (1981). On the purpose and content of secondary reading programs: Educational and ideological perspectives. *Curriculum Inquiry, 11*, 73–79.

POSTSCRIPT

Should Bilingual Education Programs Be Abandoned?

Research comparing the effectiveness of the several approaches to helping linguistically disadvantaged students remains inconclusive. At the same time, the effort is clouded by the political agendas of those who champion first-language instruction and those who insist on some version of the immersion strategy. Politics and emotional commitments aside, what must be placed first on the agenda are the needs of the students and the value of native language in a child's progress through school.

Some books to note are Jane Miller's *Many Voices: Bilingualism, Culture and Education* (1983), which includes a research review; Kenji Hakuta's *Mirror of Language: The Debate on Bilingualism* (1986); *Bilingual Education: A Sourcebook* (1985) by Alba N. Ambert and Sarah E. Melendez; and *Sink or Swim: The Politics of Bilingual Education* (1986) by Colman B. Stein, Jr. Thomas Weyr's book *Hispanic U.S.A.: Breaking the Melting Pot* (1988) presents a detailed plan of action in light of the prediction that "by the year 2000 as many people in the U.S. will be speaking Spanish as they will English." A helpful overview article is David Rosenbaum's "Bilingual Education: A Guide to the Literature," *Education Libraries* (Winter 1987).

A number of articles may be found in the March 1989 issue of *The American School Board Journal*, the March 1988 issue of *The English Journal*, and the Summer 1988 issue of *Equity and Excellence*. Some especially provocative articles are these: "Bilingual Education: A Barrier to Achievement," by Nicholas Sanchez, *Bilingual Education* (December 1987); " 'Official English': Fear or Foresight?" by Nancy Bane, *America* (December 17, 1988); and "The Language of Power," by Yolanda T. DeMola, *America* (April 22, 1989).

More recent articles include Charles L. Glenn's "Educating the Children of Immigrants," *Phi Delta Kappan* (January 1992); David Corson's "Bilingual Ed Policy and Social Justice," *Journal of Education Policy* (January–March 1992); and Mary McGroarty's "The Societal Context of Bilingual Education," *Educational Researcher* (March 1992). The Fall 1993 *Peabody Journal of Education* features a number of articles devoted to the theme "Trends in Bilingual Education at the Secondary School Level." Donaldo Macedo offers a wide-ranging critique of current educational practices in "Literacy for Stupidification: The Pedagogy of Big Lies," *Harvard Educational Review* (Summer 1993). Macedo has also had published *Literacy: Reading the Word and the World* (1987), coauthored with Paulo Freire.

ISSUE 16

Does Tracking Create Educational Inequality?

YES: Jeannie Oakes, from "Keeping Track, Part 1: The Policy and Practice of Curriculum Inequality," *Phi Delta Kappan* (September 1986)

NO: Charles Nevi, from "In Defense of Tracking," *Educational Leadership* (March 1987)

ISSUE SUMMARY

YES: Social scientist Jeannie Oakes argues that tracking exaggerates initial differences among students and contributes to mediocre schooling for many who are placed in middle or lower tracks.

NO: Charles Nevi, director of Curriculum and Instruction for the Puyallup School District in Washington, feels that tracking accommodates individual differences while making "high-status knowledge" available to all.

One of John Franklin Bobbitt's scientific management principles, designed for application to public schooling early in this century, was this: Work up the raw material into that finished product for which it is best adapted. During the first four decades of the century, public school officials became more and more captivated by the "efficiency" movement, and, according to Edward Stevens and George H. Wood, in *Justice, Ideology, and Education* (1987), "The ideal of a unified curriculum gave way to the ideal of differentiating students for predetermined places in the work force." The application of these principles of management resulted in a tracking system in schools that tended to reproduce the divisions of the social class system.

Books such as Willard Waller's *The Sociology of Teaching* (1967), Paulo Freire's *The Pedagogy of the Oppressed* (1973), and *Schooling in Capitalist America* (1976) by Samuel Bowles and Herbert Gintis, mounted a pungent criticism of this prevailing practice. In more recent times, during which a conscious effort has been made to "equalize" opportunities for all students regardless of their backgrounds, the race is still rigged. According to Stevens and Wood: "The very structure of the school, particularly its tracking and sorting function, is designed to assure the success of some at the expense of others."

Many people now realize the importance of reducing the social and racial homogeneity of the school environment. As presently structured, the schools seem unable to overcome initial differences based on social and cultural disadvantages whether or not tracking and grouping are employed. The

National Association for the Advancement of Colored People (NAACP) has officially called for the elimination of tracking and homogeneous grouping, the utilization of multimethod assessments of ability and achievement, and the assurance that high expectations will be held for all students.

In her 1985 book *Keeping Track,* Jeannie Oakes presents the results of her analysis of a wide selection of tracking studies. She found that there is little evidence that grouping improves the achievement levels of *any* group. She also found that students from disadvantaged backgrounds are given a less demanding and less rewarding set of curricular experiences and that children in the lower tracks suffer losses of self-esteem and develop negative self-concepts.

In the following articles, Oakes defines tracking, examines its underlying assumptions, and summarizes what she judges to be the disappointing effects of the practice. She contends that even as they voice commitment to equality and excellence, schools organize and deliver educational experiences in ways that advance neither. Charles Nevi counters with the argument that while students are obviously equal under the law they are not equal in ability. Tracking and grouping provide for these individual differences, he contends, whereas treating all students the same is not a formula for equity or excellence.

YES   Jeannie Oakes

KEEPING TRACK

The idea of educational equality has fallen from favor. In the 1980s policy makers, school practitioners, and the public have turned their attention instead to what many consider a competing goal: excellence. Attempts to "equalize" schooling in the Sixties and Seventies have been judged extravagant and naive. Worse, critics imply that those well-meant efforts to correct inequality may have compromised the central mission of the schools: teaching academics well. And current critics warn that, given the precarious position of the United States in the global competition for economic, technological, and military superiority, we can no longer sacrifice the quality of our schools to social goals. This view promotes the judicious spending of limited educational resources in ways that will produce the greatest return on "human capital." Phrased in these economic terms, special provisions for underachieving poor and minority students become a bad investment. In short, equality is out; academic excellence is in.

On the other hand, many people still argue vociferously that the distinction between promoting excellence and providing equality is false, that one cannot be achieved without the other. Unfortunately, whether "tight-fisted" conservatives or "fuzzy-headed" liberals are in the ascendancy, the heat of the rhetoric surrounding the argument largely obscures a more serious problem: the possibility that the unquestioned *assumptions* that drive school practice and the *basic features of schools* may themselves lock schools into patterns that make it difficult to achieve *either* excellence *or* equality.

The practice of tracking in secondary schools illustrates this possibility and provides evidence of how schools, even as they voice commitment to equality and excellence, organize and deliver curriculum in ways that advance neither. Nearly all schools track students. Because tracking enables schools to provide educational treatments matched to particular groups of students, it is believed to promote higher achievement for all students under conditions of equal educational opportunity. However, rather than promoting higher achievement, tracking contributes to mediocre schooling for *most* secondary students. And because it places the greatest obstacles to achievement in the path of those children least advantaged in American society—poor and minority children

From Jeannie Oakes, "Keeping Track, Part 1: The Policy and Practice of Curriculum Inequality," *Phi Delta Kappan* (September 1986). Copyright © 1986 by Phi Delta Kappa, Inc. Reprinted by permission.

—tracking forces schools to play an active role in perpetuating school and economic inequalities as well. Evidence about the influence of tracking on student outcomes and analyses of how tracking affects the day-to-day school experiences of young people support the argument that such basic elements of schooling can *prevent* rather than *promote* educational goals.

WHAT IS TRACKING?

Tracking is the practice of dividing students into separate classes for high-, average-, and low-achievers; it lays out different curriculum paths for students headed for college and for those who are bound directly for the workplace. In most senior high schools, students are assigned to one or another *curriculum track* that lays out sequences of courses for college-preparatory, vocational, or general track students. Junior and senior high schools also make use of *ability grouping*—that is, they divide academic subjects (typically English, mathematics, science, and social studies) into classes geared to different "levels" for students of different abilities. In many high schools these two systems overlap, as schools provide college-preparatory, general, and vocational sequences of courses and also practice ability grouping in academic subjects. More likely than not, the student in the vocational curriculum track will be in one of the lower ability groups. Because similar overlapping exists for college-bound students, the distinction between the two types of tracking is sometimes difficult to assess.

But tracking does not proceed as neatly as the description above implies. Both curriculum tracking and ability grouping vary from school to school in the number

of subjects that are tracked, in the number of levels provided, and in the ways in which students are placed. Moreover, tracking is confounded by the inflexibilities and idiosyncrasies of "master schedules," which can create unplanned tracking, generate further variations among tracking systems, and affect the courses taken by individual students as well. Elective subjects, such as art and home economics, sometimes become low-track classes because college-preparatory students rarely have time in their schedules to take them; required classes, such as drivers' training, health, or physical education, though they are intended to be heterogeneous, become tracked when the requirements of other courses that *are* tracked keep students together for large portions of the day.

Despite these variations, tracking has common and predictable characteristics:

- The intellectual performance of students is judged, and these judgments determine placement with particular groups.

- Classes and tracks are labeled according to the performance levels of the students in them (e.g., advanced, average, remedial) or according to students' postsecondary destinations (e.g., college-preparatory, vocational).

- The curriculum and instruction in various tracks are tailored to the perceived needs and abilities of the students assigned to them.

- The groups that are formed are not merely a collection of different but equally-valued instructional groups. They form a hierarchy, with the most advanced tracks (and the students in them) seen as being on top.

• Students in various tracks and ability levels experience school in very different ways.

UNDERLYING ASSUMPTIONS

First, and clearly most important, teachers and administrators generally assume that tracking promotes overall student achievement—that is, that the academic needs of all students will be better met when they learn in groups with similar capabilities or prior levels of achievement. Given the inevitable diversity of student populations, tracking is seen as the best way to address individual needs and to cope with individual differences. This assumption stems from a view of human capabilities that includes the belief that students' capacities to master schoolwork are so disparate that they require different and separate schooling experiences. The extreme position contends that some students cannot learn at all.

A second assumption that underlies tracking is that less-capable students will suffer emotional as well as educational damage from daily classroom contact and competition with their brighter peers. Lowered self-concepts and negative attitudes toward learning are widely considered to be consequences of mixed-ability grouping for slower learners. It is also widely assumed that students can be placed in tracks and groups both accurately and fairly. And finally, most teachers and administrators contend that tracking greatly eases the teaching task and is, perhaps, the *only* way to manage student differences.

THE RECORD OF TRACKING

Students clearly differ when they enter secondary schools, and these differences just as clearly influence learning. But separating students to better accommodate these differences appears to be neither necessary, effective, nor appropriate.

Does tracking work? At the risk of oversimplifying a complex body of research literature, it is safe to conclude that *there is little evidence to support any of the assumptions about tracking.* The effects of tracking on student outcomes have been widely investigated, and the bulk of this work *does not* support commonly-held beliefs that tracking increases student learning. Nor does the evidence support tracking as a way to improve students' attitudes about themselves or about schooling.[1] Although existing tracking systems *appear* to provide advantages for students who are placed in the top tracks, the literature suggests that students at all ability levels can achieve at least as well in heterogeneous classrooms.

Students who are *not* in top tracks—a group that includes about 60% of senior high school students—suffer clear and consistent disadvantages from tracking. Among students identified as average or slow, tracking often appears to retard academic progress. Indeed, one study documented the fact that the lowered I.Q. scores of senior high school students followed their placement in low tracks.[2] Students who are placed in vocational tracks do not even seem to reap any benefits in the job market. Indeed, graduates of vocational programs may be less employable and, when they do find jobs, may earn lower wages than other high school graduates.[3]

Most tracking research does not support the assumption that slow students suffer emotional strains when enrolled in mixed-ability classes. Often the opposite result has been found. Rather than helping students feel more comfortable about themselves, tracking can reduce self-esteem, lower aspirations, and foster negative attitudes toward school. Some studies have also concluded that tracking leads low-track students to misbehave and eventually to drop out altogether.[4]

The net effect of tracking is to exaggerate the initial differences among students rather than to provide the means to better accommodate them. For example, studies show that senior high school students who are initially similar in background and prior achievement become *increasingly* different in achievement and future aspirations when they are placed in different tracks.[5] Moreover, this effect is likely to be cumulative over most of the students' school careers, since track placements tend to remain fixed. Students placed in low-ability groups in elementary school are likely to continue in these groups in middle school or junior high school; in senior high school these students are typically placed in non-college-preparatory tracks. Studies that have documented increased gaps between initially comparable high school students placed in different tracks probably capture only a fraction of this effect.

Is tracking fair? Compounding the lack of empirical evidence to support tracking as a way to enhance student outcomes are compelling arguments that favor exposing all students to a common curriculum, *even if differences among them prevent all students from benefiting equally.* These arguments counter both the assumption that tracking can be carried out "fairly" and the view that tracking is a legitimate means to ease the task of teaching.

Central to the issue of fairness is the well-established link between track placements and student background characteristics. Poor and minority youngsters (principally black and Hispanic) are disproportionately placed in tracks for low-ability or non-college-bound students. By the same token, minority students are consistently underrepresented in programs for the gifted and talented. In addition, differentiation by race and class occurs within vocational tracks, with blacks and Hispanics more frequently enrolled in programs that train students for the lowest-level occupations (e.g., building maintenance, commercial sewing, and institutional care). These differences in placement by race and social class appear regardless of whether test scores, counselor and teacher recommendations, or student and parent choices are used as the basis for placement.[6]

Even if these track placements are ostensibly based on merit—that is, determined by prior school achievement rather than by race, class, or student choice—they usually come to signify judgments about supposedly fixed abilities. We might find appropriate the disproportionate placements of poor and minority students in low-track classes if these youngsters were, in fact, known to be innately less capable of learning than middle- and upper-middle-class whites. But this is not the case. Or we might think of these track placements as appropriate *if* they served to remediate the obvious educational deficiencies that many poor and minority students exhibit. If being in a low track prepared disadvantaged students for success in higher tracks and opened future educational opportunities to them, we would not question the need for tracking. However, this rarely happens.

The assumption that tracking makes teaching easier pales in importance when held up against the abundant evidence of the general ineffectiveness of tracking and the disproportionate harm it works on poor and minority students. But even if this were not the case, the assumption that tracking makes teaching easier would stand up *only if* the tracks were made up of truly homogeneous groups. In fact, they are not. Even within tracks, the variability of students' learning speed, cognitive style, interest, effort, and aptitude for various tasks is often considerable. Tracking simply masks the fact that instruction for any group of 20 to 35 people requires considerable variety in instructional strategies, tasks, materials, feedback, and guidance. It also requires multiple criteria for success and a variety of rewards. Unfortunately, for many schools and teachers, tracking deflects attention from these instructional realities. When instruction fails, the problem is too often attributed to the child or perhaps to a "wrong placement." The fact that tracking *may* make teaching easier for some teachers should not cloud our judgment about whether that teaching is best for any group of students —whatever their abilities.

Finally, a profound ethical concern emerges from all the above. In the words of educational philosopher Gary Fenstermacher, "[U]sing individual differences in aptitude, ability or interest as the basis for curricular variation denies students equal access to the knowledge and understanding available to mankind." He continues, "[I]t is possible that some students may not benefit equally from unrestricted access to knowledge, but this fact does not entitle us to control access in ways that effectively prohibit all students from encountering what Dewey called the 'funded capital of civilization.'"[7] Surely educators do not intend

any such unfairness when by tracking they seek to accommodate differences among students.

WHY SUCH DISAPPPOINTING EFFECTS?

As those of us who were working with John Goodlad on A Study of Schooling began to analyze the extensive set of data we had gathered about 38 schools across the U.S., we wanted to find out more about tracking.[8] We wanted to gather specific information about the knowledge and skills that students were taught in tracked classes, about the learning activities they experienced, about the way in which teachers managed instruction, about the classroom relationships, and about how involved students were in their learning. By studying tracked classes directly and asking over and over whether such classes differed, we hoped to begin to understand why the effects of tracking have been so disappointing for so many students. We wanted to be able to raise some reasonable hypotheses about the ways in which good intentions of practitioners seem to go wrong.

We selected a representative group of 300 English and mathematics classes. We chose these subjects because they are most often tracked and because nearly all secondary students take them. Our sample included relatively equal numbers of high-, average-, low-, and mixed-ability groups. We had a great deal of information about these classes because teachers and students had completed extensive questionnaires, teachers had been interviewed, and teachers had put together packages of materials about their classes, including lists of the topics and skills they taught, the textbooks they used, and the ways in which they evaluated student learning. Many teachers also gave us sample lesson plans, worksheets, and tests. Trained observers recorded what students and teachers were doing and documented their interactions.

The data gathered on these classes provided some clear and consistent insights. In the three areas we studied —curriculum content, instruction quality, and classroom climate—we found remarkable and disturbing differences between classes in different tracks. These included important discrepancies in student access to knowledge, in their classroom instructional opportunities, and in their classroom learning environments.

Access to knowledge. In both English and math classes, we found that students had access to considerably different types of knowledge and had opportunities to develop quite different intellectual skills. For example, students in high-track English classes were exposed to content that can be called "high-status knowledge." This included topics and skills that are required for college. High-track students studied both classic and modern fiction. They learned the characteristics of literary genres and analyzed the elements of good narrative writing. These students were expected to write thematic essays and reports of library research, and they learned vocabulary that would boost their scores on college entrance exams. It was the high-track students in our sample who had the most opportunities to think critically or to solve interesting problems.

Low-track English classes, on the other hand, rarely, if ever, encountered similar types of knowledge. Nor were they expected to learn the same skills. Instruction in basic reading skills held a prominent place in low-track classes,

and these skills were taught mostly through workbooks, kits, and "young adult" fiction. Students wrote simple paragraphs, completed worksheets on English usage, and practiced filling out applications for jobs and other kinds of forms. Their learning tasks were largely restricted to memorization or low-level comprehension.

The differences in mathematics content followed much the same pattern. High-track classes focused primarily on mathematical concepts; low-track classes stressed basic computational skills and math facts.

These differences are not merely curricular adaptations to individual needs, though they are certainly thought of as such. Differences in access to knowledge have important long-term social and educational consequences as well. For example, low-track students are probably prevented from *ever* encountering at school the knowledge our society values most. Much of the curriculum of low-track classes was likely to lock students into a continuing series of such bottom-level placements because important concepts and skills were neglected. Thus these students were denied the knowledge that would enable them to move successfully into higher-track classes.

Opportunities to learn. We also looked at two classroom conditions known to influence how much students will learn: instructional time and teaching quality. The marked differences we found in our data consistently showed that students in higher tracks had better classroom opportunities. For example, all our data on classroom time pointed to the same conclusion: students in high tracks get more; students in low tracks get less. Teachers of high-track classes set aside more class time for learning, and our observers found that more actual class time was spent on learning activities. High-track students were also expected to spend more time doing homework, fewer high-track students were observed to be off-task during class activities, and more of them told us that learning took up most of their class time, rather than discipline problems, socializing, or class routines.

Instruction in high-track classes more often included a whole range of teacher behaviors likely to enhance learning. High-track teachers were more enthusiastic, and their instruction was clearer. They used strong criticism or ridicule less frequently than did teachers of low-track classes. Classroom tasks were more various and more highly organized in high-track classes, and grades were more relevant to student learning.

These differences in learning opportunities portray a fundamental irony of schooling: those students who need more time to learn appear to be getting less; those students who have the most difficulty learning are being exposed least to the sort of teaching that best facilitates learning.

Classroom climate. We were interested in studying classroom climates in various tracks because we were convinced that supportive relationships and positive feelings in class are more than just nice accompaniments to learning. When teachers and students trust one another, classroom time and energy are freed for teaching and learning. Without this trust, students spend a great deal of time and energy establishing less productive relationships with others and interfering with the teacher's instructional agenda; teachers spend their time and energy try-

ing to maintain control. In such classes, less learning is more likely to occur.

The data from A Study of Schooling permitted us to investigate three important aspects of classroom environments: relationships between teachers and students, relationships among the students, and the intensity of student involvement in learning. Once again, we discovered a distressing pattern of advantages for high-track classes and disadvantages for low-track classes. In high-track classes students thought that their teachers were more concerned about them and less punitive. Teachers in high-track classes spent less time on student behavior, and they more often encouraged their students to become independent, questioning, critical thinkers. In low-track classes teachers were seen as less concerned and more punitive. Teachers in low-track classes emphasized matters of discipline and behavior, and they often listed such things as "following directions," "respecting my position," "punctuality," and "learning to take a direct order" as among the five most important things they wanted their class to learn during the year.

We found similar differences in the relationship that students established with one another in class. Students in low-track classes agreed far more often that "students in this class are unfriendly to me" or that "I often feel left out of class activities." They said that their classes were interrupted by problems and by arguing in class. Generally, they seemed to like each other less. Not surprisingly, given these differences in relationships, students in high-track classes appeared to be much more involved in their classwork. Students in low-track classes were more apathetic and indicated more often that they didn't care about what went on or that failing didn't bother most of their classmates.

In these data, we found once again a pattern of classroom experience that seems to enhance the possibilities of learning for those students already disposed to do well—that is, those in high-track classes. We saw even more clearly a pattern of classroom experience likely to inhibit the learning of those in the bottom tracks. As with access to knowledge and opportunities to learn, we found that those who most needed support from a positive, nurturing environment got the least.

Although these data do show clear instructional advantages for high-achieving students and clear disadvantages for their low-achieving peers, other data from our work suggest that the quality of the experience of *average* students falls somewhere between these two extremes. Average students, too, were deprived of the best circumstances schools have to offer, though their classes were typically more like those of high-track students. Taken together, these findings begin to suggest *why* students who are not in the top tracks are likely to suffer because of their placements: their education is of considerably lower quality.

It would be a serious mistake to interpret these data as the "inevitable" outcome of the differences in the students who populate the various tracks. Many of the mixed-ability classes in our study showed that high-quality experiences are very possible in classes that include all types of students. But neither should we attribute these differences to consciously mean-spirited or blatantly discriminatory actions by schoolpeople. Obviously, the content teachers decide to teach and the ways in which they teach it are greatly influenced by the students with whom they interact. And it is unlikely that students are passive participants in tracking processes. It seems more likely that students' achievements, attitudes, interests, perceptions of themselves, and behaviors (growing increasingly disparate over time) help produce some of the effects of tracking. Thus groups of students who, by conventional wisdom, seem less able and less eager to learn are very likely to affect teacher's ability or even willingness to provide the best possible learning opportunities. The obvious conclusion about the effects of these track-specific differences on the ability of the schools to achieve academic excellence is that students who are exposed to less content and lower-quality teaching are unlikely to get the full benefit out of their schooling. Yet this less-fruitful experience seems to be the norm when average- and low-achieving students are grouped together for instruction.

I believe that these data reveal frightening patterns of curricular inequality. Although these patterns would be disturbing under any circumstances (and though many white, suburban schools consign a good number of their students to mediocre experiences in low-ability and general-track classes), they become particularly distressing in light of the prevailing pattern of placing disproportionate numbers of poor and minority students in the lowest-track classes. A self-fulfilling prophecy can be seen to work at the institutional level to prevent schools from providing equal educational opportunity. Tracking appears to teach and reinforce the notion that those not defined as the best are *expected* to do less well. Few students and teachers can defy those expectations.

TRACKING, EQUALITY, AND EXCELLENCE

Tracking is assumed to promote educational excellence because it enables schools to provide students with the curriculum and instruction they need to maximize their potential and achieve excellence on their own terms. But the evidence about tracking suggests the contrary. Certainly students bring differences with them to school, but, by tracking, schools help to widen rather than narrow these differences. Students who are judged to be different from one another are separated into different classes and then provided knowledge, opportunities to learn, and classroom environments that are vastly different. Many of the students in top tracks (only about 40% of high-schoolers) do benefit from the advantages they receive in their classes. But, in their quest for higher standards and superior academic performance, schools seem to have locked themselves into a structure that may *unnecessarily* buy the achievement of a few at the expense of many. Such a structure provides but a shaky foundation for excellence.

At the same time, the evidence about tracking calls into question the widely held view that schools provide students who have the "right stuff" with a neutral environment in which they can rise to the top (with "special" classes providing an extra boost to those who might need it). Everywhere we turn we find that the differentiated structure of schools throws up barriers to achievement for poor and minority students. Measures of talent clearly seem to work against them, which leads to their disproportionate placement in groups identified as slow. Once there, their achievement seems to be further inhibited by the type of knowledge they are taught and by the quality of the learning opportunities they are afforded. Moreover, the social and psychological dimensions of classes at the bottom of the hierarchy of schooling seem to restrict their chances for school success even further.

Good intentions, including those of advocates of "excellence" and of "equity," characterize the rhetoric of schooling. Tracking, because it is usually taken to be a neutral practice and a part of the mechanics of schooling, has escaped the attention of those who mean well. But by failing to scrutinize the effects of tracking, schools unwittingly subvert their well-meant efforts to promote academic excellence and to provide conditions that will enable all students to achieve it.

NOTES

1. Some recent reviews of studies on the effects of tracking include: Robert C. Calfee and Roger Brown, "Grouping Students for Instruction," in *Classroom Management* (Chicago: 78th Yearbook of the National Society for the Study of Education, University of Chicago Press, 1979); Dominick Esposito, "Homogeneous and Heterogeneous Ability Grouping: Principal Findings and Implications for Evaluating and Designing More Effective Educational Environments," *Review of Educational Research*, vol. 43, 1973, pp. 163-79; Jeannie Oakes, "Tracking: A Contextual Perspective on How Schools Structure Differences," *Educational Psychologist*, in press; Caroline J. Persell, *Education and Inequality: The Roots and Results of Stratification in America's Schools* (New York: Free Press, 1977); and James E. Rosenbaum, "The Social Implications of Educational Grouping," in David C. Berliner, ed., *Review of Research in Education, Vol. 8* (Washington, D.C.: American Educational Research Association, 1980), pp. 361–01.

2. James E. Rosenbaum, *Making Inequality: The Hidden Curriculum of High School Tracking* (New York: Wiley, 1976).

3. See, for example, David Stern et al., *One Million Hours a Day: Vocational Education in California Public Secondary Schools* (Berkeley: Report to the California Policy Seminar, University of California School of Education, 1985).

4. Rosenbaum, "The Social Implications..."; and William E. Shafer and Carol Olexa, *Tracking and Opportunity* (Scranton, Pa.: Chandler, 1971).

5. Karl A. Alexander and Edward L. McDill, "Selection and Allocation Within Schools: Some Causes and Consequences of Curriculum Placement." *American Sociological Review,* vol. 41, 1976, pp. 969–80; Karl A. Alexander, Martha Cook, and Edward L. McDill, "Curriculum Tracking and Educational Stratification: Some Further Evidence," *American Sociological Review,* vol. 43, 1978, pp. 47–66; and Donald A. Rock et al., *Study of Excellence in High School Education: Longitudinal Study, 1980–82*

(Princeton, N.J.: Educational Testing Service, Final Report, 1985).

6. Persell, *Education and Inequality...*; and Jeannie Oakes, *Keeping Track: How Schools Structure Inequality* (New Haven, Conn.: Yale University Press, 1985).

7. Gary D. Fenstermacher, "Introduction," in Gary D. Fenstermacher and John I. Goodlad, eds., *Individual Differences and the Common Curriculum* (Chicago: 82nd Yearbook of the National Society for the Study of Education, University of Chicago Press, 1983), p. 3.

8. John I. Goodlad, *A Place Called School* (New York: McGraw-Hill, 1984).

NO

Charles Nevi

IN DEFENSE OF TRACKING

In his book, *A Place Called School*, John Goodlad presents a dire picture of low-level tracked classes. These classes, he says, are characterized by unmotivated teachers teaching uninspired students; the material has little significant content or relevance. The picture he presents is enough to embarrass any educator who has ever been associated with tracking in any way, other than to rail against it.[1]

In *Keeping Track* Jeannie Oakes takes the same data that were available to Goodlad for *A Place Called School* and adds even more dire information. In addition to considerably more verbiage, Oakes adds a historical perspective and develops the possibility that tracking is a conscious, deliberate conspiracy on the part of the capitalistic bourgeois elements in society. Oakes claims these groups seek to protect their privileges and property by providing low-level educational programs for the less advantaged to keep them content with their menial roles in society.[2]

Goodlad and Oakes muster enough data and emotion so that it is difficult to dispute them. But with a little reflection, something seems amiss in the pictures of tracking that they present. Somehow, one is reminded of a poem by Issa that goes something like this:

> The world is a drop of dew,
>
> And yet—and yet...

They are stating the obvious, and one hesitates to dispute them, and yet there still seems to be more to the issue.

Despite the criticism of tracking, ability-grouping is a common, even universal characteristic of public education. Others who have studied the issue indicate that it was being practiced at least as early as the turn of the century and that today it is established in "thousands of American schools."[3] Some observers even say that the history of education is the history of tracking. Tracking was born the first time an enterprising young teacher in a one-room schoolhouse in the 1800s divided his or her class into those who knew how to read and those who didn't. Certainly it began when teachers started organizing their students into grade- and age-level groups, a clear indication that

From Charles Nevi, "In Defense of Tracking," *Educational Leadership*, vol. 44, no. 8 (March 1987), pp. 24–26. Copyright © 1987 by The Association for Supervision and Curriculum Development.

some students were going to cover different content or the same content at a different rate.

REASONS FOR TRACKING

As education has become more complex, content more broad, and students more heterogeneous, tracking has increased. In recent years guidelines for certain federal funds—special and gifted education, Chapter 1—require that students be grouped for the purpose of different specialized instruction.

Oakes argues that tradition is one of the main reasons for the existence of tracking. And certainly this historical sorting of students into groups was done for one of the reasons that Oakes gives for tracking today: homogeneous groups are easier to teach.

A variety of additional reasons explain why tracking has become a tradition. It is one method of trying to improve the instructional setting for selected students, or what one researcher refers to as a "search for a better match between learner and instructional environment."[4] Tracking becomes a very common way of attempting to provide for individual differences. Unless everyone is going to be taught everything simultaneously, grouping is necessary. It may be as simple and obvious as putting some students in grade four, or some students into a primer and others into a novel.

Tracking is not an attempt to create differences, but to accommodate them. Not all differences are created by the schools; most differences are inherited. In reading Goodlad, and particularly Oakes, one can get the impression that all students come to school with exactly the same kinds of abilities, aptitudes, and interests. The reality, of course, is that students vary widely. Socioeconomic status does account for differences in students. Learning disabilities may make some students less able to learn than others, and even though educators seldom deal publicly with the fact, some students are more able learners than others. Some students, for whatever reasons, are just plain smarter than others. Other students come to school with a broader and deeper range of experiences, with attitudes that foster learning, and with a positive orientation to school, rather than a neutral or a negative one. The schools did not create these differences, but the schools must accommodate them, and one way is through grouping students according to their needs and abilities. Even Oakes seems to recognize this.

> Schools must concentrate on equalizing the day-to-day educational experiences for all students. This implies altering the structures and contents of schools that seem to accord greater benefits to some groups of students than to others.[5]

EQUALIZING EDUCATIONAL OPPORTUNITY

But how are educational experiences made equal? It is easy to argue that putting all students in the same classes is not going to equalize their expectations. In fact, an approach that treats all students the same and ignores the real differences among them can guarantee unequal experiences for all. Treating all students the same is not a formula for equity or excellence.

Indeed, research supports tracking. A meta-analysis of 52 studies of secondary tracking programs found "only trivial effects on the achievement of average and below average students." The researchers added that "this finding...

does not support the view of other recent reviewers who claim that grouping has unfavorable effects on the achievement of low-aptitude students. The effect is near zero on the achievement of average and below-average students; it is not negative."[6]

Despite the zero effect on achievement of average and below-average students, these studies did show some benefits for tracking.

The controlled studies that we examined gave a very different picture of the effects of grouping on student attitudes. Students seemed to like their school subjects more when they studied them with peers of similar ability, and some students in grouped classes even developed more positive attitudes about themselves and about school.[7]

Tracking is more than a tradition. In a balanced view of tracking, the issue becomes not whether tracking is good or bad, but whether any particular example of tracking accomplishes the goal of matching the learner to the instructional environment.

APPROPRIATE TRACKING

If there is such a thing as good and bad tracking, how does one tell the difference? Can we establish objective criteria? Obviously no magic formulas exist, but *Keeping Track* provides a basis for distinguishing between good and bad tracking.

Oakes cites the decision in the court case of Hobson v. Hansen, and calls it "the best known and probably still the most important rule on tracking."[8] The court's decision stated that tracking is inappropriate and unlawful when it limits educational opportunities for

certain students "on the assumption that they are capable of no more." The court also provided a definition of appropriate tracking.

Any system of ability grouping which, through a failure to include and implement the concept of compensatory education for the disadvantaged child or otherwise fails in fact to bring the great majority of children into the mainstream of public education denies the children excluded equal opportunity and thus encounters the constitutional bar.[9]

This decision suggests the characteristics of appropriate tracking. One obvious consideration is content. Oakes uses the term "high-status knowledge" which she defines initially as "a commodity whose distribution is limited" to enhance its value. But it is also defined as the knowledge that "provides access to the university."[10] For the purposes of this discussion, high-status knowledge can be thought of as the combination of skills, experiences, attitudes, and academic content needed to create an informed and productive member of society. At the risk of using a cliche: it is the idea that knowledge is power, and that the primary function of the schools is to empower students.

Goodlad and Oakes express legitimate concern that students in the lower tracks are denied access to high-status knowledge, increasing the gap between lower- and higher-tracked (or nontracked) students. Tracking is not appropriate when the intent is to provide the lower-track student with an alternative curriculum that does not lead to the high-status knowledge. An appropriate program of tracking has the same expectations for all students and uses low-level tracking only to provide remediation and to upgrade selected students.

Another consideration, not directly addressed by the court but implicit in the decision, relates to the quality of instruction. Goodlad and Oakes apparently never observed good instruction in a lower-level tracked class, and they seem to assume that quality instruction in a lower track is not possible.

It is true that the attitudes, behaviors, and abilities of the students make lower-track classes more difficult to teach. But these conditions do not magically improve when the students are scattered among untracked classes. They only become hidden from view and easier to ignore. Appropriate tracking is an attempt to structure situations in which the students' special needs and abilities can be recognized and considered. It enables students in lower-level tracks to move toward the worthwhile goal of achieving high-status knowledge.

Appropriate tracking, then, can provide the best possible match between the learner and the instructional environment. Teachers using it can build a good instructional climate and motivate students toward attaining high-status knowledge.

Inappropriate tracking assumes that low-track students are not capable of acquiring high-status knowledge, and they must be given something less.

Oakes points out that the judge in the Hobson v. Hansen decision felt he was making an educational decision that would have been better left to educators. The court's decision concluded, "It is regrettable, of course, that in deciding this case, the court must act in an area so alien to its expertise."[11] But alien or not, the court's decision against limiting educational opportunities for some provides the essential basis for distinguishing between appropriate and inappropriate tracking.

NOTES

1. John I. Goodlad, *A Place Called School* (New York: McGraw-Hill, 1983), see esp. pp. 155–57.

2. Jeannie Oakes, *Keeping Track, How Schools Structure Inequality* (New Haven: Yale University Press, 1985), see esp. pp. 191–213.

3. Chen-Lin C. Kulik and James A. Kulik, "Effects of Ability Grouping on Secondary School Students. A Meta-Analysis of Evaluation Findings." *American Educational Research Journa* (Fall 1982): 416.

4. Deborah Burnett Strather, "Adopting Instruction to Individual Needs. An Eclectic Approach." *Phi Delta Kappan* (December 1985) 309. 5. Oakes, p. 205.

5. Oakes, p. 205.

6. Kulik, p. 426.

7. Kulik, p. 426.

8. Oakes, p. 184.

9. Oakes, p. 184.

10. Oakes, pp. 199–200.

11. Oakes, p. 190.

POSTSCRIPT

Does Tracking Create Educational Inequality?

In his *Paideia Proposal*, Mortimer J. Adler argues that all students in the public schools, regardless of ability level, must be given access to the same basic curriculum. For some, the pace will be slower than for others, and in some cases the depth and extent of study in a given area of the curriculum will vary, but there will be no separation into vocational or business or "basic" tracks. The goal of the proposal is to move toward a true democratization of education.

Should the schools end the practice of ability grouping and tracking in the name of democracy and equity? The January 1989 issue of *Update*, a publication of the Association for Supervision and Curriculum Development, contains commentary by prominent educators on this basic question. Robert Slavin feels that a decision to assign a child to an ability group or track at one point in that child's school experience will greatly influence later grouping decisions; therefore, the practice should be used only when there is a clear educational justification and an absence of other alternatives. Ralph Scott contends that fair and equal opportunities should consist of *appropriate* schooling experiences for individual students; therefore, ability grouping is an essential means for effective education. Don Hindman claims that research has made it clear that homogeneous grouping has a detrimental effect on achievement and social development for students in the low and intermediate tracks; for students in the higher group, achievement effects are negligible.

Some helpful articles to consider are Ray C. Rist, "Student Social Class and Teacher Expectations: The Self-Fulfilling Prophecy in Ghetto Education," *Harvard Educational Review* (August 1970); Walter C. Parker, "The Urban Curriculum and the Allocating Function of Schools," *The Educational Forum* (Summer 1985); Jean Anyon, "Social Class and the Hidden Curriculum of Work," *Journal of Education* (Winter 1980); Kenneth A. Sirotnik, "What You See Is What You Get: Consistency, Persistency, and Mediocrity in Classrooms," *Harvard Educational Review* (vol. 53, no. 1, 1983); and "We Must Offer Equal Access to Knowledge," by John I. Goodlad and Jeannie Oakes, *Educational Leadership* (February 1988). The specific issue of separate classes for the gifted and talented is addressed by Arthur R. King, Jr., and Mary Anne Raywid in *Educational Perspectives* (vol. 26, 1989).

Other additions to the debate may be found in Samuel Brodbelt's "How Tracking Restricts Educational Opportunity," *The Clearing House* (July–August 1991); "The Realities of Un-tracking a High School," by Dennis L. Evans, *Educational Leadership* (May 1991); Ralph Scott's "Untracking Advocates Make

Incredible Claims," *Educational Leadership* (October 1993); and two articles in the October 1992 issue of *Educational Leadership*, Anne Wheelock's "The Case for Untracking" and Adam Gamoran's "Is Ability Grouping Equitable?"

Jeannie Oakes has coauthored a relevant book with Martin Lipton, *Making the Best of Schools* (1990), and the issue at hand has been thoroughly explored by Anne Wheelock in *Crossing the Tracks: How "Untracking" Can Save America's Schools* (1992). Also, the October 1992 issue of *Educational Leadership* addresses the theme "Untracking for Equity."

ISSUE 17

Do "Discipline Programs" Promote Ethical Behavior?

YES: Lee Canter, from "Assertive Discipline—More Than Names on the Board and Marbles in a Jar," *Phi Delta Kappan* (September 1989)

NO: John F. Covaleskie, from "Discipline and Morality: Beyond Rules and Consequences," *The Educational Forum* (Winter 1992)

ISSUE SUMMARY

YES: Lee Canter, developer of the Assertive Discipline program, argues for the value of a positive approach to behavior management.

NO: John F. Covaleskie of Syracuse University criticizes the behavioral approach and claims that it fails to shape character.

Discipline has always been a central problem in formal education. In centuries past the problem was handled by corporal punishment, threats, and other repressive measures. In the twentieth century a number of factors—the emergence of psychology as a dominant influence on schooling, the legal granting of broader rights to the young, the formation of a "youth culture" influenced greatly by the mass media, and the erosion of traditional authority patterns in home, school, and community—have brought new complexities to the concept of discipline.

In the past three decades, the implementation of Skinnerian behaviorism in the instructional and disciplinary procedures of public education has led to the "packaging" of techniques and strategies aimed at the improvement of classroom control, the enhancement of motivation, and the routinization of desirable patterns of student behavior. Just as Carl R. Rogers attacked B. F. Skinner's stimulus-response-reinforcement approach to motivation and self-control as being too "external" and merely expedient, so have some of today's theorists contended that we must look "inside" the behaving person in order to ground our approach to discipline.

The various contending theories of discipline on the current scene can be placed along a continuum that stretches from "noninterventionists" to "interventionists," with "interactionists" taking up the middle ground position. Noninterventionists (Harris's "I'm O.K. You're O.K." and Gordon's "teacher effectiveness training") rely mainly on observation, questioning, and nondirective statements in an effort to understand the inner workings of student behavior. Interactionists (Dreikurs's "discipline without tears" and

Glasser's "schools without failure") also probe with questions, but they add directive statements and engage in the subtle molding of student behavior. Interventionists (Axelrod's "behavior modification" and Canter's "assertive discipline") mold behavior more directly, emphasize positive reinforcement, and sometimes employ threats and physical intervention strategies. A full portrait of these and other current theories of discipline can be found in *Innovative School Discipline* by John Martin Rich (1985) and in *Building Classroom Discipline: From Models to Practice*, 3rd ed. by C. M. Charles (1989).

Probably the most widely used and controversial of the various discipline programs is Lee Canter's Assertive Discipline. This approach emphasizes teacher firmness and consistency, the clear communication of behavioral expectations, and an incentive system that rewards positive student performance.

In the pairing presented here, Canter explains the basic procedures for the successful use of Assertive Discipline in the classroom and clears up some misconceptions about his ideas. John F. Covaleskie turns attention to the ends that are served when a given discipline program is employed in the schools. His central criterion is this: Does the approach teach children to make reasoned judgments about what actions are desirable and about how actually to decide to act in those desirable ways?

YES

Lee Canter

ASSERTIVE DISCIPLINE—MORE THAN NAMES ON THE BOARD AND MARBLES IN A JAR

About a year ago I was on an airline flight, seated next to a university professor. When he found out that I had developed the Assertive Discipline program, he said, "Oh, that's where all you do is write the kids' names on the board when they're bad and drop marbles in the jar when they're good."

The university professor's response disturbed me. For some time I've been concerned about a small percentage of educators—this professor apparently among them—who have interpreted my program in a way that makes behavior management sound simplistic. More important, I'm concerned with their misguided emphasis on providing only negative consequences when students misbehave. The key to dealing effectively with student behavior is not negative—but positive—consequences. To clarify my views for *Kappan* readers, I would like to explain the background of the program and address some of the issues that are often raised about Assertive Discipline.

I developed the program about 14 years ago, when I first became aware that teachers were not trained to deal with student behavior. Teachers were taught such concepts as "Don't smile until Christmas" or "If your curriculum is good enough, you will have no behavior problems." Those concepts were out of step with the reality of student behavior in the 1970s.

When I discovered this lack of training, I began to study how effective teachers dealt with student behavior. I found that, above all, the master teachers were assertive; that is, they *taught* students how to behave. They established clear rules for the classroom, they communicated those rules to the students, and they taught the students how to follow them. These effective teachers had also mastered skills in positive reinforcement, and they praised every student at least once a day. Finally, when students chose to break the rules, these teachers used firm and consistent negative consequences—but only as a last resort.

It troubles me to find my work interpreted as suggesting that teachers need only provide negative consequences—check marks or demerits—when students misbehave. That interpretation is wrong. The key to Assertive Discipline is catching students being good: recognizing and supporting them when they behave appropriately and letting them know you like it, day in and day out.

THE DISCIPLINE PLAN

It is vital for classroom teachers to have a systematic discipline plan that explains exactly what will happen when students choose to misbehave. By telling the students at the beginning of the school year what the consequences will be, teachers insure that all students know what to expect in the classroom. Without a plan, teachers must choose an appropriate consequence at the moment when a student misbehaves. They must stop the lesson, talk to the misbehaving student, and do whatever else the situation requires, while 25 to 30 students look on. That is not an effective way to teach—or to deal with misbehavior.

Most important, without a plan teachers tend to be inconsistent. One day they may ignore students who are talking, yelling, or disrupting the class. The next day they may severely discipline students for the same behaviors. In addition, teachers may respond differently to students from different socioeconomic, ethnic, or racial backgrounds.

An effective discipline plan is applied fairly to all students. Every student who willfully disrupts the classroom and stops the teacher from teaching suffers the same consequence. And a written plan can be sent home to parents, who then know beforehand what the teacher's standards are and what will be done when students choose to misbehave. When a teacher calls a parent, there should be no surprises.

MISBEHAVIOR AND CONSEQUENCES

I suggest that a discipline plan include a maximum of five consequences for misbehavior, but teachers must choose consequences with which they are comfortable. For example, the first time a student breaks a rule, the student is warned. The second infraction brings a 10-minute timeout; the third infraction, a 15-minute timeout. The fourth time a student breaks a rule, the teacher calls the parents; the fifth time, the student goes to the principal.

No teacher should have a plan that is not appropriate for his or her needs and that is not in the best interests of the students. Most important, the consequences should never be psychologically or physically harmful to the students. Students should never be made to stand in front of the class as objects of ridicule or be degraded in any other way. Nor should they be given consequences that are inappropriate for their grade levels. I also feel strongly that corporal punishment should *never* be administered. There are more effective ways of dealing with students than hitting them.

Names and checks on the board are sometimes said to be essential to an Assertive Discipline program, but they are not. I originally suggested this particular practice because I had seen teachers interrupt their lessons to make such negative comments to misbehaving students as, "You talked out again. I've had it. You're impossible. That's 20 minutes after school." I wanted to eliminate the need to stop the lesson and issue reprimands. Writing a student's name on the board would warn the student in a calm, nondegrading manner.

It would also provide a record-keeping system for the teacher.

Unfortunately, some parents have misinterpreted the use of names and checks on the board as a way of humiliating students. I now suggest that teachers instead write an offending student's name on a clipboard or in the roll book and say to the student, "You talked out, you disrupted the class, you broke a rule. That's a warning. That's a check."

In addition to parents, some teachers have misinterpreted elements of the Assertive Discipline program. The vast majority of teachers—my staff and I have probably trained close to 750,000 teachers—have used the program to dramatically increase their reliance on positive reinforcement and verbal praise. But a small percentage of teachers have interpreted the program in a negative manner.

There are several reasons for this. First, Assertive Discipline has become a generic term, like Xerox or Kleenex. A number of educators are now conducting training in what they call Assertive Discipline without teaching *all* the competencies essential to my program. For example, I have heard reports of teachers who were taught that they had only to stand in front of their students, tell them that there were rules and consequences, display a chart listing those rules and consequences, and write the names of misbehaving students on the board. That was it. Those teachers were never introduced to the concept that positive reinforcement is the key to dealing with students. Such programs are not in the best interests of students.

Negative interpretations have also come from burned-out, overwhelmed teachers who feel they do not get the support that they need from parents or administrators and who take out their frustrations on students. Assertive Discipline is not a negative program, but it can be misused by negative teachers. The answer is not to change the program, but to change the teachers. We need to train administrators, mentor teachers, and staff developers to coach negative teachers in the use of positive reinforcement. If these teachers cannot become more positive, they should not be teaching.

POSITIVE DISCIPLINE

I recommend a three-step cycle of behavior management to establish a positive discipline system.

First, whenever teachers want students to follow certain directions, they must *teach* the specific behaviors. Teachers too often assume that students know how they are expected to behave. Teachers first need to establish specific directions for each activity during the day—lectures, small-group work, transitions between activities, and so forth. For each situation, teachers must determine the *exact* behaviors they expect from the students.

For example, teachers may want students to stay in their seats during a lecture, focusing their eyes on the lecturer, clearing their desks of all materials except paper and pencil, raising their hands when they have questions or comments, and waiting to be called on before speaking. Once teachers have determined the specific behaviors for each situation, they must teach the students how to follow the directions. They must first state the directions and, with younger students, write the behaviors on the board or on a flip chart. Then they must model the behaviors, ask the students to *restate* the directions, question the students to make sure they understand the directions, and immediately engage the students in the activity to make sure that they understand the directions.

Second, after teaching the specific directions, teachers—especially at the elementary level—must use *positive repetition* to reinforce the students when they follow the directions. Typically, teachers give directions to the students and then focus attention only on those students who do *not* obey. ("Bobby, you didn't go back to your seat. Teddy, what's wrong with you? Get back to work.") Instead, teachers should focus on those students who do follow the directions, rephrasing the original directions as a positive comment. For example, "Jason went back to his seat and got right to work."

Third, if a student is still misbehaving after a teacher has taught specific directions and has used positive repetition, only then should the teacher use the negative consequences outlined in his or her Assertive Discipline plan. As a general rule, a teacher shouldn't administer a disciplinary consequence to a student until the teacher has reinforced at least two students for the appropriate behavior. Effective teachers are always positive first. Focusing on negative behavior teaches students that negative behavior gets attention, that the teacher is a negative person, and that the classroom is a negative place.

An effective behavior management program must be built on choice. Students must know beforehand what is expected of them in the classroom, what will happen if they choose to behave, and what will happen if they choose not to behave. Students learn self-discipline and responsible behavior by being given clear, consistent choices. They learn that

their actions have an impact and that they themselves control the consequences.

I wish teachers did not need to use negative consequences at all. I wish all students came to school motivated to learn. I wish all parents supported teachers and administrators. But that's not the reality today. Many children do not come to school intrinsically motivated to behave. Their parents have never taken the time or don't have the knowledge or skills to teach them how to behave. Given these circumstances, teachers need to set firm and consistent limits in their classrooms. However, those limits must be fair, and the consequences must be seen as outcomes of behaviors that students have *chosen.*

Students need teachers who can create classroom environments in which teaching and learning can take place. Every student has the right to a learning environment that is free from disruption. Students also need teachers who help them learn how to behave appropriately in school. Many students who are categorized as behavior problems would not be so labeled if their teachers had taught them how to behave appropriately in the classroom and had raised their self-esteem.

WHY ASSERTIVE DISCIPLINE?

The average teacher never receives in-depth, competency-based training in managing the behavior of 30 students. No one teaches teachers how to keep students in their seats long enough for teachers to make good use of the skills they learned in their education classes. In most instances, behavior management is taught through a smorgasbord approach —a little bit of William Glasser, a little bit of Thomas Gordon, a little bit of Rudolf

Dreikurs, a little bit of Lee Canter. The teachers are told to find an approach that works for them.

Such an approach to training teachers in behavior management is analogous to a swimming class in which nonswimmers are briefly introduced—without practice—to the crawl stroke, the breast stroke, the back stroke, and the side stroke; then they are rowed to the middle of a lake, tossed overboard, and told to swim to shore, using whatever stroke works for them. In effect, we're telling teachers to sink or swim, and too many teachers are sinking.

The lack of ability to manage student behavior is one of the key reasons why beginning teachers drop out of teaching. Teachers must be trained thoroughly in classroom management skills. It is not sufficient for them to know how to teach content. They will never get to the content unless they know how to create a positive environment in which students know how to behave.

Assertive Discipline is not a cure-all. It is a starting point. Every teacher should also know how to use counseling skills, how to use group process skills, and how to help students with behavioral deficits learn appropriate classroom behaviors. In addition, classroom management must be part of an educator's continuing professional development. Teachers routinely attend workshops, enroll in college courses, receive feedback from administrators, and take part in regular inservice training to refine their teaching skills. Classroom management skills deserve the same attention. Unfortunately, some educators view training in Assertive Discipline as a one-shot process; they attend a one-day workshop, and that's supposed to take care of

their training needs for the rest of their careers.

One day is not enough. It takes a great deal of effort and continuing training for a teacher to master the skills of classroom management. A teacher also needs support from the building administrator. Without an administrator backing a teacher's efforts to improve behavior management, without an administrator to coach and clinically supervise a teacher's behavior management skills, that teacher is not going to receive the necessary feedback and assistance to master those skills.

Parental support for teachers' disciplinary efforts is equally important. Many teachers become frustrated and give up when they don't receive such support. We must train teachers to guarantee the support of parents by teaching teachers how to communicate effectively with parents. In teacher training programs, participants are led to believe that today's parents will act as parents did in the past and give absolute support to the school. That is rarely the case. Today's teachers call parents and are told, "He's your problem at school. You handle it. You're the professional. You take care of him. I don't know what to do. Leave me alone."

RESEARCH AND ASSERTIVE DISCIPLINE

Over the last several years, a number of dissertations, master's theses, and research projects have dealt with Assertive Discipline. The results have consistently shown that teachers dramatically improve student behavior when they use the skills as prescribed. Teachers who use Assertive Discipline reduce the frequency of disruptive behavior in their classrooms, greatly reduce the number of students they refer to administrators, and dramatically increase their students' time-on-task.[1] Other research has demonstrated that student teachers trained in Assertive Discipline are evaluated by their master teachers as more effective in classroom management.[2] Research conducted in school districts in California, Oregon, Ohio, and Arizona has shown that an overwhelming majority of teachers believe that Assertive Discipline helps to improve the climate in the schools and the behavior of students.[3]

No one should be surprised that research has verified the success of the program when teachers use the skills properly. Numerous research studies have shown that teachers need to teach students the specific behaviors that they expect from them. Research also shows that student behavior improves when teachers use positive reinforcement effectively and that the pairing of positive reinforcement with consistent disciplinary consequences effectively motivates students to behave appropriately.[4]

Any behavior management program that is taught to teachers today must have a solid foundation in research. Many so-called "experts" advocate programs that are based solely on their own opinions regarding what constitutes a proper classroom environment. When pressed, many of these experts have no research validating their opinions or perceptions, and many of their programs have never been validated for effectiveness in classrooms. We can't afford to train educators in programs based only on whim or untested theory. We have an obligation to insure that any training program in behavior management be based solidly on techniques that have been validated by research and that have been shown to work in the classroom.

Research has demonstrated that Assertive Discipline works and that it isn't just a quick-fix solution. In school districts in Lennox, California, and Troy, Ohio, teachers who were trained 10 years ago still use the program effectively.[5] The program works because it is based on practices that effective teachers have followed instinctively for a long time. It's not new to have rules in a classroom. It's not new to use positive reinforcement. It's not new to have disciplinary consequences.

Teachers who are effective year after year take the basic Assertive Discipline competencies and mold them to their individual teaching styles. They may stop using certain techniques, such as putting marbles in a jar or writing names on the board. That's fine. I don't want the legacy of Assertive Discipline to be— and I don't want teachers to believe they have to use—names and checks on the board or marbles in a jar. I want teachers to learn that they have to take charge, explain their expectations, be positive with students, and consistently employ both positive reinforcement and negative consequences. These are the skills that form the basis of Assertive Discipline and of any effective program of classroom management.

NOTES

1. Linda H. Mandlebaum et al., "Assertive Discipline: An Effective Behavior Management Program," *Behavioral Disorders Journal*, vol. 8, 1983, pp. 258–64; Carl L. Fereira, "A Positive Approach to Assertive Discipline," Martinez (Calif.) Unified School District, ERIC ED 240 058, 1983; and Sammie McCormack, "Students' Off-Task Behavior and Assertive Discipline" (Doctoral dissertation, University of Oregon, 1985).

2. Susan Smith, "The Effects of Assertive Discipline Training on Student Teachers' Self Concept and Classroom Management Skills" (Doctoral dissertation, University of South Carolina, 1983).

3. Kenneth L. Moffett et al., "Assertive Discipline," *California School Board Journal*, June/July/August 1982, pp. 24–27; Mark Y. Swanson, "Assessment of the Assertive Discipline Program," Compton (Calif.) Unified School District, Spring 1984; "Discipline Report," Cartwright (Ariz.) Elementary School District, 10 February 1982; and Confederation of Oregon School Administrators, personal letter, 28 April 1980.

4. Helen Hair et al., "Development of Internal Structure in Elementary Students: A System of Classroom Management and Class Control," ERIC ED 189 067, 1980; Edmund Emmer and Carolyn Everston, "Effective Management: At the Beginning of the School Year in Junior High Classes," Research and Development Center for Teacher Education, University of Texas, Austin, 1980; Marcia Broden et al., "Effects of Teacher Attention on Attending Behavior of Two Boys at Adjacent Desks," *Journal of Applied Behavior Analysis*, vol. 3, 1970, pp. 205–11; Hill Walker et al., "The Use of Normative Peer Data as a Standard for Evaluating Treatment Effects," *Journal of Applied Behavior Analysis*, vol. 37, 1976, pp. 145–55; Jere Brophy, "Classroom Organization and Management," *Elementary School Journal*, vol. 83, 1983, pp. 265–85; Hill Walker et al., "Experiments with Response Cost in Playground and Classroom Settings," Center for Research in Behavioral Education of the Handicapped, University of Oregon, Eugene, 1977; Thomas McLaughlin and John Malaby, "Reducing and Measuring Inappropriate Verbalizations," *Journal of Applied Behavior Analysis*, vol. 5, 1972, pp. 329–33; Charles Madsen et al., "Rules, Praise, and Ignoring: Elements of Elementary Classroom Control," *Journal of Applied Behavior Analysis*, vol. 1, 1968, pp. 139–50; Charles Greenwood et al., "Group Contingencies for Group Consequences in Classroom Management: A Further Analysis," *Journal of Applied Behavior Analysis*, vol. 7, 1974, pp. 413–25; and K. Daniel O'Leary et al., "A Token Reinforcement Program in a Public School: A Replication and Systematic Analysis," *Journal of Applied Behavior Analysis*, vol. 2, 1969, pp. 3–13.

5. Kenneth L. Moffett et al., "Training and Coaching Beginning Teachers: An Antidote to Reality Shock," *Educational Leadership*, February 1987, pp. 34–46; and Bob Murphy, "Troy High School: An Assertive Model," *Miami Valley Sunday News*, Troy, Ohio, 12 March 1989, p. 1.

NO

John F. Covaleskie

DISCIPLINE AND MORALITY: BEYOND RULES AND CONSEQUENCES

For the past two decades, at least, there has been a major concern in American education on the issue of student discipline. During that period, the emphasis has been on behavioral approaches to discipline, which by their nature tend to make discipline largely the responsibility of teachers. The so-called Assertive Discipline has become both the program of choice in many schools and a paradigm of the behavioral approach. Some recent literature reviewing this particular program made clear the extent to which the debate is about means, rather than ends.[1] Rather than endlessly continue the debate about which program best controls student behaviors, we might look at the question from the other end: What is it that we hope to teach children about being good people, and does this mean more than what schools call "discipline"? If we can better define our ends, we might have a better standard by which to evaluate the means to achieve them. This article puts forth a proposal as to the proper ends of education relative to student behavior. Only then can we rationally turn to the question of how best to achieve these ends.

Now what is interesting is that the best recent work on formation of moral character seems agreed on one thing, whatever disagreements there may exist: children do not learn to be moral by learning to obey rules that others make for them. From the fields of psychotherapy,[2] psychology,[3] and philosophy,[4] the current understandings of the formation of moral character involve children learning to think and talk about moral issues in ways that are actively discouraged by programs conceiving of discipline as obedience to authority and rules. What current conceptions of morality help us see is that children grow into morality and ethical thinking, and that they do so by engaging in moral thought and conversation. What helps children become moral is not knowledge of rules, or even obedience to rules, but discussions about the reasons for acting in certain ways. Whether conceived as based in rationality, emotion, or both, morality is not simply obedience to rules.

From John F. Covaleskie, "Discipline and Morality: Beyond Rules and Consequences," *The Educational Forum*, vol. 56, no. 2 (Winter 1992). Copyright © 1992 by Kappa Delta Pi, an international honor society in education. Reprinted by permission.

WHAT COUNTS AS "SUCCESS"?

Given the fact that education should have implications for life, the question can be rephrased. It is not, "What is the best way to control student behavior in schools?" but, "What is the best way to prepare our children to love ethical lives?" Another way of addressing this issue is to ask the opposite question: "What would we consider unsatisfactory?" There are two answers to this last question, one obvious, the other somewhat less so. The obvious answer is that no discipline program would be considered satisfactory if it did not result in children acting responsibly and in accordance with the legitimate rules of behavior established in the school.

I, however, would like to argue the case that there is a more subtle way in which a discipline program can fail. A program that teaches children that they are simply expected to obey rules, even legitimate and duly established rules, fails the children and the larger society, even if it meets the needs of the adults in a school. A discipline program cannot be judged merely by asking whether it does a good job of keeping children out of trouble in school; being a good person is more than that. Children must develop a framework within which they can make good choices about how to act, and we must help them do so.

It is important in this connection to examine the meaning of two central concepts: "good" and "choices." "Good" is used here in the sense of ethical or moral, not in the sense of practical or advantageous. Children must develop a sense of what it means to be a good person—what it means to choose to do the right thing, especially when circumstances are such that one is faced

with the possibility of doing the wrong thing to one's own advantage, and getting away with it. A good choice can, and often will, place the chooser at a disadvantage, and still be a good choice. Further, learning to be a good person is not the same as learning to obey rules; it is more complex than that.

Obviously, this is no new insight. In the *Nicomachean Ethics*, Aristotle[5] included *phronesis* (practical wisdom) as an essential attribute of the good person. In fact, his definition of a virtuous action was that which a person with practical wisdom would judge to be virtuous. This capacity for judgment was not only necessary for a person to do the right thing, it was the standard by which the right thing was defined. *Phronesis* is closer than obedience to the goal we in schools should have in mind as we help children to form their characters. In choosing how to act in any circumstance, I am making a judgment about what action is the right one to take. Much more often than not, good judgment will dictate behavior that conforms to rules for the situation, but that is not the point. The point is that I must choose and act well even where rules conflict or do not obviously apply.

To illustrate what happens when people do not learn to make and act on these kinds of judgments, we need only consider Milgram's experiment on obedience,[6] in which he discovered that most people would follow a researcher's order to administer what were apparently painful shocks to the alleged "subjects" of a learning experiment. In actuality, these victims were confederates of the researcher, and there was no shock; they were only acting as if in pain. The real purpose of this experiment was to study the behavior of those being told to administer the shocks, and the question was whether they would obey the rules established by the researcher. The results of the experiment were disturbing, to say the least. Average people, chosen at random, would administer, if told to do so by someone in a position of authority (even under no threat of penalty for refusing), what were perceived as painful (even dangerous) shocks to "suffering" victims begging them to stop. Milgram reports that these common people showed real anguish as they administered the shocks —they did not want to do so—but, nevertheless, administer the shocks they did. They followed the rules, and just in doing so, they made a bad moral choice. These were people whose training failed to help them develop effective good judgment. It is instructive to note that many of these individuals appeared to understand that what they were being asked to do was wrong; they lacked confidence in this judgment of their own to translate it into action.

To sum up, any approach to discipline is to be judged a failure not only on the obvious criterion that it fails to establish and affect appropriate standards of behavior, but also if, in establishing such standards, it does so primarily by teaching children to obey rules rather than to make reasoned judgments about what actions are desirable, and about how actually to decide to act in those desirable ways.[7]

Developing good judgment. How can we then help children develop this judgment? It is easy to state, but hard to do: we must teach children that the reason they should not do certain things is that those things are wrong; the reason they should prefer to do other things is that those things are right. We must help them see *why* one thing is wrong as

against another which is right. *Teaching children that X is wrong because there is a rule against X is not the same as teaching them that there is a rule against X because X is wrong, and helping them understand why this is so.* Children should be taught not to steal because it is wrong. They should not be taught not to steal because there is a rule against stealing. Although they certainly need to know that there is such a rule, the rule is not the reason we teach children not to steal. What they need to understand is that *the rule against stealing exists only because stealing is wrong,* and why this is so.

Some help in picturing the pedagogical implications of this comes from Strike,[8] who suggests that the way children develop a moral sense is by using moral language. That is, if we talk with children about the moral implications of their actions, they will be learning to think morally at the same time that they are learning to speak the language of morality.

The standard by which we should be judging "discipline programs" in schools is that of moral responsibility: do our children learn to think, talk, and act morally? The goal is not compliance with rules, but making the choices to live a good life, an ethical life. Further, in order to reach this goal children must learn that certain things are wrong, and should be avoided *for that reason only.* Negative consequences, fear of getting caught, self-advantage, and rules themselves should all yield before the voice of conscience, the internal voice which monitors my actions against the standard of the kind of person I hope to be. This voice of conscience, this sense of right and wrong, is what we must strive to shape in our schools, and this internal voice can best be given shape through external language that models its proper form.

OBJECTIONS CONSIDERED

Implementing this suggestion involves a practical problem of considerable dimension: what (or whose) standards of right and wrong should be taught? I would make three suggestions: (1) this question misconstrues the true nature of moral education, (2) the issue is not, in the long run, relevant, and (3) the difficulty of the task, however great it is, does not excuse us from the effort.

1) The argument against ethics education is usually based on two assumptions: (a) moral education consists merely in telling children what is right or wrong conduct, and (b) the differences of judgment over difficult moral issues make such teaching in public schools inappropriate and/or impossible. What, for example, should we teach children with respect to the rightness or wrongness of capital punishment, abortion, or sexual experimentation? Given the deep divisions within society on these and many other ethical questions, this argument goes, do schools not serve both children and the community better by avoiding discussions of moral and/or ethical behavior? While this argument may seem compelling at first, it fails upon closer examination, since it falsely presumes that moral education must be rules-based, as behavioral approaches to discipline are.

In reality, however, teaching children that there is such a thing as an ethical point of view, and helping them understand what that means, does not mean having an answer for every ethical dispute. This does not entail, or even suggest, that we cannot engage in moral conversation about such issues. Where there are sharp disagreements in society about the moral or ethical stand on an issue (and this merely demonstrates the correctness of the proposition argued earlier, namely, that acting ethically requires the exercise of judgment and that following rules will not help us in life, and should not suffice in school, either), we probably should avoid telling students that X is wrong. We still can, and probably must, make clear the nature of the issues involved that makes, for instance, the abortion choice question a moral dilemma. Similarly, it may just be the job of schools in this regard to help people see that issues of poverty, health care distribution, care for the homeless, or of war and peace are at root moral, not financial or procedural, issues.

On the other hand, most moral issues are not dilemmas; society mostly accepts the idea that it is wrong to steal, barring exceptional circumstances. The fact that there is this agreement is why "Thou shalt not steal" seems so much like a rule which we can follow. The fact that there are exceptions explains why children need to learn moral *reasoning*, not just moral *rules*. Some of our children will be put into conflict even here by the fact that their parents do not believe this, but that must not prevent us from taking the only acceptable ethical stand on that issue: it is wrong to steal, opinions to the contrary notwithstanding.

The same goes for a broad range of socially valuable "civic virtues": e.g., honesty, civic responsibility, and tolerance. The existence of racism in a society may make the teaching of tolerance controversial, even professionally risky; yet the existence of racism is precisely what makes that teaching so necessary. And this teaching must not be rule driven. We do not act tolerantly to others simply by obeying rules—it is more than that; there are no rules that will get us there. It is a matter of whom we choose to be, as individuals and as a society. Further, when we do behave tolerantly, it is not because there are rules that say we should; the rules exist because we should act so. What makes some actions right and others wrong is teachable only by example and discussion, not by dictate and as a set of rules.

2) The second point is that the issue is, in the long run, irrelevant. As they grow, children shaped by rules will discard some of the rules of their childhood while affirming others. Likewise for children raised through moral conversation. Some of what they grow up believing to be right will be denied, while some will be affirmed. What they will carry with them, however, is how they make choices. Will they follow rules, or make careful (and caring) moral judgments? It is like giving children a frame and a canvas upon which they will create themselves —we can shape the canvas, but the actual picture is up to each individual. Since following rules will not suffice in the real world, we had better teach them a better way to make their decisions while we have the opportunity. The specifics do not matter as much as the categories we create for them. Should children make decisions based on the categories of required, prohibited, and permitted, or on those of right, wrong, and neutral? This is not a trivial difference.

3) With regards to the third objection, the difficulty of the task, a simple statement will suffice. If ethically literate adults is the desired goal, and if shaping of ethical beliefs is the only way to get there, then that is what we must try to do, even if doing so is extremely difficult,

or we are unsure of how to go about the task.

4) There is a fourth objection to be considered in proposing such an approach to helping children learn ethical behavior, namely, that this way of treating children can result in narrow-minded bigotry and intolerance. A seeming case in point is what Grant graphically showed for Hamilton High School.[9] The students and faculty there had become so certain about their own values in the 1950s and early 60s that it was difficult for them to accept differences in looks, dress, race, religion, or just about anything else.

On the other hand, he also reported that by the 1980s there were no standards of behavior except what was allowed or likely to be gotten away with. There was nothing wrong with cheating, as long as one got away with it. No one had taught these young adults as children that it is wrong to cheat; they only knew that they might be punished if they were caught. The fact that there were no negative consequences for undiscovered cheating meant that it was acceptable to cheat. Grant's conclusion was that schools, in order to function, need a body of agreements that have been negotiated and accepted, and which individuals are expected to accept as a frame of acceptable behavior. He calls the existence of this area of agreement, if it is a healthy one that both allows individuality and establishes ethical boundaries, a "strong positive ethos." It is this positive ethos which we should be striving to create.

The foregoing discussion should make clear the shortcomings in any "discipline" program that sees discipline as something (1) one in authority does to subordinates, or (2) aimed at the control of behavior rather than the shaping of character. It seems clearly the case that this conception of discipline oriented to externalized control is what has driven much educational practice for the past two decades, and that this view deprives our children of the opportunity to learn what it means, and what it takes, to be good people in our society. The lessons of behavioral approaches to discipline are often precisely contrary to what we wish children to learn.

A DIFFERENT STANDARD: A WELL-FORMED CONSCIENCE

Consider an example common enough in a primary classroom: a child, say, a boy, is discovered to have told the teacher, say, a woman, a lie. A teacher trained in a behavior modification program would remind the child that there is a rule against telling lies in her class (let us make the assumption that there is such a rule), and that something will now happen as a consequence of the rule violation. What has the child learned? Perhaps not what we intend. Let us imagine the conversation from the child's point of view. His teacher has reminded him of the rule, and told him that he will now suffer negative consequences as a result of the violation. What the teacher assumes the child is learning is something like, "Don't lie." However, it seems (at least) as plausible that the child is learning something closer to, "Don't get caught lying." After all, the child is not, in fact, receiving negative consequences as a result of lying; he is receiving them only because he got caught. If he had lied better, he would have been *positively* reinforced. He has probably successfully lied on previous occasions, thus learning that there is no *necessary* connection between lying

and getting punished. These lessons are not lost on the child. The very best we can hope for is that the child is learning something like, "Don't break rules." More likely, the lesson is, "Don't get caught breaking rules."

Now in certain situations, that is, where there is adequate supervision, these lessons produce very similar results, and children will more often than not tell the truth in such circumstances. However, in other circumstances, which describe most of life, one can often successfully lie. The child who has been taught only by a behavioral approach lacks a moral compass to guide her or him in those circumstances. By definition and philosophical commitment, such approaches attempt to shape behavior only, without regard to "unnecessary" notions like a child's conscience. Having been taught not to lie because of the negative consequences that follow getting caught or positive consequences given for telling the truth, she or he has not the internal voice to help make the right choice when getting caught is unlikely. The discipline here is an external thing, which does not shape the child's actions except when regulated externally.

The question that has been ignored in the current discussion about the most effective or best discipline program is this: "Does it make a difference why students act in desirable ways?" Behaviorists will, if pressed, argue that the answer is no, and this seems wrong. It *does* matter that children are being taught to obey the rules in order to gain externally controlled positive consequences and avoid negative ones. What we want to do with children is to teach them to act morally, not because of the rewards or punishments others will give for good or bad actions, not because it will make their teachers, or others, unhappy, but because it is *wrong* to act immorally, and because they should not wish to be the kind of persons who behave in that way. It is not merely a matter of following rules; it is a matter of knowing the right, wanting to do it, and doing so. It is *caring* about the sort of person *I am*, and recognizing that what I do and who I am are connected. Most often, and in societies that are basically healthy, following rules complies with the requirements of being a good person, but sometimes one must break rules to be good; this is the message of Milgram's experiment. It also highlights the importance of constructing moral conversation in our schools, and teaching our children how to be part of it.

Proper self-esteem.   In an effort to protect a child's self-esteem, we often refuse to label a behavior as wrong, as shameful. Does this make sense? What creates the sense of true esteem, if not believing that what I do is, in fact, right and praiseworthy? But actions can only be right and praiseworthy in contrast to that which is wrong and shameful. If one is to have genuine pride in one's behavior, the person must first be capable of feeling shame. Whence comes this legitimate pride except in the message delivered by one's teachers (in the most general sense of this word) that one has acted nobly *in circumstances when one might have acted shamefully?* It is this avoidance of shame that constitutes a valid sense of self-esteem, believing that what one has done is good, is right, and is praiseworthy, *though it might have been otherwise.* Note that, once the individual has developed this sense and awareness, an audience is not necessary.

I feel shame or pride for what I know about myself, not what others know about me. It is this voice of conscience that creates in me the desire, not to obey rules, but to do the right thing, and the awareness of what that means. What matters is not just what we do, but how what we do reflects who we are. Any approach to dealing with children that explicitly attempts to treat the behavior as separate from the child is cheating the children since it relieves them of the responsibility of feeling shame for behaving shamefully.

This argument in favor of shame requires explanation in today's climate; shame is not synonymous with humiliation, though we often use the terms as though it were. Humiliation is a public shaming of someone, holding the person up to ridicule in the eyes of others. Shame is something else. The precise point of shame is that the child learns to identify his or her own shameful behavior as such. Humiliation need not, and should not, play any part in instructing children in proper behavior. It is likewise true that children should learn to be proud of their good behaviors without being boastful about them. Pride, like shame, has to do with the judgments we pass on ourselves.[10]

* * *

It will justifiably be argued by behaviorists, as Canter for one does in fact argue,[11] that an ethical approach to behavior is both time consuming and difficult. It takes much longer to obtain desired behavior by shaping thinking than by shaping behavior. However, the force of this argument rests on a false premise: that one makes no attempt to control behavior while working to shape beliefs. Addressing behavior is certainly a necessary condition for teaching children how to behave; it is not, however, sufficient. In addition to learning what to do, children must learn the reasons for so doing. Note that the reasons need to be more than the rewards granted or punishment imposed by others on the basis of behavior.

Because of the inadequacies of behavioral approaches, schools must chart a very difficult course with regard to children's behavior. We must establish the ethical foundations upon which we can agree, and teach children that these will be the bases of judgment about action in the school at all times because of the inherent value we perceive in them, not just because there are rules. We must, of course, also help them learn that these same standards of judgment should apply in their lives outside the school. One way we can do this is by seeing to it that actions that conform to or violate these standards will carry consequences, and adults must be very aware of their own actions relative to these standards as well. However, application of consequences is not enough. Along with rewards and punishments, there must be conversation, not about the rules, but about the standards. The focus, contrary to the teachings of behaviorism, should always be on the person acting and the reasons for actions, not merely the behavior. Our desire should be to help children act responsibly, not just behave manageably.

There is no doubt that this process will be arduous and time consuming. Behavioral approaches, with their more limited goals, are clearly easier and quicker to implement, and are likely to reward the teacher with quick positive reinforcement. However, this also oversimplifies the problem we face as a society.

Behavioral approaches teach conformity and compliance, obedient behavior when faced with rules based in authority. Ethical approaches can bring up children who behave well for more substantial reasons. The latter is more difficult and time consuming, but it is also necessary.

REFERENCES

1. Richard Curwin and Allen Mendler, "Packaged Discipline Programs: Let the Buyer Beware," *Educational Leadership* 46 (October 1988): 68–71; Lee Canter, "Let the Educator Beware: A Response to Curwin and Mendler," *Educational Leadership* 46 (October 1900): 71 70; Gary Render, JeNell Padilla, and H. Mark Krank, "What Research Really Shows about Assertive Discipline," *Educational Leadership* 46 (March 1989): 72–75; Sammie McCormack, "Response to Render, Padilla, and Krank: But Practitioners Say It Works!" *Educational Leadership* 46 (March 1989): 77–79; Lee Canter, "Assertive Discipline —More Than Just Names on the Board and Marbles in a Jar," *Phi Delta Kappan* 71 (September 1989): 57–61; Richard Curwin and Allen Mendler, "We Repeat, Let the Buyer Beware: A Response to Canter," *Educational Leadership* 46 (March 1989): 83.

2. Robert Coles, *The Moral Life of Children* (Boston: Houghton Mifflin, 1986).

3. Carol Gilligan, *In a Different Voice: Psychological Theory and Women's Development* (Cambridge, Massachusetts: Harvard University Press, 1982); Lawrence Kohlberg, *The Philosophy of Moral Development* (San Francisco: Harper and Row, 1981).

4. Nel Noddings, *Caring: A Feminine Approach to Ethics and Moral Education* (Berkeley, California: University of California Press, 1984); Kenneth Strike, "Virtuous Speech: An Essay on Moral Learning and Pluralism." (Paper presented at the Schools of Character Forum, Le Moyne College, Syracuse, New York, May 8, 1991).

5. Aristotle, *Nicomachean Ethics*, trans. Terence Irwin (Indianapolis: Hacket, 1985).

6. Stanley Milgram, *Obedience to Authority: An Experimental View* (New York: Harper and Row, 1973).

7. Procedural rules such as, "Hang up your coat," or, "Write your name in the top left hand corner of your page," are not the sort of rules under discussion in this essay. The point is that teachers must understand that there is a basic difference between procedural rules,

which are often somewhat arbitrary (though not therefore unreasonable), and those rules of classroom behavior that are not arbitrary but grounded in ethical principles. The former will often appropriately be taught through simple stimulus-response training; the latter should never be.

8. Strike, "Virtuous Speech."

9. Gerald Grant, *The World We Created at Hamilton High* (Cambridge, Massachusetts: Harvard University Press, 1988).

10. See Gabrielle Taylor, *Shame, Pride, and Guilt: The Emotions of Self-Assessment* (Oxford, England: Clarendon Press, 1985), for a fuller exploration.

11. Canter, "Let the Educator Beware."

POSTSCRIPT

Do "Discipline Programs" Promote Ethical Behavior?

"If we continue to follow the dead end of stimulus-response psychology and focus on the symptom rather than the cause," William Glasser contends, "our schools will never be significantly better or more 'disciplined' than they are now." If this is true, then those who hold the position must achieve the theoretical and practical precision that has been a hallmark of behaviorism and assertive discipline programs.

Although the focus of discussion on this issue has been primarily on theoretical aspects, there is a wealth of material available that attempts to translate theory into practical, situational terms. Among the more provocative works are these: R. C. Newell's "Learning to Survive in the Classroom," *American Teacher* (February 1981); "Good, Old-Fashioned Discipline: The Politics of Punitiveness," by Irwin A. Hyman and John D'Alessandro, *Phi Delta Kappan* (September 1984); and "Effective Teacher Techniques: Implications for Better Discipline," by Elizabeth M. Reis, *Clearing House* (April 1988).

The Summer 1987 issue of *Pointer* contains articles on a variety of discipline approaches, as does the January 1988 issue of the *National Association of Secondary School Principals Bulletin*. An article by Lee Canter, "Assertive Discipline and the Search for the Perfect Classroom," appears in the January 1988 issue of *Young Children*.

Other articles of interest are Thomas R. McDaniel's "Practicing Positive Reinforcement: Ten Behavioral Management Techniques," *Clearing House* (May 1987); "This 'Step System' of Discipline Helps Kids Improve Their Behavior," by Steve Black and John J. Welsh, *The American School Board Journal* (December 1985); and Larry Bartlett's "Academic Evaluation and Student Discipline Don't Mix: A Critical Review," *Journal of Law and Education* (Spring 1987).

The March 1989 issue of *Educational Leadership* offers a special feature on the topic of discipline. Of particular interest is an article entitled "What Research Really Shows About Assertive Discipline." David Hill's "Order in the Classroom," *Teacher Magazine* (April 1990) draws a provocative portrait of the Canter system. Theodore A. Chandler, in "Why Discipline Strategies Are Bound to Fail," *The Clearing House* (November–December 1990), offers some interesting observations.

Two books on the topic that are worthy of attention are *Discipline With Dignity* by Richard L. Curwin and Allen N. Mendler (1989) and *The Quality School—Managing Students Without Coercion* by William Glasser (1990).

ISSUE 18

Are Current Sex Education Programs Lacking in Moral Guidance?

YES: Kevin Ryan, from "Sex, Morals, and Schools," *Theory into Practice* (Summer 1989)

NO: Peter Scales, from "Overcoming Future Barriers to Sexuality Education," *Theory into Practice* (Summer 1989)

ISSUE SUMMARY

YES: Professor of education Kevin Ryan argues for movement toward a firmer moral grounding of sex education programs.

NO: Peter Scales, a leading advocate of sexuality education, feels that current objections to these programs are unwarranted.

As early as the middle of the nineteenth century, English philosopher Herbert Spencer was recommending that sex education be included among the school subjects that are considered essential to the leading of a complete and satisfactory life. He saw the subject as a natural part of preparing for family life that could be grounded firmly in the newly emerging body of scientific knowledge.

There are those who, still today, oppose even narrowly scientific explanations of sexual functioning in the schools. Some people object to the information itself as having a possible corrupting influence. Others contend that clinical information alone, without religiously grounded moral guidance, is misleading. Still others resent the efforts of some educators to infuse sex instruction with values that may be ideologically slanted.

On the larger cultural level, some critics of sex education feel that the recent "sexual revolution" has left many young people adrift without moral moorings and that most of the school efforts fail to counteract this situation. Church or home guidance is deemed preferable by some of these people, while inclusion of ethical considerations in the sex education curriculum is desired by others.

Some central questions are these: Are the schools qualified to handle such subject matter competently? Is there room in the public school curriculum for such studies at a time when performance in basic academic areas is weak? If the answers to these questions are affirmative, many issues stemming from the teaching of sex education need to be addressed, such as: How early should sexuality education begin? By whom should it be taught? Should it be taught separately or as a component of health or biology classes? Is it an appropriate topic for social studies courses? Are some aspects of the topic taboo? How explicit should instructional materials be? What controls on library inclusions are needed? Should parents review or approve course materials? Should parents have the right to exclude their children from such instructional programs? How early should the topic of acquired immunodeficiency syndrome (AIDS) be addressed? Should high schools provide condoms for teenagers?

Indeed, the AIDS epidemic places new urgency on increasing the schools' efforts in the area of sexuality education. A recent Gallup poll shows that 90 percent of respondents are in favor of AIDS education, with 40 percent saying it should begin in the elementary schools. A 1988 report by the Sex Information and Educational Council of the United States, titled *State Update on Sexuality Education and AIDS Education*, shows that 13 states require sexuality education and another 22 have stipulated guidelines for teaching the subject. The range of programs is indeed wide—from full K–12 treatment of the topic to a few hours of instruction on physiological aspects alone.

Although some 80 percent of parents favor sex education in the schools, many feel that values and morals must be included in the instructional program to guide young people in making sex-related decisions. Some parents express concern about the "situational ethics" tone, which some programs seem to espouse, and call for a more direct moral approach.

In the following articles, Kevin Ryan, who is the director of the Center for the Advancement of Ethics and Character at Boston University, contends that sex is not a morally neutral matter and shows how the moral dimension can be infused through the use of an experimental curriculum developed at the center. Peter Scales counters that current comprehensive programs, often run by sexuality educators and health professionals, operate from a firm base of values and ethical concerns.

YES

Kevin Ryan

SEX, MORALS, AND SCHOOLS

Sexuality is an important part of our humanity and an issue that is vital to the survival of the species. It is, therefore, a necessary part of the education we offer to the young. Yet sex has historically been an aspect of human relations shrouded in taboos and rarely talked about openly. Despite changes in this regard, parents who have tried to discuss sex with their children know that it can be an awkward topic.

Sex is controversial today because the authorities in sexual matters have changed. Until this century, many people in this country were guided in what was acceptable sexual practice and what was unacceptable by their religious leaders. Medical doctors have also been a source of advice, often being asked to give talks on sex to high school students. Today, however, authority status seems to be gained by an appearance on a TV talk show or inclusion in the reading rack at the supermarket checkout.

We have undergone a revolution in sexual attitudes and practices in a very short period of time. This change appears to be the result, in part, of our expanded individualism and in part, of easier and improved methods of birth control. Twenty years ago sex before marriage became more acceptable, as did sexual relations between people of the same sex. Many of our prohibitions and inhibitions slipped away, and more and better sex became the goal of many.

Several things have happened since then, however, to give even the most ardent of the apostles of the new sexuality pause. Our family rearing practices have been radically affected. We appear to live in a no-fault divorce climate where it is projected, for instance, that 44 percent of the marriages contracted in 1983 will end in divorce. Since 1970, marriages are down 30 percent and divorces are up 50 percent (Christensen, 1988). We have recently seen the advent of, first, herpes complex B, and now, AIDS.

More to the issue of moral education and sex education, we have the highest levels of teenage sexuality ever recorded in this country. More than one-half of our nation's young people have had sexual intercourse by the time they are 17 (Bennett, 1987, p. 134). In 1980, two professors from Johns Hopkins University reported that 49.8 percent of girls between 15 and 19

From Kevin Ryan, "Sex, Morals, and Schools," *Theory into Practice*, vol. 28, no. 3 (Summer 1989), pp. 217–220. Copyright © 1989 by The College of Education, Ohio State University. Reprinted by permission.

had premarital sex, compared with 30 percent when they began their study in 1971 (cited in Lickona, 1983, p. 367). Between 1940 and 1985 the rate of out-of-wedlock births to adolescents rose 621 percent (ASCD, 1988, p. 7). In this nation, the sexual landscape for children and adolescents has changed dramatically.

THE MORAL NATURE OF SEX

Teaching the young about sex raises concerns among parents due to its traditional sense of sacredness and taboo, and to the dramatic changes in sexual attitudes and practices. Schools have reacted to this social context by putting more effort and devoting more of students' time-on-task to sex (Kasun, 1979). Critics, however, are contending that our sex education programs are simply feeding the fires of sexual interest and activities among the young (Anchell, 1986; Kasun, 1979). Cuban (1986) states: "Decade after decade... statistics have demonstrated the ineffectiveness of such courses in reducing sexual activity, unwanted pregnancy, and venereal disease among teenagers. Before the reformers mindlessly expand school programs aimed at preventing teenage pregnancy, they ought to ask some hard questions" (p. 321). The problem seems to be that while school boards, parents, and teachers know "something is wrong" with this increase in sexual activity among adolescents, they do not approach it as the moral issue it is.

Sexual intercourse is not simply a physical value-free activity. Nor is sexual activity merely a matter of personal taste and choice, although this has been the view among many sex educators. Exemplifying this value-neutral, individualistic approach are the words of a well-known sex educator and author of a sex education curriculum guide for the state of California: 'Right' or 'wrong' in so intimate a matter as sexual behavior is as personal as one's own name and address. No textbook or classroom teacher can teach it" (cited in Cronenwett, 1982, p. 101).

By its very nature, sexual intercourse is moral. It is moral because it is social, involving another person with human dignity and rights. Sex is a mutual giving and mutual taking. It affects body and mind, a person's physical and psychological well-being.

Like all human action, sex is subject to moral judgment. Sexual activities and practices must be open to the question, "What is the right thing to do?" Because sex can have profound consequences for individuals (i.e., birth), it has traditionally been part of a society's rules of behavior, its moral code. Since sex carries the source of a community's existence, it is also natural that it is seen as part of the community's moral code.

All cultures have an overriding mission to endure. The adults in a community are committed to passing on to the young the rules they believe will enable them to endure and to live well. Schools from the time of the Greeks have been seen as one of a society's primary vehicles to pass on to its young its values and moral code (Pratte, 1988; Ryan, 1986). A culture that fails to tell its adolescents these larger facts-of-life and does not think its young have the capacity for sexual self-restraint is one that is giving up the fight.

Nevertheless, as Kasun (1979) and Bennett (1987) point out, the older generation, particularly in our schools, is hesitant to teach sex in its full moral context. A possible reason for this is that sexual morality has traditionally been intertwined with religious morality and, as Vitz (1986) has demonstrated, our public schools in recent years act as if religion is not part of our cultural life or even our history. It appears that since the moral nature of sex is of concern to many people of traditional religious beliefs, public school educators have shied away from examining the moral dimension of sex in their programs. Certainly, no major denomination in our nation's very pluralistic patchwork of churches supports sexual activity among unmarried teenagers. But neither does any responsible group of non-religious people. Most people, religious and non-religious, decry what Jesse Jackson calls, "Babies having babies" (cited in Read, 1988). What, then, keeps sex education programs from taking a strong pro-chastity, pro-abstinence stance?

Our failure to confront the young with moral arguments against engaging in sexual intercourse may be due to adults, including teachers, not wanting to be seen as old-fashioned or out-of-step with views that up until recently have been perceived as progressive and sophisticated. In our media-saturated world where sexual images are continually portrayed, attitudes valuing youth and sexual freedom are easy to acquire. Descriptions like "sexually active" connote vitality and freedom, often leaving the average monogamous married adult feeling vaguely inert and out-of-step, while chaste single adults may well perceive themselves as relics from our puritan past.

Whatever the reason for teaching sex from a biological and value-free psychological manner, it needs reconsideration. Sex is not a morally neutral matter. The dangers it holds in terms of AIDS, other diseases, and unwanted preg-

nancy are well known. Eunice Kennedy Shriver (1986), who for several years has been working closely with unwed teenaged mothers, has written about how teenagers want sex dealt with in a value context—values such as self-restraint, compassionate understanding of the other, and fidelity. Shriver states:

> Over the years I have discovered that teenagers would rather be given standards than contraceptives.... They are thirsting for someone to teach them... to tell them that for their own good and the good of society it is not wise for them to have sexual intercourse at 12, 13, 14, or 15... that sex at this age is not necessary for a caring relationship to develop and endure. (p. 7E)

Thus, teenagers as well as adults would welcome having the morality of sex joined with the biological content.

SUGGESTIONS FOR SEX EDUCATION

Since our children will and should come to know and understand sex, it is in everyone's interest that they "get the story right." While it would be comforting to be guided in this by empirically verified procedures, how we conduct sex education must currently rely on good judgment. The following suggestions are offered in the hope that they might contribute to sound school policies in this area.

First, sex education should be taught within a moral, though not necessarily religious, context. While teachers should not be moralistic, they should join moral perspectives to the biological information. They should ensure, as Shriver (1986) and Mast (1986) have urged, that sex be a matter of reflection and moral discourse, and that the biological knowledge and issues are infused with the ethical.

Second, the teacher or the school should not be the lone arbiter of what is taught around this topic. One of a school's goals is to meet the needs of the local community. A sex education course, therefore, should reinforce what the community believes to be correct. It should not be used to separate the young from their families' values. If teachers feel unduly constrained, they should try to educate parents to their views and intentions or, if they fail, find a more accommodating school-community.

Individual parents who are uncomfortable with what their community has decided should be taught may want to find another school for their children. However, allowance has to be made for those parents who object to the school's sexual messages and mores but cannot afford to change schools. Given the many sensitivities around this issue, it is imperative that the public schools and parents find a common moral ground for the sex education programs presented in the schools.

Third, teachers should urge children to talk to their parents about the rightness and wrongness of sexual attitudes and practices. The school could also provide an important service to parents if it shared information with parents on how to talk with their children about these issues. In the same vein, while not teaching the sexual views of a particular religion, the public school could suggest to students an investigation of what their religion has to say about sexual behavior. To teach about religion as a source of knowing and guidance is not a violation of our separation of church and state.

Fourth, the schools should receive the best guidance possible about the biology and morality of sex. The secretary of education and the 50 chief state school officers ought to request a special commission composed of members of the National Academy of Science, other learned associations, and the National Council of Christians and Jews to give guidance to the public schools about what to teach and how to teach it. The state boards of education could then translate these recommendations into educational policy.

Fifth, sex education should not be the sole province of health educators. The question, "What is sex and what should we do with our sexuality?" like other great questions, such as "What is human nature?" and "What is most worth knowing?" does not yield to easy answers. The nature of human sexuality has been the subject of reflection by philosophers, theologians, poets, novelists, sociologists, biologists, and even economists, to name but a few of the groups that have given systematic attention to this topic.

In most American schools today sex education falls to health educators and sometimes physical educators. Their training tends to lean heavily on physiology and psychology. A relatively new discipline, psychology has certainly enriched our understanding of humans, and indeed, of human sexuality. However, psychology has spent much of its brief history jumping from one set of sexual verities to another, and health educators should be cautious about relying on this discipline for guidance.

If health educators continue to be given the major responsibility for sex education, they ought to be educated to draw on several disciplines in their understanding of and teaching about sex. For example, while literature has been largely ignored, much of what we as a human community have learned about sexuality is embedded in our myths, stories, and poems. In literature, sex is more than "the facts of life." It is, rather, a quality of people's lives, charged with energy and meaning, with subtleties and shadings. Literature addresses sexuality in its full complexity of love and jealousy, arousal and rejection, fulfillment and betrayal. Our poems and short stores are "case studies" of what we have learned.

Given this awareness, a group of us at Boston University constructed a literature based curriculum that tries to put the adolescent student's emerging interest in sex in a fuller context than mechanical sexual behavior. Entitled *Loving Well*, this experimental curriculum attempts to engage the student's moral imagination through old and new stories of falling in love, dating, infatuation, romantic betrayal, and the emotional roller coaster of love. Some of the stories and poems involve sexual acts, albeit the descriptions are more suggestive than clinical. However, the sexual situations are framed by lives—lives that must deal with the consequences of these acts, lives that demonstrate how these acts are permeated with ethical considerations. The purpose of the *Loving Well* curriculum, which is currently being tested in classrooms in Massachusetts and Maine, is to get students thinking about their sexuality in this larger context and to discuss the stories and their implications with other students, their teachers, and their parents. While quite preliminary, the initial reactions from students, teachers, and parents have been extremely positive. However, even if effective, we see this curriculum as only one component of a fuller, richer program of sex education.

A final suggestion is that sex education should actively promote sexual abstinence among unmarried teenagers. Sexual abstinence should be presented to the young as an ideal, just as we present honesty as an ideal to be sought after. The self-control involved with sexual abstinence, coupled as it often is with concern for the well-being of another person (i.e., the potentially pregnant teenaged girl or the young man with a venereal disease), can be an important part of character formation for a young person.

But from where does the ideal of sexual abstinence gain its authority? Good sexual attitudes and habits should serve both the individual and the society. Most Americans, regardless of their religious or ethnic affiliation, believe that it is unwise for high school students to be sexually active. A national poll (Leo, 1986) found that two-thirds of our citizens want the schools to "urge teenagers not to have sexual intercourse" and that 76 percent of American adults old enough to have adolescent children considered it "morally wrong for (unmarried) teenagers to have sexual relations."

Thus, it seems reasonable to propose that the schools criticize promiscuity and support sexual abstinence during adolescence. Rather than a value-free approach that advances condoms, abortion, and sexual experimentation, our schools should promote a sex education that not only has the support of the community, but contributes to the development of character and moral maturity.

REFERENCES

Anchell, M. (1986, June 20). Psychoanalysis vs. sex education. *National Review*, 33–61.

Association for Supervision and Curriculum Development (ASCD). (1988). *Moral education in the life of the school*. Alexandria, VA: Author.

Bennett, W. (1987). *Sex and the education of our children*. Washington, DC: U.S. Department of Education.

Christensen, B. (1988, Spring). The costly retreat from marriage. *The Public Interest, 91,* 62.

Cronenwett, S. (1982). Response to symposium on sex and children and adolescents. In E. A. Wynne (Ed.), *Character policy: An emerging issue* (p. 101). Washington, DC: University Press of America.

Cuban, L. (1986). Sex and school reform. *Phi Delta Kappan, 68,* 319–321.

Kasun, J. (1976, Spring). Turning children into sex experts. *The Public Interest, 55,* 3–14.

Leo, J. (1986, November 24). Sex and schools. *Time,* p. 321.

Lickona, T. (1983). *Raising good children*. New York: Bantam.

Mast, C. (1986). *Sex respect*. Bradley, IL: Respect, Inc.

Pratte, R. (1988). *The civil imperative: Examining the need for civic education*. New York: Teachers College Press.

Read, E. W. (1988, March 17). Birth cycle: Teenage pregnancy becomes rite of passage in ghetto. *The Wall Street Journal,* p. 13.

Ryan, K. (1986). The new moral education. *Phi Delta Kappan, 68,* 228–233.

Shriver, E. K. (1986, July 10). Teenage pregnancy: Something can be done. *Philadelphia Inquirer,* p. 7E.

Vitz, P. C. (1986, Fall). The role of religion in public school textbooks. *Religion and Public Education, 13,* 48–56.

NO

Peter Scales

OVERCOMING FUTURE BARRIERS TO SEXUALITY EDUCATION

In the late 1970s, the U.S. Centers for Disease Control embarked on an extensive research effort to understand and improve sexuality education. Part of that effort was funding for the Mathtech research corporation to conduct a national study of the barriers to sexuality education. Based on studying 23 communities' experiences through the 1960s and 1970s, the Mathtech study concluded that (a) administrators' fear of opposition, more than opposition itself, and (b) supporters' inadequate political skills were a central explanation for the widespread lack and/or superficiality of most sexuality education programs in the United States (Scales, 1984).

Some of those barriers have been surmounted. The '80s have seen an expansion of sexuality education, in and out of schools, and more young people seem to be participating in some type of sexuality education. However, the comprehensiveness and timing have not appeared to have changed much from the late '70s. Sonenstein and Pittman (1984) found that perhaps 15 percent of U.S. students experienced a comprehensive sexuality education course in school, as compared with the Mathtech estimate of no more than 10 percent in the late 1970s (Kirby, Alter, & Scales, 1979). This reflects an increase, but is still a distinct minority.

Most differences in when sexuality education is offered may be explained by sexual abuse prevention units in the early grades, as compared to formal sex education in the junior and senior high grades. AIDS prevention efforts do not appear to have taken hold yet below the junior high school level ("Local Districts," 1987). Also, only 10 states require sexuality education today ("Sexuality Education," 1988), as compared to 2 states in 1981 (Kirby & Scales, 1981).

The opposition to sexuality education continues to be a force, most notably in the debate over school based or school linked health clinics, and some old battles are still being fought. For instance, it took until 1987 for Tennessee to pass a law saying it is not a crime to answer relevant questions in sexuality education classes ("Highlights," 1987). However, opponents seem less likely today to succeed in restricting sexuality education, and supporters seem to have broadened their base.

Those in support had always been the majority, at least since the first Gallup poll on the issue in 1943. The opinion polls today express a popular will to improve and expand sexuality education to a degree unthinkable a generation ago. For example, not only are the usual 80–90 percent in support of comprehensive sexuality education content in the public schools, fully two-thirds of U.S. adults say they think schools should be *required* to establish links with family planning clinics ("Teen Pregnancy," 1986).

In 1988, the theme of the annual meeting of the Society for the Scientific Study of Sex was "sexual literacy." To be sexually literate, the society's program stated, is "to possess the basic sexual information and skills to thrive in a modern world; a comprehensive knowledge of sex and sexuality; the ability to understand alternative sides of a sexual issue; tolerance for ambiguity and paradox; and understanding of the advantages and limitations of different methodologies used in the study of sex" ("Sexual Literacy," 1988). In this broad sense, few would suggest that our nation has become sexually literate.

While barriers to the offering of sexuality education have decreased, many barriers to the effectiveness of sexuality education remain or are likely to appear in the next two decades.[1] If improvement is to occur, the following barriers will have to be overcome.

BARRIER 1. TAKING A NARROW VIEW OF SEXUALITY EDUCATION

In the 1970s, sexuality educators strived to broaden understanding of the field as something more than "sex" education. The focus in many programs had been on reproductive anatomy, or what Gordon (1981) called the "relentless pursuit of the fallopian tubes" (p. 214). To counteract this approach, the term "sexuality" education was emphasized, embracing not just the physical but also the social, emotional, psychological, and spiritual aspects of being human.

Narrowness remains, however, in at least three key ways: (a) overselling the impact of school instruction alone on behavior as contrasted with the impact of broader social actions; (b) basing judgments of sexuality education only on its measurable impact; and (c) taking a "back to the basics" approach to sexuality education.

Overselling sexuality education's impact. The impact of school curriculum on teenage pregnancy and AIDS tends to be oversold, particularly in light of the small part sexuality education courses play in the everyday life of students. Teen pregnancy reduction can occur, but reaching this goal requires going beyond the school curriculum.

School based health clinics, comprehensive programs combining dropout prevention, job opportunities, recreation, and other components, and mentor programs with adults and older youth helping younger persons all have been shown to have better impact on pregnancy reduction than sexuality education alone, although sexuality education is almost always a component in these multifaceted efforts.[2] New Jersey's commissioner of human resources notes that their $6 million pilot investment in comprehensive "youth services in the schools" programs was made because the "boundaries between education and human services don't work anymore" (Sullivan, 1988, p. A23).

Sexuality education courses can make a difference, but their impact is limited. Regarding teen pregnancy prevention, for example, the impact seems to occur through promoting greater contraceptive use among those who would be having sexual intercourse anyway, rather than by reducing sexual activity rates (Kirby, 1985). Given that all of schooling takes up just 8 percent of a person's life by age 18 (Finn, 1986), and the most comprehensive sexuality education programs take up just a fraction of that, the impact of school curriculum alone should not be oversold.

The "measurement" factor. Justifying sexuality education only on the basis of its measurable "impact" instead of its intrinsic value is a second type of narrowness. This is a more subtle barrier because of the emphasis the education reform movement of the last several years has placed on "results" in the form of higher test scores, readiness of youth for the workforce, and other instrumental impacts. In contrast, sexuality education may deserve a prominent place in the curriculum because we define such knowledge as an essential part of being fully human.

A broader barrier to truly comprehensive sexuality education may be the absence of a genuinely "liberal" ethic for education, in the non-political sense of the word. Such an ethic would support education for the sake of well-roundedness, a belief that, apart from what economic purpose they serve, certain areas of human experience and knowledge must comprise the common understanding of people in our society. In the debate about what it means to be educated, we must include an answer to a new fundamental question: What place do human sexuality and gender issues have within that common understanding of "being educated"?

The "back-to-the-basics" approach. Thinking about educational excellence as "back to the basics" is a third type of narrowness, which needs to be replaced with a "forward to the basics" framework (Scales, 1987a). A new set of "basics" is required for the future demands young people will face as they deal with collisions of emerging technology, enduring values, and changing national and world politics. AIDS, surrogate parenthood, global population pressures, and myriad other issues involving sexuality and family concerns will require citizens with well-developed critical thinking skills.

These skills should include the ability to challenge one's own assumptions, set priorities, make difficult choices among competing values, negotiate differing points of view, evaluate information brought to bear on a question, and communicate clearly and effectively. All young people need these skills for the future, not only those who go on to college. Instead of toughening standards and focusing on the college bound, a genuine reconstruction of the curriculum is needed based on rethinking the basics for the future of all children.

BARRIER 2. FAILURE TO UNDERSTAND THE IMPORTANCE OF SELF-EFFICACY

For decades, sexuality educators have held that self-esteem is a key element in behavioral change, and thus must be a key goal in sexuality education curricula. Numerous curriculum guides contain exercises teachers are supposed to use to increase students' self-esteem.[3] Mostly, however, self-esteem in this context has referred to the self-worth part of the construct, rather than what researchers believe may be a more relevant component for behavioral change, the self-efficacy aspect.

Briefly, self-efficacy refers to an individual's perception that he or she is able to do or accomplish what is desired or expected. It has to do with the sense that one can make things happen. Theorists believe that a better understanding of self-efficacy can help educators promote decisions to use contraception or avoid unprotected intercourse (Lawrance & McLeroy, 1986; Rosenstock, Strecher, & Brecher, 1988).

A problem is that neither self-worth nor self-efficacy can really be *taught*, as may be inferred from the generally disappointing results of evaluations showing little increase in self-esteem from a sexuality education program (Kirby, 1985; cf. with the contrasting construct of "sexual self-concept" in Winter, 1988). Self-worth can perhaps be nurtured through self-talk and cheerleading. Years ago, I chanted "I am somebody" along with hundreds of others at a national conference for teenagers in Atlanta, led by Jesse Jackson. I have no doubt that saying "I am somebody" helps. But it doesn't instantly give people the sense that they can make things happen in the world.

Social action must be part of the equation. Perhaps the best we as educators, helpers, and policymakers can do is to maintain the conditions in which that personal sense of self-efficacy can flourish. The sense that we can make things happen doesn't come from slogans, no matter how helpful they are to self-image. It comes only from making things happen.

BARRIER 3. FAILURE TO RESOLVE THE ROLE OF PUBLIC SCHOOLS AS "SURROGATE PARENTS"

As Dryfoos and Klerman (1988) point out, the movement to use schools as "surrogate parents" is burgeoning as schools seek help with this role. Principals in Alaska use the term "second responsibility" to describe the schools' increasing responsibility for the social, physical, and emotional well-being of children. We must acknowledge, however, that all of us—not just the schools—have responsibility for the society we live in.

To expect "the schools" to miraculously solve societal problems without a thorough rethinking of the roles families and other institutions play in the development of our young, and how we invest in those families and institutions, is ludicrous. We need to move beyond this narrow view of the schools' role. To do this, we can restructure the curriculum, as discussed earlier, and improve young people's understanding of common social needs by addressing the sexism and racism that characterize much sexuality education today.

For example, Fine (1988) calls for greater attention beyond gender roles to a "discourse on desire." Fine asks whether our focus on education through fear (in this case, fear of pregnancy) is ideologically perpetuating females as "the potential victim of male sexuality." In this setting, she says, "there is little possibility" of anyone developing "a critique of gender or sexual arrangements" (p. 31). How does the absence of that critique affect our ability to lessen interpersonal violence and promote broader equality between the sexes? Does the focus and language of current sexuality education merely reinforce the victimization of females and prevent growth in self-worth and self-efficacy for many young women, especially low-income women?

This kind of discussion in sexuality education goes beyond preventing pregnancy and points toward a more fundamental examination of human rights and human potential. Perhaps the continuing need for such discussion is best illustrated by the results of a 1987 Rhode Island survey of 1,700 sixth–ninth graders. About 25 percent of the boys and 17 percent of the girls thought it was acceptable for a man to force a woman to have sex if he had spent money on her; and an astonishing 65 percent of the boys and 57 percent of the girls said such rape was acceptable if a couple had been dating for more than 6 months ("Youths in Study," 1988).

We need to call for social action as well as education. While AIDS captures our caring and our headlines, and is a life and death issue, less dramatic events consign millions of people to a slower, no less anguished death. Racism may be at the core here, for minorities are disproportionately the victims in our society, whether we talk about poverty, rates of violence, teenage parenthood, dropping out of school, or alcohol and other drug abuse (Scales, 1988).

BARRIER 4. AIDS AND THE DECLINE OF PLURALISM

Kelly (1987) notes that the anti-sexuality messages associated with AIDS prevention may already be producing, as fallout, a decline in our national acceptance of a pluralism of values that has been a fundamental tenet of modern sex education and democracy. In its extreme, this decline of pluralism can lead to (and from some reports [Greer, 1986; Kin, 1988] has

already led to) an increase in discrimination as the debate over personal liberty and public safety prompts some people to accept apparently easy answers to these complex dilemmas.

How this personal liberty versus public safety dilemma is handled will have a deep impact on many levels. The President's AIDS Commission understood this and enunciated clearly that non-discrimination is the cornerstone of any effective and ethical approach to AIDS in our democratic society. However, former President Reagan's rejection of this anti-discrimination language killed any legislative attempts to reduce AIDS discrimination in 1988 ("Presidential Rejection," 1988).

On a less noticeable level to many, but equally pernicious in its ultimate impact, the decline of pluralism will end up expressing itself in broader censorship and restrictions on freedom of speech. This danger can be expressed in subtle and sometimes not so subtle ways. For example, Sen. Alan Simpson (R-WY) was quoted as being sore at the "thousands of creative staff people" who are "cooking them [issues] up ... all of it cranked up with special interest groups" (Lovison, 1988, p. 40). Yet, listening to that cacophony of special interest groups, not being irritated by them but welcoming them and reflecting on their messages, is part of the responsibility of governance. After all, we all belong to at least one "special interest group."

Each of us, liberal or conservative, must build honest, guiding values that are strong but still flexible enough to be open to reflection and change. If we honor this democratic process, we will find the right answers to vexing questions. This starts with a simple enough proposition; that, in a democracy, ideas, values, and people are the same. Banning an idea and discriminating against a person are just different sides of the same coin. It is only a small step from going after Anne Frank's diary to going after Anne Frank.

BARRIER 5. INADEQUATE POLITICAL SKILLS

Political savvy has improved among sexuality education advocates. Like children's advocates more generally, they are more aggressive today than 10 years ago. However, political skills still need to be developed in the following areas: (a) translating beliefs into budgets, (b) setting the right agenda, and (c) speaking for ourselves.

As former Centers for Disease Control leader Ogden (1986) wrote, the political battle is about resource allocation. On the most basic economic level, we've only just begun to translate our beliefs into budgets. Through our budgets, we express our public policy values— a different type of "values" than the sex education community has historically focused on. For example, just one Stealth bomber costs about three times as much as our entire federal family planning program (the Stealth is variously put at between $380–450 million each, while Title X stands at $138 million for fiscal year 1989 ["Appropriations," 1988]).

Seeing budgets reflect advocates' beliefs involves avoiding the wrong agenda. The wrong agenda is having just more sexuality education, or earlier, or with better trained teachers. The right agenda, on the other hand, focuses on all the issues discussed in this article, and places sexuality education into a more realistic perspective.

Such an agenda must be based on (a) a broad head start for *all* children; (b) ac-

tion to lessen poverty and welfare dependence through policies that empower people; (c) greater attention to the life skills needs of the 70 percent of children who will not get a college degree; and (d) expanded opportunities for young people to become better linked with their communities through service and voluntarism, among other principles (Hamburg, 1987; Scales, 1988; Schorr & Schorr, 1988; Weckstein, 1988).

All those things achieve the goal sexuality educators have had for years: to promote healthy, capable people who have purpose, high expectations, and lots of support. These people are more likely to avoid teen pregnancy, substance abuse, suicide, and other problems.

Finally, sexuality education advocates must not allow others to say what advocates believe. To do so is to be "reactive," always being in a position of saying "no, wait a minute, what we really mean is ..." or "no, we didn't mean that." We should not let others say what we believe in, what we stand for. We should say it ourselves. That is our first—and our final—responsibility.

NOTES

1. An update on the extent of sex education and obstacles to providing it was released just prior to publication of this article. The Alan Guttmacher Institute study of 4,200 junior and senior high teachers, superintendents of 162 of the nation's largest school districts, and all state education agencies found some improvement in the scope of sexuality education, but not dramatic improvement, so numerous inadequacies and barriers remain, including those selected for discussion here (*Risk and Responsibility*, 1989).

2. See reviews in Scales, 1987b; Scales, 1988, as well as a program example in Carrera and Dempsey, 1988, and an example of a successful community "saturation" model in Vincent, Clearie, & Schluchter, 1987.

3. Two widely used examples are "K–12 Family Life Education Curriculum" (1987) and "Family Life Education" (1980).

REFERENCES

Appropriations Fiscal 89: Labor, HHS, Education & HUD. (1988). *Youth Policy, 10*(9), 47.

Carrera, M., & Dempsey, P. (1988). Restructuring public policy priorities in teenage pregnancy. *SIECUS Report, 16*(3), 6–9.

Dryfoos, J. G., & Klerman, L. V. (1988). School-based clinics: Their role in helping students meet the 1990 objectives. *Health Education Quarterly, 15,* 71–80.

Family life education: Curriculum guide. (1980). Santa Cruz, CA: Network Publications.

Fine, M. (1988). Sexuality, schooling, and adolescent females; The missing discourse of desire. *Harvard Educational Review, 58,* 29–53.

Finn, C. (1986). Educational excellence: Eight elements. *Foundations News, 27*(2), 40–45.

Gordon, S. (1981). The case for a moral sex education in the schools. *Journal of School Health, 51,* 214–218.

Greer, W. R. (1986, November 23). Violence against homosexuals rising, groups say in seeking protections. *New York Times,* p. 15.

Hamburg, D. (1987). *Fundamental building blocks of life.* New York: Carnegie Corporation (president's annual essay).

Highlights of state-level victories for children, 1987. (1987). *Children's Defense Fund Reports, 9*(6), 3–8.

K–12 family life education curriculum (1987). Burlington, VT: Planned Parenthood of Northern New England.

Kelly, G. (1987). On being attacked by sex education foes. *Journal of Sex Education and Therapy, 13*(2), 3–4.

Kim, J. (1988, July 3). Are homosexuals facing an ever more hostile world? *New York Times,* p. E16.

Kirby, D. (1985). The effects of selected sexuality education programs: Toward a more realistic view. *Journal of School Health, 11,* 28–37.

Kirby, D., Alter, J., & Scales, P. (1979). *An analysis of U.S. sex education programs and evaluation methods.* Springfield, VA: National Technical Information Service.

Kirby, D., & Scales, P. (1981). State guidelines for sex education instruction in the public schools. *Family Relations, 30,* 229–237.

Lawrance, L., & McLeroy, K. R. (1986). Self-efficacy and health education. *Journal of School Health, 56,* 317–321.

Local districts active in AIDS education. (1987). *Family Life Educator, 5*(4), 4–12.

Lovison, D. (1988). State legislatures: The proving ground for national leadership. *State Legislatures, 14*(6), 40–44.

Ogden, H. (1986). The politics of health education: Do we constrain ourselves? *Health Education Quarterly, 13,* 1–7.

Presidential rejection of AIDS anti-bias law dashes hopes for action in 100th Congress. (1988). *The Nation's Health, 18*(9), 4.

Risk and responsibility: Teaching sex education in American schools today. (1989). New York: Alan Guttmacher Institute.

Rosenstock, I. M., Strecher, V. J., & Brecher, M. H. (1988). Social learning and the health belief model. *Health Education Quarterly, 15*(2), 175–184.

Scales, P. (1984). *The front lines of sexuality education: A guide to building and maintaining community support.* Santa Cruz, CA: Network Publications.

Scales, P. (1987a). Forward to the basics. Life skills education for today's youth. *Family Life Educator, 5*(3), 4–9.

Scales, P. (1987b). How we can prevent teenage pregnancy (and why it's not the real problem). *Journal of Sex Education and Therapy, 13*(1), 12–15.

Scales, P. (1988). An agenda for investing in children and youth. *Youth Policy, 10*(4), 3–7.

Schorr, L., & Schorr, D. (1988). *Within our reach: Breaking the cycle of disadvantage.* New York: Anchor/Doubleday.

Sexual literacy 88. (1988). Mount Vernon, IA: Society for the Scientific Study of Sex. (November 1988 annual meeting program.)

Sexuality education. (1988). New York: Planned Parenthood Federation of America Fact Sheet.

Sonenstein, F. L., & Pittman, K. J. (1984). The availability of sex education in large city school districts. *Family Planning Perspectives, 16,* 19–25.

Sullivan, J. (1988, January 10). 29 Jersey schools will offer program to aid troubled youths. *New York Times,* p. A23.

Teen pregnancy: Over one million teens become pregnant each year. (1986). *Children and Teens Today, 6*(7), 5–6.

Vincent, M. L., Clearie, A. F., & Schluchter, M. D. (1987). Reducing adolescent pregnancy through school and community-based education. *Journal of the American Medical Association, 257*(24), 3382–3386.

Weckstein, P. (1988). Youth, education and the economy. *Youth Policy, 10*(6), 4–24.

Winter, L. (1988). The role of sexual self-concept in the use of contraception. *Family Planning Perspectives, 20*(3), 123–127.

Youths in study say rape acceptable in some instances. (1988). *The Network, 3*(3), 3. (Newsletter of the North Carolina Coalition on Adolescent Pregnancy).

POSTSCRIPT

Are Current Sex Education Programs Lacking in Moral Guidance?

Protests against sex education practices in the public schools often originate through local efforts on the part of a group of parents who resent intrusions by the schools into what they consider to be very private aspects of life. The demarcation of appropriate provinces of parental and school influence has been difficult to draw—and probably always will be. As long as the schools only *offer* instruction in human sexuality without demanding that all students participate, parental protests of this sort would seem to be unjustified. When sexual topics are infused throughout the required curriculum, the problem is compounded.

Joseph Fay and Sol Gordon treat this problem in "Moral Sexuality Education and Democratic Values," *Theory into Practice* (Summer 1989), in which they explore the differences between a *moral* approach and a *moralistic* approach to human sexuality. They state that, while one cannot escape the fact that values are a major component of sexuality education, the moralistic "just say no" strategy is simplistic and ineffective in that it fails to "appreciate the complexity of sexuality and the many factors that may influence a young person's decision to become sexually active."

The Summer 1989 issue of *Theory into Practice* has additional valuable material, namely "Sexuality Education in the U.S.: What It Is, What It Is Meant to Be," by Ann Welbourne-Moglia and Ronald J. Moglia, and "AIDS and Sexuality Education," by Debra W. Haffner, the executive director of the Sex Information and Education Council of the United States (SIECUS). Questions regarding the content of AIDS instruction and the rights of HIV-infected children have been addressed recently. Some important views can be found in "AIDS: Students in Glass Houses," by Perry A. Zirkel, *Phi Delta Kappan* (April 1989); "The Legacy of Ryan White for AIDS Education," by Stephen R. Sroka, *Education Week* (May 23, 1990); and "The Social Dimensions of AIDS," by Harvey V. Fineberg, *Scientific American* (October 1988).

Among relevant publications are D. L. Kirp's book *Learning By Heart: AIDS and Schoolchildren in America's Communities* (1989); the Children's Defense Fund's *A Vision for America's Future* (1989); and "A Battle Lost," by Madelon Zady and Kenneth Cuckworth, *The American School Board Journal* (February 1991).

In the last analysis, this issue must be resolved in the context of the purposes of education. If schooling is designed to address the needs of the "whole person," then sex education, including the problems of human sexuality, morality, and love, would seem to be of central importance.

ISSUE 19

Should Schools Offer Condoms to Students?

YES: Margaret Pruitt Clark, from "Condom Availability Promotes Health, Saves Lives," *The School Administrator* (September 1992)

NO: Edwin J. Delattre, from "Apply Peer Pressure, Not Latex, Against Casual Sex," *The School Administrator* (September 1992)

ISSUE SUMMARY

YES: Margaret Pruitt Clark, director of the Center for Population Options, argues that increasing teen pregnancy rates and the growing threat of acquiring sexually transmitted diseases through unprotected sexual activity make condom availability in the schools absolutely necessary.

NO: Education dean Edwin J. Delattre asserts that a policy of distributing condoms through the schools sends to students the misguided message that "a questionable expediency is more important than mature judgment [and] personal restraint."

Sexuality education programs in general currently receive wide community support. Specific aspects of the schools' efforts to deal with adolescent sexual behavior, however, have prompted major disputes in many areas. Problems such as the persistent increase in teenage pregnancy rates, the growing number of adolescents being infected with the human immunodeficiency virus (HIV)—the virus that causes acquired immunodeficiency syndrome (AIDS) —and other sexually transmitted diseases, and evidence that far too many teenagers engage in unprotected sexual activity have led school administrators to take more drastic measures than they ever have before.

To combat teen pregnancy, some school districts offer prevention programs that include one or more of the following aspects: family planning information, the encouragement of sexual abstinence, birth control information, and the provision of contraceptive devices. School-based clinics—usually jointly sponsored by various health agencies—have been established in quite a few locales to carry out the more elaborate prevention programs. Approximately 30 percent of these clinics dispense condoms to students.

Specific programs designed to fight the spread of AIDS include guidance on such matters as the use of condoms, advocation of sexual monogamy, and warnings against the sharing of needles and syringes for intravenous drug use. The extent of public concern about AIDS is evident in the fact that more states now specifically require AIDS education in the schools than general sexuality education. However, approximately one-half of local programs require parental permission for student participation. That is, many parents maintain control over what their children learn about the deadly disease. One reason why parents retain this control may be that the nature of the content of these preventive programs raises religious and moral issues, as well as issues of constitutionally protected individual rights and of privacy.

One concern about AIDS prevention programs is that some of them make condoms available to students as a preventative measure. In New York City religious officials have termed the dispensing of condoms a "betrayal of fundamental parental rights." Also, a number of parents feel that school-based clinics, especially those that provide condoms, are legitimizing and even promoting undesirable sexual behavior among teenagers. Court cases addressing this and other concerns are reviewed and analyzed by Patricia F. First in "Sex Education in the Public Schools: A Clash of Religious Freedom and the General Welfare," *The Educational Forum* (Fall 1992). As First notes, state and district courts have protected sexuality education programs against challenges from a variety of legal standpoints, including violation of free exercise of religion, the equal protection clause, parental rights, and family privacy. But the legal system has by no means supported only the one side: courts have advised schools regarding the appropriateness of some content, and they have allowed states to prohibit sexuality education as well as to permit it. Furthermore, state legislatures have permitted parents to withdraw their children from sexuality education classes because of religious objections. And in most jurisdictions, parents are allowed to examine materials used in sexuality education programs.

Despite the growth of sexuality education and AIDS prevention programs, the spread of HIV has become epidemic. If infection by HIV could, by some unimaginable miracle, be totally prevented starting tomorrow, the number of Americans who are currently HIV-positive and would end up dying from AIDS would be greater than the number of Americans who were killed in the Vietnam War, the Korean War, World War I, World War II, and the Civil War combined, according to W. James Popham in "Wanted: AIDS Education That Works," *Phi Delta Kappan* (March 1993). Even by conservative estimates, he claims, all but a small percentage of the more than 1 million currently infected Americans will die within the next decade, and most of these people do not even know they are infected.

This serious situation and the measures that need to be taken to correct it are discussed in the selections that follow. Margaret Pruitt Clark strongly supports condom distribution as a necessary and effective way to diminish the rates of teen pregnancy and HIV infection. Edwin J. Delattre argues that condom distribution advocates such as Clark fail to consider all of the moral questions involved in protecting young people from HIV infection.

YES

Margaret Pruitt Clark

CONDOM AVAILABILITY PROMOTES HEALTH, SAVES LIVES

In 1990 a group of high school students in Cambridge, Mass., received intensive training to learn to counsel their peers about HIV/AIDS and how it is transmitted. They hoped friends would take their message of prevention to heart. They were convinced it was a message that could save lives.

But feelings of frustration and futility gradually replaced their natural optimism. Despite their best efforts, they continued to hear stories of friends and classmates risking their lives and futures through unprotected intercourse, unknowing or nonchalant about the dangers of sexually transmitted diseases, pregnancy, and even AIDS.

How could they get the attention of these other young people? How could their friends know the facts about AIDS and still have unprotected sex? What could keep them from foolishly, needlessly, thoughtlessly, throwing away their lives?

With the idealism and courage of young people who believe in a cause, the students started handing out plain white envelopes containing condoms and written materials about AIDS prevention. They weren't sure what to expect from school authorities and realized the reaction could be harsh. But they were willing to take the risk because of what was at stake.

The actions of this student group and others who collected signatures on a petition to the school board opened an important debate in the community. Ultimately, the Cambridge school board altered an existing policy and permitted the school clinic to make condoms available to sexually active students.

GROWING AWARENESS

No longer is condom distribution in schools a novel idea, though it continues to generate controversy. A growing number of communities are adopting policies and developing plans to help young people understand the seriousness of the risks they face and reduce risk-taking behavior.

A surprising but important benefit of the controversy over school condom availability programs is the way it has engaged entire communities in the debate and increased public awareness at the local level.

Schools are conducting surveys of teenage students to determine their level of risk-taking. Students themselves also are being heard on this issue, sometimes for the first time. Parents and community members are becoming involved in the early stages of the debate, and their help is being enlisted in designing the programs. Typically, school condom availability programs involve collaborative efforts among schools, health agencies, and youth-serving organizations.

The stakes in the controversy are considerable. According to the national school-based Youth Risk Behavior Survey by the Centers for Disease Control (CDC), 31.9 percent of ninth-grade girls and 48.7 percent of ninth-grade boys have had sexual intercourse. By the time they are seniors, the figures rise to 66.6 and 76.3 percent, respectively.

Another survey of inner-city black males found an average age of first intercourse under 12 years old. The younger the age at which an individual becomes sexually active, the more likely he or she is to have multiple partners, substantially increasing the risk of acquiring a sexually transmitted disease, including the AIDS virus.

Two and one-half million adolescents are infected with sexually transmitted diseases, and one in 10 teen-age girls becomes pregnant every year. A recent study by CDC at the National Children's Medical Center in Washington, D.C., shows a five-fold increase since 1987 in the number of HIV-positive adolescents who are treated there. Since this study involved a limited population, we can assume that these known cases are just the tip of the iceberg.

DESERVE PROTECTION

When faced with the facts, most adults agree the threat to young people has reached crisis proportions and that strong measures are required to control the spread of HIV among adolescents. Every tool at our disposal must be used to help students make healthier choices. Every one of our institutions, not just the schools, must be mobilized in the effort to control the triple threat of pregnancy, sexually transmitted diseases, and AIDS.

While only sexual abstinence and abstinence from intravenous drugs and other judgment-impairing substances, including alcohol, guarantee non-transmission, teens who are exposed to risks need and deserve the best means possible for protecting themselves: knowledge, skills, and access to latex condoms. School personnel can and should provide these to in-school youth.

Condoms are legally available to teenagers in a variety of settings, and condom use among sexually active teenagers is increasing. Nevertheless, in 1988 only 26 percent of sexually active teen women reported condom use at last intercourse. Young people often cite confidentiality, cost, and access as reasons for failing to use contraceptives. Other reasons include lack of transportation, embarrassment, objection by a partner, and lack of perceived risk of pregnancy and infection.

School condom availability programs, whether as part of comprehensive health services at the school site or in the context of school-based HIV/AIDS and sexuality education, address each of these barriers and help to establish condom use as a norm with both peer and cultural acceptance.

The ground-breaking proposal by New York City Schools Chancellor Joseph Fernandez to make condoms available upon request in all 120 public high schools moved the issue of condoms in schools onto the national stage. Part of the goal of this program is not just to make condoms available, but to change adolescent culture.

The comprehensive HIV/AIDS education program in New York seeks to make condom use the norm rather than the exception for sexually active young people and to provide a setting in which adolescents can talk openly about their behavior and their concerns with adults they trust.

Students' fear of being judged, embarrassed, sanctioned, or "hassled," as one student put it, needs to be overcome for the programs to be effective. Recent news coverage about the program suggests that since the novelty has worn off, most teen-agers are using the program to ask questions and get counseling.

COMMUNITY BACKING

Since December 1990, the Center for Population Options' (CPO) National School Condom Availability Campaign and Clearinghouse has monitored developments across the country and provided information, assistance, and referrals to communities. In many cities, such as Baltimore, Chicago, and Portland, Ore., condoms are available through school-based health centers that provide primary health care to students. CPO is aware of almost 50 (out of more than 300) school-based health centers that provide condoms to sexually active students.

These programs have the strong support of the communities they serve. Surveys conducted by Baltimore and Portland health officials (prior to decisions by local policymakers to permit condoms to be dispensed in the clinics) showed a majority of parents in both cities support condom availability for sexually active students.

In some schools with no health facility on site, condoms are made available by specially trained school staff or local health professions as part of school- or districtwide AIDS/HIV prevention and education programs. School officials in Los Angeles, San Francisco, and Philadelphia approved both clinic-based and education-based programs. These are now being implemented.

Earlier this year the District of Columbia announced a citywide campaign to control the spread of AIDS, including condom availability in all 16 public high schools. With one in 57 D.C. males between the ages of 20 and 64 infected with HIV and one in 67 babies being born to mothers with HIV, there is no room for cautious response. As one D.C. City Council member put it, "Abstinence is preferable, but AIDS kills." One thousand and six hundred students signed petitions asking for condoms in their schools.

School condom availability programs are not limited to urban school systems. One of the first programs started in 1988 in Commerce City, Colo., a district with 6,000 students, nearly half living in poverty. This program uses specially trained, volunteer teachers who are available to students at times and locations posted prominently in the school.

In addition, the Massachusetts Board of Education last year passed a resolution to become the first state agency urging all school districts to consider making condoms available as part of HIV prevention and education for students. As of early summer, 10 local school boards had approved the concept and now are planning or implementing a program.

SINGLE ANSWER

Schools contemplating condom distribution have many issues to resolve, such as whether availability will be part of comprehensive health services or part of an intensive HIV/AIDS and sexuality education program. How will costs be covered? What sort of education and counseling will be provided to students? Who will actually be trained to give out the condoms? How, ultimately, will the effectiveness of the program be evaluated?

No one would argue that making condoms available in high schools alone will eliminate the threat of AIDS and adolescent pregnancy or miraculously change adolescent behavior. Yet easy access to latex condoms is an important strand in the safety net of services, care, and education for teen-agers.

NO
Edwin J. Delattre

APPLY PEER PRESSURE, NOT LATEX, AGAINST CASUAL SEX

We are told by condom distribution advocates that school distribution of condoms is not a moral issue but rather an issue of life and death. We are told by the same people we have a moral obligation to do everything in our power, at all times, to save lives.

The incoherence—indeed, contradiction—between these claims reflects the failure of condom distribution advocates to perceive that all life-and-death issues and all questions of what schools do in the interest of their students are moral questions.

If our only moral duty were to save lives—at whatever cost to other ideals of life—we would raise the legal age for acquiring a driver's license to at least 25; reduce speed limits to 35 mph or less; mandate annual physical examinations; outlaw tobacco and foods that contribute to bad health; and so on.

Even if saving lives were our only moral concern, distributing condoms in schools is not the best way to save lives. Abstinence has greater life-saving power than any piece of latex can have. We have a duty to make clear to students the danger they face if they become sexually involved with someone who may be HIV positive and has not had the decency to seek out a medical test. That person is, in principle, willing to kill.

We have a duty to explain to students that it is morally wrong to cause needless suffering and to be indifferent to the suffering we may cause.

INDULGENT BEHAVIOR

Condom distribution in our schools promotes casual sex, casual indifference to the seriousness of sexual life, and casual disregard and contempt for others. Casual sex is promiscuous sex.

Where promiscuity is calculated, it is crudely exploitative and selfish; where it is impulsive, it is immature. A person who is promiscuous treats others as objects to be used for gratification, ignoring the possibility of

From Edwin J. Delattre, "Apply Peer Pressure, Not Latex, Against Casual Sex," *The School Administrator* (September 1992). Copyright © 1992 by The American Association of School Administrators. Reprinted by permission.

pregnancies that may result in an unwanted child whose lot in life will be unfair from the beginning.

Those who are promiscuous usually exert peer pressure in favor of their form of indulgence, just as drug users do. Such persons say condoms make sex "less dangerous," that sexual activity is only a health issue and not a moral issue.

That leaves to us, the teachers, the duty to tell our students about the rate of failure of condoms in preventing pregnancy when used by young unmarried women—36.3 percent. The Family Research Council stresses this figure is probably too low in protecting against AIDS, since the HIV virus is 1/450 the size of a sperm and is less than 1/10 the size of open channels that routinely pass entirely through latex products such as gloves.

The behavior of health professions with respect to "less dangerous" sex ought to be described to students as well. The Richmond, Va., *Times-Dispatch* reported recently on a speech given by Dr. Theresa Crenshaw, a member of the national AIDS Commission and past president of the American Association of Sex Education, Counselors, and Therapists, to an international gathering of 800 sexologists.

"Most of them," Crenshaw said, "recommended condoms to their clients and students. I asked them if they had available the partner of their dreams and knew that person carried the virus, would they have sex, depending on a condom for protection? No one raised their hand. After a long delay, one timid hand surfaced from the back of the room. I told them that it was irresponsible to give advice to others that they would not follow themselves. The point is, putting a mere balloon between a healthy body and a deadly disease is not safe."

By distributing condoms to children and adolescents, we convey the false message that we do not care about the moral dimensions of sexual life, and that there is no reason for them to care either. Those who tell them, and us, that we are not faced with a moral issue betray the young to expediency.

MISGUIDED MESSAGES

Condom distribution advocates will reply that sexual activity among the young is inevitable, even natural. To protect themselves from pregnancy, AIDS, and other sexually transmitted diseases, students must use condoms. At the same time, these advocates deny that the availability of condoms will increase sexual activity.

But if we teach the young we expect them to be sexually active, they are likely to expect if of themselves. We have no right to exhibit such low expectations—or to encourage the young in sexual activity that is promiscuous and, thus, necessarily devoid of the emotional and spiritual intimacy that anchor genuine love.

We must ask ourselves whether we really want to encourage the young to engage in sexual activity that, by its nature, undermines the sanctity of the family as the model of loving sexual intimacy between adults committed to one another and to their offspring.

And for those who are sexually promiscuous—whether to aggrandize themselves, or exert power over others, or gain prestige or physical pleasure or peer approval—does it follow that we should give them the condoms in the high school?

Even if promiscuity with condoms and dental dams is physically less dangerous than promiscuity without them, should we be in the business of distributing them? Filtered cigarettes are less harmful than unfiltered ones, but we do not distribute free filtered cigarettes.

We should instead stand on the side of peer pressure against casual sex, because it is morally right and because it has the power to save lives.

Some condom distribution advocates insist that we defer to experts in health care on this subject. They claim these experts do not try to tell us what we should do as educators, and we should not tell them what to do in matters of health.

This argument is based on the false premise that what health officials do in the high school contains no educational lessons. Health and social service providers attempt to teach students the high school is an appropriate condom distribution site, while dismissing as irrelevant questions of morality and educational mission. In this, they exceed their competence.

Furthermore, as if qualified not only in ethics but also in law, these health professionals and social service personnel dismiss the prospect of legal liability for our institutions. Yet it is well understood by all of us that condoms are quite fallible.

On this weak foundation of flawed arguments about educational policy, about ethical life, and about the law, too many school boards across the country have voted in favor of the distribution of condoms in their schools. In doing so, they have made it possible for students to believe that even a questionable expediency is more important than mature judgment, personal restraint, and respect for the well-being of other people—and they have placed teachers and administrators in a position that runs counter to sound educational policy.

NECESSARY LIMITS

In these schools, it is necessary to make the best of bad policy by imposing requirements on the distribution of condoms:

- First, only the most reliable condoms manufactured should be distributed, whatever the cost.
- Second, indemnification should be provided for the school and the city for all malpractice or other legal liability.
- Third, the high school should send a letter to all parents describing the services offered by the health clinic and informing them condoms do not make sex safe.
- Fourth, under no circumstances should any teacher or school administrator be involved in the distribution of condoms.
- Fifth, these condoms should be distributed only in conjunction with qualified counseling in their use and qualified instruction in ethics—both to be provided by health personnel in the clinic. The instruction should first be prepared in general form in writing—in English and other languages—for review and approval by those qualified in such matters.
- Sixth, the counseling should include instruction about all sexually transmitted diseases and their consequences, not only in suffering and possible death of those infected but also in endangering pregnancies and in harming or killing offspring. This instruction should include education about all conditions under which AIDS can be transmitted by intercourse and oral sex, by transfusions, by shared use of contaminated needles, by intrusive medical treatments performed by afflicted health

care professionals, and by other varieties of behavior against which condoms and dental dams afford no protection.

- Seventh, students should be given a written examination, and be required to pass it, on these subjects before receiving condoms.
- Eighth, no student should ever be excused from classes or study periods to receive such counseling and instruction. Only lunch period or time before and after school should be available for this purpose—in keeping with the educational mission and priorities of the schools.
- Ninth, any student who requests condoms, and is not exempt by statute from requirements of parental consent for medical treatment, should be made to bring a signed letter from a parent or guardian approving distribution of condoms to this daughter or son—and explicitly absolving the school and city and all of their personnel from all legal liability for any consequences —all liability. The letter should be confirmed by telephone or by a written receipt sent by return mail.

If the parent or guardian cannot, for any reason, provide such a letter, then legally satisfactory approval should be given in person, witnessed and recorded. All letters and visitation and telephone logs should be kept permanently on file to safeguard against legal actions.

RESPONSIBLE ACTIONS

If we are forced to distribute condoms, we should do so in a way that shows our understanding of the duties and aspiration central to a life well and honorably lived—the respect for others and the effort to make the best possible people of ourselves.

Students should understand we are not willing to grant free rein to peer pressure that obstructs their self-interest and jeopardizes their happiness. They should understand we cannot save their lives —only they can do that for themselves —and we are working to advance their ability to do so, in the short run and in the long run, as they assume progressively greater responsibility for their own destinies.

I cannot forget the youngest in a group of students who spoke publicly in favor of condom distribution in the local high school. Although she had not yet reached high school age, she beseeched us to distribute condoms in the high school because if we did not, students would die. The sincerity of her belief was clear in her tone and in her eyes, which glistened with tears.

I want that child to be told the truth.

I want her to learn that those students do not have to die in youth; that many of her peers will not die of sexually transmitted diseases but will learn to avoid casual sex because it is irreducibly dangerous and because it diminishes self-respect; that untimely sexual activity is not inevitable unless individuals make it so, by their own decisions and actions; that there are many safeguards against destructive diseases available to the young; and that the most trustworthy of these are not condoms and dental dams.

I want her to learn that among the better safeguards are a due regard for personal safety, an unwillingness to put loved ones at risk, a rejection of promiscuity as a way of life, and a choice of friends and possible spouses who deserve trust and love.

HIGH-RISK GAMBLE

These safeguards also include the courage to rise above adverse peer pressure, the maturity of self-determination, the acquisition of habits of learning that open the doors of opportunity and dramatically expand the domain of future friendships and loves, and the patience to deter gratification until it is timely, healthy, and warranted.

And I want students to know that betting their life—or letting someone else bet their life—on a condom is a gamble only one in 800 experts on sexual behavior is willing to risk, and if our own students behave otherwise, they make a mockery of the commitment they expressed over and over again to saving lives.

If we fail to do all this, we will have been incompetent and immoral teachers. Such incompetence would be far more shameful than being forced to distribute condoms, and every student, every citizen, deserves to learn that we know it.

POSTSCRIPT

Should Schools Offer Condoms to Students?

Consider the following statistics on teenage sexual activity in the United States:

- Each year more than 200,000 babies are born to girls under 18, and 96 percent of these girls keep their babies.
- Over 25 percent of sexually active teens *never* use contraceptives, and only one-third of them use contraceptives consistently.
- The average age of first sexual intercourse for American males is 15.7; the average age for females is 16.2.
- The average age of first sexual intercourse for inner-city black males is under 12.
- There are currently 2.5 million adolescents who are infected with various sexually transmitted diseases.
- One in ten teenage girls becomes pregnant every year.

Figures like these—culled from such sources as the Center for Population Options, the Planned Parenthood Federation, the Centers for Disease Control, the Alan Guttmacher Institute, and the Sex Information and Education Council of the United States—demand attention and action. The questions for educators to wrestle with involve the appropriate role of the schools and the limitations that must be placed on what the schools can do about the problem. Some articles that address these and similar questions are the following: Dana Mack, "What the Sex Educators Teach," *Commentary* (August 1993); Patricia Donovan, "Sex Education in America's Schools: Progress and Obstacles," *USA Today Magazine* (July 1992); and Barbara D. Whitehead, "Dan Quayle Was Right," *Atlantic Monthly* (April 1993).

Some other worthwhile sources of ideas are *Teenage Parenthood: The School's Response* by L. M. Bonjean and D. C. Rittenmeyer (1987); Susan Eaton, "AIDS Education Must Go Beyond the Condom Wars," *The Harvard Education Letter* (September–October 1993); Steve Sroka, "Condom Sense," *Teacher Magazine* (November–December 1991); Donna Harrington-Leuker, "Kids and Condoms," *American School Board Journal* (May 1991); and the Urban Institute Policy and Research Report *Educating Teenage Males About Sex and AIDS* (Fall 1992), which contains recommendations for prevention programs.

Teenage pregnancy is also given a thorough airing in "Schools, Society, and 'Teen' Pregnancy," by Mike Males, *Phi Delta Kappan* (March 1993), and in two articles in the January 1994 issue of *Phi Delta Kappan* by Stephen J. Caldas and by Mike Males.

ISSUE 20

Can Outcome-Based Education Transform America's Schools?

YES: William G. Spady, from "Choosing Outcomes of Significance," *Educational Leadership* (March 1994)

NO: John O'Neil, from "Aiming for New Outcomes: The Promise and the Reality," *Educational Leadership* (March 1994)

ISSUE SUMMARY

YES: William G. Spady, director of the High Success Network and a leader of the outcome-based education (OBE) movement, advocates an approach to teaching that leads students through "traditional, transitional, and transformational" zones of performance.

NO: Journalist John O'Neil examines OBE practices, notes prevailing criticisms, and concludes that there is little evidence that OBE will lead to major changes in the schools.

Recently, there has been much discussion about the major effort to reform instructional methodology and curriculum in American schools known as outcome-based education (OBE). OBE is the latest in a line of efficiency-oriented educational approaches and has its roots in three previous movements: behavioral objectives, competency-based education, and mastery learning. The behavioral objectives movement placed emphasis on the achievement of specific observable or measurable skills. Competency-based education focused on student demonstration of clustered knowledge and skills. In mastery learning, students' objectives were achieved through a series of learning sequences, with slower learners given more time and varied approaches to achieve positive results and faster learners given enrichment activities.

OBE draws on each of these prior reform movements. According to Floyd Boschee and Mark A. Baron, in "OBE: Some Answers for the Uninitiated," *The Clearing House* (March–April 1994), outcome-based education is a "student-centered, results-oriented design based on the belief that all individuals can learn, that calls for education agencies to determine the skills, knowledge, and ways of thinking that a person needs to function in the world [also called "competencies"] and then to adapt the curriculum and instruction so that students attain those desired outcomes."

William G. Spady, one of the leaders of the OBE movement, feels that the emphasis in education has shifted from microconceptions (behavioral specifics) to macroconceptions (complex role performances). In an interview with Ron Brandt in *Educational Leadership* (December 1992/January 1993), Spady states that he thinks of the competencies that students are expected to demonstrate in the OBE system as large constructs that integrate and apply a lot of related skills. These "life skills" are similar to what Spady calls "transformational outcomes." In Spady's approach, these transformational outcomes replace the traditional subject-based curriculum as the basic definer and organizer of educational activities.

Although OBE is the fastest-growing educational reform of the 1990s, it is being fiercely opposed by conservative parents, religious activists, taxpayer groups, and some state legislators. Many see the outcomes defined by the movement (for example, "tolerance," "global awareness," and "self-respect") as too broad or too vague. Some see OBE as a vehicle for political indoctrination and the inculcation of beliefs that conflict with those of parents. Others see OBE as usurping local control of schools. These and other objections are detailed by Bill Zlatos in "Outcomes-Based Outrage Runs Both Ways," *The Executive Educator* (September 1993).

Other recent writings show the variety of criticisms that people have for OBE. For example, George R. Kaplan notes that religious fundamentalists have campaigned vigorously against OBE, calling it "a cornucopia of value-laden curricula, affective concepts run amok, and institutional boundary-crossing," in "Shotgun Wedding: Notes on Public Education's Encounter With the New Christian Right," *Phi Delta Kappan* (May 1994). In "Outcomes-Based Education: Toxic Teaching?" *Family Voice* (April 1993), Janet Parshall portrays the movement as a lethal shift away from fact-based skills to a focus on "politically correct" feelings and emotions. And in *Reinventing America's Schools* (1992), Kathi Hudson describes OBE as "a method of manipulating students through behavior modification based on B. F. Skinner's methods of repetitive reinforcement."

In the selections that follow, Spady describes the instructional journey toward the successful completion of real-life performances through OBE techniques, while John O'Neil looks at some criticisms of the approach and examines what he sees as the potential pitfalls of OBE.

YES

William G. Spady

CHOOSING OUTCOMES OF SIGNIFICANCE

The term *outcomes* has come of age. Reformers from coast to coast agree that measures other than student grades and Carnegie units must be used for determining student and district achievement. But what outcomes *are* and what kinds should be expected of high school graduates are still disputed. Determining what students in the '90s need to learn and successfully demonstrate is further complicated by the emerging work on national standards, authentic tasks, and portfolio assessments.

The overriding issue affecting the development and implementation of outcomes today is *significance*. Do the outcomes we expect students to demonstrate matter in the long run—in life after formal schooling? This issue has stimulated a dramatic evolution in approaches to outcome-based education at the local level since the mid-1980s. In its simplest form, this evolution has been a shift away from small, relatively simple curriculum-focused segments of learning to much more complex and comprehensive learning experiences focused on life roles, which I call *role performances*. Why? Because evidence overwhelmingly shows that much classroom learning never makes it out the door, either into other classrooms or into the world beyond the school.

WHAT IS AN OUTCOME?

Before leaping into a discussion of role performances, we need to establish what outcomes are and aren't. Outcomes are high-quality, culminating demonstrations of significant learning in context. *Demonstration* is the key word; an outcome is not a score or a grade, but the end product of a clearly defined process that students carry out.

First, the demonstration must be *high quality*, which, at a minimum, means thorough and complete. (This criterion calls into question conventional grading practices that accept and label all student performances, whether complete or not.)

Second, the demonstration comes at the *culminating* point of the student's learning experiences, literally "at or after the end"—not "during the experi-

From William G. Spady, "Choosing Outcomes of Significance," *Educational Leadership*, vol. 51, no. 7 (March 1994), pp. 18–22. Copyright © 1994 by The Association for Supervision and Curriculum Development. Reprinted by permission. All rights reserved.

ence" as most people seem to assume. The term *exit outcomes* has emerged for those outcomes that occur at the close of a student's academic career, and students in more advanced outcome-based districts are going to be expected to demonstrate significant, high-quality learning with that ultimate culminating point in mind.

Third, the demonstration must show *significant learning;* significant content is essential. Content alone, however, cannot be an outcome because it is inherently inert. Much like potential energy, it must be manifested through a demonstration process.

Finally, all demonstrations of learning occur in some *context* or performance setting. The conditions and circumstances students face when performing affect what they need to know, do, and be like in order to succeed, quite apart from the cognitive, technical, or interpersonal nature of the task itself. We need only consider the difference between in-seat classroom demonstrations and public, on-stage performances to recognize how important this factor can be.

THE DEMONSTRATION MOUNTAIN

The metaphor that we use in the High Success Network to explain differences in learning outcomes is the Demonstration Mountain. The mountain represents the act of climbing from basic demonstrations of classroom learning up to demonstrations that involve living effectively in the face of real-world challenges at home, at work, and in the community....

The mountain consists of three major zones and six different forms of learning demonstrations. The complexity, generalizability, and significance of each form of

demonstration increase as we climb from the lowest level to the highest. Also increasing as we move up the mountain are the ownership, self-direction, and self-assessment that students must apply to a demonstration.

The least complex forms of demonstrations fall in the Traditional Zone and are grounded primarily in subject matter content. These forms and their classroom context are relatively simple and limited to traditional subject categories. Because of their strong content grounding, these demonstrations are not generalizable across other areas of the curriculum or other performance contexts; school is the only place where they are typically performed.

Midway up the mountain lies the Transitional Zone, in which demonstrations are relatively complex and grounded in the kinds of competence that transcend given subject areas and that can be applied in a variety of relatively demanding performance contexts and settings. In this zone, demonstrations are generalizable across content areas and require substantial degrees of integration, synthesis, and functional application, thereby encouraging interdisciplinary approaches to developing the outcomes.

At the highest level of the mountain is the Transformational Zone. In this zone, demonstrations require the highest degrees of ownership, integration, synthesis, and functional application of prior learning because they must respond to the complexity of real-life performance contexts.

BEGINNING OUR CLIMB

Within each of the three major zones on the mountain are two different levels of learning demonstrations. At the bottom in the Traditional Zone are *Discrete Content Skills.* Concrete and content-dependent, these microforms of learning demonstrations are narrow in scope, tightly structured by the teacher, and linked to small, specific segments of curriculum content. The skills demonstrated are virtually inseparable from their content, as in reading passages for meaning, spelling specific words, carrying out specific mathematical operations, drawing particular objects, or locating specific features on a map.

While some of these Discrete Content Skills do eventually serve as enabling outcomes for demonstrations higher on the mountain, most of them are *discrete objectives*—small and detailed pieces of learning that constitute components in a larger block of curriculum content. An example of a Discrete Content Skill used by Spence Rogers of the High Success Network is:

> All students will correctly identify local government procedures for initiating new laws.

The next level of demonstrations, *Structured Task Performances,* may be the most prevalent and misinterpreted form of demonstration on the mountain. These performances include a broad range of demonstrations that vary substantially in the degree of mental processing required for their execution. Examples include: writing a paper explaining a specific topic; carrying out a laboratory experiment and comparing its results with established theory; or drawing a map of a region at a specific point in history and contrasting it with a contemporary map of the same region.

These Structured Task Performances represent most day-to-day classroom activities, homework assignments, and work tasks. They typically involve completing a series of steps that the teacher has defined (hence, the term *structured*), and they use Discrete Content Skills as performance enablers. In most cases, adding to the number of steps required in a Structured Task Performance does not change the nature of this form of demonstration, though it may make its execution more difficult. An example from Rogers for this level is:

> All students will conduct a research project on methods of initiating new laws at the local level and present their findings to the class and/or to their parents.

MIDWAY UP THE MOUNTAIN

Climbing to the Transitional Zone of the mountain, we encounter *Higher-Order Competencies.* Higher-Order Competencies include analyzing concepts and their interrelations; proposing solutions to multifaceted problems; using complex arrays of data and information to make decisions; planning complex structures, processes, or events; and communicating effectively with public audiences. All of these demonstrations can involve many kinds of content. Although they are more generalizable across different kinds of subject areas and performance contexts than outcomes in the Traditional Zone, they do rely on some Content Skills and Structured Tasks as enablers. The example from Rogers for this kind of demonstration is:

> All students will teach an adult civic group how to initiate new laws in the community.

In the next level of demonstration, *Complex Unstructured Task Performances,* personal ownership, self-direction, and self-assessment intensifies. Students create their own projects, defining the parameters, criteria, standards, and modes of execution and evaluation. These are the broad, complex demonstrations one finds in independent research and high-level applied projects, and they frequently require the integration of knowledge from many different sources and disciplines. At their core, Complex Unstructured Task Performances embody what Theodore Sizer characterizes as significant "exhibitions" of learning (1983, 1984). Almost by definition, these demonstrations involve much higher degrees of latitude and independence than in the Traditional Zone of the mountain. An example of a Complex Unstructured Task Performance is:

All students will design and carry out a project on a major issue or problem that uses data to heighten community awareness and proposes feasible ways to address it by initiating new laws.

HEADING TOWARD THE TOP

To enter the Transformational Zone of the mountain is to depart from the formal curriculum and its content categories as the starting point and purpose of learning. Here we enter the realm of Role Performances. Operating with authentic life contexts as the backdrop, students demonstrate what real people do to be successful *on a continuing basis* in their career, family, and community. Almost all real-life role performances require complex applications of many kinds of knowledge and all kinds of competence as people confront the challenges surrounding them in their social systems.

Grounded in these real-world contexts are *Complex Role Performances*. These performances occur and recur as people carry out their responsibilities; they involve a high degree of generalizability across time and situations; and they demand a high degree of ownership, self-direction, and self-assessment on the part of their practitioners. Complex Role Performers have the motivation and commitment to continually carry out their role responsibilities, not just perform isolated tasks on demand.

Because this zone of the mountain seems to lie beyond the structures and frames of reference used most often in schools, we might ask two questions: Are Complex Role Performances possible in school? What Role Performances link the world of schooling to real life? Figure 1 sets forth 10 Fundamental Life Performance Roles that will help us answer these questions. The figure can also serve as a template for implementing transformational outcome-based education (Spady 1991, 1992; Brandt 1992/1993).

The framework shown in Figure 1 outlines 10 clusters of performance roles that are essential to almost all of the major life roles students will face once they leave school—citizen, employer, worker, parent, and civic leader. Consistent with the SCANS Report of 1991, which has been used to shape the outcome frameworks for the states of Florida and Oregon, Figure 1 serves as a design template for many districts throughout Canada and the United States. The bottom section of the framework deals with technical and strategic Life Performance Roles, while the top contains social and interpersonal roles. All of these roles can be carried out in Transformational classrooms just

Figure 1
Fundamental Life Performance Roles

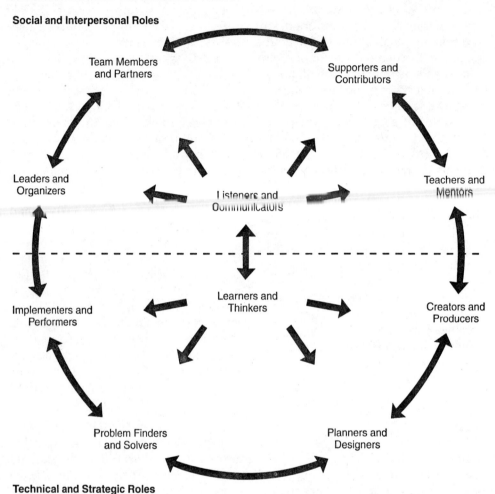

Social and Interpersonal Roles

Team Members and Partners

Supporters and Contributors

Leaders and Organizers

Listeners and Communicators

Teachers and Mentors

Learners and Thinkers

Implementers and Performers

Creators and Producers

Problem Finders and Solvers

Planners and Designers

Technical and Strategic Roles

as they can in authentic life contexts. An example of such a demonstration is:

> All students will organize and participate in a community service team that monitors major community issues and problems, develops alternatives—including proposed changes in laws—for addressing them, and explains potential solutions to key community groups.

Working with students on a continuous basis, schools can prepare them to be:

- *Implementers and Performers*, who can apply basic and advanced ideas, information, skills, tools, and technologies as they carry out the responsibilities associated with all life roles. They grasp the demands of a particular situation and use available resources to get things done.

- *Problem Finders and Solvers,* who can anticipate, explore, analyze, and resolve problems, examining underlying causes from a variety of perspectives and developing potential solutions.
- *Planners and Designers,* who develop effective methods and strategies for resolving issues and problems.
- *Creators and Producers,* who seek new possibilities for understanding or doing things and who transform those possibilities into original, workable products or processes that change the operating environment.
- *Learners and Thinkers,* who develop and use cognitive tools and strategies to translate new information and experiences into sound action, and who use their repertoire of knowledge and strategies to extend their capacities for successful action by assimilating, analyzing, and synthesizing new experiences.
- *Listeners and Communicators,* who can grasp and express ideas, information, intention, feeling, and concern for others in ways that are clearly understood and appreciated. They accurately comprehend and use words, pictures, gestures, deeds, styles, symbols, and mannerisms to receive and convey thoughts.
- *Teachers and Mentors,* who can enhance the thinking, skills, performance orientations, and motivation of others through the explanations they provide, the counsel they give, and the example they set. They share the information, time, perspectives, and skills at their disposal.
- *Supporters and Contributors,* who invest time and resources to improve the quality of life of those around them.
- *Team Members and Partners,* who contribute their best efforts to collaborative

endeavors and who seek agreement on goals, procedures, responsibilities, and rewards, setting aside personal preferences in order to accomplish mutual aims.
- *Leaders and Organizers,* who can initiate, coordinate, and facilitate the accomplishment of collective tasks by perceiving and defining intended results, determining how they might be accomplished, anticipating roadblocks, and enlisting and supporting the participation of others to achieve the results.

If preparing students for this constellation of 10 Life Performance Roles looks like a major expansion of the school's vision and priorities beyond the practices of the Traditional and Transitional Zones of the mountain, *it is.* To provide this level of learning will require a transformation of what schools are and how they spend their time. But our young people deserve the significant learning experiences and capabilities that the Life Performance Roles represent.

The learning environments that continuously involve students in all 10 sets of Performance Roles are not impossible to conceive, design, and implement. The key is to continually engage students in both individual and team activities that explore important issues or phenomena, use multiple media and technologies, create products that embody the results of students' explorations, and call for students to explain their work and products to adult and student audiences. In short, the classroom becomes an active, high-challenge learning environment and performance center.

The question that remains, however, is whether schools can address and support the *Life-Role Functioning* outcomes at the top of the Transformational Zone. Can students carry out the requirements of adult citizens, workers, employers, and parents while still young and in school? To say no is easy; performances at that level require that people be in those life-roles and deal with the conditions and challenges that they encounter in those real-life contexts.

On the other hand, states and districts can design learning experiences and performances that can serve as exit outcomes based on the realities faced by today's adults and on the realities that we anticipate will face the adults of tomorrow. These performances can be simulated in both typical educational settings and in the real-world contexts with which schools are connecting more and more through business partnerships and service learning programs. Frameworks like those in Figure 1 can serve as guides.

If schools can't guarantee successful Life-Role Functioning, they can come close by helping students become com-petent Complex Role Performers with extensive experiences drawn from real-life contexts. Accomplishing this will make the climb up the Demonstration Mountain both compelling and rewarding for schools, their students, and their communities.

REFERENCES

Brandt, R. (December 1992/January 1993). "On Outcome-Based Education: A Conversation with Bill Spady." *Educational Leadership* 50, 4: 66–70.

Secretary's Commission on Achieving Necessary Skills (SCANS). (1991). *What Work Requires of Schools.* Washington, D.C.. U.S. Department of Labor.

Sizer, T. (June 1983). "High School Reform: The Need for Engineering." *Phi Delta Kappan* 64, 10: 679–683.

Sizer, T. (1984). *Horace's Compromise: The Dilemma of the American High School.* Boston: Houghton Mifflin Co.

Spady, W. G. (Spring 1991). "Shifting the Grading Paradigm That Pervades Education." *Outcomes* 9, 4: 39–45.

Spady, W. G. (Summer 1992). "It's Time to Take a Close Look at Outcome-Based Education." *Outcomes* 11, 2: 6–13.

NO

John O'Neil

AIMING FOR NEW OUTCOMES:
THE PROMISE AND THE REALITY

Just two years ago, the rhetoric supporting a massive American shift to an education system organized around student outcomes was cresting.

From Congress to the State House, politicians and educators advocated higher standards for student learning. One expert after another opined that consensus was needed on what students "should know and be able to do" at the culmination of their K–12 experience. Then, the thinking went, schools would refocus their programs to help students attain these desired outcomes. Ultimately, students would earn a diploma not by merely sitting through a series of required courses—they would have to demonstrate their proficiency in these common outcomes. "Outcome-based education" (OBE) was the label loosely applied to this results-oriented thinking.

The talk sparked a spate of activity. Acting on the impetus provided by national education goals, a national process was launched to describe outcomes in the major subject areas. State after state undertook to craft common learner outcomes, or to require districts to do so. One state, Pennsylvania, pledged to phase out the traditional Carnegie unit, saying that within several years the state's high school graduates would have to demonstrate attainment of outcomes, not merely accrue the necessary clock hours in required courses. If put into practice, the changes proposed in Pennsylvania and elsewhere would have marked a dramatic shift in the way schools do business.

Since then, however, the OBE bandwagon has stalled. In Pennsylvania, the state was forced to curtail its ambitious OBE plan in the wake of fierce opposition, much of it mobilized by organized religious conservative groups. Among their criticisms, opponents claimed that the state's proposed outcomes watered down academics in favor of ill-defined values and process skills. Similar charges were lobbed against OBE plans in other states, and state officials in Minnesota, Ohio, Iowa, and Virginia have been forced to revise, delay, or drop their efforts.

In the face of the opposition, many OBE enthusiasts are retrenching, pondering how an idea that, on its face, appears so sensible, proved to be so controversial. "I think OBE is largely done for as a saleable public term," a

From John O'Neil, "Aiming for New Outcomes: The Promise and the Reality," *Educational Leadership*, vol. 51, no. 7 (March 1994), pp. 6–10. Copyright © 1994 by The Association for Supervision and Curriculum Development. Reprinted by permission. All rights reserved.

former Pennsylvania official who played a key role in the state's OBE plan says darkly. "Now, nobody can use the O-word," jokes Bob Marzano, senior program director at the Mid-continent Regional Education Laboratory (McREL).

WHAT IS OBE ANYWAY?

One reason OBE has sparked differences of opinion is that many people—even within the camps of proponents and opponents—define the term differently.

At one level, outcome-based education is the simple principle that decisions about curriculum and instruction should be driven by the outcomes we'd like children to display at the end of their educational experiences. "It's a simple matter of making sure that you're clear on what teaching should accomplish . . . and adjusting your teaching and assessing as necessary to accomplish what you set out to accomplish," says Grant Wiggins, director of programs for the Center on Learning, Assessment, and School Structure. "Viewed that way, nobody in their right mind would have objections to it." In this sense, outcome-based education is a process, and one could use it to come up with schools as unlike one another as Summerhill or one E. D. Hirsch dreamed up.

At another level, policymakers increasingly talk about creating outcome-driven education "systems" that would redefine traditional approaches to accountability. In policyese this means that schools should be accountable for demonstrating that students have mastered important outcomes (so-called "outputs") not for their per-pupil ratio or the number of books in the school library (so-called "inputs").

Both the outcome-based philosophy and the notion that schools should have more autonomy (site-based management) have been adopted as the new conventional wisdom guiding accountability, despite the lack of compelling research evidence supporting either reform, points out Thomas Guskey, professor of education policy studies at the University of Kentucky. Policy wonks love the crystal clear logic of OBE and Site-Based Management—at least on paper. "Outcome-based education gives them the 'what' and site-based management gives them the 'who'" in their accountability system, Guskey says.

Parents and educators familiar with a specific version of outcome-based education often equate all OBE with the model they've heard most about. But the models differ. The Johnson City, New York, public schools, for example, have gained a national reputation for their outcome-based education program. The Outcomes-Driven Developmental Model, as they refer to their model, has contributed to impressive gains in student achievement of desired outcomes over the past two decades. Another highly visible model of outcome-based education is that espoused by Bill Spady and the High Success Network.

The different interpretations of outcome-based education help explain why, even among those who support an outcomes-driven education system, sharp divisions persist over what it would look like. For example, business leaders and policymakers appear to strongly support the idea of outcome-based accountability systems. But their conception of desirable learning outcomes appears to be very different from that offered by educators.

The very nature of outcome-based education forces one to address inherently controversial issues. "The questions ultimately get down to the fundamentals —what's worth knowing and what's the purpose of schooling," says Jay McTighe, an observer of the OBE movement who directs the Maryland Assessment Consortium. "Outcome-based education gets to the heart of the matter."

CURRENT CONDITIONS

Proponents of OBE suggest that an outcome-based education system would help to address some of the problematic conditions confronting contemporary schools.

Numerous experts, for example, believe that the currently expressed outcomes for student learning are neither sufficiently rigorous nor appropriate for the requirements of students' adult lives. One national study after another has shown that graduates of U.S. schools are able to demonstrate very basic levels of skill and knowledge, but that they lack higher-order thinking skills. Put simply, many students can (and do) make it through the education system without learning needed skills and knowledge, even though they've earned the requisite number of Carnegie units and passed minimum competency exams and classroom tests. Under OBE, students would be required to *demonstrate* these necessary outcomes before graduation. Just as pilots are required to demonstrate their facility at flying an aircraft (not merely sit through the required instruction), students would be pushed to display the outcomes society holds important.

This raises the related equity issue. The futures of many students are compromised because the outcomes held for them are low or unclear. As they progress through school, such students are frequently tracked into low-level courses where they are not held responsible for the outcomes necessary for success after graduation. As long as the credentialing system is based on seat time, one student may earn a diploma by taking advanced placement history and calculus, while another makes it through the system taking watered-down academic fare. Put another way, some students —and some schools—are held to high standards, while many others are not. According to the OBE philosophy, all students will be held responsible for attaining common outcomes. And schools will be responsible for altering present conditions to prepare them to do it.

In addition, OBE can bring some needed focus to the way schools are organized. Currently, state and district regulations—including graduation requirements, competency tests, textbook adoption policies, local curriculum guides, special mandates to teach about AIDS or gun safety—combine in a patchwork of diffuse and oftentimes contradictory signals to which teachers must attend as they plan instruction. In the system envisioned by OBE enthusiasts, the desired learner outcomes become the foundation upon which decisions about curriculum, instruction, assessment, staff development, and so on are based. Presumably, such a system would be better aligned and focused and, thus, more efficient than the system now operating.

WHAT OUTCOMES?

As promising an approach as OBE may be, even proponents have struggled to explain how schools can successfully act upon the implications of their philosophy. Few schools appear to have actually reorganized their curriculum and overhauled their assessment and reporting schemes to reflect new, higher outcomes. More commonly, schools and districts draft outcomes based on the present curriculum or write ambitious and far-reaching new outcomes while changing the curriculum very little.

The reason seems to be that schools, districts, and states that have attempted to use OBE philosophy very quickly find themselves struggling with some difficult challenges.

The first is deciding what outcomes should form the heart of an OBE plan —and no aspect of OBE has proven quite so contentious. Opponents of OBE have consistently charged that traditional academic content is omitted or buried in a morass of pedagogic claptrap in the OBE plans that have emerged to date.

For example, a draft plan in Virginia, since shelved, contained six major areas of student outcomes: environmental stewardship, personal well-being and accomplishment, interpersonal relationships, lifelong learning, cultural and creative endeavors, work and economic well-being, and local and global civic participation. According to the draft, a student outcome for personal well-being and accomplishment was "a responsible individual who has a good sense of his or her abilities and needs, and uses that knowledge consistently to make choices likely to lead to a healthy, productive, and fulfilling life." A worthy aim, to be sure, but critics convinced the general public that such outcomes would lead to more "touchy feely" exercises and less history and math in the schools.

Supporters of OBE find themselves in a precarious position. Many of them believe strongly that an educated graduate is not just someone who has absorbed a set of discrete experiences in the traditional academic domains. The OBE movement "has taken shape around the idea that the educational experience is too fragmented, and that important outcomes not easily pegged to typical subject area divisions and pedagogical approaches are falling through the cracks," says Wiggins. But architects of OBE plans find it extraordinarily difficult to weave the academic content into the broad outcomes. "If you say that the purpose of school is not control over the disciplines, but control over these more generic capacities," then there is a danger that traditional rigor will be diminished, says Wiggins. "Because if you now say that the purpose of a literature program, for example, is to teach people to communicate effectively, you are now saying, implicitly to some people, that it doesn't matter if you read Judy Blume or Shakespeare to accomplish that end."

OBE advocates have struggled mightily with the question of whether one set of outcomes will fit the needs of all students; those who will go on to Harvard as well as those who will clerk at K-Mart. One option would be to craft outcomes based on the kind of curriculum taken by students in the advanced college-prep track—outcomes derived from physics, U.S. history, and so on—and push more students to attain such outcomes. But the more common approach taken by OBE planners has been to frame outcomes that describe students as "effective communicators or problem-solvers." Parents of high-achieving students, in particular, fear that such nebulous outcomes will result in less academic rigor in their children's program.

Good outcomes have to have three elements: the content knowledge, the competence (what the student is *doing*), and the setting (under what conditions the student is performing), says Kit Marshall, associate director and co-founder of the High Success Network, Inc. Content is *essential*, she says: "you can't demonstrate anything without the basics." But the field has fallen short in defining what a good outcome is, she says. "Many so-called outcomes are really more like goals, and they aren't assessable as such," says Marshall. "We have not clearly defined in a large enough sense what an outcome is, or what a demonstration of an outcome looks like. The field has not done that well enough."

The drafting of common outcomes for an OBE system requires enormous time and care. Even then, outcomes will appear too vague for some or too specific for others. If outcomes are too "global," McTighe notes, critics ask "Where's the beef?" But if a state specifies dozens or hundreds of outcomes, it is attacked for "prescribing the curriculum" and treading on local initiative.

HOW TO ASSESS

A second major challenge facing any move to an outcome-based system is redesigning student assessment and reporting programs. Since OBE requires students to demonstrate their knowledge and skills, the assessments used to evaluate their performances become critically important.

But are the student assessments currently available up to the task? Although assessment experts know how to measure basic levels of skill and knowledge, they have less proven experience measuring higher-order outcomes within the subject area domains and almost no track record with the transformational, cross-disciplinary outcomes that some OBE plans envision.

Many experts say that performance-based assessments—not standardized, multiple-choice tests—are necessary to measure student attainment of outcomes. "Many outcomes demand a type of assessment that is more performance-oriented" because most current tests fail to measure the applications of knowledge described in new outcomes, says McTighe.

David Hornbeck, a former state school superintendent in Maryland who has advised states on outcome-based systems, believes the field is making progress on designing assessments that measure complex tasks. "We can measure much higher levels of knowledge and skills than we try to measure routinely now," he says, citing improvements in the assessment of student writing. But most experts agree that designing assessments linked to high-level and broadly written outcomes present enormous technical challenges.

One reason assessment is so critical, of course, is that OBE philosophy suggests that students should *demonstrate* their attainment of outcomes before receiving a diploma, a notion some experts referred to as "performance-based graduation." But even OBE proponents suggest moving very cautiously in considering whether to deny students a diploma based on their failure to demonstrate their proficiency on the assessments currently available. On certain outcomes, it's probably wise to give students feedback on their performance, but not to deny advancement or a diploma to students who fail, suggests Marzano.

Dubious outcomes and the prospect that assessment of those outcomes would be used in a high-stakes fashion fueled the criticisms about OBE in states such as Pennsylvania. But *not* holding students accountable to outcomes carries consequences, too. The Kentucky accountability system measures schools on their ability to help students to attain state-defined learner outcomes. Schools are held accountable (and can be taken over by the state if they show insufficient improvement), but students are not, says Guskey of the University of Kentucky. In fact, the state-required assessment of 12th graders is administered during the spring of their senior year, and is not connected with graduation requirements, "so students can just blow it off" without consequences, says Guskey.

BUILDING SCHOOL CAPACITY

A third major challenge facing those wishing to move to an OBE system involves building the capacity of schools to make the changes necessary for students to master required outcomes. On paper, OBE suggests that each school's curriculum and instruction would be reorganized to support agreed-upon student outcomes. In reality, many practices and traditions—mandatory standardized testing programs and college admissions requirements, for example—combine to create an inertia preventing local schools from changing very substantively in response to the precepts of OBE. This is true of other reforms besides OBE, notes Wiggins: faced with the prospects of a major new reform, educators often "retitle what they are already inclined to do."

For example, many of the schools claiming to practice OBE appear to offer the same set of courses as before, even though they've drafted new outcomes. A real tension exists between the curriculum educators might wish to implement and the one that responds to current conditions and constraints. For example,

"Right now, given our transitional education system, we've got to respect and respond to the fact that algebra is still a door to college," says Marshall. "So regardless of whether or not someone thinks that you'll ever use algebra, we've got to see to it that we're holding ourselves accountable, that we're expanding students' options, not limiting them."

Because drafting new outcomes and developing new assessments linked to them are such difficult tasks, they have drawn more attention than the question of what can be done to build schools' capacity to help students attain new outcomes, believes John Champlin, executive director of the National Center for Outcomes-Based Education and the former superintendent in Johnson City, New York. "Outcomes are what we want, but what we have to do is to change the capacity of schools" to help students attain them. States need to place as much attention on the capacity-building side of outcome-based systems as on the accountability side, he says.

FUTURE DIRECTIONS

Although it's impossible to predict precisely what the future of outcome-based education is, there are several likely trends.

OBE plans will probably rely more heavily on outcomes defined in traditional subject areas, rather than the "transformational" outcomes that cross the disciplines. "The starting point and the emphasis should be on the academic disciplines," says Hornbeck. This is the model of the national standards for content and student performance, which are being crafted in all of the major disciplines and which will be published over the next year or two (mathematics standards have already been written). States that have defined outcomes within the subject areas, as in Kentucky, for example, have not encountered the same degree of opposition as states that attempted to create cross-disciplinary outcomes.

Another likely trend is that states will move slowly on attaching high stakes to outcome-based education plans. Few states, for example, are likely to abolish the Carnegie unit as the basis for graduation, as Pennsylvania plans to do. Instead, bet on more states attempting to define learner outcomes, aligning assessment programs with those outcomes, and compiling student assessment data with other indicators of school performance as part of the accountability system. Until (and unless) performance-based assessments shore up their technical qualities, or the outcomes are more clearly defined, high-stakes uses are likely to be frowned upon.

A third trend is more systematic attempts to communicate with the public what outcome-based education is about. Educators substantially underestimated the degree of public confusion and disagreement with OBE in several of the states that attempted to launch programs.

"There has to be an awful lot of attention to communicating in simple terms," says James Cooper, dean of the Curry School of Education at the University of Virginia. Virginia's OBE plan foundered, he says, in part because opponents convinced the middle ground of citizens that OBE (as defined in the state's proposed "common core" of learning outcomes) would mean lower academic standards. "The vagueness [of the plan] was a real political problem," says Cooper. State officials, "try as they might, could not say simply and clearly enough what this common core was. Then the opposition defined it in their terms as 'mushy-headed.'"

It may be that the public believes that the present performance of schools does not warrant the restructuring that would result from a true application of OBE's precepts. "People are really not that dissatisfied with what's going on" in schools, Cooper believes. "People are interested in school improvement, but not necessarily in break-the-mold schools or break-the-mold education." As a result, "major sweeping changes are exceedingly difficult," and modest, incremental changes seem the only plausible route.

POSTSCRIPT

Can Outcome-Based Education Transform America's Schools?

Outcome-based education, like most major reform efforts (even going all the way back to John Dewey's "new education"), is being worshipped and vilified, overestimated and underappreciated. The present shakedown period will determine the level of acceptance by the profession and the public and the extent of modifications needed to solidify support.

For further insight into the OBE controversy, the following articles are recommended: "Outcome-Based Education: Another Educational Bandwagon?" by James M. Towers, *The Educational Forum* (Spring 1992); "The Biggest Reform of All," by Chester E. Finn, Jr., *Phi Delta Kappan* (April 1990); William G. Spady, "Organizing for Results: The Basis of Authentic Restructuring and Reform," *Educational Leadership* (October 1988); Gail Chase Furman, "Outcome-Based Education and Accountability," *Education and Urban Society* (August 1994); Outcome-Based Education: Skinnerian Conditioning in the Classroom," by W. F. Jasper, *The New American* (August 23, 1993); and "Outcomes-Based Education Reexamined: From Structural Functionalism to Poststructuralism," by Colleen A. Capper and Michael T. Jamison, *Educational Policy* (December 1993).

Also worthwhile are "The Perils of Outcome-Based Teacher Education," by James M. Towers, *Phi Delta Kappan* (April 1994); "Education for Outcomes Puts Preparation Up for Grabs," by Judith Renyi, *Basic Education* (February 1993); and Colleen A. Capper, " 'And Justice for All': Critical Perspectives on Outcomes-Based Education in the Context of Secondary School Restructuring," *Journal of School Leadership* (March 1994). Also, the March 1994 issue of *Educational Leadership* contains a number of articles on the topic, among them Arnold Burron, "Traditionalist Christians and OBE: What's the Problem?" and Randy Zitterkopf, "A Fundamentalist's Defense of OBE."

Mastery learning, the principles and techniques of which lie at the heart of outcome-based education, was developed by John B. Carroll and Benjamin Bloom in the 1960s and 1970s. For a look at these origins, see Carroll, "A Model of School Learning," *Teachers College Record* (September 1963); Bloom, *Human Characteristics and School Learning* (1976); and Thomas R. Guskey, *Implementing Mastery Learning* (1985).

ISSUE 21

Is Mandatory Community Service Desirable and Legal?

YES: Vito Perrone, from "Learning for Life: When Do We Begin?" *Equity and Excellence in Education* (September 1993)

NO: Institute for Justice, from " 'Compulsory Volunteering': Constitutional Challenges to Mandatory Community Service," *Litigation Backgrounder* (1994)

ISSUE SUMMARY

YES: Education professor Vito Perrone makes the case for community service learning as a mechanism for revitalizing schools and building a service ethic in students.

NO: The Institute for Justice, a nonprofit public interest law center in Washington, D.C., argues that government-mandated service is unconstitutional and negates the spirit of voluntarism.

In recent years governmental action at the state and national levels has aimed to generate altruism among America's youth through programs of community service. State and local policymakers have added new high school graduation requirements that stipulate the completion of a given number of community service hours. At the federal level, Congress has passed the National and Community Service Trust Act of 1993 (P.L. 103–82), a reauthorization of P.L. 101–610, passed in 1990, and the Domestic Volunteer Service Act. The new legislation, which was strongly promoted by President Bill Clinton, established the Corporation for National and Community Service "to engage Americans of all ages and backgrounds in community-based service" in order to deal with the nation's "education, human, public safety, and environmental needs" while fostering civic responsibility and providing educational opportunity for those who make a substantial contribution to service. Although participation is not compulsory, the federal effort is being driven by the same principles that are animating the more binding state and local programs.

Supporters of state-mandated community service echo the Aristotelian sentiment "We become just by doing just acts." Kathleen Kennedy Townsend, executive director of the Maryland Student Service Alliance, contends that "required service is the best strategy for graduating smart, thoughtful, and committed citizens. Without a requirement whether a student becomes involved in service activities depends on happenstance. With a requirement all young people will learn that they can be effective and powerful, that they can solve problems, and that helping others can be enjoyable." Roland MacNichol, a teacher, claims that service learning is "the right thing to do in helping make our schools thoughtful, caring places with strong belief systems based on service and on young people making a difference." In "The Sleeping Giant of School Reform," *Phi Delta Kappan* (June 1991), Joe Nathan and Jim Kielsmeier contend that "combining classroom work with service/social action projects can help produce dramatic improvements in student attitudes, motivation, and achievement."

The movement, however, is not without its detractors. Williamson Evers, for example, argues that students who are not up to grade level in math should not be spending time in a mandatory service program, that a "service learning" program gives teachers a license to instill partisan doctrines, and that the movement is "a chintzy way for politicians to get cheap labor out of young people." Evers further argues that the program's coercion aspect takes the spirit of generosity out of service.

Lawsuits stemming from mandatory service programs have been initiated in a number of localities, including Chapel Hill, North Carolina; Mamaroneck, New York; and Bethlehem, Pennsylvania. The legal challengers have held that mandatory, uncompensated service violates the constitutional prohibition of involuntary servitude and that the policy intrudes improperly on parental responsibility. Harry C. Boyte, director of Project Public Life, argues that community service programs, which are widely touted as the cure for young people's political apathy, in fact teach little about the art of participation in public life. In "What Is Wrong With National Service?" *Social Policy* (Fall 1993), Claudia Horwitz maintains that the federal effort is "sapping the energy of many of our nation's most powerful young leaders" and drawing attention away from the real causes of and possible solutions to very critical problems.

In the selections that follow, Vito Perrone draws on his own positive experiences in making the case for expanding the various types of community service learning practices that are currently in effect. The Institute for Justice, which has provided legal support for those who have challenged the constitutionality of mandatory service programs, maintains that the decision to serve others is not a choice that should be made by the state.

YES   Vito Perrone

LEARNING FOR LIFE:
WHEN DO WE BEGIN?

While service learning is currently assuming the role of innovation, seen as a means for enhancing citizenship education and informing reform within schools by encouraging flexibility of schedules and a more active pedagogy, I trust we know that there is a history of consequence. John Dewey, for example, wrote eloquently at an earlier time in this century about the need for education to be seen as active—about doing and acting and being connected to the world. The Dewey School, which existed during the period 1896–1904, had an important outwardness as did many other early 20th century schools that assumed a progressive orientation.

The revival of interest in service learning has many roots—concerns about a growing age stratification, a youth culture that has too few connections to civic life, feelings among youth of having no critical and acknowledged place in the society, disturbing voting patterns in the 18- to 24-year-old population, growing schoolwork transitional difficulties, a deterioration of communities as settings for social growth, an enlarging set of social service needs, increased pessimism about the future, and a belief that schooling is not powerful enough to evoke deep commitments to learning, among others.

The revival of service learning has not, though, been smooth, even as federal legislation and some state actions have given it a big boost. In most settings, service learning is an add-on. It is not a set of activities or orientation integral to the ongoing life of schools. It is often framed as a modest requirement for graduation with accompanying debates about whether 15 hours, 20 hours, or 40 hours should be the standard. And the issue is in the courts as well. The Bethlehem case—about a 40-hour service requirement over four years—is now in the Court of Appeals in Philadelphia, the challenge being rooted in the 13th Amendment which deals with involuntary servitude.

I have long been attracted to service learning as a means of revitalizing schools and their connections to communities. It is an important way of fully engaging students, of pushing what is done in and around schools toward the *use* of knowledge and not just the *possession* of information. It is also a process directed toward the full integration of all persons, young and old, into the

From Vito Perrone, "Learning for Life: When Do We Begin?" *Equity and Excellence in Education*, vol. 26, no. 2 (September 1993). Copyright © 1993 by *Equity and Excellence in Education*. Reprinted by permission.

civic and economic aspects of life in their various communities. I invoke this broader view to make sure that we understand clearly the need for service learning to be more than a single activity. It needs to be more than another course, another requirement or another onetime event. Thinking about many forms of outreach is helpful. Connecting outreach to work, as in cooperative education, which we have long done and are familiar with, is also useful.

CSL [COMMUNITY SERVICE LEARNING] BUILDS ENGAGEMENT

Currently, children and young people tend to describe their school learning as having very little to do with their lives beyond school. When students speak of the "remoteness" of school, they are really talking about the lack of connection between school and the world outside. They are acknowledging what Alfred North Whitehead noted—that most of what is taught in school is not about life "as it is known in the midst of living it."

Students see homelessness and poverty in the streets around them, they know about immigration as they hear so many languages being spoken. They are aware of racial discord, of community violence, of drugs, of war, of famine and environmental degradation. When schools do not explore such issues deeply, or even ignore them, it reinforces for students that the schools are about something other than the realities of the world. This division is unfortunate.

Further, the content of schools seldom relates to what people in a particular community are worried about or care deeply about. For example, the schools do not often make the local community architecture, its historical and cultural roots, or its economic and political structures a focus of study. The community's storytellers, craftspersons, builders, day-care and health providers are not common visitors. The literature that is read has generally not been selected because it illuminates the life that students see day in and day out outside of the school. Neither is it generally chosen because it helps them assume a larger sense of responsibility for some aspect of the social good or makes it possible for them to engage a non-school mentor more productively or assist a person in need. This disconnectedness trivializes much of what students are asked to learn.

We know all of this intuitively. Indeed, this knowledge causes many in schools to make occasional forays into the community: Students take a walk to the park in relation to a science project; classes go to the local library so that every student will get a library card; teachers invite a couple of persons each year to share some aspect of their experience or host a cultural awareness day related to the special ethnic origins of a dominant community group; or students go sporadically to a senior citizen center or read to children in a lower grade level. These activities tend to be viewed as special events surrounding the *real* work of the school. This is the case even as teachers and their students often view these efforts as the *highlights* of the school year. The real work of school could, of course, be centered a good deal more on aspects of and interaction with the local setting. That could be the principal starting point of learning.

In relation to the aforementioned, I am reminded of the project week organized by a Boston high school a couple of years ago. The week, which involved all the students and teachers, focused on the question: "Is Boston a livable city?" Students conducted a large number of interviews and surveys, visited cultural sites, read city and state crime, health and environmental studies, and the like. They concluded the week with various oral and written reports, what Ted Sizer calls "exhibitions of learning" and many at Harvard call "understanding performances." The intensity *was* very high. It *was*, without question, the highlight of the year, causing many students to ask why this kind of intensive study around authentic issues could not be more the norm, rather than being just an enrichment activity. It seemed to me a reasonable question.

COMMUNITIES AS CLASSROOMS

As I reflect on this kind of outwardness, I am quickly drawn back to Richard Wurman's *Yellow Pages of Learning Resources.* I loved that book when I first read it. It affirmed so much of my outlook about the need to reconceptualize schooling. While many conditions have changed since the book was originally published, the potential for connecting schools with their wider communities remains large. Service learning is, of course, about enlarging those connections.

Wurman provides a number of entry points for using one's city or town as an extended school house. He writes: "Education has been thought of as taking place mainly within the confines of the classroom, and school buildings have been regarded as the citadels of knowledge. However, the most extensive facility imaginable for learning is [beyond the school]" (Wurman, 1972, p. 1). He stresses the need for teachers to become careful observers of their environments, to find in the reality of the world addi-

tional learning possibilities. He suggests that "the city is everywhere around us, and it is ripe with learning resources.... But in order to realize the vast learning potential of their resources, we must learn to learn from them... learn not to overlook the obvious,... hear when we listen, see when we look... realize that good questions are better than brilliant answers."

Any place where something special occurs can be a classroom of consequence. For example, churches, medical facilities, museums, libraries, bakeries, day care settings, senior centers, soup kitchens, social service centers, Ys, city halls, park and recreation facilities, among others, are all possible classrooms of consequence. The people who work in and around these special settings and around the community are teachers as well as workers.

A course I taught several years ago in a secondary school drew heavily on Wurman's understandings of the potential of a community serving as a larger schoolhouse, providing much of the content for an intensive education. Entitled "Growing Up in Grand Forks," its primary purpose, along with enlarging writing and inquiry skills and understandings of how historians and sociologists go about their work, was to enlarge students' consciousness about their own community and their place in it.

As juniors and seniors, most could not, when we began, really describe their community in much detail. They had not observed carefully the special Romanesque architecture of the downtown buildings or taken note of the community's statues or their origins. Most had never been inside the federal court house, the city hall, the Jewish synagogue, the state mill, the downtown art gallery, or the university museum of art, to name only a few sites. They could not identify most of the trees and knew little about city government, tax structures, or the city's development plans. Issues that people cared about—water purity, flood control, recreational uses of the river and its banks, low-income housing policies, the deterioration of the downtown, economic stagnation and tax rates—these were not part of their studies. Few had ever gone to a public hearing about any community issue. Though many were eighteen, they had not really thought much about voting. They knew they could, but most told me they did not really know anything about the issues.

I believe we owe it to our young people to assure that they are deeply involved *with* their communities, that they leave us eager to take an active part in the political and cultural systems that surround them. Enlarging our vision of the school is, therefore, important.

PREPARING PRODUCTIVE CITIZENS

A point of connection in secondary schools that has not been tapped well relates to student work. Close to 70 percent of secondary school students are employed, principally in the burgeoning service sector of the economy. Rather than viewing this work as positive, and as contributing to student responsibility and a sense of usefulness, those in schools speak of it primarily as lessening student commitments to the school's academic and extracurricular programs. They also see it as fostering what they believe to be an unhealthy materialism (Perrone et al., 1981). These perceptions place the work of the school and the work of the larger world in conflict. It denies the possibility that there are connecting points of consequence that actually affect students and their learning.

While I acknowledge that students who work over 20 hours a week tend to suffer academically within the current structure of schools, the work of students and the structure of schools could be thought about more constructively. Many students speak of what they do in their work as "being useful," "being independent" and "responsible." They also tend to enjoy their work. Employers see them as reliable and competent (Perrone et al., 1981). Are such perspectives to be negated? Is there no way to use such awareness?

Why do teachers not have students maintain journals of their work experience? Why not make the kinds of employment students are engaged in the focus of study in courses in health, nutrition, science, economics, mathematics, government, history, and literature? Why do teachers not engage their classrooms in a closer look at the materialist culture which is such a potent force in American society and which also contributes heavily to student employment? Cannot the world that these students have entered into so fully be connected to the ongoing and important work of the schools? While not directly service, it is a starting point for seeing their lives as connected to the world—as tied to the social and economic aspects of their communities. Making such a tie conscious is important.

Those in the schools talk a great deal about preparing their students for social and civic responsibility, but the opportunities to gain experience in these directions are limited, if they exist at all. It is possible for students to complete their schooling and never be involved deeply, in or outside the school, in any service-oriented activity. Too few students are tutoring younger children or classmates, working with the elderly, constructing or maintaining a playground, monitoring a public hearing, completing a community survey, or teaching at a Boy's Club or Y. The absence of connections is notable. In most settings, teaching for social responsibility and active citizenship is merely rhetoric.

Children have a disposition toward outwardness from their very early years. They have a need to learn *about* the world and participate actively in its ongoing life. They have a natural desire to engage others, to be helpful. If this desire to engage others is nurtured in the home and in the schools, such a disposition can develop into a fuller form of social and civic responsibility.

Some of the wonderful remembrances of teens I have talked with are of particular trees they planted as children and which now bring so much pleasure to communities. The trees stand as visible reminders of their earlier service.

The isolation in students' lives between what they do in and outside of schools is being addressed as many schools become centers for community service. Increasing numbers of schools, in fact, have made service an integral part of their curriculum. All schools, though, need to build a service ethic.

Central Park East Secondary School, in New York City, has a school-wide service program that involves all of its students *during* the school day. Approximately one in eight students are involved in a service activity each morning and afternoon, Monday through Thursday. Their placements include such settings as the Museum of the City of New York, the Studio Museum of Harlem, Mount Sinai Medical Center, the Association to Benefit Children, the 92nd Street YMHA, the Jewish Guild for the Blind, the Union Settlement House, the Community Planning Board, the Center for Collaborative Education, Headstart programs, and local elementary schools. Increasingly students are taking roles on school and community decision-making boards.

Efforts are made at Central Park East to integrate the experience students are having in their service placements with their ongoing coursework. This service-academic connection must be an important goal of all service programs. Without it, service is a peripheral activity and the curriculum remains insular. Central Park East is an exceptional school in regard to service. Its example should not be so unique. Every school could do what Central Park East does if it chose to do so.

ENLARGING POSSIBILITIES

The service I have concentrated on has been beyond the school. The larger, out-of-school community has been my focus in this presentation. Service can also be directed back to the school. It can be aimed at building the community of the school. A social and civic responsibility orientation can certainly be fostered within a school as efforts are made to build its community, to develop more fully its democratic character.

Let me provide one example that has impressed me. Several years ago, at an elementary school in Revere, Massachusetts, the principal of an all-White, fully English-speaking school, learned that a large number of Cambodian children would enter the school that fall. When the 100 Cambodian children arrived, the school was ready. They were greeted with outstretched hands of welcome and friendship.

The principal had earlier decided that it was critical for *everyone* in the school—children, teachers, custodians, secretaries, lunch workers—to know who these Cambodian children were, where they had come from, and why they were coming to Revere. Getting ready for the Cambodian children became the curriculum. It was real and as a result it was vital. Those in the school community learned how to speak to Cambodian children and also gained knowledge about some of their cultural patterns as well as their suffering. As part of their preparation, those in the school learned about prejudice and the harm that prejudice brings to persons who are different. They also learned about how prejudice disrupts communities both in the schools and in the neighborhoods.

Given the heavy flow of immigrant children into the schools, possibly the largest we have had in our history, engaging a school community as was

done in the Revere elementary school is exemplary. It addresses an important citizenship responsibility. And, of course, there are many related projects beyond immigration.

My concern has been about enlarging possibilities for students to construct a more productive community-oriented life and helping them to see their learning in more than school terms. That calls for connecting the school and the world beyond the school more directly. It calls for blurring wherever possible the lines which separate them. It calls for providing the ground for a service ethic to be constructed. That is our task. Service Massachusetts needs to be our future.

REFERENCES

Perrone, V., et al. (1981). *Secondary school students and employment.* Grand Forks, ND: Bureau of Educational Research and Services, University of North Dakota.

Wurman, R. (Ed.). (1972). *Yellow pages of learning resources.* Cambridge: MIT Press.

"COMPULSORY VOLUNTEERING": CONSTITUTIONAL CHALLENGES TO MANDATORY COMMUNITY SERVICE

INTRODUCTION

Ninth-grader Aric Herndon of Chapel Hill, North Carolina will soon receive his Eagle Scout award. He faithfully serves the Chapel Hill community through his work on Scout-sponsored projects and merit badge requirements.

But Aric may not graduate from high school—not because of any academic failings, but because he does not conform to the Chapel Hill School District's ideal of model citizenship. The community service that Aric performs for the Boy Scouts does not qualify for credit under the school district's new mandatory community service program. In the school district's judgment, since Aric receives an independent "benefit" from his service, such as an award or merit badge, the work does not rise to the level of "true" and selfless community service.

The Chapel Hill School District's twisted logic exemplifies the growing number of public schools around the country that require community service as a condition of graduation. Approximately 21 percent of public schools surveyed impose some type of community service requirement while an additional 10 percent will implement programs in the next year.[1] Like many other mandatory community service plans, the Chapel Hill program requires high school students to "serve" 50 hours in the community as a condition of graduation. The work must be performed after school hours, on weekends, or over summer vacation, and the students cannot receive compensation for their services.

Rye Neck High School in Mamaroneck, New York similarly conditions the receipt of a high school diploma on students performing 40 hours of labor in the community. Daniel Immediato, a student at Rye Neck, currently does not perform community service as defined by the school. Although Daniel does not object to helping others, he instead works as a lifeguard at a public pool and contributes to the modest earnings of the family. Daniel's lifeguarding, while certainly a service to the community, does not count toward the community service requirement since he receives compensation for his work.

Regardless of whether Aric or Daniel's community service qualified for credit, the students and their parents believe that the decision to serve others must come from within, not through government edict. The parents fundamentally object to their sons being forced to participate in a government-created program intended to inculcate a sense of obligation to the community. So they have joined other families in challenging the constitutionality of mandatory community service.

On April 19, 1994, the Institute for Justice will file two lawsuits challenging mandatory community service for public high school students in Chapel Hill and Mamaroneck as a violation of constitutional rights.

The issue of mandatory community service raises important and fundamental questions about the obligations of individuals in a free society to serve others and the role of the government in determining what individuals owe to the "community." The question of whether students can be drafted into a government-mandated community service program goes directly to the heart of the Institute for Justice's commitment to individual liberty and to the principle that voluntarism, not government coercion, is the basis of a free society.

THE NATIONAL FIGHT AGAINST MANDATORY COMMUNITY SERVICE

Mandatory community service was first challenged in a lawsuit filed in 1990 by the Steirer and Moralis families in Bethlehem, Pennsylvania.[2] Lynn Steirer pioneered the fight against mandatory community service. An avid volunteer and now a senior at Liberty High School in Bethlehem, Lynn compellingly captures the unintended consequences of coerced community service: "People should volunteer because they want to, not because of a government threat. So many kids who do this treat it like a joke; they do the minimum to get the credit."[3]

The lawsuit was unsuccessful in the lower courts and last summer, when the families' resources were exhausted, the Institute for Justice took on their case. The Institute filed a petition for certiorari in the U.S. Supreme Court, which declined to hear the case. This result was not surprising as the Court often lets issues ripen for several years in multiple court cases before addressing them.

The Third Circuit Court of Appeal's ruling in the *Steirer* case emboldened school districts nationwide. More and more school districts now condition the receipt of a high school diploma on students performing community service. And students are not the only targets for the "mandatory volunteering" juggernaut. The Tulsa, Oklahoma school district, citing the *Steirer* opinion as authority, wants to adopt a community service requirement not only for students, but for their parents as well. Under the proposed plan, if the parents do not perform the service, the students do not graduate.

Many community service advocates view mandatory programs as necessary to counter what they perceive as excessive selfishness and materialism in young people today. Recent polls, however, debunk the myth of selfish and lazy youths: a surprising six out of ten 12- to 17-year-olds volunteer their time to others.[4] This outpouring of good will and voluntarism on the part of today's youth counts for naught among community service proponents. Kathleen Kennedy Townsend, one of the most outspoken advocates of the first state-wide service program in Maryland, declared, "You don't choose to do good unless you learn to do good. A lot of people who are forced to do something learn to like it."[5]

In 1993, Maryland imposed the first statewide community service requirement, covering nearly 200,000 public high school students. Much public discussion and debate surrounded the adoption of Maryland's program. Indeed, all but one of Maryland's local school districts adamantly opposed the state-wide program. Because of the outcry by the public and school officials alike, the state board of education granted local schools broad discretion to craft their own programs. As a result, the local school districts in Maryland do not aggressively enforce this new graduation requirement.

Even with local school officials' unenthusiastic acceptance and enforcement of mandatory community service, the Maryland program already exhibits one of the most disturbing aspects of school-sponsored community service: the increasing politicization of programs and service opportunities. The Maryland program teaches that political activism is the highest form of community service.[6] Even the promotional posters for community service produced by the Maryland Department of Education demonstrate the overt emphasis upon political action as a means of solving community problems. One poster depicts a student climbing the mountain of community service. On each layer of the mountain is a type of community service. At the pinnacle of the mountain, above such service as caring for the sick and the aged, rests the form of service Maryland deems most important: lobbying. Another poster shows students in the service program demonstrating outside Maryland's capital for greater public education funding.

Unlike the heated controversy surrounding the Maryland program, the Chapel Hill School District unceremoniously imposed its mandatory community service requirement with little fanfare and seemingly no public discussion. The school district merely notified parents of this great expansion of government power through a letter sent at the beginning of the 1993–94 school year. However, two families in Chapel Hill refused to accept the school district's new intrusion into their lives and have instead joined in a constitutional challenge to mandatory community service.

Several years ago, the Rye Neck School District in Mamaroneck, New York imposed community service after many far wealthier school districts in Westchester County adopted service requirements. Compulsory community service typically exists in public schools with privileged children from wealthy families. Families in Rye Neck, however, have more modest incomes and struggle to provide a good education for their children. Also, many students in Rye Neck, including the Institute's clients, work part-time after school and contribute to the family income. Not surprisingly, these families want their children to concentrate on their studies, rather than be subjected to experiments requiring children to engage in out-of-school activities the authorities deem good for them.

The Institute's new challenges to mandatory community service aim to prevent the dilemma now confronting Bethlehem students Lynn Steirer and

David Moralis as their senior year draws to a close. They must either participate in a program that violates their fundamental beliefs about the nature of helping others, or not receive a crucial stepping stone to success in life: a high school diploma. No student should have to face this Hobson's choice in the future.

LITIGATION STRATEGY

The Institute challenges the Chapel Hill and Rye Neck coerced service programs under the 13th Amendment's guarantee against involuntary servitude and the Ninth and 14th Amendment rights to parental liberty and due process of law.... While a 13th Amendment claim was raised in the Bethlehem case, a 14th Amendment challenge to mandatory community service has thus far not been presented to a court. With the filing of these lawsuits in the Fourth and Second U.S. Circuit Courts of Appeal, the Institute seeks a "circuit split" among the federal appellate courts, thereby increasing the chances of Supreme Court review.

It is widely known that the 13th Amendment banned the institution of slavery throughout the United States. However, the amendment also prohibits "involuntary servitude," except as punishment for a crime. While slavery involves the ownership and complete control of one individual by another, the U.S. Supreme Court defines involuntary servitude as a "condition of enforced compulsory service of one to another."[7] Mandatory community service programs fit this definition by requiring students to work for others against their will without compensation. The requirement for providing free labor to others, either organizations or individuals, distinguishes service programs from other mandatory school activities, such as gym classes, chemistry labs, and so on.

The Third Circuit Court of Appeals in the *Steirer* case virtually admitted that the program constituted a textbook definition of servitude. However, the court decided to ignore the constitutional text and instead opted for a "contextual" approach to the 13th Amendment. Furthermore, the court held that even if the program was a form of servitude, it was not "involuntary" because students had the "option" of quitting school, going to a private school, or receiving their G.E.D. Logically, this ruling means that the 13th Amendment has no applicability to the public school setting. Under the court's reasoning, public schools could require any type of student labor, from building a new addition to the school to mowing the lawns of school board members, and the students could not raise a claim under the 13th Amendment because they could always leave the public schools. The Institute's new challenges to coerced community service place this unprecedented holding directly at issue.

The 14th Amendment guarantees to parents the right to direct and control the upbringing and education of their children. The U.S. Supreme Court recognized this important right in two landmark U.S. Supreme Court cases: *Meyer v. Nebraska*[8] and *Pierce v. Society of Sisters*.[9] The Court held in those cases that certain "ideas touching the relation of the individual and the state [are] wholly different from those upon which our institutions rest" and do "violence to both the letter and spirit of the Constitution."[10] The decision to help others under our system of law has always been left to the conscience of the individual and to the moral education of children by parents. Programs that require service to others are foreign to the relationship between the individual and the state under the U.S. Constitution and the *Meyer* and *Pierce* cases.

Courts have consistently held that in public schools, mere exposure to ideas or beliefs with which parents disagree does not normally give rise to a constitutional violation.[11] However, when public schools require students to *act* on the basis of those values or beliefs, especially outside of the public school setting, constitutional limits apply. For instance, while public schools can teach the values of thrift and the importance of saving money, could schools require students as a condition of graduation to save a certain percentage of any money they earned? To stress the importance of abstinence to students, could schools require them to sign a pledge stating that they will remain virgins until they graduate? To underscore the importance of participating in our democratic system, could schools condition graduation on proof that students voted in the first election in which they were eligible?

All of the above-described programs would no doubt raise very serious constitutional concerns since in each instance the government intrudes into areas that have always been left to the private domain of individuals and to the relationship between parents and their children. Moreover, mandatory community service programs require students to act in programs that directly clash with their parents' fundamental belief that the decision to help others must be a voluntary one and cannot be imposed by the state.

Under the *Meyer* and *Pierce* cases, intrusion by the government into the relationship between parent and child requires a showing of a compelling state interest. In the mandatory community service context, the government must demonstrate that the programs are justified by such compelling interests. This task will be made difficult for the government by the lack of empirical studies showing mandatory community service programs having any serious educational value, especially when compared to the harm coercive programs do to recognized parental rights. Indeed, a 1991 survey of community service programs concluded that "much of the initiative for school-based service comes from policy makers and politicians—not educators."[12]

The Institute's litigation team in these lawsuits is headed by staff attorney Scott G. Bullock. Local counsel for the challenge in Chapel Hill, North Carolina is Robert H. Edmunds, Jr., former U.S. Attorney for the Middle District of North Carolina, and a partner at the Greensboro law firm of Stern, Graham & Klepfer, L.L.P. Local counsel for the Mamaroneck challenge is Lance Gotko, an attorney in New York.

CONCLUSION

People across the political spectrum share the desire to build strong and interconnected communities. But the hallmark of community is voluntarism. Too many people today confuse the ideal of community with what government officials deem the community's interest. In today's highly regulated society, individuals endure many government intrusions into their lives. By filing lawsuits that will have nationwide ramifications, families in Chapel Hill and Mamaroneck draw a line and proclaim that certain decisions, especially the decision to serve others, must be between an individual and his conscience, not the individual and the state. Through this principled stand, the families reinforce institutions that unquestionably build well-functioning communities: true voluntarism and private charitable efforts.

NOTES

1. Gordon Cawelti, *High School Restructuring: A National Study,* Educational Research Service, pp. 32–35 (1994).

2. The court opinions are reported in *Steirer v. Bethlehem Area School District,* 987 F.2d 989 (3rd Cir. 1993) and 789 F. Supp. 1337 (E.D. Pa. 1992).

3. Michael Winerip, "Required Volunteerism: School Programs Tested," *The New York Times,* Sept. 23, 1993.

4. "Schools Shouldn't Force Community Service," *USA Today,* Sept. 15, 1993.

5. Aaron Epstein, "Forced Community Service Likened to Slavery," *Phil. Inquirer,* Sept. 3, 1993.

6. For an enlightening article on the workings of the Maryland program, *see* Mark Parenti, "Lobbying School," *Reason,* pp. 56–57 (April 1994).

7. *Hodges v. United States,* 203 U.S. 1, 16 (1906).

8. 262 U.S. 390 (1923).

9. 268 U.S. 510 (1925).

10. *Meyer,* 262 U.S. at 401-02.

11. *See,* for example, *Mozert v. Hawkins County Board of Education,* 827 F.2d 1058 (6th Cir. 1987).

12. Dan Conrad & Diane Hedin, "School-Based Community Service: What We Know From Research and Theory," *Phi Delta Kappan,* p. 744 (June 1991).

POSTSCRIPT

Is Mandatory Community Service Desirable and Legal?

The Civilian Conservation Corps, the National Youth Conservation Corps, the Peace Corps, Volunteers in Service to America (VISTA), and now AmeriCorps, an action group sponsored by the new Corporation for National and Community Service, all attest to the success of federal efforts to kindle and reward altruism and idealism. However, the manifestation of this effort at the state and local levels has become far more controversial since "voluntary" service has evolved into "required." In addition to the organizations mentioned above, many advocacy groups support the community service movement, including Youth Service America, the Points of Light Foundation, the National Center for Service Learning in Early Adolescence, and the Community Service Learning Center. But the central questions remain: Can bureaucratically run volunteer programs fulfill their intentions? and, Can community service be a legal requirement for high school graduation?

Books that address the first of these related questions include Donald J. Eberly, ed., *National Youth Service: A Democratic Institution for the Twenty-First Century* (1990); *National Service: Pro and Con* edited by Williamson M. Evers (1990); *A Call to Civic Service* by Charles C. Moskos (1988); and E. B. Gorham, *National Service, Citizenship, and Political Education* (1992). Theme issues of journals addressing many aspects of the total controversy include *Phi Delta Kappan* (June 1991), *Social Policy* (Fall 1993), and *Equity and Excellence in Education* (September 1993).

Some interesting articles, most of them supportive of community service, include "Youth Service: A Profile of Those Who Give More Than They Take," by John Backes, *High School Journal* (April–May 1992); "Making a Difference: Students and Community Service," by Derek Bok and Frank Newman, *Change* (July–August 1992); "School-Based Community Service Programs: An Imperative for Effective Schools," by Harry Silcox, *NASSP Bulletin* (February 1993); Deborah Hirsch, "Politics Through Action: Student Service and Activism in the '90s," *Change* (September–October 1993); and Rogers M. Smith, "American Conceptions of Citizenship and National Service," *The Responsive Community* (Summer 1993).

Somewhat more critical perspectives are offered in Harry C. Boyte, "Community Service and Civic Education," *Phi Delta Kappan* (June 1991); Jonathan Schorr, "Class Action: What Clinton's National Service Program Could Learn from 'Teach America'," *Phi Delta Kappan* (December 1993); and "National Service and the Ideal of Community: A Commentary on *What You Can Do for Your Country*," *Journal of Education Policy* (May–June 1994).

CONTRIBUTORS
TO THIS VOLUME

EDITOR

JAMES WM. NOLL is an associate professor emeritus in the College of Education at the University of Maryland in College Park, Maryland, and a member of the American Educational Studies Association, the National Society for the Study of Education, the Association for Supervision and Curriculum Development, and the World Future Society. He received a B.A. in English from the University of Wisconsin, an M.S. in Educational Administration from the University of Wisconsin, and a Ph.D. in Philosophy of Education from the University of Chicago. His articles have appeared in several education journals, and he is the coeditor, with Sam P. Kelly, of *Foundations of Education in America: An Anthology of Major Thought and Significant Actions* (Harper & Row, 1970). He has also served on the editorial boards for The Dushkin Publishing Group's *Annual Editions: Education* and *Computer Studies: Computers in Education* for many years.

STAFF

Mimi Egan   Publisher
Brenda S. Filley   Production Manager
Libra Ann Cusack   Typesetting Supervisor
Juliana Arbo   Typesetter
Lara Johnson   Graphics
Diane Barker   Proofreader
David Brackley   Copy Editor
David Dean   Administrative Editor
Richard Tietjen   Systems Manager

AUTHORS

AMERICAN ASSOCIATION OF UNIVERSITY WOMEN is an organization of college and university graduates that was founded in 1881 to work for the advancement of women.

JEAN B. ARNOLD is an attorney with McGuire, Woods, Battle, and Boothe in Charlottesville, Virginia.

ZITA AROCHA is a freelance writer in Bethesda, Maryland, who focuses on education and social issues.

STEPHEN ARONS is an attorney and a professor of legal studies at the University of Massachusetts–Amherst. His research interests focus on individual and cultural freedoms in school and society, and he has written widely on cultural freedom and on law and education.

MOLEFI KETE ASANTE is a professor in and the chair of the Department of African American Studies at Temple University in Philadelphia, Pennsylvania. A leading proponent of the Afrocentric philosophy, he is the author of 33 books, including *Kemet, Afrocentricity, and Knowledge* (Africa World, 1992).

JAMES A. BANKS is a professor of education and the director of the Center for Multicultural Education at the University of Washington in Seattle, Washington. He is also a former president of the National Council for the Social Studies. His publications include *Multiethnic Education: Theory and Practice*, 4th ed. (Allyn & Bacon, 1994).

R. FREEMAN BUTTS is the William F. Russell Professor Emeritus in the Foundations of Education at Columbia University's Teachers College in New York City. His publications include *The Civic Mission in Educational Reform: Perspectives for the Public and the Profession* (Hoover Institute Press, 1989).

LEE CANTER is the president of Lee Canter & Associates in Santa Monica, California, and the developer of the Assertive Discipline program. His publications include *Assertive Discipline: A Take-Charge Approach for Today's Educator* (Canter & Associates, 1976), coauthored with Marlene Canter, and *Assertive Discipline for Parents* (Canter & Associates, 1982).

LINDA CHAVEZ, a political commentator, policy analyst, and author, is a John M. Olin Fellow of the Manhattan Institute for Policy Research in Washington, D.C., and the chair of the National Commission on Migrant Education. She has held several positions in the U.S. government, including professional staff member of the House of Representatives' Subcommittee on Civil and Constitutional Rights (1972–1974) and staff director of the U.S. Commission on Civil Rights (1983–1985). Her articles have appeared in such publications as *Fortune*, the *Wall Street Journal*, and the *Los Angeles Times*.

JOHN E. CHUBB is a senior fellow in the Governmental Studies Program at the Brookings Institution, a private nonprofit organization devoted to research, education, and publication in economics, government, foreign policy, and the social sciences. He is also a partner in the Edison Project in Knoxville, Tennessee, and he has held academic appointments at Princeton University, the Johns Hopkins University, and Stanford University. His publications include *Can the Government Govern?* (Brookings Institution, 1989), coauthored with Paul E. Peterson, and *Politics, Markets, and America's Schools* (Brookings Institution, 1990), coauthored with Terry M. Moe.

MARGARET PRUITT CLARK is the executive director of the Center for Population Options in Washington, D.C.

ROBERT L. CORD is a professor of political science and the University Distinguished Professor at Northeastern University in Boston, Massachusetts. He is the author of several books and articles about the U.S. Constitution, including *Separation of Church and State: Historical Fact and Current Fiction* (Baker Book House, 1988), which has been cited in numerous constitutional law books and in the opinions of U.S. Supreme Court justices for cases involving the church and the state.

JOHN F. COVALESKIE is a doctoral candidate of the cultural foundation of education and curriculum in the School of Education at Syracuse University in Syracuse, New York.

EDWIN J. DELATTRE is the dean of the School of Education and a professor of education and philosophy in the College of Liberal Arts at Boston University in Boston, Massachusetts. President emeritus of St. John's College, he is well known nationally for his work on ethics in daily public and private life. His publications include *Education and the Public Trust: The Imperative for Common Purposes* (Ethics and Public Policy, 1988) and *Character and Cops: Ethics in Policing* (American Enterprise Institute, 1989).

JOHN DEWEY (1859–1952) was a philosopher and a leader in the field of education. He emphasized the importance of "learning by doing," and his writings and teachings profoundly affected such diverse fields as philosophy, educational theory, psychology, law, and political science. His many works include *The School and Society* (1899), *Democracy and Education* (1916), and *Experience and Education* (1938).

HAROLD W. DODGE is the superintendent of schools in Cumberland County, Virginia.

CLIFTON FADIMAN, a writer and editor, has been a member of the board of editors for *Encyclopaedia Brittanica* since 1959. He also served as an editorial consultant to the Encyclopaedia Brittanica Education Corporation from 1963 to 1970, and he is the author of *The Lifetime Reading Plan*, 3rd ed. (HarperCollins, 1988).

FRANCES C. FOWLER is an assistant professor in the Department of Educational Leadership at Miami University in Oxford, Ohio. She received a B.A. from Cornell University, an M.A. from the University of Illinois, and a Ph.D. from the University of Tennessee. Her research interests include educational policy analysis and comparative educational policy.

JOHN HOLT (1923–1985) was an educator and a critic of public schooling. He authored several influential books on education, including *How Children Fail* (Pittman, 1964); *Escape from Childhood* (E. P. Dutton, 1974); and *Instead of Education: Ways to Help People Do Things Better* (Holt Associates, 1976).

ROBERT M. HUTCHINS (1879–1977) was a chancellor of the University of Chicago, a cocompiler of Encyclopaedia Britannica, Inc.'s *The Great Books of the Western World,* and a director of the Center for the Study of Democratic Institutions. His publications include *The Higher Learning in America* (Yale

University Press, 1936) and *The Conflict in Education* (Harper & Row, 1953).

INSTITUTE FOR JUSTICE is a non-profit public interest law center in Washington, D.C., that seeks to promote a free and responsible society.

EDWARD M. KENNEDY, senator (D) from Massachusetts (1962–present; term ends 2001), is the chair of the Senate Immigration and Refugee Affairs Subcommittee and has been the ranking Democratic member of the Labor and Human Resources Committee since 1981.

JONATHAN KOZOL, a graduate of Harvard University and a former teacher, is a writer and social commentator who writes on the problems of the American education system. His publications include *Death at an Early Age: The Destruction of the Hearts and Minds of Negro Children in the Boston Public Schools* (Plume Books, 1968), which was the winner of the National Book Award in 1968, and *Savage Inequalities: Children in America's Schools* (Harper-Perennial, 1991).

RITA KRAMER is an author whose publications include *Ed School Follies: The Miseducation of American Teachers* (Free Press, 1991).

THOMAS LICKONA is a professor of education at the State University of New York College at Cortland, in Cortland, New York, the director of the State University of New York's Center for the Fourth and Fifth Rs (Respect and Responsibility), and a member of the board of directors of the Character Education Partnership, a national coalition working to promote character development in schools and communities. He is a frequent consultant to schools throughout the United States, and he has lectured in

Canada, Japan, Switzerland, Ireland, and Latin America on teaching moral values in the school and home.

ALAN L. LOCKWOOD is a professor in and the chair of the Department of Curriculum and Instruction at the University of Wisconsin–Madison. He received a Ph.D. from Harvard University's Graduate School of Education, and he has written extensively on the role of values in education.

DONALDO MACEDO is an associate professor of linguistics at the University of Massachusetts–Boston. He is the author of *Literacies of Power: What Americans Are Not Allowed to Know* (Westview, 1994) and the coauthor, with Paulo Freire, of *Literacy: Reading the Word and the World* (Greenwood, 1987).

TERRY M. MOE is a professor of political science at Stanford University in Stanford, California, where he has been teaching since 1981. He has written extensively on a variety of topics, including public bureaucracy, the presidency, and the education system, and his book *Politics, Markets, and America's Schools* (Brookings Institution, 1990), coauthored with John E. Chubb, has received national attention for its institutional critique of the American school system and its market-based proposal for bringing about sweeping institutional change.

CHARLES NEVI is the executive director of curriculum and instruction for the Puyallup School District in Puyallup, Washington. He received an Ed.D. from Seattle University.

JEANNIE OAKES is a professor of education in the Graduate School of Education at the University of California, Los Angeles. She is the author of *Keeping*

Track: How Schools Structure Inequality (Yale University Press, 1985), which was chosen as one of the "Ten Most Read Books of 1985" by *The American School Board Journal*, and the coauthor, with Martin Lipton, of *Making the Best of Schools: A Handbook for Parents, Teachers, and Policymakers* (Yale University Press, 1990).

JOHN O'NEIL is a contributing editor to *Educational Leadership*.

VITO PERRONE is the chair of the Department of Teaching Curriculum and Learning Environment at Harvard University in Cambridge, Massachusetts, and the director of the university's Teacher Education Program.

DIANE RAVITCH is the senior research scholar at New York University in New York City and a fellow of the Brookings Institution, a private nonprofit organization devoted to research, education, and publication in economics, government, foreign policy, and the social sciences. She also served as assistant secretary of education during the Bush administration. She is the author of *The Schools We Deserve* (Basic Books, 1985) and the coauthor with Chester E. Finn, Jr., of *What Do Our Seventeen-Year-Olds Know?* (Harper-Collins, 1987).

RALPH E. REED, JR., is the executive director of the Christian Coalition in Chesapeake, Virginia.

CARL R. ROGERS (1902–1987) was a noted psychologist and educator who taught at the University of Chicago and the University of Wisconsin–Madison. He introduced the client-directed approach to psychotherapy in 1942, stressing the importance of a personal doctor-patient relationship, and he was the first psychologist to record and transcribe therapy sessions verbatim, a practice now standard with psychotherapy. His publications include *On Becoming a Person* (Houghton Mifflin, 1972).

KEVIN RYAN is the director of the Center for the Advancement of Ethics and Character at Boston University in Boston, Massachusetts. He has been in teacher education for more than 30 years.

PETER SCALES is the director of national initiatives for the Center for Early Adolescence in the School of Medicine at the University of North Carolina at Chapel Hill, where he is also an associate professor in the School of Social Work. He has been the director of education for the Planned Parenthood Federation of America and a research director of Syracuse University's Institute for Family Research and Education. He has published more than 100 articles, essays, and books, and he serves on the editorial boards of *Child Welfare* and the *Middle School Journal*.

ARTHUR M. SCHLESINGER, JR., is the Albert Schweitzer Professor of the Humanities at the City University of New York and the author of prize-winning books on Presidents Andrew Jackson, Franklin Roosevelt, and John F. Kennedy. His publications include *The Cycles of American History* (Houghton Mifflin, 1986).

PETER SCHRAG is a writer and an editor who has been associated with such journals as *Saturday Review, Change,* and *Social Policy.* His publications include *Voices in the Classroom* (Beacon Press, 1965) and *The End of the American Future* (Simon & Schuster, 1987).

ALBERT SHANKER is the president of the American Federation of Teachers in Washington, D.C., an organization that works with teachers and other educational employees at the state and local levels in organizing, collective bargaining, research, educational issues, and public relations. A leader in the educational reform movement, he is recognized as the first labor leader elected to the National Academy of Education.

RUTH SIDEL is a professor of sociology at Hunter College in New York City. She received an M.S.W. at the Boston University School of Social Work and a Ph.D. at Union Graduate School. Her publications include *Women and Children Last: The Plight of Poor Women in Affluent America* (Viking Penguin, 1987).

ROBERT L. SIMONDS is the president of Citizens for Excellence in Education in Costa Mesa, California.

B. F. SKINNER (1904–1990), noted psychologist and an influential exponent of behaviorism, was the holder of the William James Chair in the Department of Psychology at Harvard University in Cambridge, Massachusetts. His major works include *Beyond Freedom and Dignity* (Alfred A. Knopf, 1971); *About Behaviorism* (Random House, 1976); and *Reflections on Behaviorism and Society* (Random House, 1978).

WILLIAM G. SPADY is the founder and the director of the High Success Network in Eagle, Colorado. He has served on the faculties of Harvard University and the Ontario Institute for Studies in Education, and he has held positions at the National Institute of Education and the American Association of School Administrators. He is the author of *Excellence in Our Schoools: Making it Happen* (Far West Lab, 1984) and *Outcome-Based Education: Critical Issues and Answers*.

ROGER WILKINS is a professor of history at George Mason University and an editorial board member of *The Nation*.

INDEX